D1212871

The
Political System
of Pakistan

Sayeed

Under the editorship of

DAYTON D. McKEAN

University of Colorado

OTHER TITLES IN THE SERIES

The Government of Republican Italy
JOHN CLARKE ADAMS and PAOLO BARILE

British Parliamentary Democracy
SYDNEY D. BAILEY

The Federal Government of Switzerland
GEORGE A. CODDING, JR.

The Political System of Chile
FEDERICO G. GIL

Government and Politics in Israel
OSCAR KRAINES

Contemporary Government of Japan
THEODORE MCNELLY

Government and Politics in Malaysia
R. S. MILNE

The Mexican Political System
L. VINCENT PADGETT

The Indian Political System
NORMAN D. PALMER

Contemporary Government of Germany
ELMER PLISCHKE

South Vietnam: Nation Under Stress
ROBERT SCIGLIANO

Norwegian Democracy
JAMES A. STORING

❀

The Political System

of Pakistan

❀

KHALID B. SAYEED

QUEEN'S UNIVERSITY

HOUGHTON MIFFLIN COMPANY · BOSTON

CONTENTS

Copy 2

JQ
242
S38
Copy 2

TABLES

PREFACE

In the first three chapters of this book an attempt is made to delineate the origins and growth of the Pakistan movement culminating in the creation of the state of Pakistan. I have drawn freely on the material presented in my earlier book, *Pakistan, The Formative Phase,* but with the significant difference that in this book my primary concern has been to explain the kind of political process that operated under the British with the Congress and Muslim League as the two major contestants for political power. In addition, I have had the advantage of consulting the Minto Papers and the papers of the late Sir George Cunningham (Governor of the N.-W.F.P., 1937–45 and 1947–48) and Sir Francis Mudie (Governor of Sind, 1946–47, and Governor of West Punjab, 1947–49).

Chapters 4–11 deal more directly with the political system of Pakistan. In Chapters 5 and 6 there is more emphasis on the output process and the capabilities of the government in coping with political and social change. Chapter 7 is concerned with what is often regarded as the *raison d'être* of Pakistan, namely, Islam, and how it has influenced Pakistan's political culture. The demands that are made on and the cues that are intimated to the political system have been explored in Chapters 8 and 9 (Politics of Regionalism, and Parties and Elections). Development in the rural sector is examined in Chapter 10. The final chapter on Foreign Relations explores the impact of Pakistan's external environment on the capabilities of its government in maintaining national security and unity and in promoting economic development. The author has tried to interpret the Pakistani point of view. An attempt of this kind is essential if one is to understand how Pakistan's political system is shaped by Pakistani attitudes, their beliefs and their reactions to certain external forces.

President Ayub and his government take great pride in having created a political system which has ensured both political stability and economic development. But one still wonders whether the unabsorbed regional and other political demands and the new forces generated by economic development will dislocate the existing system. Another crucial variable is the availability of a leader like Ayub who can keep institutions such as the army and the bureaucracy united for the purpose of mobilizing support and commitment for economic and social development.

Sir Francis Mudie and the late Sir George Cunningham have placed me in considerable debt by letting me read their diaries and papers. I cannot thank adequately those scholars and students who have helped

viii PREFACE

me at various stages in the writing of this book. Dr. Percival Spear and Professor W. H. Morris-Jones have read the first four chapters of the book. My students at Queen's University have been a creative audience. I am grateful to the Canada Council and the Queen's University Arts Research Committee for the financial support they have provided for my field research in Pakistan. My thanks are also due to the Nuffield Foundation for a summer grant which enabled me to improve the material presented in the early chapters. In the final stages of editing and publication, the help rendered by Professor Dayton D. McKean, editor of this series, and the editorial staff of Houghton Mifflin Company has been generous and indispensable. Considerable as these debts are, that owed to my wife is even greater for the entire progress of the book has been shaped by her wholehearted and creative cooperation.

KHALID B. SAYEED

Queen's University
Kingston, Ontario
November 27, 1966

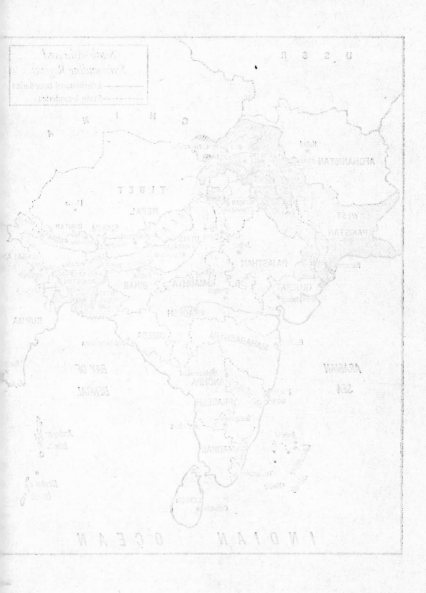

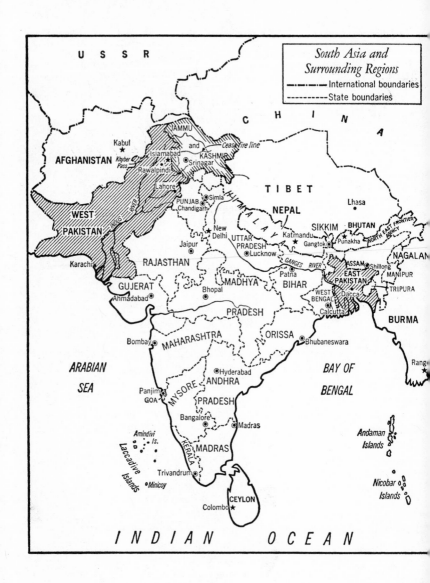

South Asia and
Surrounding Regions
— · —· International boundaries
— — — State boundaries

U S S R

C H I N A

AFGHANISTAN

Kabul ★

Khyber Pass

JAMMU

and KASHMIR

Cease fire line

Islamabad

Rawalpindi

⊙ Srinagar

TIBET

Lhasa

WEST PAKISTAN

Lahore

INDUS RIVER

PUNJAB ⊙ Simla

Chandigarh

New Delhi ★

H I M A L A Y A

NEPAL

Katmandu

SIKKIM

BHUTAN

Gangtok ⊙ Punakha

NORTH EAST FRONTIER AGENCY

Jaipur ⊙

UTTAR PRADESH

⊙ Lucknow

GANGES RIVER

NAGALAND

Karachi ⊙

RAJASTHAN

Patna ⊙

ASSAM ⊙ Shillong

MANIPUR

GUJERAT

Ahmadabad ⊙

Bhopal ⊙

MADHYA

PRADESH

BIHAR

WEST BENGAL

EAST PAKISTAN

⊙ Dacca

TRIPURA

Calcutta ⊙

BURMA

ARABIAN
SEA

Bombay ⊙

MAHARASHTRA

ORISSA

Bhubaneswara ⊙

BAY OF
BENGAL

Rang

Panjim ⊙
GOA

MYSORE

⊙ Hyderabad

ANDHRA
PRADESH

Bangalore ⊙

⊙ Madras

Amindivi
Is.

Laccadive Islands

KERALA

MADRAS

Andaman
Islands

Trivandrum ⊙

• Minicoy

CEYLON

Colombo ★

Nicobar
Islands

I N D I A N   O C E A N

1

The Origins of Pakistan

The origins of Pakistan lie entangled in prejudices. Those of us who have witnessed its gestation and later its final emergence have been led to believe in theories which either deride it as the crown and consummation of the British policy of "divide and rule" in India or in theories which glorify it as the final fulfilment of a clear, uninterrupted and separate stream of Muslim political consciousness in Indian history. An objective study of the origins of Pakistan and a willingness to face facts will reveal that many of the weaknesses and tensions that Pakistan has been encountering recently existed in their embryonic form during the period of Pakistan's gestation. Similarly, a dispassionate analysis of the factors which helped the formation of Pakistan should dispel a good deal of mutual misunderstanding and ill will that still exists in the minds of Indians and Pakistanis. Pakistan, like any other state, is a product of both negative and positive forces. It would be unfair to attribute its establishment entirely to Hindu communalism; Muslim separatism, sometimes bordering on hostility towards Hindus, was perhaps even a more important cause. Thus, a readiness to see each other's shortcomings ought to contribute to a better relationship and understanding between India and Pakistan.

Mahatma Gandhi, while speaking in the second session of the Round Table Conference in London in 1931, said that the quarrel between Hindus and Muslims was "coeval with the British advent" in India. The record of history is that the conflict between Hindus and Muslims had started long before the British arrival in India. Perhaps Emperor Aurangzeb (1658–1707) was responsible for increasing Hindu-Muslim tension by trying to Islamicize the Mughal government. Several Muslim historians have glorified Aurangzeb for making Muslims conscious of their separate religious and ideological identity. But the fact remains that under Aurangzeb, Maratha and Sikh leaders raised their banners

1

of revolt precisely because in trying to organize his government on Islamic lines, Aurangzeb was acting against their interests. Sir Jadunath Sarkar's observation on the role of Shivaji is revealing:

> Shivaji has shown that the tree of Hinduism is not really dead, that it can rise from beneath the seemingly crushing load of centuries of political bondage, exclusion from the administration, and legal repression; it can put forth new leaves and branches; it can again lift its head up to the skies.[1]

After Aurangzeb's death, Muslim power started disintegrating. How powerful had non-Muslims become and how desperate had become the Muslim position is revealed in the letters of Shah Waliullah (1703–81). Here was the son of a Sufi scholar, who would have normally passed his life either in meditation or teaching Islamic theology, but who felt that he should resort to every possible means to save Muslims from disaster. He did not hesitate to write to Ahmad Shah Abdali to come to the rescue of Muslims in India even though the latter was an Afghan outsider.

> In short, the Muslim community is in a pitiable condition. All control of the machinery of government is in the hands of Hindus because they are the only people who are capable and industrious. Wealth and prosperity are concentrated in their hands, while the share of Muslims is nothing but poverty and misery. . . . At this time you are the only King who is powerful, far-sighted, and capable of defeating the enemy forces. Certainly it is incumbent upon you to march to India, destroy Maratha domination and rescue weak and old Muslims from the clutches of non-Muslims. If, God forbid, domination by infidels continues, Muslims will forget Islam and within a short time become such a nation that there will be nothing left to distinguish them from non-Muslims.[2]

It has also been alleged that a separate Muslim political movement really started after the British conceded separate electorates to Muslims. The argument runs that here was a deliberate attempt on the part of the British to divide the electorate and thereby the Nationalist movement itself. The point which merits some examination is whether separate electorates were mainly responsible for creating differences between Hindus and Muslims or whether the granting of separate electorates recognized the cultural and religious differences that already existed between Hindus and Muslims. Prior to 1909, when separate

[1] Sir Jadunath Sarkar, *Shivaji and His Times* (Calcutta: Sarkar, 1952), p. 390.

[2] Khaliq Ahmad Nizami, ed., *Shah Waliullah Ke Siyasi Maktubat* (Political Letters of Shah Waliullah) (Aligarh: 1951), p. 106.

electorates were granted, no two books were more representative of Muslim and Hindu ways of thinking than Altaf Husain Hali's *Musaddas* (*The Ebb and Flow of Islam*, 1879) and Bankim Chandra Chatterjee's *Anandamath* (*The Abbey of Bliss*, 1882). Hali, in a lucid and flowing verse, described the rise and fall of Islam as a political and cultural force in the world. "With my unskillful hands," he wrote in the preface, "I have constructed a house of mirrors, in which Muslims will find their face and stature reflected and can see what they were and what they have become."[3] The entire burden of Hali's *Musaddas* was to appeal to Indian Muslims to discard their ignorance, indolence, selfishness, and forge ahead as a disciplined, industrious and united nation. *Anandamath*, portraying the rise of Hindu nationalism during the decline of Muslim power in Bengal, sounded a clarion call to Hindus to arise from their languor and take up arms against the degenerate and oppressive Muslim rule. Hindu leaders in the novel made it clear that their struggle was not against the British government, who had really come to India as liberators, but against Muslim tyranny and misrule. Though the plot of *Anandamath* dealt with the themes of a bygone age, yet it left a clear impression on the minds of its readers that Hindus were still bitter towards Muslims.

It may be argued that even if it were admitted that the conflict between Hindus and Muslims existed both before the establishment of British power in India and the introduction of separate electorates in 1909, the British could have used their imperial power to compose these differences and help Hindus and Muslims evolve a common nationality. The British not only failed to do this, but actually tried through separate electorates to widen the gap that existed between the two communities. These are very formidable arguments. But it may be pointed out that no imperial power in history has displayed such a benevolent behavior as to bring about a rapprochement between two rival communities. The traditional British approach to their colonies has been very largely that of laissez-faire. Furthermore, there was no guarantee that joint electorates would have necessarily helped Hindus and Muslims to develop a national outlook in political matters. On the contrary, it may be argued that joint electorates, particularly when Muslim political leaders were thinking primarily in communal terms, might have worsened the relations between the two communities. At every election in each constituency where Muslims were in substantial numbers, communal riots might have flared up. Even if some of the harmful effects of separate electorates were conceded, it could still be argued that a generous attitude on the part of the majority community could have

[3] Altaf Husain Hali, *Musaddas-i-Hali* (*The Ebb and Flow of Islam*) (Lahore & Karachi: Taj, n.d.), p. 5.

easily nullified most of these harmful effects. For example, if the Indian National Congress had agreed to include representatives of the Muslim League in the provincial Congress Cabinets in 1937, much communal rancor and bitterness might have been avoided. Thus, if the British had planned to divide Hindus and Muslims, it seems that the Congress and Muslim League leaders did very little to frustrate British designs. It may be stated in passing that some writers in their keenness to prove the "divide and rule" thesis, tend to forget the unifying influences of British rule in India — namely, modernization of Indian life through education, commerce and industry, and the establishment of centripetal institutions like the civil service, the army and the judiciary.

The Hindu-Muslim conflict was further heightened when more and more political power was placed on the counter by the British after 1919 and Hindu and Muslim leaders appeared as rival contenders to grab as much of it as possible for their respective communities. Unfortunately, progressive realization of responsible government turned out to be progressive aggravation of the Hindu-Muslim conflict. It was Maulana Muhammad Ali, at one time an ardent Indian Nationalist and the famous leader of the Khilafat movement, who told the British government in the Round Table Conference in 1930, "We divide and you rule."

The British were also caught in a vicious circle which was not entirely of their own making and from which there was probably no easy way out. The problem of administering justice between Hindus and Muslims was not a problem of holding balance between two equal communities. Muslims were not only smaller in number, but lagged behind the Hindus in education, in commerce, and political leadership. To start with, when the British arrived, Muslims were sulky and not very malleable to their policy of Westernization. The British impact on Hindu areas was not only earlier but was received with great enthusiasm. The Hindus, unlike the Muslims, took to the learning of English with great readiness and proficiency and soon supplanted the Muslims in every office of administration. When Muslims found that they were being reduced to an inferior economic and social status, they tried to acquire English education and assure the British that they also would be loyal to their rule. The British, on the other hand, felt that they had probably been unfair to Muslims, and impressed by their pledges of loyalty, tried to help them. This created resentment among the Hindu intelligentsia, and particularly when Lord Curzon inaugurated his scheme of the partition of Bengal in 1905, there was a hue and cry throughout Hindu India. The British yielded to Hindu agitation and revoked partition. In the wake of this, there followed a series of events in the Middle East which confirmed Muslim fears and suspicions regarding the British policy towards Muslims in general and Muslim powers like Turkey in particular. A barometer of Muslim anger was the Khilafat movement (1920–22) in which Hindu and Muslim cooperation reached its high-water mark. Later differences arose between Hindus and Muslims which will be dealt with in Chapter 2.

The pendulum of British policy continued to oscillate between the two points — recognition of Hindu demands and support of Muslim interests. In 1937, Congress governments were installed in office in seven provinces, and Muslims became resentful and suspicious once again. In August, 1940, when the Congress refused to cooperate with the British war effort, the Muslims were given a solemn assurance by the British that no constitutional advance in India would be contemplated without their assent and approval. It would indeed be a daring historian who would single out the British for all blame because they were not complete masters of the circumstances in which they were placed. They occupied the apex, but the other two points of the triangle were held by Hindus and Muslims.

For the Congress, the establishment of Pakistan was a crushing blow to their claim of being a Nationalist organization. It meant that Muslims did not trust the Hindus as a majority community to be just and generous to Muslim interests and culture. For that reason, there has been a tendency on the part of Congress leaders to attribute the creation of Pakistan entirely to the British policy of "divide and rule." But Muslim Leaguers believe that to accept this view not only belittles the tenacity and brilliant strategy of Jinnah and the Muslim League, but also questions their thesis that Pakistan came into being because Muslims were a separate nation. Truth should lie somewhere between the two positions. The creation of Pakistan was probably helped by the British unwillingness, matched by their inability, to compose the differences between Hindus and Muslims. In the main, however, Pakistan was the end product of Muslim anxiety at first to attain cultural and political autonomy within the framework of a federal India and later of their bold assertion that Muslims, being a separate nation, must have a sovereign state.

Popular among Muslims is the view that Pakistan emerged because the Hindu community in India was intolerant and exclusive. They argue that just as caste Hindus have kept inferior castes at arm's length, the Hindu community, dominated by Brahmins, has always regarded Muslims, who came from outside and brought with them an alien culture, as *melechas* (unclean). Hindus, on the other hand, have also remembered the alleged indignities and the occasional religious persecution that they suffered under Muslim rule in India. Jawaharlal Nehru himself pointed out that many a Congressman was a communalist under a national cloak.[4] The latest verdict is that of a bitter opponent of the Muslim League, Maulana Abul Kalam Azad. He has pointed out that Jinnah cannot be blamed entirely for the turn of events that brought about the creation of Pakistan. It was Sardar Patel who had been communal-minded from the beginning and later, as a result of the non-cooperative attitude of the Muslim League in the Interim Government, became convinced that Muslims and Hindus were separate nations and that partition was the only solution. According to Azad, if the Congress had shown sufficient patience and far-sightedness and had followed Lord Wavell's advice on the matter, Pakistan would not have been inevitable.[5]

Muslims often take the view that since Hindus were the majority community, all generosity and far-sightedness should have emanated from them. It should also be stressed that the sense of Muslim separatism, which is a dominant theme in the Qur'an (Koran), was an equally potent factor which prevented the growth of a common Indian nationalism. In addition, memories of Muslim rule in India not only remained alive, particularly among the upper-class Muslims, but were constantly used by them to impress upon the Muslim masses that having ruled India, Muslims should not allow themselves to be ruled by the Hindu majority. It was because of such separatist tendencies and memories of former Muslim rule in India that there was little deep-seated or sustained love for India as their motherland on the part of the Muslim elite.

The fact that a large number of Muslims were descendants of Hindu forebears who had been converted was often advanced as the most formidable argument against the existence of a separate Muslim nation. It was also suggested that there was hardly any cultural difference between Hindus and Muslims who lived in Indian villages. But Islam was not merely a religion confined to the sort of relationship that should exist between man and his God. It was also a code of social ethics which implied a distinct way of life. How strong and comprehensive had been the influence of Islam on the culture of its converted followers was well demonstrated in what constitutes today West Pakistan. In that part of the country the dominant culture was clearly

---

[4] Jawaharlal Nehru, *An Autobiography* (London: The Bodley Head, 1958), p. 136. A communalist in the context of Indian politics during the British period was one whose loyalty to his own community, Hindu or Muslim, was supposed to be so intense and complete that he often ignored or underrated the existence of a common Indian nationalism which was supposed to embrace all communities, castes and creeds.

[5] Maulana Abul Kalam Azad, *India Wins Freedom* (Calcutta: Orient Longmans, 1959), see pp. 15, 177–178, 185.

Islamic. As Sir Denzil Ibbetson observed: "Where that tone and feeling is that of the country beyond the Indus, as it is on the Panjab frontier, the Hindu even is almost as the Musalman."[6] It was true that as one moved away from the Indus basin, the Islamic cultural stream lost some of its vigor and identity, except at Muslim cultural centers like those in the United Provinces and Hyderabad. But it must be noted that ever since the disintegration of the Muslim empire, Muslim religious reformers tried to purify Muslims of Hindu idolatrous customs and superstitions because they were against the spirit of Islam. The *Faraiziyah* movement[7] among the Muslims of Bengal was perhaps the best example.

Another popular view regards Pakistan as solely the creation of Quaid-i-Azam (the Great Leader) Muhammad Ali Jinnah. It was his dogged determination and sheer fanaticism which brought about the partition of the subcontinent. Some even go so far as to say that had Jinnah died earlier, there would not have been Pakistan.[8] It was true that Jinnah's tenacity of purpose and superb organizing capacity were highly important contributory factors, but without intense Muslim consciousness and zeal for an Islamic state on the part of Muslim masses, Jinnah could not have created a Pakistan. Khilafat leaders like Maulana Muhammad Ali and Maulana Abul Kalam Azad and poets like Hali, Akbar Allahabadi, and Iqbal were mainly responsible for creating Muslim consciousness among the Muslim masses. Thus, when the message of Pakistan was brought to the masses, it fell on fertile soil. Jinnah, who did not know Urdu, could not have achieved Pakistan without able and missionary lieutenants and without the vision of an Islamic state as an intoxicating stimulant. One may even go so far as to say that the Muslim League, led largely by middle-class Muslim leaders, would have probably come to some sort of a compromise on the issue of Pakistan had they not been swept off their feet by the intense Islamic fervor of the masses and the astounding success that the Muslim League achieved during the elections of 1945–46.[9]

[6] Sir Denzil Ibbetson, *Punjab Castes* (Lahore: Government Printing, Punjab, 1916), p. 14. See also Muhammad Miyan, *Jamiyat al Ulama Kia Hai?* (*What is Jamiyat al Ulama?*) (U. P.: Jamiyat al Ulama, n.d.), p. 45.

[7] This was a puritanical movement, the aim of which was to take the Muslims back to the essentials of their faith and purify Islam as practiced in India of Hindu idolatrous practices.

[8] Michael Brecher, *Jawaharlal Nehru: A Political Biography* (London: Oxford University Press, 1959), p. 353.

[9] The Muslim League did accept the Cabinet Mission Plan of 1946 which rejected the Pakistan scheme. It withdrew its acceptance when the Congress acceptance of the Cabinet Mission Plan turned out to be a conditional acceptance with its own interpretations of the Cabinet Mission proposals.

It has been reported that the Quaid-i-Azam himself never expected to see Pakistan in his lifetime.[10]

Each view taken by itself is a highly exaggerated account of the origin of Pakistan, for the country was brought about by a multiplicity of factors. But perhaps the principal reason for the existence of Pakistan is that there has never been a confluence of the two civilizations in India — the Hindu and the Muslim. They may have meandered towards each other here and there, but on the whole the two have flowed their separate courses — sometimes parallel and sometimes contrary to one another.

[10] Hector Bolitho, *Jinnah, Creator of Pakistan* (London: John Murray, 1954), p. 195.

❀ *2* ❀

Muslim Separatism and Indian Nationalism[1]

We have already indicated that even before the advent of British power in India, Muslims had become aware that their religious, cultural, and political interests were in danger as a result of the growing weakness of the Mughal empire and the growing strength of the Marathas, the Sikhs, and other non-Muslim groups. Amidst such diverse antagonisms, there did not exist any Indian nationalism which the British had to combat. The story of the British acquisition of the Indian empire can very largely be related in terms of how the British successfully dealt with one cultural or religious group after another.

After the British power became consolidated and India came under the British Crown in 1858, the British continued to be impressed and influenced by India's cultural and political diversity. One could say that they felt that they could maintain a sense of justice and fair play between the various communities by not letting any major group dominate the rest of India. This policy soon ran counter to the nationalism that was ushered in after the establishment of the Indian National Congress in 1885. The Indian National Congress leaders from the beginning made earnest efforts to build Indian nationalism on the bedrock of Hindu-Muslim accord. But the Congress failed to erase the impression that it was predominantly a Hindu body. The British had to protect their own interests and at the same time maintain a balance between the two communities. The failure of the Indian National Congress in evolving an Indian nationalism which embraced the whole

[1] For more detailed background material, see Khalid Bin Sayeed, *Pakistan, The Formative Phase* (Karachi: Pakistan Publishing House, 1960), Chapters II and III.

of the Indian subcontinent can perhaps be explained more by the political mistakes they made and the growing sense of Muslim separatism than in terms of British machinations to accentuate the existing conflict between the two communities. Penderel Moon, commenting on the role of the Congress, observed: "They passionately desired to preserve the unity of India. They consistently acted so as to make its partition certain."[2]

Muslim separatism, originating from cultural and religious factors, obtained its first nourishment from the feeling among the Muslim leaders that their community, having lost political power, was being deprived of its rightful share of administrative jobs and was lagging far behind the Hindus in education and material prospects. In a province like Bengal, Muslim landowners were replaced by Hindus to whom the collection of land revenue had been assigned by the British. The Muslim legal system was replaced by that of the British, and Persian gave way to English. "From having monopolised the posts of pleaders of the High Court even as late as 1851 . . . out of 240 natives admitted between 1852 and 1869 there was only one Mussalman."[3] The collapse of the Indian Mutiny of 1857 with its storm centers in Muslim areas of Delhi and Oudh darkened Muslim fears, for they suspected that the British would now embark on a policy of deliberate discrimination against Muslims in civil administration and in the army.

Hindus, on the other hand, had forged ahead in acquiring British education and securing jobs in the administration. Hindu areas of India were not only exposed first to the influence of British ideas and culture, but the impact created forward-looking and progressive reformist movements as that of Raja Ram Mohan Roy. The universities of Calcutta, Madras, and Bombay were established in 1857. In contrast, the first impact of British power on Muslims was in an inward-looking direction in the sense that the Muslims felt that they might have lost political power because they had deviated from the true path of Islam. It was later under Sir Syed Ahmad Khan that one detects a progressive trend in Muslim culture.

Hindu and Muslim reaction to British political ideas and institutions is also a study in contrast. Speeches made in the first session of the Indian National Congress in 1885 disclose that the Congress leaders were optimistic about the growing sense of Indian nationalism and the establishment of representative institutions in India. One of the great benefits of British rule was "that for the first time in the history of the

[2] Penderel Moon, *Divide and Quit* (Berkeley and Los Angeles: University of California Press, 1962), p. 14.

[3] Cited in Sir Percival Griffiths, *The British Impact on India* (London: Macdonald & Co., 1952), p. 306.

Indian populations there is to be beheld the phenomenon of national unity among them, of a sense of national existence." Another speaker said that they had learned from "the English people how necessary representation is for good government." Sir Syed Ahmad Khan (1817–98), a retired government servant who had sprung from a Mughal family of noble lineage, emerged as an outstanding leader of the Indian Muslims. He put forward an entirely opposite point of view from that expressed by the Congress leaders.

> So long as differences of race and creed and the distinctions of caste form an important element in the socio-political life of India, and influence her inhabitants in matters connected with the administration and welfare of the country at large, the system of election, pure and simple, cannot be safely adopted. The larger community would totally override the interests of the smaller community, and the ignorant public would hold Government responsible for introducing measures which might make the differences of race and creed more violent than ever.[4]

Hindu leaders were becoming conscious of their Indian identity and perhaps felt they would be called upon as leaders of the majority community to lead the Indian Nationalist movement. On the other hand, Muslim leaders, drawn from the landowning classes of the Punjab, Delhi, and other areas of northern India, regarded themselves as descendants of the Mughals from whom the British had seized political power. They were not quite as conscious of India as their country as they were proud of their Mughal forebears and Muslim culture. Shah Waliullah, a famous eighteenth-century Muslim thinker, had described Muslims as travellers sojourning in a foreign land, and the famous poet, Hali, an associate of Sir Syed, in his ode on the plight of the Muslim community in the Indian subcontinent, wrote: "A faith which left its home with so much glory is now reduced to being a stranger of strangers in a foreign land."[5]

Sir Syed's Leadership and British Concessions to Muslims

Sir Syed constantly pleaded with the Muslims to remain loyal to the British and not participate in the Congress movement. He felt that the Muslim community should remain aloof from all kinds of political

---

[4] Cited in R. Coupland, *The Indian Problem 1833–1935* (New York: Oxford University Press, 1944), I, p. 156.

[5] Cited in Ishtiaq Husain Qureshi, "The Background of Some Trends in Islamic Political Thought," in *Tradition, Values and Socio-Development,* Ralph Braibanti and Joseph J. Spengler, eds. (Durham: Duke University Press, 1961), p. 216.

agitation because by taking an active role in the Indian Mutiny of 1857 they had already placed themselves in danger by arousing British antagonism. The only path that lay before the Muslims, according to Sir Syed, was that of equipping themselves with English education. He established the Anglo-Oriental College in 1875 which later became the well-known Muslim university of Aligarh.

In his attempts to dissuade the Muslims from joining the Congress, the arguments that Sir Syed employed and the alliances that he built up were destined to have a decisive influence on the subsequent growth of the Muslim separatist movement. In one of his speeches, he cited the Qur'an and said that "the command of God was that Mussalmans could not be friends of non-Muslims. They could cooperate with Christians who were people of the Book. If they could be friends, it could only be with Christians."[6] Congress was dubbed a Hindu organization. According to one account, at a meeting in which Sir Syed bitterly attacked the Congress, all the influentials of the Muslim community were present.

> There were present the Taluqdars of Oudh, members of the Government services, the Army, the profession of the Law, the press, and the priesthood; Syeds, Sheikhs, Moghals, Pathans, belonging to some of the noblest families of India; representatives of every school of thought from orthodox Sunni and Shiah Muslims to the young men, trained in the Indian colleges and in England.[7]

It was significant that the British at this time had become aware that they had not been quite fair to Muslim interests. Sir William Hunter in his well-known book, *The Indian Mussalmans,* published in 1871, pointed out that Muslims had suffered grave injustices, particularly in the matter of administrative and judicial jobs in Bengal. He urged that the British should try to rectify the situation and also adopt a wise and far-sighted policy to save the Muslims from the dangerous influences of their religious agitators. The British civil servants in the United Provinces and in the Punjab were by and large sympathetic towards Muslims. Sleeman's *Rambles and Recollections of an Indian Official,* which every British official used to read as an instructive and engaging guide on Indian customs and manners, admired Muslims for their learning and suggested that they should be distinguished from the superstitious and idolatrous Hindus.[8] The Muslim areas of the

[6] Cited in Husain B. Tyabji, *Badruddin Tyabji* (Bombay: Thacker & Co., 1951), p. 204.

[7] *Ibid.,* p. 197.

[8] Major-General Sir W. H. Sleeman, *Rambles and Recollections of An Indian Official* (London: Archibald Constable & Co., 1893).

Punjab and the Frontier lay on the strategic routes through which the feared Russians might penetrate India. British Governors and officials of these areas persuaded the government to introduce the Punjab Alienation of Land Act, 1900, which, while allowing free transfer of land within the agricultural tribe or group of tribes, prohibited permanent alienation of the land of agricultural tribes to non-agriculturalists like the Hindu moneylenders and other urban interests except in those rare cases where the revenue authorities were satisfied. One of the architects of this legislation was S. S. Thorburn, who wrote:

> If it be remembered that the Musalman peasantry of the Panjab, to the number of four millions, are chiefly congregated in the western districts between the Chenab and Afghanistan, are probably, except in some Trans-Indus tracts, more indebted and expropriated than any of the agricultural races in India, and have, in their own opinion at least, small reason to be satisfied with our rule, — the unsettling effect upon their minds of the near approach of a "liberator" will be realised.[9]

It may also be pointed out that these areas provided the bulk of the manpower in the Indian army. Both political and strategic considerations and sympathy for their Muslim charges had influenced the British officials in offering protection to the Muslim peasantry. The editor of the *Amrita Bazar Patrika* complained to the Secretary of Lord Curzon that "the British had got into India on the shoulders of the Bengali," but had discarded their old friends "and took to your hearts the Northerners."[10]

It was on October 1, 1906, that a delegation of about seventy Muslims led by the Aga Khan was received in the ballroom of the Viceroy's house at Simla by Lord Minto. The delegation had brought with it an address signed by "nobles, ministers of various states, great landowners, lawyers, merchants, and of many other of His Majesty's Mahommedan subjects." They asked for separate representation of Muslims in all levels of government — District Boards, Municipalities, and Legislative Councils. They drew the attention of the Viceroy to the fact that in the United Provinces, where Muslims constituted 14 per cent of the population, they had not secured a single seat by joint franchise. And if by chance they were to win any seats, Muslim candidates would have to pander to the views of the Hindu majority and thus go against the interests of their own community. Lord Minto

---

[9] S. S. Thorburn, *Asiatic Neighbours* (Edinburgh & London: William Blackwood & Sons, 1894), p. 51.

[10] Sir Walter R. Lawrence, *The India We Served* (London: Cassell & Company, 1928), pp. 264–265.

assured the delegation that he was entirely in accord with their case. Muslims had won separate representation for themselves. It was well known, and this has been confirmed by the Minto Papers, that the persons who engineered the Muslim deputation to the Viceroy were the landowning Muslim aristocrats of Bengal and the United Provinces, others holding high administrative ranks in the state of Hyderabad, the English principal of the Muslim college that Sir Syed had established at Aligarh, and the Viceroy's Secretary, who had all corresponded with one another. Muhammad Ali, who later became a leader of the Khilafat (Caliphate) movement,[11] dubbed the delegation as a "command performance." Separate electorates were given statutory recognition in the Indian Councils Act of 1909. Muslims were accorded not only the right to elect their representatives by separate electorates, but also the right to vote in general constituencies. In addition, they were also given weightage in representation. In spite of these concessions, one could see how politically weak they were in the Legislative Councils set up under the Act of 1909. In Bengal, where they were in the majority, there were only five Muslim representatives out of twenty-eight elected members. In the United Provinces, where they were in a minority but where their position was politically stronger than it was in Bengal, they had four representatives out of twenty-one elected members. Ironically, in the Punjab, where they were supposed to be in the majority and had therefore not been given any special protection under the Act, not one of the eight elected members was a Muslim.

It had become increasingly apparent to the Muslim leaders that they could not extract concessions from the government by merely remaining aloof from the Congress. It looked as if the British government had decided to extend the principle of representation in measured stages. The Councils Act of 1892 enlarged the Provincial Councils and allowed the discussion of the budget and the raising of administrative questions, though the right to vote on them was not extended. In view of all this, a separate political organization for Muslims — the All-India Muslim League — was created on December 30, 1906, nearly three months after the Muslim deputation had called on Lord Minto. In addition to the well-known Muslim leaders from the landowning classes, several young Muslim lawyers were also present. The first resolution stated the three objectives of the League as follows: (1) To foster a sense of loyalty to the British government among the Muslims of India; (2) to look after the political interests of Indian Muslims; (3) to bring about better understanding between Muslims and other communities.

[11] See pp. 22–26.

The alliance between the Muslim landed gentry and British civil servants continued to flourish. The British civil servants perhaps took a liking to the landed gentry as a whole, and particularly to the Muslims, for several reasons. Indian landowners in northern India, both Hindu and Muslim, still behaved like cultured Mughal noblemen, and British civil servants treated the landowners as natural leaders in their respective districts. These leaders figured prominently in the local *Durbars*[12] and hunting parties, which were arranged for visiting British dignitaries like the Commissioner, the Governor, and on rare occasions, even the Viceroy. Cordiality on the part of British civil servants towards Muslim landowners continued right until the transfer of power; Sir Francis Mudie, Governor of Sind during 1946–47, in his letter to Lord Wavell, reported:

> So far I have been struck by the high morale of the superior services. Most of them, especially the Europeans, get on well personally with the Ministers who are gentlemen by birth and tradition, very unlike the Congress Ministers we had in the U.P.[13]

In contrast to their regard for the landowners, British civil servants were not sympathetic towards the new urban, educated leaders like lawyers and teachers who actively supported the Congress Party in its demand for representative government. Edwyn Bevan was very perceptive when he wrote, "I feel sure that the very same man who would give his life to keep people alive in famine, might behave to an educated Indian in a manner which could not fail to wound, and be unconscious of anything wrong."[14]

Since Sir Syed, supported by many well-known members of the Muslim landed aristocracy in the North, had advised the Muslims to stay away from the Congress and remain loyal to the British, it was obvious that British civil servants would be sympathetic towards the Muslims. In 1909 the Viceroy wanted to consult a body of representative Muslims from the different provinces regarding the special representation to be accorded to Muslims on the new Councils. He asked the Lieutenant-Governors of various provinces to recommend the names of Muslim representative leaders. In all, the names of fifty-one Muslim leaders were sent to the Viceroy by the Lieutenant-

[12] A court held by an Indian or Muslim prince for administering justice or on ceremonial occasions. This practice was sometimes followed by the British Governors and officers.

[13] Sir Francis Mudie's letter to Lord Wavell, DO No. 98/FR dated 21st February, 1946. These letters have been shown to the author by Sir Francis who has them in his personal possession.

[14] Edwyn Bevan, *Indian Nationalism* (London: Macmillan & Co., 1913), p. 66.

Governors of Bengal, Eastern Bengal and Assam, the United Provinces, the Punjab, and the Governor of Bombay. Of these fifty-one representative leaders forty-one were titled landowners and government officials. Out of the remaining ten, six were merchants from the province of Bombay.[15]

Even though this alliance between the British and the Muslim landed gentry remained strong, British civil servants were not completely confident that Muslims would continue to remain politically passive and loyal. Sir Syed had hoped that English education would enable Muslims to compete effectively for government jobs and also make them conscious of their social obligations to their community as well as to other classes of citizens. But he did not realize that education, besides ushering in such healthy benefits, would also make Muslims politically conscious and that they, like Hindus, might also claim due recognition of their civil and political rights. There is evidence to suggest that as early as 1907 the provincial government of the United Provinces was becoming concerned about the restiveness of students in the Muslim college at Aligarh.[16] In 1910 the Lieutenant-Governor of the United Provinces wrote to Lord Minto:

> I have felt frightened lest the lawyer party, mainly consisting of young and irresponsible persons, would attain a predominant position in the League, and that they might at some time coalesce with the advanced Hindu politicians against the Government on one or more questions and later on rue the fact that they had done so. I think that the Aga Khan has put an effectual check to this, and that the League may be expected to be much more conservative and stable than it once promised to be.[17]

Hindu-Muslim Tension and the Partition of Bengal

The Indian National Congress was conscious of the fact that it had not attracted a large number of Muslims to its fold, but it had made earnest efforts to enlist Muslim membership. It elected a Muslim, Badruddin Tyabji, as the president of its third annual session in 1887. Congress leaders sometimes offered to pay the fares of Muslim delegates so that a larger number of them might attend its sessions. But the Muslim leadership it had attracted came mostly from Muslim-

[15] The Earl of Minto, *Correspondence With Persons In India. Volume I. 1909, January-June,* pp. 214–219 and 221. These papers are in the National Library of Scotland, Edinburgh.

[16] The Earl of Minto, *Correspondence With Persons In India. Volume I. 1907, January-June,* p. 62.

[17] The Earl of Minto, *Correspondence With Persons In India. Volume I. 1910, January-June,* p. 58.

minority areas and a few of the urban centers in Bengal and northern India, and they were mostly lawyers and a few merchants from Bombay and Madras. Lawyers like Muhammad Ali Jinnah from Bombay, Mazhar-ul-Huq and Syed Hasan Imam from Bihar were well known in Congress circles and had gone on record to deprecate the extension of communal representation to local bodies. Why had the Congress not succeeded in enlisting Muslim support and creating Hindu-Muslim accord with the help of such leaders?

Two factors explained the Congress failure. First of all, the existing Muslim leaders from the landowning classes were successful in persuading Muslims that under a democratic or representative government, the Muslims, who until recently had ruled India, would be swamped and subjugated by the Hindu majority. Secondly, in Maharashtra and Bengal, Congress leaders in order to win grass-roots support for their political movements used Hindu religious symbols and slogans and thereby aroused Muslim suspicions regarding the secular character of the Indian National Congress.

Maharashtra produced two great Brahmin leaders, Tilak and Gokhale, who dominated Congress politics before the arrival of Gandhi on the Indian scene. Gokhale was a great admirer of British institutions and believed that given British good will, India would be able to win responsible government by adopting constitutional methods. Tilak disagreed with this point of view and felt that Indians, and particularly the Hindus, had gone too far in imitating British culture. He disagreed with those Hindu reformists who had tried to change some of the Hindu customs and institutions under the influence of British ideas. He also strongly believed that the British favored the Muslims over the Hindus and that this had increased Muslim arrogance and violence. Tilak used his journal, *Kesari,* to propagate his ideas. In 1893 he started a Hindu revivalist movement and the two weapons he sought to employ for this purpose were the festival of Ganesh, the Elephant God, and that of Shivaji. The latter festival associated with Shivaji was bound to provoke Muslim hostility for Shivaji had led the Marathas against the Muslim Mughal empire. Tilak had two objectives in his use of religion for political purposes. Under the cloak of religion, he thought he could carry on his anti-British propaganda because it would be difficult for the British government to ban religious meetings as easily as they could suppress political meetings. Secondly, he thought such festivals would solidify the Hindu community against the Muslims. However, Tilak could not be dubbed as an outright Hindu communalist. He played an important role in the Hindu-Muslim Lucknow Pact of 1916, but he did not realize the harmful consequences of injecting religion into politics. Indian leaders like Tilak wanted to organize mass movements by using Hindu religious symbols and slogans to dislodge the British; at the same time they wanted to build Indian nationalism on the basis of Hindu-Muslim understanding. They did not seem to realize that by trying to achieve the first objective through religious methods they were making the attainment of Hindu-Muslim accord almost impossible. This was because both Hindu and Muslim urban leaders often lived in two different worlds. In the world of universities, law courts and bar associations, they were in agreement regarding the constitutional liberties to be given Indians by the British. Jinnah defended Tilak against the government which had charged him with sedition. But when confronted with the world of villages and family, leaders like Tilak seemed to be under the spell of the traditional Hindu mores, customs, and ideas.

The British government were of the opinion that Bengal, with an area of nearly 200,000 square miles and with a population of 78.5 million, was too large a province for efficient administration. They also suggested that the districts of East Bengal had been neglected and the neighboring province of Assam was too small an area to be governed as a province. The partition of Bengal was announced on September 1, 1905. The new province, called Eastern Bengal and Assam, consisted of Assam and Eastern and Northern Bengal — an area of 106,650 square miles with a population of 31 million of which 18 million were Muslims and 12 million were Hindus. Congress and other Hindu leaders in Bengal interpreted this decision as a deliberate blow aimed at the growing solidarity and self-consciousness of the Bengali-speaking population. The Congress movement was largely led by Hindu lawyers, merchants and landlords who were determined to oppose the partition of Bengal because it would also disrupt Calcutta's commercial and professional life in which they had so much at stake. The anti-partition leaders employed two weapons to bring pressure to bear upon the government in India and in Britain. Taking the cue of the Chinese boycott of American goods, the Bengalis launched the Swadeshi movement whose sole purpose was to organize a boycott of British goods. Their aim was to bring pressure on important textile interests in Britain who, the agitators thought, would in their turn pressure the home government into abandoning the partition scheme. The other weapon used was mass meetings of protest. In the Minto Papers, there is clear evidence based on letters circulated by Congress leaders in India and their supporters in Britain that mass meetings were used to pressure the Secretary of State for India into revoking the partition scheme.

Since both these weapons involved mass participation, the agitators had to employ religious symbols and slogans both in their speeches and editorials because this was perhaps the most effective way of arousing public indignation. Hindu goddesses and gods were appealed to and oaths were taken in the temple of Kali. India was represented as Kali, the grim goddess, dark and naked, bearing a garland of human heads around her neck — heads from which blood was dripping. It was obvious that these Hindu symbols and slogans were not likely to make the movement popular among the Muslims, particularly when it was becoming increasingly apparent to the Muslims that the partition had given them a province in which they constituted a majority. In Bengali political literature, Indian nationalism had often been presented in a Hindu setting. The editor of the Bengali paper, *Bande Mataram*, wrote:

> The ground work of what may well be called the composite culture of India is undoubtedly Hindu. Though the present Indian nationality is composed of many races, and the present Indian culture of more than one world civilisation, yet it must be admitted that the Hindu forms its base and centre. . . . And the type of spirituality that it seeks to develop, is essentially Hindu.[18]

The economic and administrative setup in rural East Bengal was such that the anti-partition movement directed by Bengali leaders from Calcutta was bound to increase Hindu-Muslim tension. A large number of the wealthy land revenue collecting landlords were Hindus and the bulk of the police and other services at the lower levels were mostly Hindus. The Lieutenant-Governor of East Bengal in his letter to Lord Minto reported:

> In Mymensingh and in Sylhet, to a lesser degree, the Hindu landlords are persecuting all Mohammedan tenants who have been concerned in any way with the recent Mohammedan riots, or have given evidence in the Courts with respect to them.[19]

In another letter the same Governor wrote that if the government could only be pressured through mass meetings, Muslims were also capable of organizing demonstrations. "The Mohammedan organization, through the Moulavies, and based on religious practices is far and away in advance of the Hindu organization, which is only a political organization."[20] Such Muslim meetings did take place and were well attended — "twenty thousand in Dacca, ten thousand at

[18] Haridas Mukherjee and Uma Mukherjee, *'Bande Mataram' and Indian Nationalism* (1906–1908) (Calcutta: Firma K. L. Mukhopadhyay, 1957), pp. 93–94.
[19] The Earl of Minto, *Correspondence With Persons in India. Volume II. 1906, July–December*, p. 101.
[20] *Ibid.*, p. 72.

Mymensingh, six thousand at Faridpur, one thousand at Sylhet." Bengali newspapers alleged that government officials were behind such meetings. There is no clear evidence to establish these charges. But one could see that Hindu-Muslim relations had suffered a severe setback. A highly sensitive Hindu writer, recording his impressions of those days, has pointed out:

A cold dislike for the Muslim settled down in our hearts, putting an end to all real intimacy of relationship. Curiously enough, with us, the boys of Kishorganj, it found visible expression in the division of our class into two sections, one composed purely of Hindus and the other of Muslims. . . . Compartmentalization by communities came into our education before it was introduced into our politics.[21]

The Lucknow Pact

Muslims did derive a number of advantages from Sir Syed's policy. But it suffered from three major weaknesses. It could not succeed indefinitely because the British government had their own interests to pursue and protect. Having tried to educate and influence Indians on Western lines, the British government could not indefinitely withhold from them parliamentary institutions. It soon became clear that they would have not only to concede representative government but also pay heed to the demands and grievances of the Hindus. Revocation of the partition of Bengal in 1911 was an example. Secondly, as the Muslim community came increasingly under the impact of British education and culture, the educated Muslim elite felt that Hindus and Muslims should get together to evolve a common nationality and to serve their country by awakening public opinion in support of political reforms. A man like Jinnah, who had studied closely the lives of British political leaders like Gladstone and Disraeli, probably was impatient to play a role in his country as great and useful as they had done in theirs. But two obstacles stood in the way of such people — the British reluctance to concede political reforms and the lack of any genuine understanding between Hindus and Muslims. Third, there was an anti-British tradition in Muslim religious thought which continued unabated among orthodox religious circles. It was not necessarily reactionary. It did not reject Western ideas out of hand. It felt that Muslims could form a political alliance with Hindus without going either against the dictates of their faith or their interests. Its best exponent was perhaps Maulana Shibli Nomani (1857–1914). He was followed by Maulana Abul Kalam Azad (1888–1958). Muhammad Ali (1878–1931) stood between the two schools, that of Westernized

[21] Nirad C. Chaudhuri, *The Autobiography of An Unknown Indian* (New York: Macmillan, 1951), p. 232.

parliamentarians like Jinnah and religious leaders like Maulana Shibli and Maulana Azad.

The annulment of the partition of Bengal in 1911 severely shocked the followers of Sir Syed. As one of them pointed out, "It is now manifest like the midday sun, that after seeing what has happened lately, it is futile to ask the Muslims to place their reliance on Government." But despite such a rebuff, he would not recommend what he called "the way to suicide," namely, joining the Congress as a result of such disappointments.[22]

It seemed that the liberal wing of the Muslim League, led by Muhammad Ali Jinnah, was becoming increasingly powerful. Jinnah had joined the Muslim League in the autumn of 1913 after making absolutely clear that his loyalty to the Muslim League would in no way imply any disloyalty to the larger national cause espoused by the Congress. The liberal wing of the League succeeded in persuading both the Congress and the Muslim League parties to hold their annual sessions in Bombay in 1915. A large number of Muslims felt that the British government was turning against the Muslims once again. The British were not only fighting against Turkey in the war but also making Muslim soldiers in the Indian army fight against their fellow Muslim Turks. Muhammad Ali, Shaukat Ali, and Abul Kalam Azad had all been interned under the Defense of India Act and their papers suppressed under the Press Act. Thus the anti-British feeling among the Muslims enabled Jinnah and Mazhar-ul-Huq to persuade the Muslim League to think in terms of coming to a long-term settlement with the Congress. The war was on, and both the League and the Congress expected that the government would soon be compelled to concede constitutional reforms to placate the political interests in the country.

The atmosphere in Lucknow in 1916, where once again the All-India Muslim League and the Indian National Congress met to hold their annual sessions, was even more cordial. It was at Lucknow that the famous Congress-League Pact, otherwise known as the Lucknow Pact, was signed. Congress conceded separate Muslim electorates and was even agreeable to their introduction in provinces like Punjab and the Central Provinces where they had not existed before. Muslims were to get nine-tenths of the seats in Punjab to which they were entitled on a purely numerical basis. The result was that Muslim representation in Punjab rose from 25 per cent (under the reforms of 1909) to 50 per cent (as a result of the Pact). Similarly, in the Lucknow Pact, Muslims in Bengal were given only three-quarters of the seats to which they were entitled on their population basis. Mus-

[22] A. H. Albiruni, *Makers of Pakistan and Modern Muslim India* (Lahore: Ashraf, 1950), pp. 110–112.

lims were to complain later that particularly in Bengal (though also in Punjab) they were deprived of their majority position. The answer was that separate electorates had been conceded by the British to the Muslims as a minority; therefore, they were not entitled to have separate electorates in provinces where they were in majority. The Muslim complaint was that they were backward and grossly under-represented even in the majority provinces. However, in Muslim-minority provinces, according to the Lucknow Pact, Muslims obtained a representation almost double that of what they would have got on a purely numerical basis. Similarly, at the Center they obtained one-third representation in the Council by separate Muslim constituencies. They, of course, had to give up their right to vote in general consti-tuencies which had been accorded to them by the Reforms of 1909. The Congress also went so far as to concede that no bill or resolution concerning a community could be passed if three-fourths of the repre-sentatives of that community were opposed to it.

Most of these principles, as well as other constitutional features of the Lucknow Pact, were later incorporated in the Government of India Act, 1919. The Hindu-Muslim concordat of Lucknow was the high-water mark of Hindu-Muslim unity. It was obvious that it was all the work and creation of constitutionalists, both in the Congress and in the League. All this was to be swept away by tides which followed in the wake of the Amritsar tragedy and particularly the Khilafat agitation.

The Khilafat Movement

The Lucknow Pact showed that it was possible for middle-class, English-educated Muslims and Hindus to arrive at an amicable settle-ment of Hindu-Muslim constitutional and political problems. Tilak had once shrewdly observed: "The real dispute is not between the educated leaders of the two communities; it is to be found among the uneducated and the illiterate."[23] According to Jawaharlal Nehru, Jinnah "suggested once privately that only matriculates should be taken into the Congress."[24] This shows that some of the English-educated, middle-class lawyers were not too happy at the prospect of mass participation in politics. Indian politics after the First World War, under the impact of short-sighted government policies and the resulting noncooperation and Khilafat movements, was so tempestuous that the constitutional captains could no longer chart its course. The

[23] D. V. Tahmankar, *Lokamanya Tilak* (London: John Murray, 1956), p. 55.
[24] Jawaharlal Nehru, *An Autobiography* (London: The Bodley Head, 1958), p. 68.

political skills that were needed were possessed only by men like Gandhi and Muhammad Ali who had received Western education but had remained basically loyal to the religious and spiritual traditions of their respective communities. The tragedy was that gifted as these men were in the art of mobilizing mass support for political agitation, they could not control or channelize the energy and emotions generated by the mass movements. Religious feelings that were aroused, when thwarted by the superior might of the government forces, sought outlet and vengeance in the form of Hindu-Muslim riots.

During the First World War, Indians of all classes had cooperated with the British, and toward the end of the war they had begun to hope that India would soon achieve a considerable degree of freedom and emerge as a Dominion in the British Commonwealth. But soon after the war, the government policy, as manifested in the Rowlatt Act and the Amritsar tragedy, dealt a deadly blow to such expectations. There was a wave of indignation among political circles when the Rowlatt Act was passed in 1919. According to this Act, the government, when faced with anarchical and revolutionary movements, could take action against any individual and interne him. The protest meetings against the Act culminated in the Jallianwalla Bagh massacre on April 13, 1919. The military opened fire on the densely packed crowd, killing 379 people and wounding at least 1,200. Gandhi declared that it had become painfully clear to him that "the British Ministers or the Government of India have never meant well by the people of India." In cooperation with the Muslim demand for the preservation of the Khilafat (Caliphate) in Turkey, Gandhi persuaded the Congress to launch a civil disobedience movement on September 8, 1920.

So far as Muslims were concerned, they were as interested in the territorial integrity of the Turkish empire as they were in Indian independence. In the eyes of the Muslims, Turkey occupied a special place, for the Khalifa (Caliph), who was theoretically the religious and political ruler of all Muslims, resided in Turkey. Before the First World War, all the Muslim Holy Places in the Middle East were within the Turkish empire. The British government, when informed of Indian Muslim concern over the fate of Turkey in the First World War, declared in January, 1918, that Turkey would be left in possession of her capital and lands in Asia Minor and Thrace. But toward the end of the war, Indian leaders felt that the British government had gone back on its promises when Greek armies were allowed to invade Turkey and the Holy Places were to be placed under non-Muslim mandates.

Muslim leaders like Muhammad Ali, his brother, Shaukat Ali, and Abul Kalam Azad urged the Muslims to cooperate with the Congress, which, under Gandhi's leadership, had embarked on a civil disobedience movement. The Congress declaration of "progressive, nonviolent, noncooperation" involved total noncooperation with all government institutions like local bodies, the Reformed Councils announced under the Government of India Act, 1919, and courts of justice, gradual withdrawal of children from government schools and colleges, and boycott of foreign goods. Gandhi thought that this was a capital opportunity for building Hindu-Muslim unity at the grass-roots level. "I claim that with us both the Khilafat is the central fact, with Maulana Mahomed Ali because it is his religion, with me because, in laying down my life for the Khilafat, I ensure safety of the cow, that is my religion, from the Mussalman knife."[25]

Gandhi, accompanied by the Ali brothers and Azad, undertook extensive tours of the country to mobilize popular support. The Khilafat movement had captured the public imagination and most of the moderate leaders had either veered round to Gandhi's point of view or had been rendered ineffective. Jinnah seemed lonely in furrowing his constitutional path. His view was that Gandhi's "extreme programme has for the moment struck the imagination mostly of the inexperienced youth and the ignorant and the illiterate. All this means complete disorganization and chaos."

For Muslims, Khilafat meant the honor and glory of Islam. They had been watching with mounting dismay the gradual and steady decline of Muslim political power throughout the world. They regarded this as an opportunity to pour forth all their energy and fervor for the cause of Islam. Hundreds of *ulama* (learned men in Islamic religion) issued *fatwas* (religious decrees) sanctioning the program of nonviolent noncooperation. Another *fatwa* forbade Muslims from serving the government in any capacity — particularly service in the police or the army was declared an unpardonable sin. Resolutions to the effect that religious duty forbade Muslims from joining the Indian army or continuing to serve in it were passed by the All-India Khilafat Conference which met in Karachi in July, 1921. This resulted in the imprisonment of the Ali brothers. The idea that owing to the flagrant disregard of the law of Islam by the British government, India had become a *dar-ul-harb* (zone of war) spread widely, particularly in the North-West Frontier Province and Sind. The result was that thousands of Muslims — as many as 18,000 in the month of August, 1920 — sold all their belongings and migrated to Afghanistan. They had been told that the Afghan government would welcome them with open arms and fertile fields. Afghan authorities, alarmed by such an enormous influx, were compelled to turn the emigrants back.

[25] M. K. Gandhi, *Communal Unity* (Ahmedabad: Navajivan, 1949), p. 26.

It was obvious that the whole Khilafat movement had taken a religious turn and it was extremely doubtful whether Muslims could conduct their agitation and demonstrations purely on nonviolent lines. It has been alleged that Muhammad Ali in one of his speeches had said that if the Afghans were to invade India, Muslims would offer their help to them against the British. A Hindu leader was equally concerned about the Khilafat movement taking an anti-Hindu turn, even though it had started as an anti-British movement.

> There was another prominent fact to which I drew the attention of Mahatma Gandhi. Both of us went together one night to the Khilafat Conference at Nagpur. The Ayats (verses) of the Quoran recited by the Maulanas on that occasion, contained frequent references to Jihad and against, [sic] killing of the Kaffirs. But when I drew his attention to this phase of the Khilafat movement Mahatmaji smiled and said, "They are alluding to the British Bureaucracy." In reply I said that it was all subversive of the idea of non-violence and when the reversion of feeling came the Mahomedan Maulanas would not refrain from using these verses against the Hindus.[26]

Hindu-Muslim cooperation for the Khilafat movement registered a severe setback when the Moplahs (Muslim inhabitants of Malabar in South India) rioted against their Hindu landlords. In addition to destroying government property and attacking European planters, they sacked Hindu houses, desecrated temples, and converted thousands of Hindus by force. They declared their objective to be the establishment of a Khilafat. The Moplah riots alienated a considerable body of Hindu opinion. These riots were followed by Hindu-Muslim clashes in several parts of India. Several Hindu communal organizations started Hindu movements to reconvert those Hindus who had recently embraced Islam. Muslims retaliated by launching similar movements. It was becoming increasingly obvious that the Khilafat movement was petering out. In February, 1922, horrified by an incident in which twenty-one policemen were murdered and for which the Congress volunteers were held mainly responsible, Gandhi called off the national movement. The final blow was struck by the Turkish government on March 3, 1924, which under its President, Kemal Pasha, exiled the Khalifa and abolished the Khilafat.

The Khilafat movement was the first and the only movement in which both Hindus and Muslims had played a joint role on a mass scale. But as suggested earlier, freedom of India was not the first and only objective of the Muslim struggle. Muslims seemed to suggest to the Hindus through the Khilafat movement that they could become

[26] Cited in B. R. Ambedkar, *Pakistan or The Partition of India* (Bombay: Thackers, 1946), p. 149.

passionately interested in the freedom of their country only if it ensured the safety and glory of Islam both in India and Muslim countries. No one was more acutely aware of this than Gandhi.

> We both have now an opportunity of a life-time. The Khilafat question will not recur for another hundred years. If the Hindus wish to cultivate eternal friendship with the Mussalmans, they must perish with them in the attempt to vindicate the honour of Islam.[27]

Constitutional Proposals — Nehru Report and Government of India Act, 1935

It was apparent that after the collapse of the Khilafat movement, there was Hindu-Muslim antagonism in the air. Communalism had even penetrated the ranks of the Congress itself. Commenting on the elections of 1926, Motilal Nehru wrote to his son:

> It was simply beyond me to meet the kind of propaganda started against me under the auspices of the Malaviya-Lala gang. Publicly I was denounced as an anti-Hindu and pro-Mohammedan but privately almost every individual voter was told that I was a beef-eater in league with the Mohammedans to legalise cow slaughter in public places at all times.[28]

The Government of India Act, 1919, under its system of dyarchy, had introduced a measure of autonomy in the provinces. The Congress refused to cooperate with this scheme and whenever its representatives were present in the provincial legislatures, they attempted to paralyze the machinery of the provincial government by moving motions of no-confidence against the Ministers who were in charge of transferred subjects like education, agriculture, public health, and local government.

The British government set up a commission under Sir John Simon in November, 1927, to investigate India's constitutional problems and make recommendations to the government on the future constitution of India. There was no Indian member on the commission. The Nehru Report was an answer to the challenge thrown to Indians by the British government that the composition of the Simon Commission had to be purely British because Indians were incapable of arriving at an agreed solution regarding the constitutional problem of India. The committee which was called upon to draft a constitution for India was set up under the chairmanship of Pandit Motilal Nehru, with

[27] Gandhi, pp. 5–6.

[28] Jawaharlal Nehru, *A Bunch of Old Letters* (Bombay: Asia Publishing House, 1958), p. 49.

Jawaharlal Nehru as Secretary, and was drawn from all parties — the Congress, Muslim League, Mahasabha, Sikh League, Liberals, etc. The Report recommended that the central government be constructed on a unitary basis and that separate electorates and weightage for minorities be rejected. It referred to what it considered the illogical fear of Muslims of being dominated by the Hindu majority. But what was significant was the way Muslims were thinking of tackling this problem. They had made a novel suggestion that "they should at least dominate in some parts of India." Hindus, on the other hand, in spite of enjoying an all-India majority, were fearful of Muslim majorities in Bengal, Punjab, Sind, Baluchistan, and the North-West Frontier Province. The Report ended, however, on an optimistic note saying that once alien authority and intervention were withdrawn from India, people would start thinking in terms of the larger economic and political problems. In such a climate, political parties based mainly on economic grounds were a natural outcome.

A convention of all parties known as the All-Parties Conference met in Calcutta in the last week of December, 1928, to consider the Nehru Report. Jinnah, who was at that time president of the Muslim League, put forward his famous Fourteen Points, which were amendments to the Report, before the open session of the Conference on December 28, 1928. His basic amendments were: (1) Representation of communal groups should continue to be by means of separate electorates as at present. (2) There should be a Federal constitution with the residuary powers vested in the provinces. (3) In the central legislature Muslims should have one-third representation. (4) No cabinet, either central or provincial, should be formed without there being at least one-third Muslim Ministers. (5) The Muslim majority in the Punjab, Bengal, and the North-West Frontier Province should not be disturbed.

These proposals were rejected in their entirety by the Conference. Congress leaders felt that Muslims were divided, and Jinnah was representing only a faction. There were other Muslims led by Abul Kalam Azad who were in agreement with the proposals of the Nehru Report. Another reason why the Congress leaders adopted a rigid attitude was because a considerable section of Hindu opinion would have been alienated if they had made any concessions to the Muslims. But it must be emphasized that Motilal Nehru, the chairman, stood solidly behind his Report, not merely because it was politically wise to do so. He was a lawyer who believed in a liberal, democratic, and constitutional government. To him, separate electorates were not only antithetical to basic principles of responsible government; they also had accentuated the animosities that prevailed between the two communities. Jinnah himself at one time had held such views. In the author's opinion, herein lay the crux of the problem. Leaders like Motilal Nehru in their total adherence to Western modes of thinking and forms of government were not taking into account the peculiar political conditions in India: although India was a heterogeneous subcontinent, they were drawing on the practices and traditions of a unitary and homogeneous country like the United Kingdom in order to solve its problems.

During 1930 and 1931, a series of meetings of British government leaders and Indian representatives of all parties and communities, known as the Round Table Conference, were held. The Congress Party, before taking part in such a Conference, wanted a clear commitment from the government that the purpose of the Round Table Conference would be to draft a scheme for Dominion status which would be implemented by the British government. The Viceroy's refusal to give such a commitment resulted in the Congress launching a campaign of civil disobedience, including nonpayment of taxes, in March-April, 1930.

It was significant that Muhammad Ali, who had so far taken an active part in the Congress movement, called upon Muslims to remain aloof from the Congress civil disobedience campaign. He declared: "Mr. Gandhi is working under the influence of the communalist Mahasabha. He is fighting for the supremacy of Hinduism and the submergence of Muslims." This was strong language, and this view regarding the role of the Congress and Gandhi, as we shall see later, became the official and accepted view of the Muslim League under Jinnah. This bitterness also cast its shadow over the Round Table Conference. Gandhi was absent in the first session, November-January, 1931. He was present in the second session of the Round Table Conference in the autumn of 1931, after having suspended the civil disobedience movement in accordance with the agreement reached between himself and the Viceroy, Lord Irwin.

In the Round Table Conference a long and bitter conflict regarding the number of seats that minorities should be given in various legislatures took place. Muslim representatives asked for one-third representation for Muslims in the central legislature of British India. Similarly, they argued strongly for Muslim majority representation in Punjab and Bengal since these provinces were to be given provincial autonomy. But no agreement could be reached on the question of minority representation. Gandhi tried his best, but "with deep sorrow and deeper humiliation" he announced "utter failure to secure an agreed solution of the communal question."

On August 16, 1932, Prime Minister Ramsay MacDonald announced the Communal Award. Referring to separate electorates, he said that the government must "face facts as they are, and must maintain this exceptional form of representation." Muslim representation in various provinces under the Award may be seen in Table 1.

Table 1

Muslim Representation in Indian Provinces During the British Period

Province	Muslim Percentage of Population	Total Number of Seats	Number of Seats Reserved for Muslims
Madras	7.9	215	29
Bombay excluding Sind	9.2	175	30
Bengal	54.7	250	119
The United Provinces	15.3	228	66
The Punjab	57.0	175	86
The Central Provinces	4.7	112	14
Assam	33.7	108	34
Sind	70.7	60	34
N.-W. F. Province	91.8	50	36
Bihar and Orissa	10.8	175	42

The Government of India Act, 1935, was a compromise between the views put forward by various Indian representatives and those of the government. At the federal level, dyarchy was introduced under which matters like defense and external affairs were placed under the control of the Governor-General responsible to the Secretary of State for India and Britain. The Governor-General was also empowered with special responsibilities which extended his authority over matters like maintenance of law and order, safeguarding of the financial stability of the government, and safeguarding of the rights and interests of minorities. For matters other than defense, external affairs, and special responsibilities, he was to act in accordance with the advice of his Council of Ministers. There was to be a bicameral legislature. Members representing British India were to be elected and those representing the Indian states were to be appointed by their rulers. At the provincial level, on the other hand, dyarchy of the Government of India Act, 1919, was replaced by provincial autonomy whereby genuine power was to be transferred to popularly elected provincial ministries. Governors were armed with certain discretionary powers and special responsibilities which extended their authority over matters like threats to law and order, safeguarding of minority interests, and protection of the rights of civil servants.

Owing to the unwillingness of the Princes to accede to the federation contemplated in the Government of India Act, 1935, as well as the opposition of the Congress and the League to what they considered an undemocratic and an irresponsible Center in the Act, the British government decided to postpone the implementation of the federal part of the Act. Instead, it was decided to put into effect only the section in the Act dealing with the British Indian provinces.

It could not be said that the Act had resolved the Hindu-Muslim conflict. The question which hung in the balance was: Would the Act, as a result of the transfer of power at the provincial level, heighten Hindu-Muslim differences or provide a machinery whereby such differences could remain within bounds and the legitimate interests and grievances of minorities be accommodated? The Congress at that time did not rate the danger of Muslim separatism high. Leaders like Jawaharlal Nehru felt that most of the genuine grievances could be accommodated and that the Congress organization had grown so strong and efficient that whatever hold Muslim League leaders had over the Muslim masses, it could effectively challenge and undermine by its own Muslim mass contact campaign. The Congress wanted to win the provincial elections and use the power so gained to combat the reactionary features in the Act and ultimately wrest independence from British hands. Congress inability to resolve the Hindu-Muslim conflict and the growing strength of the Muslim League under the leadership of Jinnah created a chain of events which seemed to lead inexorably to the partition of India.

3

Strength and Weaknesses
of the
Pakistan Movement[1]

We have already seen that the politics of the Hindu-Muslim conflict had come out in the open during the twenties and the thirties of this century. There had been earlier political movements in Bengal and Maharashtra in which this conflict was present, but compared to the Khilafat movement, the earlier manifestations were provincial. We have also seen in the Khilafat movement that Muslim religious feelings were aroused as a weapon against the British government, but the movement could not retain its purely anti-British direction and deteriorated into Hindu-Muslim conflicts. The conflict that took place between the Indian National Congress and the Muslim League during 1937–39, following the formation of Congress governments in seven of the eleven provinces, accentuated the conflict between Hindus and Muslims at two levels. First, since more power was placed on the counter under the scheme of provincial autonomy under the 1935 Act, the conflict between the Hindu and the Muslim intelligentsia and commercial classes increased. Secondly, since political power under the new reforms could only be organized and acquired through political parties competing for support from electorates divided communally, there was a two-way communication of the conflicts — the conflict of the intelligentsia infecting and accentuating Hindu-Muslim differences

[1] For more detailed background material, see Khalid Bin Sayeed, *Pakistan The Formative Phase* (Karachi: Pakistan Publishing House, 1960), Chapters III-VI.

at the mass level and a feed-back from the mass and the rural level to the legislative chambers.

How does one spell out these conflicts in concrete terms? In the northwestern parts of the Indian subcontinent, in the Punjab and Sind, Hindus were the moneylenders and the Muslims were peasants, whereas in the east, in the province of Bengal, Hindus were often landowners with Muslims as tenants. In East Bengal, despite its greater concentration of Muslim majority, the professional classes were mostly Hindus. This conflict had caught the Congress in different provinces in contradictory positions. In the United Provinces, they were in favor of land reforms directed against big landowners, great numbers of whom were Muslim, whereas in Bengal they were opposed to land reforms where the great majority of big landowners happened to be Hindu. In the Punjab and Sind, they often opposed legislation designed against the moneylenders.

It was well known that Muslims, because of their backwardness in Western education, had lagged behind the Hindus in obtaining positions in the all-Indian services like the Indian Civil Service, the Indian Police Service, and others. In order that Muslims might be able to make up this handicap, the British had introduced the quota system in the recruitment of the central services. This competition for jobs, particularly at the provincial level, aggravated Hindu-Muslim tension among the intelligentsia. The provincial civil servants came in close contact with the rural people in matters like land records, payment of land revenue, and maintenance of law and order. Whether a Muslim or Hindu villager felt secure or apprehensive depended upon the religious affiliation of the officer. In the United Provinces, where Muslims were in the minority, they occupied a favored position in the provincial services; whereas in Bengal, where they were in the majority, the Hindus held most of the posts in the provincial services. In the United Provinces, the Muslim League could point out that under the Congress regime, Hindus were determined to oust the Muslims from their favored positions, and in Bengal the Muslim League could point the accusing finger at the Hindus for having deprived the Muslims of their share in public services, even though the latter were in the majority.

The question that may be raised is: Were Muslims merely interested in cataloguing their grievances against the Hindus and reiterating the plea that under a perpetual Hindu majority, the Muslim minority could not be confident of fair play and justice? In other words, was Muslim nationalism a mere product of negative forces, or did it have intellectual and ideological content? According to Sir Muhammad Iqbal (1873–1938), one of the greatest poets of Indian Islam and often described as the national poet of Pakistan, Muslims of India did not have to struggle to become a nation for they were already a nation.

> We are seventy millions and far more homogeneous than any other people in India. . . . The Hindus, though ahead of us in almost all respects, have not yet been able to achieve the kind of homogeneity which is necessary for a nation, and which Islam has given you as a free gift.[2]

There was no doubt that Muslim leaders could evoke enthusiastic support for a political cause from Muslim masses by invoking the name of Islam. The problem was whether Islam would continue to have the same appeal for the Muslim intelligentsia who were coming under the spell of Western rationalism. Sir Syed went to great lengths in showing that Islam was basically a rational system and that the superstitious beliefs and practices which had arisen among Muslims were based upon an erroneous and fanciful interpretation of the Qur'an and the Traditions of the Prophet. Ameer Ali's *The Spirit of Islam* was perhaps even a more elaborate and painstaking effort to persuade both Muslim and Western readers that Islam in its days of glory had been ahead of other religions in its spirit of tolerance towards minorities and liberal in protecting the rights of individuals — women, slaves, etc. The spirit of philosophical and scientific inquiry had always been prized by Muslim rulers. But Ameer Ali wrote in an apologetic vein. It was Sir Muhammad Iqbal who pointed out that there was no need for Muslims to emulate the Western example in politics or philosophy because the West itself had grown disenchanted with its thinking and philosophy which had produced the inequitable capitalist system and horrible global conflicts. Iqbal claimed that as opposed to Western nationalism, Islam preached international brotherhood, and in contrast to the Western capitalist system, Islam was vibrant with a sense of social justice and humanitarianism. However, all these values needed to be reinterpreted in the light of modern times. Iqbal thought that Indian Islam could undertake this task of reinterpretation. The most important instrument that Indian Islam needed for fulfilling this role was a separate Muslim polity. In his famous presidential address to the annual session of the All-India Muslim League in 1930, Iqbal declared:

> I would like to see the Punjab, North-West Frontier Province, Sind, and Baluchistan amalgamated into a single state. Self-government within the British Empire or without the British Empire, the formation of a consolidated North-West Indian Muslim State appears to me to be the final destiny of the Muslims, at least of North-West India.

[2] "Shamloo," *Speeches and Statements of Iqbal,* 2nd ed. (Lahore: Al-Manar Academy, 1948), p. 31.

Congress-League Antagonism

The elections that were fought during 1936–37 were not marked by any increase in Hindu-Muslim tension. On the contrary, the Muslim League under Jinnah produced a program which was not too dissimilar from that of the Congress. But it was clear that the Muslim League was determined to maintain its separate identity as an organization representing the Muslims of India. Jinnah had become quite convinced that the only way of resolving the Hindu-Muslim conflict was for the two representative bodies, the Indian National Congress and the Muslim League, to enter into negotiations with each other. This was how the Lucknow Pact was arrived at, and Jinnah, as a lawyer and political leader, regarded political settlement as essentially a compromise arrived at between two negotiating parties. The Congress, on the other hand, because of its growing strength and efficient organization, thought that there were only two parties in the country — the British government and the Congress. Jinnah, who was trying to build the Muslim League under his leadership, made his position clear.

> Pandit Jawaharlal Nehru is reported to have said in Calcutta that there are only two parties in the country, namely, the Government and the Congress, and the others must line up. I refuse to line up with the Congress. There is a third party in this country and that is the Moslems. We are not going to be dictated to by anybody.[3]

It may also be pointed out that Congress intellectuals and particularly Jawaharlal Nehru held the view that India as an historic and cultural entity had absorbed many outside forces and thereby grown richer, and, despite its apparent diversity, there had been an inner spirit in India which rolled through all ages. Thus, to them Islam could also be absorbed, and India's unity could flow in an uninterrupted fashion. Furthermore, to a socialist like Nehru, religion was a somewhat reactionary force and all communities in modern India should think primarily in economic terms.

The election results indicated that Congress victories were won mainly in Hindu constituencies. Out of 1,585 seats, the Congress captured 714. Of these, only 26 were Muslim seats. On the other hand, the Muslim League showing was not very impressive. Out of 485 Muslim seats, the Muslim League captured only 109 seats. It won a substantial number of seats in the Hindu-majority provinces, but in the Muslim-majority provinces, it did not create much of an impression. In Bengal, out of 117 Muslim seats, it won only 40. In Punjab, it won only two seats out of 86 Muslim seats. And in the N.-W.F.P. and

[3] *The Statesman* (Calcutta) (weekly overseas edition), January 7, 1937.

Sind, out of 36 Muslim seats in each, it won none at all. The Congress was successful in forming governments in 7 out of the 11 provinces. Of the 26 Muslim seats it had won throughout India 19 were in the N.-W.F.P. It could form a government in this province, where the Muslims were in the majority, because the other 23 Muslim seats in a house of 50 were divided among a number of parties and groups.

The Muslim League claim that it was the sole spokesman of the Muslims was first challenged in the United Provinces. The Muslim League expected that each provincial cabinet would have a representative of the minorities, as the Governor under the 1935 Act had been called upon to make every effort to include minority representatives in the cabinet. They were even more confident in the case of the U.P., where the Congress and the League had fought the provincial elections on a common platform. Out of 64 Muslim seats, the Muslim League had won 27, the Independent Muslims 27, the National Agricultural Party 9, and the Congress only 1. The Congress ministry was prepared to include a representative from the Muslim League, but it demanded that the Muslim League Party should merge itself in the Congress Party and that the Muslim League should not set up any candidates in later by-elections. The Muslim League refused to join the cabinet under such conditions. The Congress, by refusing to include non-Congress Muslim leaders who represented the majority opinion among Muslims, created the impression that the Congress organization and governments were predominantly Hindu in character. Abul Kalam Azad, a Congress leader, thought that this was a serious mistake which strengthened the League and "ultimately led to Pakistan."[4] Nehru, while replying to Azad's criticism, remarked that in 1937 he was eager that the Congress should introduce land reforms in the United Provinces and therefore was averse to the idea of the Muslim League, which represented some big landowners, joining the Cabinet. He conceded, however, that the Muslim League had agreed to abide by the majority decisions of the Cabinet.[5] Like his father, Motilal Nehru (in the case of the Nehru Report), Jawaharlal regarded the British parliamentary system as a model. The situation in India, however, was not the same as it was in a homogeneous and unitary state like the United Kingdom. In India, because of its infinite diversities, a coalition Cabinet drawn from more than one political party would have created better confidence among the minorities.

Nehru felt that the Congress under the leadership of socialists like himself could look after the genuine interests of Muslims better than

[4] Maulana Abul Kalam Azad, *India Wins Freedom* (Calcutta: Orient Longmans, 1959), p. 161.

[5] *The New York Times,* February 8, 1959.

the Muslim League, which was dominated by landowning classes and therefore reactionary.

> I come into greater touch with the Moslem masses than most of the members of the Muslim League. I know more about their hunger and poverty and misery than those who talk in terms of percentages and seats in the Councils and places in the State service.[6]

But this view of Muslim politics grossly underrated the enormous appeal that religion had for the Muslim masses. It also ignored the fact that a number of Congress leaders were not as secular-minded and generous towards Muslims as Jawaharlal Nehru. Such mistakes could have been avoided if the Congress had been able to consult representatives of Muslim majority opinion. This it could have done if it had included such representatives in the provincial governments.

The Congress, by launching its Muslim mass contact movement and pointing out to the Muslims that the real fight was for bread and butter, hurled a challenge at the Muslim League to which the Muslim League responded with considerable vigor. The first indication that Muslims were disturbed by the Congress challenge came in the annual session of the Muslim League in Lucknow in October, 1937. The Muslim League had won less than a quarter of the Muslim seats in the provincial elections. Particularly its showing in the Muslim-majority provinces was most unimpressive. But at Lucknow it looked as if Jinnah had snatched victory from the jaws of defeat. On the day he appealed to the Muslims to get organized — for "politics meant power and not relying only on cries of justice or fair-play or good will" — Sir Sikander Hyat Khan, the Premier of Punjab, Fazlul Huq, Premier of Bengal, and Sir Muhammad Saadulla, Premier of Assam, declared in the League session that they were advising the Muslim members of their respective parties to join the Muslim League. This again was a demonstration of the unifying capacity of Islam.

Jinnah was determined to create a well-organized and broad-based political movement to face the Congress challenge. If the Congress could employ its own Muslim *ulama,* so could the Muslim League, and, in addition, it could discredit the Congress *ulama* as men who had been bribed by Hindu money. The Muslim League went a step further and accused the Congress governments of being determined to destroy Muslim culture and impose Hindu culture and ideology on the helpless Muslim minority. The Muslim League organization published a series of reports cataloguing cases of alleged Congress persecution of Muslims in the Congress-ruled provinces. Cases of such persecution included the forcing of Muslim children to sing *Bande Mataram* (a song found in

[6] *The Statesman,* January 7, 1937.

the anti-Muslim Bengali novel, *Anandamath*) and offer reverence before Mahatma Gandhi's portrait, the prohibition of cow slaughter, the elimination of Urdu and imposition of Hindi, etc. The Muslim League propagandists were capable of describing this alleged Congress persecution of Muslims in lurid terms. "Here and there the worm did turn, and not all the conflicts were onesided. But so indeed could the German historian accuse the Poles of turning upon the aggressive and death-dealing Nazi hordes!"[7]

It was true that the Congress governments did put forward some of their ideas and social and educational schemes in terms derived from the Hindu religion and Hindu scriptures. They probably did this to evoke popular support from the bulk of the population which happened to be Hindu. In addition, the great majority of Congress Hindu leaders who had emerged in the provinces were much less Westernized than some of the all-India leaders. The Congress educational scheme introduced in the Central Provinces was given a Hindu name and a Hindu form. The scheme of *Vidya Mandirs* (Temples of Learning) was bitterly opposed by the 3 per cent Muslim minority in the Central Provinces, but their protests were disregarded. Their complaint was that how could Muslims cooperate with a scheme which bore such a Hindu name as *Mandirs* (Hindu temples). For Muslims, a Hindu temple was a place where idols were worshipped and this, they thought, was a deliberate affront to Islam's prohibition and condemnation of idolatry. Even Gandhi, who strove unceasingly for Hindu-Muslim unity, was in the habit of using Hindu phrases in politics. Thus, according to Nehru:

Even some of Gandhiji's phrases sometimes jarred upon me — thus his frequent reference to Ram Raj as a golden age which was to return. But I was powerless to intervene, and I consoled myself with the thought that Gandhiji used the words because they were well known and understood by the masses.[8]

As indicated earlier, the Congress insistence on forming one-party cabinets in the provinces was a serious mistake. The Swiss pattern where racial and linguistic groups were represented in a composite cabinet was not unknown to the Congress. There was also a suggestion that matters which were of particular significance to certain communities, such as their social customs, religious establishments, language and

---

[7] *It Shall Never Happen Again* (Delhi: All-India Muslim League, 1946), p. 3.

[8] Jawaharlal Nehru, *An Autobiography* (London: The Bodley Head, 1958), p. 72. See also A. R. Desai, *Social Background of Indian Nationalism* (Bombay: Geoffrey Cumberlege, 1948), pp. 366–367.

literary traditions, should not be subject to legislation by the common central or provincial legislature, but should fall within the domain of special bodies or guilds, each of which represented one cultural or religious group.[9]

It is difficult to establish the degree of truth in the charges levelled by the Muslim League against the Congress governments. The Muslim League did not respond to a Congress offer to have the charges investigated by the Chief Justice of the Federal Court (an Englishman). Moreover, the evidence offered by pro-Congress Muslim leaders was conflicting. The president of the pro-Congress *Jamiyat al Ulama-i-Hind* suggested that in view of the fact that Muslims were dissatisfied with the treatment meted out to them in certain Congress provinces, the Congress should appoint a nonofficial committee to look into the charges. He also protested at the increasing use of Sanskrit words in the Hindustani language.[10] Abul Kalam Azad felt the Muslim League charges "were absolutely unfounded."[11] The point that one has to bear in mind is not whether the Muslim grievances were true or exaggerated but whether a great majority of Muslims believed them. Had not the Qur'an reminded them time and again that the infidel could never be expected to bear any good will toward Muslims? When the Congress Ministers resigned their offices in October, 1939, on the plea that India had been dragged into war with Germany by the British government without consulting Indian leaders, Jinnah seized this occasion to call upon the Muslims to celebrate what he designated the "Deliverance Day" on December 22, 1939. The resolution that was passed by Muslim League meetings in various provinces on this day said:

> The Congress Ministry both in the discharge of their duties of the administration and in the Legislatures have done their best to flout the Muslim opinion, to destroy Muslim culture, and have interfered with their religious and social life, and trampled upon their economic and political rights. . . .[12]

The Emergence of Pakistan

One could say that several writers and political leaders had predicted the division of India into several states.[13] But so far as Muslim leaders were concerned, they started groping toward the idea of a separate

[9] See Percival Spear, *Communal Harmony* (Bombay: Oxford University Press, 1940).

[10] *The Indian Annual Register. 1939.* (Calcutta), I, 382.

[11] Azad, p. 21.

[12] Jamil-ud-Din Ahmad, ed., *Some Recent Speeches and Writings of Mr. Jinnah* (Lahore: Ashraf, 1952), I, pp. 118–119.

[13] For an outline of these views and theories, see Sayeed, pp. 110–122.

Muslim state during the early twenties of this century. We have already referred to Iqbal's conception of a separate and independent Muslim state in northwest India which he put forward at a Muslim League session in December, 1930. Iqbal was thinking only of northwest India and not of Bengal. He was also agreeable to the idea of this northwestern Muslim state entering into a federal arrangement with the rest of India for a clearly agreed purpose like joint defense. Choudhry Rahmat Ali, when he was a student at Cambridge, suggested the word *Pakistan* in a pamphlet published in January, 1933. He pointed out that *Pakistan* was both a Persian and an Urdu word and that he had composed it by taking certain letters from the names of Muslim homelands in India and Asia. According to him, the word *Pakistan* was composed in the following manner: *P*unjab, *A*fghania (North-West Frontier Province), *K*ashmir, *I*ran, *S*indh (including Kachch and Kathiawar), *T*ukharistan, *A*fghanistan and Balochista*N*.[14]

Soon after the outbreak of the war, it was clear to the Muslim League that in view of the opposition of the Princes and the Congress, the chances of implementing the federal part of the Government of India Act, 1935, had become very dim. In his statement of October 18, 1939, the Viceroy had made it clear that the British government would be prepared to consider any modifications of the Act that the various Indian parties would like to propose. The Muslim League wanted a clear undertaking from the British government that they would not put forward any constitutional scheme without obtaining the approval and consent of the Muslims of India. The only commitment Jinnah could extract from the Viceroy, however, was that Muslims would be consulted before the British government made any declaration regarding the constitution. The Muslim League was not entirely satisfied with this position.

On March 26, 1939, it was announced that the Working Committee of the All-India Muslim League had set up a committee to examine the various constitutional proposals which had already been made regarding the future constitution of India. This committee was also to consider constitutions of other countries and was then to report its conclusions at an early date to the working committee. Several schemes had been put forward by Muslim leaders: some suggested two or three separate federations while others recommended an all-India federation of the regions comprising Muslim, Hindu, and other areas.[15]

The way Jinnah's mind was working was revealed in an article he published in *The Time and Tide* of London on January 19, 1940. He

[14] Choudhry Rahmat Ali, *Pakistan The Fatherland of the Pak Nation* (London: The Pak National Liberation Movement, 1947), p. 225.

[15] See Sayeed, pp. 117–121.

pointed out that the Muslim League was irrevocably opposed to any federal objective because it would bring about Hindu majority rule. He suggested that the British government should revise the entire problem of India's future constitution *de novo:* "To conclude, a constitution must be evolved that recognizes that there are in India two nations who both must share the governance of their common motherland."[16]

A day before the famous Lahore Resolution was passed on March 23, 1940, Jinnah's presidential address spelled out the two-nation theory which became the bedrock of the Muslim League ideology.

> It is extremely difficult to appreciate why our Hindu friends fail to understand the real nature of Islam and Hinduism. They are not religions in the strict sense of the word, but are in fact different and distinct social orders, and it is a dream that the Hindus and Muslims can ever evolve a common nationality. . . . They neither intermarry, nor interdine together and, indeed they belong to two different civilisations which are based mainly on conflicting ideas and conceptions. Their aspects on life and of life are different. It is quite clear that Hindus and Mussalmans derive their inspirations from different sources of history. They have different epics, their heroes are different, and different episodes. Very often, the Hero of one is a foe of the other and likewise their victories and defeats overlap. To yoke together two such nations under a single state, one as a numerical minority and the other as a majority, must lead to growing discontent and final destruction of any fabric that may be so built up for the government of such a state.[17]

The resolution which was passed at the Lahore session of the All-India Muslim League on March 23, 1940, stated:

> Resolved, that it is the considered view of this Session of the All-India Muslim League that no constitutional plan would be workable in this country or acceptable to the Muslims unless it is designed on the following basic principles, viz. that geographically contiguous units are demarcated into regions which should be so constituted, with such territorial readjustments as may be necessary, that the areas in which the Muslims are numerically in a majority as in the North-Western and Eastern zones of India should be grouped to constitute "Independent States" in which the constituent units shall be autonomous and sovereign.

The resolution clearly stated that "North-Western and Eastern zones of India should be grouped to constitute 'Independent States.' " Later the resolution again stated that the respective regions would assume

[16] Jamil-ud-Din Ahmad, I, p. 138.
[17] *Ibid.,* I, pp. 160–161.

"all powers such as defence, external affairs, communications, customs, and such other matters as may be necessary." Was the Muslim League deliberately making provision for the establishment of two states? Did the Working Committee think that since the two zones were separated from each other by Indian territory, it would not be easy to make them units of a single federation and, therefore, each of them was to be an independent state? There is evidence to suggest that the idea of two separate federations of Muslim provinces and states, one in the north-west and the other consisting of East Bengal and Assam, had been considered by League leaders.[18] However, since the Lahore Resolution could be interpreted to mean that it envisaged the creation of two independent Muslim states, it later created confusion and misunderstanding. Those Bengali leaders who felt after Partition that the Center, dominated by West Pakistanis, was not looking after the interests of Bengal, claimed that the original Lahore Resolution visualized two independent Muslim states, one of West Pakistan and the other of East Bengal.

So far as the official position of the Muslim League as expressed by Jinnah was concerned, it was clear that it interpreted the Lahore Resolution to mean that the Pakistan state would constitute a single federation consisting of the northwestern provinces of India (the North-West Frontier, Baluchistan, Sind, and the Punjab) and the eastern provinces of Bengal and Assam. This was outlined by Jinnah in an interview with the Associated Press of America soon after the Lahore Resolution was passed. Referring to the difficulties of defending the two separate areas of Pakistan, the League president pointed out that the two halves of Pakistan would be more closely knit than the British Commonwealth of Nations.[19] The Muslim League did not use the word *Pakistan* in the Lahore Resolution, but it came to be known as the Pakistan Resolution, and, as Jinnah explained it later, "We wanted a word, and it was foisted on us, and we found it convenient to use it as a synonym for Lahore Resolution."

During 1940–47, Jinnah played his hand with consummate skill. He exploited every opportunity that presented itself and capitalized fully on the weaknesses and tactical mistakes made by the Congress. After the passage of the Lahore Resolution, there were several factors working in his favor. The Congress ministries had resigned. The Muslim League, by obtaining the support of independent Muslims and other groups, continued to be in power at one time or another in Bengal, the

[18] Choudhry Khaliquzzaman, *Pathway to Pakistan* (Lahore: Longmans, 1961), pp. 206–207.
[19] A. B. Rajput, *Muslim League Yesterday and To-day* (Lahore: Muhammad Ashraf, 1948), pp. 75–77.

Punjab, Sind, the North-West Frontier Province and Assam. In the remaining provinces, the Assemblies had been prorogued and the administration was under British Governors. Some of the big Congress leaders like Nehru, Gandhi, and Patel were often in prison during 1940–45. Again, soon after the Lahore Resolution was passed, Jinnah's position was strengthened by the Viceroy's statement of August 8, 1940, which clearly stated that the British government "could not contemplate the transfer of their present responsibilities for the peace and welfare of India to any system of government whose authority is directly denied by large and powerful elements in India's national life."

Jinnah's strategy was simple. He was in no hurry to come to a settlement as he needed time to strengthen the Muslim League organization as a disciplined force which spoke not only on behalf of what he called the hundred million Muslims of India but also stood completely behind its supreme leader, the Quaid-i-Azam. It was a rare phenomenon even in the long history of India that a Westernized cold-blooded logician and lawyer, who did not speak any of the languages of his community fluently, at the age of sixty-four (in 1940) had captured the imagination of a highly religious people like the Muslims. During 1940–45, a series of negotiations and proposals were shipwrecked on the rock of Hindu-Muslim differences. But with each failure, Jinnah's prestige soared, the Muslims blaming the enemy, the Hindu Congress, or the British, and displaying increasing zeal to struggle for Pakistan under his leadership. There was no pronounced anti-British strand in Muslim nationalism under Jinnah's leadership. Perhaps the Muslim League leaders were shrewd enough to know that if they were to arouse any anti-British feeling, particularly among the Muslims inhabiting the Punjab and the North-West Frontier, the British would regard this as a deliberate move directed at undermining their defense effort during the war.[20] The Muslim League could not afford to antagonize the British in this manner as they were not strong enough to take on two enemies at the same time. Above all, Jinnah knew that the Muslim League in the Punjab, the Frontier, and Sind was in the hands of the titled gentry, most of whom took pride in having rendered faithful services to the British government.

In April, 1942, Sir Stafford Cripps, a British Cabinet Minister, brought with him to India certain specific proposals regarding the Interim Government and the future constitution of India to be implemented at the end of the war. The negotiations that Cripps held with the Congress and League leaders ended in failure, but the cause of

[20] See Khalid B. Sayeed, "Pathan Regionalism," Reprint No. 13, Duke University Commonwealth Studies Center (1964).

Pakistan was advanced because the British government for the first time had recognized the right of individual provinces to stay out of the proposed Indian Union and to form a separate federation.

The Gandhi-Jinnah talks took place during the month of September, 1944. They were brought about largely by the efforts of C. Rajago-palachari, a former Congress Premier of Madras, to resolve the Congress-League deadlock on the issue of Pakistan. Throughout the talks, Jinnah contended that the Rajagopalachari formula, on the basis of which Gandhi wanted to continue his discussions, did not fully concede the basic demands of the Lahore Resolution. The formula suggested that the northwestern and eastern areas of India should be demarcated so that the wishes of the inhabitants of the area might be ascertained. But Jinnah insisted that Gandhi should first concede that the two zones of Pakistan would comprise the six provinces of Sind, Baluchistan, the North-West Frontier Province, the Punjab, Bengal, and Assam. Gandhi's position was that Muslims could claim only those parts of the Punjab, Bengal, and Assam where they were in absolute majority. Jinnah did not agree to this proposal and said that if it were accepted, the area of Pakistan would be maimed and mutilated. However, what Jinnah described as a truncated and moth-eaten Pakistan had to be accepted by the Muslim League in August, 1947, when Muslims were given only those contiguous districts of Punjab, Bengal, and a part of Assam where they constituted a majority.

The more basic difference between the two leaders was over the question of federal and confederal arrangements between the two states. Jinnah took his stand on a separate and independent national state of Muslims with complete sovereignty over matters like defense and foreign affairs. Gandhi, on the other hand, was willing to accord to the Muslims the right of separation not because they formed a separate nation but only because they wanted to separate themselves from "one family consisting of many members." According to Gandhi, such a separation would still imply that matters like foreign affairs, defense, internal communications, etc., "must necessarily continue to be the matters of common interest between the contracting parties."[21] The impression one gathers from this correspondence is that Jinnah distrusted Gandhi as a wily politician and thought the talks would not bear any fruit unless the British were made a party to the settlement. He had agreed to hold these talks with Gandhi for the great tactical and political advantages that he would be able to snatch from these negotiations. For the first time it was clearly and publicly recognized

[21] For a more detailed account of the Gandhi-Jinnah talks, see Sayeed, pp. 130–134.

that here were two leaders, Gandhi representing the Hindus, and Jinnah representing the Muslims, meeting, as it were, at the summit to resolve the political deadlock in India.

The next stage was reached when the Viceroy, Lord Wavell, called a conference of Indian leaders in June, 1945. The purpose of this conference was to hold discussions regarding the reconstitution of the Viceroy's Executive Council to include leaders of Indian political parties in such a way that a balanced representation was given to the main communities. Muslims and Caste Hindus were to be accorded equal representation. Again the crucial difference between the Congress and the Muslim League was with regard to the League's claim that it alone had the right to nominate all the Muslim members of the Executive Council, since it was the sole spokesman of the Muslims of India. This meant that the Congress could only nominate Caste Hindu members in its quota for the Executive Council. There were to be representatives of other communities like the Sikhs and the Scheduled Castes. Another sore point with Jinnah was that the Viceroy also suggested the inclusion of Malik Khizr Hyat Khan Tiwana, the Muslim Premier of the Punjab, who had broken with Jinnah. This meant that the Executive Council under this arrangement would have two non-League Muslim members, one, the Muslim Premier of the Punjab, and the other, a Muslim member from the Congress Party, who, the Congress insisted, would be included in its quota. Though Lord Wavell, announcing the failure of the Simla Conference in July, 1945, assumed full responsibility for the failure of the Conference, it was clear the Conference had been wrecked by Jinnah's uncompromising attitude. Jinnah knew that once the various Muslim leaders — and particularly the Muslim leaders of the Punjab — realized they were not likely to get any prize offices by remaining outside the Muslim League, they would all have to flock to the Muslim League. Such a stand by Jinnah was bound to win for him great admiration among the Muslims, for he was satisfying a very deep and religious urge of his community, namely, that for the unity and solidarity of the *millat* (community of believers).

On July 26, 1945, a Labor Government was established in Britain. Congress circles were jubilant, but the Muslim League suspected the new British government to be of pro-Congress sympathies. The new government wanted elections to be held so that the elected representatives might form a Constituent Assembly to formulate a new constitution for India. The government made it clear that it would not be right to force the Muslim-majority provinces into joining a new constitutional arrangement against their wishes, but, at the same time, it would not be proper to allow any minority, however large and important, to veto the attainment of self-government for the rest of India.

In the elections that were held for the central and provincial legislatures, both the Congress and the Muslim League emerged with resounding successes. The Congress showing was very impressive in general constituencies. In the provinces, Congress successes enabled it to form ministries in Assam, Bihar, the United Provinces, Bombay, Madras, the Central Provinces, Orissa, and the North-West Frontier Province. The Muslim League won every Muslim seat in the central legislature, and the Congress or non-League Muslim candidates who opposed it forfeited their deposits in many cases. It won 460 out of the 533 Muslim seats in the central and provincial Assemblies. The Muslim League could form governments only in Bengal and Sind. In the Punjab the Muslim League obtained 79 out of a total of 86 Muslim seats, but since the 79 Muslim seats it had won did not have a clear majority in a house of 175, and since it was opposed by other non-Muslim parties, the Muslim League could not form a ministry. A ministry was formed by Khizr Hyat Khan with the help of Congress and Sikh support. It should also be noted that the Congress success in forming a ministry in the North-West Frontier Province was a serious blow to the Muslim League. The Congress had won 19 Muslim seats as opposed to 17 Muslim seats won by the League. The League, however, claimed that the personal influence of the Khan brothers was largely responsible for this and succeeded in making the ministry unpopular by launching a province-wide agitation later on the issue of Pakistan.

In order to hold discussions with the elected representatives and other political leaders regarding the future constitutional setup, the British government sent a Cabinet Mission consisting of three Cabinet Ministers, including the Secretary of State for India and Sir Stafford Cripps. The Cabinet Mission arrived in New Delhi on March 24, 1946, and held a series of discussions with Indian leaders. But the differences between the Congress and the Muslim League could not be bridged.

The Cabinet Mission announced their plan on May 16, 1946. They turned down the demand for a sovereign state of Pakistan as impracticable and unworkable. First of all, the six provinces claimed by the League would have a non-Muslim minority of 37.93 per cent in the northwestern areas and 48.31 per cent in the eastern areas. Another argument against Pakistan in the view of the Mission was that even if it were established, twenty million Muslim minorities would still remain dispersed in the remainder of British India. The Cabinet Mission pointed out that they had also considered a smaller sovereign Pakistan confined to the Muslim-majority areas alone, but they found the Muslim League opposed to such a scheme. The Cabinet Mission was not prepared to recommend it either because it would involve a radical partition of the Punjab and Bengal and stressed the serious administrative, economic, and military disadvantages of dividing the country in this fashion.

The salient proposals outlined in the Cabinet Mission's Plan for the future constitution of India were as follows:

1. A Union of India comprising both British India and the States with its domain over foreign affairs, defense, and communications and with powers necessary to raise the finances required for these subjects.

2. Union executive and legislature to be constituted from the British India and States' representatives. The provision regarding parity of representation in the union legislature and executive between Hindu and Muslim majority provinces or groups was deleted. The Muslim fear of a Hindu majority was met by the provision that on a major communal issue a decision by the legislature would require a majority of the representatives present and voting of each of the two major communities as well as a majority of all the members present and voting.

3. All the residuary subjects would vest in the provinces.

4. Provinces would have a right to join groups and each group would be allowed to determine the provincial subjects to be administered in common.

5. In the Cabinet Mission Plan itself three sections were provided, each having its own provinces. Section A had Madras, Bombay, the United Provinces, Bihar, the Central Provinces and Orissa. Out of 187 representatives in Section A, 167 were general or non-Muslim, and 20 Muslim. Section B had the Punjab, the N.-W. F. P. and Sind in which, out of 35 representatives, Muslims had 22, Sikhs 4 and general 9. Section C had Bengal and Assam in which out of 70 representatives, Muslims had 36 and general 34. Thus, the total number of representatives for British India was 292 on the basis of one representative for every million of the adult population. The maximum for Indian States, provided on the same basis, was 93.

6. The representatives chosen above would meet to draft the new constitution. After the preliminary business like the election of the chairman, other officers, and an Advisory Committee on the Rights of Citizens, Minorities and Tribal and Excluded Areas, the provincial representatives would divide into three sections as indicated above —A, B, and C.

Thereafter, these sections would formulate provincial constitutions for the provinces included in each section. The question whether there should be any group constitution for those provinces and what provincial subjects would be entrusted to the group would also be taken up by these sections. It was also laid down that provinces could opt out of groups in which they were placed if the legislatures of those provinces decided to do so after the first general election under the new constitution.[22]

Even though the Cabinet Mission had rejected Pakistan, the Muslim League accepted the Plan. The Muslim League thought that the battle for Pakistan could not be won immediately. The Cabinet Mission had offered the Muslim League a great tactical advantage in the form of compulsory grouping of the six Muslim provinces in Sections B and C. It was true that these provinces had to join a Center, but the provinces were given considerable autonomy, and, above all, the big provinces like the Punjab and Bengal, in which the Muslims did not have a considerable majority, were to be left intact. Thus, the Muslim League thought that it had won the substance of Pakistan, if not the whole of it.[23]

The Congress, on the other hand, was not happy regarding the compulsory grouping of provinces, but they were confident that it would not work. Section A, which had Hindu-majority provinces, would decide against grouping and even in Sections B and C, which had Muslim-majority provinces — the North-West Frontier Province with its Congress government, and Assam with its Hindu majority — would not tolerate compulsory grouping. In a letter to Lord Wavell, the Congress president, Azad, wrote: "While adhering to our views we accept your proposals and are prepared to work them with a view to achieve our objective."[24] It was thus apparent that the Muslim League and the Congress were accepting the Cabinet Mission Plan, hoping they would be able to maneuver within its framework in such a way that they would attain their respective objectives.

The Cabinet Mission Plan also provided for the formation of an Interim Government to carry on the administration until a new constitution was framed and brought into being. During the negotiations for an Interim Government that look place between the Congress and Muslim League, it was apparent that the crucial issue between the two organizations was whether the Congress had the right to nominate a Muslim from their party as a member of the Interim Government. Jinnah was always at his best in extracting concessions in such negotiations. The Viceroy at first conceded the Muslim League claim that

[22] For the statement by the Cabinet Mission, see Sir Maurice Gwyer and A. Appadorai, eds., *Speeches and Documents on the Indian Constitution 1921–47* (London: Oxford University Press, 1957), II, pp. 577–584.

[23] For Resolution passed by the Council of the All-India Muslim League, see *ibid.*, II, pp. 600–602.

[24] For Congress and League statements and correspondence regarding the Cabinet Mission Plan, see *ibid,* II, pp. 603–624.

it alone would have the right to nominate all the Muslims in the Interim Government. Consequently, the Congress refused to join the Interim Government and the Muslim League demanded that it alone should be allowed to form the Interim Government. The Viceroy tried to extricate himself from such an uncomfortable position by reopening the negotiations. Later, he gave the Congress the right to nominate a Muslim, and it decided to join the Interim Government. But Jinnah declared that he would resort to "direct action" and withdrew the League acceptance of the Cabinet Mission Plan. The League then called on Muslims throughout India to celebrate August 16, 1946, as Direct Action Day. Jinnah said that he was bidding good-bye to constitutional methods, pointing out that the British government, faced with the prospect of the Congress launching a civil disobedience movement, had decided to appease the Congress. Noncooperation, he argued, was the only weapon the Muslim League possessed to obtain acceptance of its demands.

Even though the League called upon the Muslims to celebrate Direct Action Day of August 16 in a peaceful manner, it resulted in Hindu-Muslim riots in Calcutta. Lieutenant-General Sir Francis Tuker, who was in charge of the military operations during the riots, not only held the Muslim League, the Congress, and the Sikhs responsible for the riots in Calcutta, but noted that Hindu-Muslim antagonism had infected the officers of the Indian army.[25] This was indeed an alarming situation because it was well known that the police officers could not rise above their communal leanings at the time of the riots. When communal carnage and killing could not be controlled by the civilian authorities, the only recourse open to the government was to call in the army. The Calcutta riots were later followed by riots in Noakhali in East Bengal during the second week of October, 1946, which took a heavy toll of Hindu lives, and the Bihar riots towards the end of October and early November in which a large number of Muslims died.

It was apparent that the Muslim League civil disobedience movement would finally deteriorate into an all-India Hindu-Muslim civil war. The Congress was in the Interim Government, but there were Muslim governments in Bengal and Sind. With communalism infecting both the police and the army, the British were not in a strong position to maintain peace. The Viceroy, therefore, was eager to persuade the Muslim League to join the Interim Government. And Jinnah knew that the battle for Pakistan could best be fought by the Muslim League occupying positions of vantage in the central government.

Again, Jinnah played his hand with such adroitness in the negotiations that took place between the Muslim League and the Viceroy that

---

[25] Lieut.-General Sir Francis Tuker, *While Memory Serves* (London: Cassell, 1950), pp. 156 and 162.

he scored two tactical victories. First, he claimed that just as the Congress had a right to include a Muslim in their quota, he could also nominate a representative of the Scheduled Castes in the League quota. Secondly, since the Congress was not willing to hand over the portfolios of Defense and Home to the Muslim League representatives, the Muslim League was given perhaps an even more important portfolio, that of Finance. This, as Azad has written, was a serious mistake of the Congress, for the Muslim League Finance Minister, Liaquat Ali Khan, obtained possession of the key to government. "Every proposal of every Department was subject to scrutiny by his Department. In addition he had the power of veto."[26]

It was obvious that the Interim Government was not working as a united Cabinet. The Congress and the Muslim League were merely using the power they had acquired in the Interim Government to fight against each other. Whenever Nehru tried to hold informal meetings of the Executive Council at his residence, League members would absent themselves and attend informal meetings of League members of the Interim Government at Liaquat's residence. The first budget which Liaquat as Finance Minister brought before the Assembly announced heavy taxes on the war profits of the rich industrialists, a great majority of whom were Hindus, and who financed the Congress.

Even though the Muslim League had joined the Interim Government, it still had not withdrawn its rejection of the Cabinet Mission Plan nor sent its representatives to the Constituent Assembly which was meeting in Delhi. The Congress demanded the Muslim League to either accept the Cabinet Mission Plan or resign from the Interim Government. The Muslim League replied that the Congress had never accepted the Cabinet Mission Plan in its entirety, for the Congress was determined in its opposition to the compulsory grouping of provinces. The British Labor Government felt that in such circumstances a bold policy as well as a new Viceroy was needed to save the situation. On February 20, 1947, the appointment of Lord Mountbatten as Viceroy was announced. In his statement of February 20, 1947, Prime Minister Attlee set the time limit of the British withdrawal following the transfer of power as June, 1948. Thus, Mountbatten arrived with set targets.

> If by the 1st October Mountbatten considers there is no prospect of reaching a settlement on the basis of unitary Government, he is to report to the British Government on the steps he considers should be taken for the hand-over of power on the due date.[27]

[26] Azad, p. 167.
[27] Alan Campbell-Johnson, *Mission With Mountbatten* (London: Robert Hale, 1951), p. 31.

There is considerable evidence which goes to suggest that soon after Mountbatten's arrival in Delhi on March 22, 1947, most of the opponents of Partition had veered round to the idea that Pakistan was inevitable. Azad, who met Patel soon after Mountbatten's arrival, "was surprised and pained when Patel in reply said that whether we liked it or not, there were two nations in India." Similarly, "Jawaharlal Nehru asked me in despair what other alternative there was to accepting partition." As for Gandhi, at first he said that Partition "will be over my dead body." But within a few days, "he too had changed."[28] This change in Gandhi took place on April 2, 1947. Both Patel and Nehru were impressed by the argument that it would be better to hand over a few small strips of territory in the northwest and in the east to Muslims than to endanger Indian unity and strength by trying to work with the Muslim League.[29] Thus, barely two weeks after Mountbatten's arrival it became clear that India would be divided.

It was clear that Partition could not be avoided; only the mechanics of Pakistan had to be worked out. These were spelled out in the British government's statement of June 3, 1947. The provincial Legislative Assemblies of the Punjab and Bengal were to meet in two parts, one consisting of the representatives of the Muslim-majority districts and the other representing the rest of the province, to decide by a simple majority whether the province concerned should be partitioned. If either part decided in favor of Partition, the province would be partitioned. A commission for each of the two provinces was to be set up by the Governor-General to demarcate the boundaries of the two parts of the Punjab and Bengal on the basis of ascertaining the contiguous majority areas of Muslims and non-Muslims. The commission was also to be instructed to take other factors into account. A referendum was to be held in the North-West Frontier Province in the event the whole or any part of the Punjab decided not to join the existing Constituent Assembly to ascertain the wishes of the people of the province regarding which Constituent Assembly they would like to join. British Baluchistan was also to be given an opportunity to decide whether it would like to join the existing Constituent Assembly or a new Constituent Assembly consisting of Muslim-majority areas. A referendum was also to be held in the district of Sylhet to determine whether in the event of the partition of Bengal, the people of Sylhet would like to be amalgamated with the Muslim part of Bengal.

The Indian Independence Act, 1947, brought into being the two Dominions of India and Pakistan. The transfer of power was to take

[28] For these statements, see Azad, pp. 185–187.
[29] *Ibid.*, pp. 187–188.

place on August 15, 1947, and after that date the British government would have no responsibility in areas which were included in British India; British paramountcy over the Indian states would also lapse. The lawmaking power in each Dominion would belong to the legislature of that Dominion and, until the constitution was framed, the Government of India Act, 1935, with certain modifications would be the constitution of each Dominion. A provision was made for the appointment of a separate Governor-General for each of the two Dominions. Thus, Indian states were expected to make their own future arrangements with their new Dominion governments.

When Mountbatten arrived in India, he found that the country was faced with a desperate situation. The central government, infected by the Congress-League struggle for power, stood paralyzed before the mounting lawlessness and communal warfare in the country. In the Punjab, the provincial government under the Unionist Party was being toppled by the fierce attacks of the Muslim League. The Muslim League had launched a civil disobedience movement against the Congress government in the North-West Frontier Province. Mountbatten decided in favor of what Lord Wavell had called a major surgical operation. And he, as the principal surgeon, thought that he would save the patient from additional pain by performing the operation immediately. But the pains that afflicted the body politic of the subcontinent were of an historical and fundamental nature. The communal carnage, the slaughter of thousands, and the transmigration of millions of Muslims and Hindus across the two borders were some of the excruciating pains that both Indian and Pakistan had to go through on the morrow of Partition.

The Muslim League: Ideology and Organization

The Muslim League, by constantly reminding the Muslims that they would lose their cultural and religious identity under Hindu domination, was successful in uniting the Muslims under its banner. When it put forward the ideal of Pakistan before the Muslims, the question arose as to what kind of state would be established after the achievement of Pakistan. Would it be an Islamic state based on an Islamic ideology? What kind of Islam would be established? Would it be the same Islam in its pristine purity as the Prophet had brought into being or would there be a reinterpretation of the Qur'an and the Traditions of the Prophet in the light of modern times?

The Western-educated lawyers, landowners, merchants, doctors, journalists, and civil servants did not find these questions disturbing or complicated. To them, Pakistan meant a state where Muslims would constitute the great majority and where industries, banks, the army and the bureaucracy would all be under the control of Muslims. Most of them in their day-to-day struggle against Hindu competition had not given too much thought to problems of social philosophy or political ideology. It was from this group that the Muslim League drew most of its articulate and influential supporters.

During 1945–46, when the Muslim League campaigned in the central and provincial elections on the issue of Pakistan, the Muslim League leadership had to seek the assistance of the *ulama, pirs* (spiritual guides), and other religious leaders. The opponents of the League were described as enemies of Islam, and Muslims were told that Pakistan would be an Islamic state drawing its inspiration and guidance from the principles of the Qur'an and the Traditions of the Holy Prophet. Those Muslim Unionists, who had been defeated in the elections in Punjab, charged that the Muslim League had indulged in the corrupt practice of invoking divine displeasure against those Muslim voters who did not vote for Muslim League candidates. It was well known that some of the *mullahs* (preachers) campaigning for the Muslim League in Punjab tried to pressure Muslim voters into voting for the League by threatening that those who opposed the League might be excluded from burial in a Muslim cemetery and consigned to hell after their death. Again, the *ulama* were called in when the referenda were held in Sylhet and the North-West Frontier Province in 1947 where the people were asked to decide whether they would like to join Pakistan or India.

There was a small group of Muslim intellectuals and young political leaders who were concerned about the ideology of Pakistan. Iqbal had raised the hopes of some of the socialists by suggesting that "social democracy in some suitable form and consistent with the legal principles of Islam is not a revolution but a return to the original purity of Islam."[30] In his moving and lyrical poetry, he had constantly championed the cause of the poor peasants and the downtrodden masses throughout Asia. But other strands in Iqbal's thought clearly indicated that despite his stress on Islam's dynamism, he was conservative and in favor of religious revivalism.[31] However, there were many young intellectuals and political leaders who had been impressed by Iqbal's criticism of Western social and economic systems. They were also attracted by the Soviet experiment in economic planning designed to bring about a better distribution of wealth. They rejected Marxian

[30] Mohammed Noman, ed., *Our Struggle, 1857–1947* (Karachi: Pakistan Publications, n.d.). Appendix II. Letters of Iqbal to the Quaid-i-Azam M. A. Jinnah, p. 27.

[31] One can detect his conservatism even in his oft-quoted lecture, "The Principle of Movement in the Structure of Islam." Sir Mohammad Iqbal, *The Reconstruction of Religious Thought in Islam* (Lahore: Shaikh Muhammad Ashraf, 1960), pp. 146–180.

materialist dialectics as antithetical to Islam, but were not disturbed by Soviet totalitarianism. For example, Ishtiaq Husain Qureshi, who later became Minister of Education in Pakistan, wrote in a Muslim League publication:

> The Russian experiment has a great deal to teach us in the methods of increasing our industrial and material power in spite of lack of capital. . . . All our population will have to be regimented for the purpose of reconstruction which will have to be planned.[32]

During 1945–46, some of the well-known Muslim socialists left the Congress because of mounting Hindu-Muslim antagonism. (Mian Iftikharuddin, a well-known political leader in Punjab, who became the publisher of *The Pakistan Times,* was one of them.) To these socialists, economic planning, nationalization of key industries, land reforms, and a more equitable distribution of wealth were more relevant and vital for the future of Pakistan than the issue of an Islamic state. The manifesto of the Punjab Provincial Muslim League was published and probably written by a left-wing leader, Danyal Latifi. It declared that there should be nationalization of key industries and banks beginning with immediate nationalization of all public utility services, public control of private industry, a ceiling placed on land holdings, and an equalization of taxation involving the imposition of additional taxes on large landowners.[33] Similarly, it was reported that Abul Hashim, the general secretary of the Bengal Provincial Muslim League, had socialist leanings. G. M. Sayed, president of the Sind Provincial Muslim League during 1943–45, had been expelled from the Muslim League because of his outspoken criticism of Sind's landowning politicians and the Central High Command. He had argued that Islam was being used by the Muslim League to maintain a reactionary and corrupt social and political system in Sind.

> Do not forget that Islamic society actually in existence is that in which religious head is an ignorant Mulla, spiritual leader an immoral Pir, political guide a power intoxicated feudal lord and whose helpless members are subjected to all the worldly forces of money and influence. If the really important question about the abolition of Jagirdari and Zamindari system crops up or the prohibition of intoxicants becomes the issue of the day, what would not a rich Jagirdar or an aristocratic member of a sophisticated club do to use his influence, as also that of the Mulla and the Pir, to resist this threat to what is essentially an immoral and un-Islamic cause?[34]

[32] Ishtiaq Husain Qureshi, *The Future Development of Islamic Polity* (Lahore: Shaikh Muhammad Ashraf, 1946), p. 23.

[33] *Manifesto of the Punjab Provincial Muslim League 1944* (Delhi: Danyal Latifi), pp. 13–14, 19, and 24.

[34] G. M. Sayed, *Struggle for New Sind* (Karachi: 1949), p. 216.

54 THE PAKISTAN MOVEMENT

Thus, a number of young idealists and socialists among the lower echelons of the Muslim League leadership soon became disenchanted with the League after the formation of Pakistan when the men at the top ignored their demands for economic and social reforms. The disappointment of the *ulama* and other orthodox elements was equally acute, for the promised Islamic state in Pakistan was in no way a reality.

The Congress and the Muslim League were not political parties in the normal sense of the term. They were national movements engaged in waging their respective struggle for national independence. Gandhi, addressing a Congress session, had declared: "When we march as an army, we are no longer a democracy. As soldiers we have got to take orders from the General and obey him implicitly. His word must be law. I am your General."[35] Though the Muslim League, unlike the Congress, did not put forward an economic or social program before the Muslims, its task of building a disciplined and united national movement was perhaps easier. Muslims were not only fearful of the Hindu majority, but Islam had made them conscious of their separate cultural and political identity. Jinnah's slogans of faith, unity, and discipline were designed precisely to appeal to the Muslim sense of national solidarity. During the elections of 1945–46 he declared: "Vote for a Muslim Leaguer even if it be a lamp-post." When his mission of achieving Pakistan was accomplished in June, 1947, he was reported to have said, "I have done my job. When the Field Marshal leads his army into victory, it is for the civil authority to take over."[36]

As one reads through the constitutions of the All-India Muslim League of 1940, 1941, 1942, and 1944, one notices a steady centralization of power in the hands of the president and his Working Committee. The Working Committee could control, direct, and regulate all the activities of the various provincial Leagues. It could suspend, dissolve, or disaffiliate any provincial League which failed in its duties or acted contrary to the directions of the Working Committee or the Council of the All-India Muslim League. The Working Committee was a creature of the president in the sense that its members were nominees of the president. It was well known that Jinnah ruled his Working Committee with a rod of iron. "He is said to tell them what's what, and that they invariably fall into line."[37]

Landowners represented the largest single group in the Muslim

[35] Cited in R. Coupland, *The Indian Problem* (New York: Oxford University Press), III, 92.

[36] *Dawn* (Delhi), August 18, 1947.

[37] R. G. Casey, *An Australian in India* (London: Hollis & Carter, 1947), pp. 64–65.

League Council. Out of a total membership of 503 members, there were as many as 163 landlords. Punjab contributed the largest share of 51, followed by the United Provinces. Proportionately, Sind's share was the highest in the sense that out of 25 members in the Council, 15 were landlords. But the twin cries of Islam in danger and Pakistan had put so much power in the hands of Jinnah that no landowner could hope to defy his authority without losing political support. The next largest group in the Muslim League Council was that of lawyers, about 145 in number.[38] In the task of popularizing the message of the League among the masses and winning their support in the elections, one of the main instruments that Jinnah relied upon was the students. In Lasswell's words, they found in him "the supreme leader, who is the one capable of doing all that the child once thought the physical father could do."[39] Coming from a middle or low middle-class background, Jinnah personified in their eyes all that they aspired for — an elegantly dressed, highly successful lawyer, an adroit parliamentarian, and the Quaid-i-Azam of the Muslim nation.

In 1944 the Muslim League officially claimed a membership of some two million people. During the elections of 1945–46, it polled about 4.5 million or 75 per cent of the Muslim votes in the election.[40] When the struggle for Pakistan was being waged, it was expected that all Muslims would close their ranks and subordinate their selfish or parochial interests to the national cause. And it was true that by and large Muslims throughout India did display this sense of national cohesion. But over more mundane matters, of day-to-day provincial politics, the Muslim League like any other party was divided by factions and feuds. In addition, some of the fissures and weaknesses associated with the politics of Muslims in India were also reflected in the internal politics of the Muslim League. Strong-armed tactics and violence were endemic in the politics of several provinces, but they had a special place in the feudal politics of Sind and the Punjab.

[38] *List of the Members of the Council of the All India Muslim League 1942* (Delhi: n.d.). The figures have been worked out from this list. One can only be approximately correct in these figures because the particulars regarding the profession of each Councillor are not given in each case. Therefore, the author had to draw on the information given to him by former office-bearers and members of the Working Committee of the All-India Muslim League. A few of the Councillors, who had legal qualifications and are therefore listed as lawyers, were not practicing lawyers.

[39] Harold D. Lasswell, *Psychopathology and Politics* (New York: The Viking Press, 1960), p. 174.

[40] The 4.5 million votes cast for the Muslim League do not indicate the total number of votes that might have been cast in favor of the League if the 40 uncontested seats had been contested. See the table of these election results in *The Indian Annual Register. 1946.* (Calcutta), Vol. I.

In the Punjab and Sind, landowners constantly employed rough elements, either to keep the tenants under control or to help them in their fights against rival landlords. It was said that a number of crimes reported to the police were actually a trial of strength between the rival landlords. Sir Francis Mudie, Governor of Sind (1946–47) in a letter to Lord Wavell, said about Muhammad Ayub Khuhro, a Minister in Sind at that time, "Like most large zamindars [landlords] in this country, and not only in this Province, he probably is in contact with a number of bad characters whom he finds useful if his tenants get out of hand."[41] In large cities like Calcutta, Delhi, Lahore, and Bombay, Muslim League politicians were involved in protecting the lives of Muslim citizens living in Muslim localities during Hindu-Muslim riots. This was probably equally true of Hindu politicians. This meant that they too had to associate with rough elements on whom an ordinary Muslim very often depended for his protection during the time of communal riots. All this was bound to inject a certain amount of violence in Muslim politics. It was alleged, for instance, that the president of the Punjab Provincial Muslim League and other members of the Working Committee had been busy in October, 1946, purchasing and collecting arms because they feared the outbreak of communal riots in that province.[42]

Several provincial rivalries and cleavages, which became endemic in Pakistan's politics later, had already cropped up during the pre-independence period. Sindhi Ministers not only wanted most of the high officials to be Muslims, but preferably Sindhi Muslims.[43] There were similar jealousies between the Pathans of the Frontier and the Punjabi Muslims. In Bengal, the local Bengali Muslims resented the commercial prosperity of the Urdu-speaking non-Bengalis.[44] H. S. Suhrawardy, Premier of Bengal (1946–47), supported by several Congress leaders, put forward during the time of Partition talks in early 1947 the idea of a "sovereign independent and undivided Bengal in a divided India."[45]

A Minister in a parliamentary system has to display two kinds of political skills. First, he should know how to keep his party together behind his party program, and secondly, he should provide leadership

[41] Sir Francis Mudie's letter to Lord Wavell, DO No. 98/FR, dated 21st February, 1946.

[42] *Dawn* (Karachi), October 22, 1949.

[43] Sir Francis Mudie's letter to Lord Wavell, DO No. 298/FR, dated 11th June, 1946.

[44] *Bengal Legislative Assembly Proceedings.* Fifth session, (1939), LIX, 29–30.

[45] V. P. Menon, *The Transfer of Power in India* (Princeton: Princeton University Press, 1957), p. 355, and also Campbell-Johnson, p. 65.

and control over the civil servants in the matter of policy formulation and the management of his department. Most of the Muslim League politicians were unable to develop or display such political skills during the pre-Partition period. The majority that the Muslims had in the Provincial Assemblies in Bengal and the Punjab was very slender, not only because of the slight majority the Muslim population had over the Hindu population, but also because the non-Muslims were given weightage. (Similar weightage had been accorded to Muslims in the Hindu-majority provinces.) As a result, the Muslim League, even after its impressive success in the elections of 1945–46, could not by itself command a majority in either of the Assemblies. Thus, Muslim leaders, in order to maintain a stable majority in these Assemblies, had to form alliances with non-Muslim groups and parties. Such alliances, however, became increasingly difficult after the Muslim League committed itself to the goal of Pakistan. During 1937–42, Sir Sikander Hyat maintained his Unionist ministry (an alliance between Muslim, Hindu and Sikh landlords) in the Punjab by entering into a pact with Jinnah. According to the pact Muslim members of the Unionist Party would join the Muslim League and support the Muslim League in all-India matters; the central Muslim League, in its turn, would not interfere in provincial politics. But after the Muslim League adopted the Pakistan Resolution, the Punjab Premier was not able to insulate his province from the gusts of all-India politics. It was reported "that unless he walked warily and kept on the right side of Jinnah he would be swept away by a wave of fanaticism. . . ."[46] After the elections of 1945–46 in Punjab, the Muslim League was able to command the support of 79 Muslim members out of a total of 86, but was unable to form a ministry because the Sikhs and Hindus would not cooperate. When a Unionist ministry was formed under a Muslim Premier, however, the Muslim League launched a civil disobedience campaign which succeeded in paralyzing the administration and brought about the resignation of the ministry.

Bengal was faced with a similar situation; namely, Muslims could not maintain a stable government without the support of non-Muslim members. It was difficult for Fazlul Huq, the Premier of Bengal (1937–43), to remain in office after he antagonized the Muslim League by turning against Jinnah. His successor, Khwaja Nazimuddin, was loyal to Jinnah but was swept out of office in 1945 when his administration was faced with successive crises like the Bengal famine and the soaring prices of cloth and foodstuffs. After the elections, Suhrawardy formed his ministry in 1946 with the support of inde-

[46] Penderel Moon, *Divide and Quit* (Berkeley and Los Angeles: University of California Press, 1962), p. 38.

pendent elements. The Muslim League ministry, however, found it difficult to do any constructive work. Communal riots broke out in August, 1946, in Calcutta, followed later by riots in Noakhali. In such an atmosphere, the traditions and conventions of parliamentary government could hardly thrive.

In the Frontier and Sind, the record of the Muslim League in parliamentary politics was even more unimpressive. The Muslim League failed to win a majority in both the elections of 1937 and 1945 in the North-West Frontier Province. It was the Congress Party led by the two Khan brothers which enjoyed grass-roots support, whereas the Muslim League was aligned with landowners. The Congress Party continued to be popular until the Muslim League in 1946 launched a civil disobedience movement against the Congress ministry on the issue of Pakistan. In Sind, politics was a game of musical chairs among the big landlords. Sir Francis Mudie, who observed the political scene as Governor of that province during 1945–46, criticized the administrative capabilities of most of the Sindhi Ministers in his letters to Lord Wavell. Commenting on political intrigues, Sir Francis wrote:

> I don't know what will happen when our Assembly meets at the end of this month or in July. There are the usual stories that Khuhro, in league with Sayed, will try to upset Sir Ghulam. On the other hand, Khuhro is afraid that Sir Ghulam will intrigue with Sayed and the Hindus of his party to oust him. It is possible, too, that Bendeh Ali will try some more of his tricks as he is dissatisfied at not being Home Minister.[47]

As we pointed out in Chapter 2, British civil servants found it relatively easier to work with Muslim politicians, who were mostly landowners, than with Congress politicians. The pathetic contentment of the Muslim peasantry was left relatively undisturbed. The landowning politicians were absorbed in intrigues, and the civil servants were thus "guardians" of both tenants and their landlords. Jinnah is reported to have complained bitterly in 1932: "The Muslim camp is full of those spineless people, who whatever they may say to me, will consult the Deputy Commissioner about what they should do!"[48] By 1945–46 the situation had so changed that Muslim League politicians won the 1946 provincial elections in Punjab and Bengal largely by campaigning on the issues of Pakistan and Islam. This meant that in

[47] Sir Francis Mudie's letter to Lord Wavell, DO No. 298/FR, dated 11th June, 1946.

[48] A. H. Albiruni, *Makers of Pakistan and Modern Muslim India* (Lahore: Muhammad Ashraf, 1950), p. 209.

a province like Punjab, where the Deputy Commissioners were very powerful, the Muslim League politicians had established their own contacts with the rural masses instead of depending upon the District Officers. However, this popularity of the Muslim League was short-lived, for it was not based on a strong party organization or on a concrete program. The civil servants continued to be very powerful both in the districts and in the Secretariat after the formation of Pakistan.

The leadership contests and jealousies that took place during the pre-Partition period continued in Pakistan. Jinnah tried to assemble as many groups as possible to achieve Pakistan. His advice was:

> We shall have time to quarrel ourselves and we shall have time when these differences will have to be settled, when wrongs and injuries will have to be remedied. We shall have time for domestic programme and policies, but first get the Government. This is a nation without any territory or any government.[49]

The Muslim League could have remained a viable organization if it had inherited from Jinnah a group of strong provincial leaders and a clear program. The structure of leadership in the League, however, was weak, consisting of the supreme leader, Jinnah, and under him subleaders who were supported by their own tribes or tenants. By eliminating strong leaders and planting pliable men in the provinces Jinnah made it extremely difficult for a collective leadership to emerge after his death. Indeed, he died soon after Pakistan was formed and the groups that had been hastily strung together fell apart.

These feuds and intrigues were not unique to the politics of the Muslims of India. Students of comparative politics have no doubt discerned these traits in the politics of other transitional societies. But the chief difference between countries like India which were successful in maintaining political stability and countries like Pakistan which were not successful lay in the fact that a nationalist movement like the Indian National Congress was able to devise and develop ways of dealing with conflicts and cleavages. The Muslim League merely had one supreme arbitrator — Jinnah. After he died and Prime Minister Liaquat Ali Khan was assassinated, there was no machinery left to settle or adjust intra-party disputes.

[49] Jamil-ud-Din Ahmad, (1964), II, p. 199.

4

Politics of Conflict (1947-58) and Martial Law (1958-62)

Struggle for Survival, 1947–51

Very few states in the world started with greater handicaps than Pakistan did on August 14, 1947. It was common knowledge that Muslims lagged behind Hindus in administrative services, in commerce and finance, and in political leadership. A number of political and economic experts had ruled Pakistan out as a practicable proposition.[1] Its territory cleft into two physically and culturally separate parts would have created difficulties even for a state blessed with far greater resources and much better administrative and political leadership.

As if all this were not enough, Pakistan was faced with even greater problems which came not in single file but in battalions. The outbreak of communal riots not only took a heavy toll of human life in both India and Pakistan; these riots also deprived Pakistan of essential personnel, office equipment, and records when trains carrying men and supplies were burned. All these difficulties, however, were dwarfed by the gigantic problem of the refugees. It was not only a question of feeding and settling the millions who had come in; an equally formidable task was that of protecting the lives and property of about 3.5 million Hindus and Sikhs who were leaving West Punjab for India.

[1] See the verdict of the British Cabinet Mission cited in the previous chapter and also *Constitutional Proposals of The Sapru Committee* (Bombay: Kunwar Sir Jagdish Prasad, n.d.), pp. 143–147.

According to the 1951 census, there were 7.2 million refugees in the country out of a total population of 75.6 million. In West Pakistan there were 6.5 million refugees out of a population of 33.7 million, which meant that one out of every five persons in West Pakistan was a refugee.

In August, 1947, the entire machinery of the central government had to be created. Unlike Delhi, Karachi was the capital of the small provincial government of Sind. The central secretariat had to be created and adequately staffed. There were Ministers, but not every Minister had either a well-equipped office or a Secretary in charge of his department. The financial position of the government was extremely precarious. Soon after the outbreak of the Kashmir conflict with India in October, 1947, the Indian government decided to withhold the payment to Pakistan of Rs. 550 million which represented Pakistan's unpaid share of the cash balances under the Partition agreements.[2] Pakistan was also denied its share of the large stocks of reserve arms, equipment, stores, etc., belonging to the former Indian army.[3] When the Indian government sent its troops to Kashmir in answer to the ruler's appeal for help against Pathan tribesmen, Jinnah, the Governor-General of Pakistan, ordered the British Commander-in-Chief of the Pakistan army to send troops into Kashmir. These orders were not obeyed, and the Governor-General was told that if he insisted on carrying out his orders, the British officers in the Pakistan army would be withdrawn.[4]

The situation in West Punjab was even more depressing. Lahore, the capital city, looked very much like blitzed London. The economic and commercial life of the province was in a state of paralysis because all of the Hindu traders, moneylenders, accountants and clerks had fled to India. West Punjab was the first province to face the full impact of millions of refugees. The governor, Sir Francis Mudie, frantically wrote to Jinnah that he did not have enough administrators to cope with the situation. The refugees were not only a burden on the economy of the province; the harrowing tales of slaughter and carnage they brought with them incited the local Muslims to retaliate against the fleeing Hindus and Sikhs. The provincial government, in its attempts to maintain law and order, was bound to become unpopular.

The province of East Bengal did not face a comparable refugee problem, but its administrative and economic resources were much poorer than those of West Punjab. A British Governor of the undivided Province of Bengal had warned that East Bengal after Parti-

---

[2] The cash balances were released in January, 1948.
[3] John Connell, *Auchinleck* (London: Cassell & Co., 1959), p. 921.
[4] *Ibid.*, p. 931.

tion might become a rural slum.[5] All the key positions in the East Bengal administration were held by either Punjabi civil servants or Urdu-speaking Muslim civil servants who had migrated from India. A large number of Hindu lawyers, doctors, university teachers, and merchants had fled. "There was a time when over fifty per cent of the civil and criminal courts could not function owing to the shortage of judicial and executive officers."[6]

Pakistan's rulers were not merely interested in restoring its administrative machinery to a level of efficiency attained during the British period; they were determined to make it a modern industrialized state. However, the infra-structure needed for industrialization was woefully inadequate. A central bank, the Pakistan State Bank, and a commercial bank, the National Bank of Pakistan, were established. Muslim commercial communities like the Memons, the Khojas, the Bohras, and the Chiniotis were mostly merchants and were reluctant to take risks with their capital for the long-term investment needed for industrialization. Thus, the initiative and leadership came largely from a few Pakistani civil servants who established the Pakistan Industrial Development Corporation.

As long as Jinnah was alive (he died September, 1948), he was Pakistan. He held the position of Governor-General, but the powers and influence that he exercised were far beyond those normally associated with that office. The Cabinet rarely functioned without his directives. He was the supreme arbitrator between the Center and the provinces. His Prime Minister, Liaquat Ali Khan, emerged as *de facto* Prime Minister only after his death.

Both Jinnah and Liaquat relied very heavily on the civil servants. Particularly in the provinces, where most of the Ministers had assumed office for the first time, the Governors and civil servants were extremely powerful. Governors of three of the four provinces (North-West Frontier Province, West Punjab, and East Bengal) were British and members of the former Indian Civil Service. None of the Ministers in the central government had had much experience in administering government departments. The only model of government that Pakistani leaders had known was that of the British viceregal system in India under which the bureaucrats had exercised their power most of the time without any interference from politicians. Faced with gigantic problems of refugee rehabilitation and law and order and being dependent upon British Governors and civil servants, who were steeped

[5] Alan Campbell-Johnson, *Mission With Mountbatten* (London: Robert Hale Limited, 1953), p. 65.

[6] Khwaja Nazimuddin's address as the Governor-General. *Constituent Assembly (Legislature) of Pakistan Debates,* II, No. 2 (December 16, 1948), p. 4.

in viceregal traditions of bureaucratic government, it was not surprising that Pakistani leaders thought that Pakistan could do no better than to follow the British viceregal pattern.

Like the former Viceroys, Jinnah received fortnightly letters from his Governors which gave him a detailed account of everything ranging from intrigues in the provincial cabinets to details of refugee rehabilitation or the food problem. The Government of India Act, 1935, had been criticized as an act not very conducive to the growth of democratic government or provincial autonomy. Now that the alien rulers had been replaced by a Pakistan government, it was deemed proper that the central government, under the adapted 1935 Act, should arm itself with powers to dismiss ministries and clamp Governor's rule on the provinces. Under the Public and Representative Offices (Disqualification) Act, 1949, popularly known as the PRODA, the central or a provincial government could dismiss a Minister found guilty of corruption or misconduct by a tribunal of Federal or High Court judges set up by the government. The Premier of Sind was dismissed on charges of corruption and misconduct in April, 1948, and the West Punjab ministry was dismissed in January, 1949. There were several dismissals and ministerial changes in Sind during 1948–51.

It was obvious that there was bound to be a clash between civil servants, who were armed with extraordinary powers, and politicians, who were eager to mobilize political support. One could see how the minds of civil servants were working. According to *The Report of the Sind Special Court of Enquiry*, Secretaries should be allowed to draw the attention of the Governor if the Ministers disregarded the rules of business by granting favors to members of their party. The Court had been set up to investigate charges of misconduct and corruption against M. A. Khuhro, the Chief Minister of Sind. It reported:

> In making these suggestions we are not unmindful of the fact that the Ministers have to satisfy the members of their party and the latter do not realise that the grant of their unlawful or unusual requests does affect the administration of the province. We feel that it will be a help to the Ministers themselves if the Constitution Act makes their position clear with regard to the day to day administration, as the members of their party would then not expect from them what, under the law, is not permissible.[7]

This was how the civil servants wanted to eliminate corruption, but they did not understand or care how the political process in a democratic system worked. If all forms of political patronage were elimi-

[7] *The Report of the Sind Special Court of Enquiry* (n.d.), p. 186. One of the signatories was Justice Shahabuddin, a member of the former Indian Civil Service.

nated, it was difficult to see how, particularly in an underdeveloped country with very little industrialization, politicians would be able to build or maintain political support.

There was a head-on clash between the politically ambitious Hamidul Huq Choudhury, Minister for Finance, Commerce and Industries in the government of East Bengal and the dyed-in-the-wool bureaucrat, Aziz Ahmad, the Chief Secretary, who wanted to maintain the best traditions of the Indian Civil Service. During the inquiry conducted against Hamidul Huq Choudhury, it was alleged that the Chief Secretary had appointed the Commissioner of Sales Tax without consulting the Finance Minister and that several other Secretaries were appointed without the approval of the Ministers concerned.[8] Another allegation was that the Chief Secretary had taken over the Accommodation Board which allocated houses to officials and non-officials in the province under his jurisdiction when it should have been the responsibility of the Minister for Revenue, at that time Hamidul Huq Choudhury.[9] The Chief Secretary, who was the head of the entire civil service of the province, was amassing an enormous amount of power for the purposes of efficiency and better coordination. In justification of his action, he could have pleaded that he acquired these powers at a time when the entire administrative structure of East Bengal had to be built up. On the other hand, Hamidul Huq Choudhury could argue that he was also interested in the rapid economic development of East Bengal and that to attain such an objective as a politician he needed political support, which could not be acquired without some patronage at his disposal. Unfortunately, there was no meeting of minds. The Chief Secretary was a Punjabi, and all the key posts in the East Bengal Secretariat were in the hands of Punjabis or Urdu-speaking civil servants from outside Bengal. All this was bound to create considerable resentment among the local Bengalis. Thus, as early as 1948 it was reported: "A feeling is growing among the Eastern Pakistanis that Eastern Pakistan is being neglected and treated merely as a 'colony' of Western Pakistan."[10]

Prime Minister Liaquat Ali Khan did try to politicize the bureaucratic viceregal system that he had inherited from Jinnah. But he had been overshadowed by Jinnah's domineering personality. After Jin-

---

[8] For these allegations, see the testimony of Mr. Aziz Ahmad in the *High Court of Judicature at Dacca in East Bengal in the Matter of An Enquiry Against Hamidul Huq Choudhury Under the Public and Representative Offices (Disqualification) Act, 1949.* Typescript (September, 1950). For these allegations, see pp. 59–60.

[9] *Ibid.*, p. 54.

[10] *Constituent Assembly of Pakistan Debates,* II, No. 1 (February 24, 1948), pp. 6–7.

nah's death in September, 1948, Liaquat was not only a powerful Prime Minister; he was also the president of the Pakistan Muslim League. He was a persuasive and eloquent speaker and had considerable hold over the masses. His advantage also lay in the fact that he himself was neither a Punjabi nor a Bengali and therefore could function as an umpire between the various provincial interests that existed in Pakistan, and particularly between the feuding Punjabi and Bengali Ministers. His basic weakness, however, lay in the fact that apart from his courageous stands against the alleged aggressive intentions of India, he did not capture the popular imagination by offering a program of economic and social reforms.

As we have noted in the previous chapter, there were young men in the Muslim League who had eagerly looked forward to Pakistan becoming a modern progressive state. But they were disappointed, for land reforms were not introduced even when Pakistan was faced with an enormous inflow of refugees who were mostly agriculturalists from East Punjab. Indeed, Mian Iftikharuddin, Minister for Rehabilitation of Refugees in the West Punjab government, resigned because his proposal for resettling refugees on the estates of the large landowners was turned down. Many young lawyers and students in East Bengal wanted to win power and influence in the Muslim League in order to pressure that organization into adopting a vigorous stand in support of the demands of Bengalis, particularly over the matter of recognizing Bengali as one of the state languages. The old guard, however, supported by the Prime Minister, resisted such efforts. After the death of Jinnah, Nazimuddin, who was the Chief Minister of East Bengal, became Governor-General. The Muslim League Party in the East Bengal Legislature wanted to elect a leader who would be nominated as Chief Minister. They did not get such an opportunity, for the provincial governor was instructed by the Governor-General to appoint Nurul Amin as the Chief Minister. As a result, Suhrawardy, who had been unsuccessful against Nazimuddin in the contest for the Chief ministership of East Bengal, was able to enlist support in forming his Awami League Party from a number of disenchanted Muslim Leaguers.

Regional Conflicts, 1951-56

Before all the provinces, states and other areas in West Pakistan were integrated into the province of West Pakistan in 1955, there were in all four provinces in Pakistan. In the eastern region, there was East Bengal. In the west, there were West Punjab, Sind, and the North-West Frontier Province. There were also states like Bahawalpur, Khairpur, and Baluchistan in West Pakistan. In addition, there were areas like the Tribal Areas in the North-West Frontier Province,

Baluchistan, and Karachi, which were under the jurisdiction of the central government. The population of East Bengal in 1951 was 41.9 million and that of West Pakistan 33.7 million. In terms of area, West Pakistan was slightly more than five times as large as East Bengal.

It has almost become a truism to say that the politics of a developing country very often revolves around regional loyalties and that emergent countries are claiming to be states without having become nations. Muslim League leaders during the pre-independence period, absorbed in the heat and excitement of the struggle for Pakistan, grossly underestimated the potency of regional and linguistic forces. They were successful in driving home the point that for a Muslim, whether a Punjabi or a Bengali, the common enemy was the Hindu. They also pointed out that Islam recognized no regional or linguistic loyalties — particularly in India, where there was a danger of their faith and culture being submerged in a Hindu sea, Muslims could not afford to think in terms of parochial or provincial loyalties. Before Pakistan, Jinnah's cry was, "First get the government, this is a nation without any territory or any government." After Pakistan was achieved, one could say that Pakistan had a government, but one often wondered whether a strong sense of national consciousness had emerged. Nearly nine years after the establishment of Pakistan, an East Bengal leader, commenting on this problem, observed: "It is a country which in reality is not one country. We are going to form one State out of two countries. We are going to form one nation out of two peoples."[11]

Any government in Pakistan was under the influence of three institutional groups — the Constituent Assembly, the civil service, and the army. There were other forces such as religion, landowning classes, and general public opinion, but their impact was not always decisive; above all, they were often represented by the three major groups that we have mentioned. How were the two regional groups represented in the three major institutions in Pakistan?

In 1953, in the Constituent Assembly of 79 members, the Muslim League Parliamentary Party had 60 members, 33 of whom were Bengalis. In addition to this, there was a Dacca-Karachi-Peshawar axis. Bengalis had been able to win the support of the Frontier and Sindhi groups because of the resentment that they often displayed towards Punjabi domination. The Punjabis dominated the civil service, and in the army, next to the Punjabis, the Pathans were influential. Under the quota system in civil service recruitment, East Bengalis could hope to occupy some of the key positions in the future; whereas in the army West Pakistani domination was so complete that East Bengalis could

[11] *Constituent Assembly of Pakistan Debates,* I (January 16, 1956), p. 1816.

not hope to alter the situation for a long time to come. The Bengalis pointed out that it was because of the preponderance of West Pakistanis in the army and the civil service that there was economic disparity between the two wings. Economic policy, formulated under the influence of West Pakistani civil servants, had been such that industrialization in West Pakistan had forged ahead leaving East Bengal far behind. In addition, central government expenditure, because of the location of Karachi and the concentration of the army in West Pakistan, was much greater in West Pakistan than in East Bengal. East Bengal contributed much more to foreign exchange earnings of the country than the West and yet it was lagging far behind West Pakistan in economic development. The Center's plea was that scarce resources were being invested in West Pakistan because its developed economy would yield higher returns than that of East Bengal. The only course open to the Bengalis was to use their majority in the Constituent Assembly in such a way that government decisions with regard to allocation of economic resources were not unduly influenced by the West Pakistani groups. Bengali Muslim Leaguers knew that it was not easy for them to build a united Bengali front because there were eleven Congress (Hindu) members in the Bengali group. Therefore, they were eager to form an alliance with the Sindhi and Frontier groups.

The major constitutional conflicts that took place in Pakistan arose largely over the question of representation to be accorded to these major regional groups in the central legislature of Pakistan. Since it was the task of the Constituent Assembly to draft the constitution of Pakistan, it became the main arena of conflict. The Constituent Assembly set up the Basic Principles Committee in March, 1949, to report on the main principles on which the constitution of Pakistan was to be framed. In the Interim Report of the Basic Principles Committee, produced in 1950 during Liaquat's Prime Ministership, the lower house was to be elected on the basis of population.[12] In the upper house, the existing provinces, namely, East Bengal, West Punjab, the North-West Frontier Province and Sind, and Baluchistan (which was given the status of a province) were given equal representation. For purposes of representation, states and areas were attached to the province with which they were contiguous. The two houses were given equal powers in all matters including the budget and money bills. In cases of dispute, decisions were to be taken by joint sessions of both the houses. This meant that even though East Bengal representation would be higher in the lower house, West Pakistan representation would

[12] *Basic Principles Committee Interim Report* (Karachi: September 7, 1950).

be four times that of East Bengal in the upper house. No mention was made of the state language, but the Bengalis feared that Urdu alone might enjoy that status. There was considerable opposition from East Bengal, and Liaquat withdrew the Report, suggesting that its consideration should be postponed. The Prime Minister invited the people at large to send concrete and definite proposals to the Basic Principles Committee of the Constituent Assembly.

In the Basic Principles Committee Report produced in 1952, it was apparent that the Bengalis had gained the upper hand.[13] Parity was the principal feature of the Basic Principles Committee Report. The upper house of the federal legislature was to have sixty members from East Bengal and sixty others from West Pakistan distributed among the various units. The lower house would have two hundred members from each of the two wings. East Bengal was one unit, but West Pakistan consisted of three provinces and several states and areas — West Punjab, Sind, North-West Frontier Province, Baluchistan, the Tribal Areas, Bahawalpur, Khairpur, the Baluchistan States, and Karachi. The Punjabis opposed these proposals on the ground that they were designed to establish Bengali domination over the whole country.[14] The argument was that the Bengalis would come as a united group; by winning support from the smaller West Pakistan provinces of Sind and the N.-W. F. P. and by isolating Punjab, they would have sufficient majority to rule the country.

In addition to these regional conflicts, Pakistan was faced with a religious controversy. We have already seen that the Muslim League during the pre-Partition period had sought the assistance of the *ulama* and other religious leaders in the election campaigns and had promised the voters that Pakistan would be an Islamic state. The Objectives Resolution passed by the Constituent Assembly in 1949 also stated that Muslims would be enabled to mould their lives in accordance with the teachings and requirements of Islam. After the establishment of Pakistan, the *ulama* and other religious groups felt that the ideal of an Islamic state was in no way near being established and that the state was run by Westernized politicians and civil servants, most of whom, according to the religious groups, were not good practicing Muslims. During 1952–53, religious groups in Punjab launched demonstrations and propaganda against the Ahmadis, a religious sect among Muslims

[13] *Report of the Basic Principles Committee* (Karachi: Manager of Publication, 1952).

[14] This sharp conflict is disclosed in *Report of The Court of Inquiry Constituted Under Punjab Act II of 1954 to Enquire into the Punjab Disturbances of 1953.* (Lahore: 1954), p. 285. This Report is popularly known as the Munir Report because the president of the Court of Inquiry was Justice M. Munir.

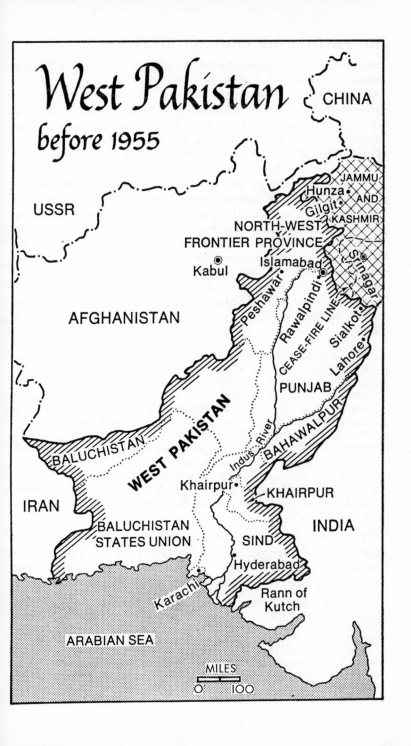

West Pakistan
before 1955

CHINA

USSR

JAMMU
Hunza•
Gilgit• AND

NORTH-WEST KASHMIR
FRONTIER PROVINCE

Kabul Islamabad Srinagar

AFGHANISTAN Peshawar•

Rawalpindi•

Sialkot•
CEASE-FIRE LINE
Lahore•

PUNJAB

WEST PAKISTAN

BALUCHISTAN

BAHAWALPUR

Indus River

Khairpur• KHAIRPUR

IRAN

BALUCHISTAN INDIA
STATES UNION

SIND

Hyderabad•

Karachi• Rann of
Kutch

ARABIAN SEA

MILES

0   100

who questioned the universally held Muslim doctrine that the Prophet Muhammad was the last of the prophets. Their demands were that the Ahmadis should be declared a religious minority and the Foreign Minister, Zafrullah Khan, and other civil and military officers belonging to the Ahmadi sect should be dismissed. (This controversy is also discussed in Chapter 7.) Khwaja Nazimuddin, who was then the Prime Minister, was in sympathy with these demands but was not willing to concede them, probably because such an action would lower the prestige of Pakistan in international circles, particularly in the United States whence Pakistan expected help to tide over its existing food scarcity. The Chief Minister of West Punjab, Daultana, having found that religious agitation was assuming alarming proportions in the province, wanted to divert the whole movement to Karachi. He thought it would be unwise on his part to suppress such a religious movement which had become so popular among the masses. In addition, Daultana, who was the spokesman of the Punjabi group, was not particularly fond of Prime Minister Khwaja Nazimuddin, who represented the Bengali interests. In the graphic language of the Munir Report:

> If the demands be compared to a baby, the whole subject of responsibility can be put into a single sentence and that is that the Ahrar gave birth to a baby and offered it to the *ulama* for adoption who agreed to father it, and that anticipating that the baby would cause mischief if it grew up in the Province, Mr. Daultana cast it on a canal, dug with the assistance of Mir Nur Ahmad and watered by the press and Mr. Daultana himself, to flow down Moses-like to Khwaja Nazim-ud-Din who in the apparent good looks of the baby noticed a frown and something indefinably sinister and therefore refusing to take it in his lap threw it away, with the result that the baby kicked and raised up a row which enveloped the Province of its birth and threw both Khwaja Nazim-ud-Din and Mr. Daultana out of office.[15]

The central Cabinet, when faced with the outbreak of lawlessness and rioting in Punjab, was forced into taking drastic action by imposing martial law on March 6, 1953. The initiative for this strong action came mostly from civil servants, and particularly from Iskander Mirza,

[15] *Ibid.*, p. 286. The Ahrar was formerly a pro-Congress and anti-Muslim League political group in the Punjab. The government circles in Pakistan felt that the aim of the Ahrar group in trying to exploit the religious feelings of the majority of Muslims against the Ahmadis, was to discredit the Muslim League Government in the eyes of the people. The movement, though started by the Ahrars, was joined later by several other groups, including the Jamaat-i-Islami and a number of Muslim Leaguers. For details, see the Munir Report.

who was then Defense Secretary. Martial law in Lahore gave an opportunity both to the army and to the public to see what could be accomplished by strong and speedy measures. It was reported that the streets of Lahore, for the first time in many years, looked clean, and that essential commodities were available to the public at controlled prices. Martial law in Lahore also led to the resignation of the Chief Minister, Daultana. Later, in April, 1953, Prime Minister Khwaja Nazimuddin was dismissed by the Punjabi Governor-General, Ghulam Muhammad. The Governor-General, in justification of his decision, pointed out that the Cabinet of Khwaja Nazimuddin had proved itself to be incapable of maintaining law and order and of arresting the deteriorating food situation.

One could see how the political process was working in Pakistan. In the case of martial law in Lahore, the decision was prompted largely by the pressure of the civil service and carried out by the army. The dismissal of Khwaja Nazimuddin was obviously a decision not taken by the central legislature. It was clear that the Prime Minister enjoyed the confidence of the legislature because the budget of his government had been recently approved by that body. It was brought home to the Bengali group in the Muslim League Parliamentary Party that even though they and their supporters from the smaller provinces of West Pakistan might control the majority in the party, the ultimate power was with the Punjabi group, supported by the civil servants and the army. Why did the Muslim League Parliamentary Party, led by the Bengali group, choose to surrender to the arbitrary action of the Governor-General? What prevented the Muslim League Parliamentary Party from refusing to accept Muhammad Ali Bogra as the new Prime Minister? The Bengali-led Parliamentary Party probably thought that they neither had enough public opinion behind them nor that the country cared enough for parliamentary institutions to support them in a fight against the Governor-General. It may be pointed out that as a result of the Prime Minister's statement in Dacca that Urdu alone would be the state language of Pakistan, there were demonstrations by students in Dacca in February, 1952. The police opened fire, a student died, and several others were injured. There was a wave of indignation and protest throughout the province and it looked as if leaders like Suhrawardy and Fazlul Huq were gathering support. Khwaja Nazimuddin, the Prime Minister and leader of the Bengali group, had clearly lost considerable support in his own province.

The Constituent Assembly had been indirectly elected in 1947 by the members of the various provincial assemblies. By 1953, it was apparent that a large number of them had lost grass-roots support. They were trying to formulate a constitution, but the regional conflicts and particularly the Punjabi-Bengali conflict was such that no solution had emerged. Governor-General Ghulam Muhammad, a former member of the Indian Audit and Accounts Service, was probably confident that his autocratic action would not provoke a storm of protest throughout the country. Those politicians in East Bengal who had been urging the people to agitate against the Muslim League government of East Bengal and the Muslim League representatives in the Constituent Assembly for having failed to champion the cause of Bengali autonomy must have derived satisfaction from the fact that their opponents had been placed in such an embarrassing position.

The constitutional proposals that the new Prime Minister, Muhammad Ali Bogra (like his predecessor, also from Bengal), announced in the Constituent Assembly in October, 1953, tried to meet most of the objections that the Punjabi group had brought against the Basic Principles Committee Report.[16] The upper house would consist of an equal number of representatives from each of the five units, a concession to the Punjabi point of view. The lower house would be composed on the basis of population of each of the five units. This arrangement satisfied the Bengalis. In a joint sitting, each of the two wings would have equal representation. Equal powers were given to both houses and deadlocks were to be resolved by a joint sitting. In such a joint sitting, the majority vote must include at least 30 per cent of the total members belonging to each zone. This meant that Bengalis could not carry a proposal with a mere majority in the joint sitting. They would have to enlist the support of at least 30 per cent of the members representing the West Pakistan zone. Still the Punjabi group could have the feeling that the Bengalis would come as a united team to enlist support from the western zone in order to produce the requisite majority. The Bengalis could plead that they were not as united as they were being made out to be because nearly a quarter of their population consisted of Hindus. However, the Prime Minister announced that the new proposals had been unanimously accepted by his colleagues, by the Chief Ministers of East Bengal, West Punjab, Sind, the N.-W. F. P. and Bahawalpur, and by all the members of the Muslim League Parliamentary Party.

The crushing defeat of the Muslim League in East Bengal elections in March, 1954, altered the situation. The defeat brought home to the Bengali members of the Constituent Assembly the fact that the voters had given a clear verdict against them. In the eyes of the voters, they had not properly represented the interests of East Bengal. The protest vote also reflected the indignation of the people against the

[16] These proposals were incorporated in *Draft Constitution of the Islamic Republic of Pakistan* (Karachi: Manager, Government Press, 1954).

provincial government of East Bengal for having allowed the police to open fire against Dacca University students who were agitating for the recognition of Bengali as a state language. The defeat of the Muslim League also meant that the Bengali members of the Constituent Assembly, who had formerly been elected by an assembly with a preponderant Muslim League majority, were no longer true representatives of their province. Muhammad Ali Bogra, who had campaigned extensively in the elections, came to realize the passionate intensity that lay behind Bengal's demand for the recognition of Bengali as one of the state languages. In May, 1954, he accordingly moved an amendment to the Basic Principles Committee Report to the effect that Urdu and Bengali should be recognized as state languages. This amendment was adopted by the Constituent Assembly.

In East Bengal, where the United Front Party had won an overwhelming majority in the elections during the spring of 1954, a United Front ministry under A. K. Fazlul Huq came to power. Soon after the ministry was installed, there were riots in industrialized areas between Bengali and non-Bengali Muslims. In one of these riots, as many as four hundred people were killed. It was reported that the provincial ministry was unwilling to take stern action to restore law and order. The Chief Minister was summoned to Karachi for consultation, but his statements advocating extreme autonomy amounting to independence antagonized the Center. The ministry was dismissed on May 29, 1954, and Governor's rule was clamped on the province. The Defense Secretary, Iskander Mirza, was sent to East Bengal as Governor. Prime Minister Muhammad Ali Bogra, in a broadcast, said: "One thing is certain — the Centre will never allow this province to again incur the danger of disintegration."

All this must have caused considerable alarm among West Pakistani leaders. Particularly the Punjabis were apprehensive that even under the parity system of representation in the Assembly, Bengalis might exploit the differences among the provinces in West Pakistan. They proposed that all the provinces and areas in West Pakistan be integrated into one single province. When they found that they could not get much support for their proposal in the Assembly, they suggested a zonal subfederation of West Pakistan, again to unite West Pakistan.[17] The Governor-General tried to pressure some of the influential members from the smaller provinces of West Pakistan into lending their support to the zonal subfederation plan. It was reported he threatened that if they did not support the zonal subfederation plan, PRODA [Public and Representative Offices (Disqualification) Act] proceedings

[17] *Constituent Assembly of Pakistan Debates,* XVI (September 15, 1954), p. 361.

would be started against them.[18] A member of the Constituent Assembly, describing the alignment of forces in the Assembly, commented later:

> So strained became the relation between them that many meetings of the Constituent Assembly had to be postponed, and at times the Bengalis used to sit alone here while the Punjab members whiled away their time in having tea in the room of Chaudhri Mohamad Ali.[19]

During September and October, 1954, there was a chain of dramatic events which resulted in a final showdown between the Governor-General and the Bengal-Sind-Frontier group in the Assembly led by the Prime Minister. On September 20, the Public and Representative Offices (Disqualification) Act was repealed by the Constituent Assembly. The Prime Minister and his supporters expected that the Governor-General would dismiss the Prime Minister and form a new Cabinet. On September 21, therefore, an amendment bill to the Government of India Act, 1935, was moved to make sure that the Governor-General did not use the Act in any way to dismiss a ministry which enjoyed the confidence of the house. In April, 1953, the Governor-General, in dismissing Nazimuddin's Cabinet, had invoked Section 10 of the 1935 Act which stated that Ministers held office during the pleasure of the Governor-General. The Prime Minister thought the Governor-General, being a sick man, had more or less reconciled himself to his reduced status and left the country to negotiate a loan agreement with the United States. But by October 24, 1954, he had been brought back to Karachi to give his support to the Governor-General's decision to dissolve the Constituent Assembly.

Again, it was clear that the Governor-General had relied on his supporters in the Punjabi group, the civil service, and the army. *Dawn*'s colorful comments were not too far off the mark:

> There have indeed been times — such as that October night in 1954 — when, with a General to the right of him and a General to the left of him, a half-mad Governor General imposed upon a captured Prime Minister the dissolution of the Constituent Assembly and the virtual setting up of a semi-dictatorial Executive.[20]

[18] The Public and Representative Offices (Disqualification) Act, 1949, under which the government could start legal proceedings against Ministers or members of the Assembly on charges of misconduct or corruption.

[19] *Constituent Assembly of Pakistan Debates*, I (September 9, 1955), p. 630.

[20] Editorial, "Revolution," *Dawn*, August 11, 1957.

The president of the Constituent Assembly appealed to the Sind Chief Court to issue writs declaring that the central government had no right to prevent the Constituent Assembly from carrying on its functions. When the Sind Court gave its verdict in favor of the president of the Constituent Assembly, the central government appealed to the Federal Court. The ruling of the Federal Court given on March 26, 1955, was that the Act under which the president of the Constituent Assembly had appealed to the Sind Chief Court for the issue of writs had not received the assent of the Governor-General and therefore was illegal. Later, when the Governor-General made a reference to the Federal Court seeking its advisory opinion with regard to the legality of his action in dissolving the Constituent Assembly, the Federal Court declared that the Governor-General was within his rights in dissolving the Constituent Assembly because he felt that the Constituent Assembly had not performed the duty assigned to it by the Indian Independence Act, namely, that of providing a constitution for the country.[21]

The ministry that had assumed office after the dissolution of the Constituent Assembly on October 24, 1954, was called the ministry of "all talents." The Prime Minister was still Muhammad Ali Bogra, who had lost all effective power. It could be said that real power was in the hands of administrators with the army standing behind the government. The Governor-General himself had been a civil servant. The Minister of the Interior, Iskander Mirza, had been Secretary of the Ministry of Defense, and later Governor of Bengal. General Ayub Khan, the Commander-in-Chief of the army, was the Defense Minister. Chaudhri Muhammad Ali, a former head of the civil service, continued to be the Finance Minister, an office to which he was first appointed in 1951. Expounding the political philosophy of the new regime, the Minister of the Interior declared:

> Some undeveloped countries have to learn democracy, and until they do so they have to be controlled. With so many illiterate people, politicians could make a mess of things. There was nothing undemocratic in declaring the State of Emergency, because 95 per cent of the people welcomed it.[22]

We have suggested earlier that there was a basic conflict between the interests of bureaucrats and those of the politicians. The Pakistani bureaucrat, as a successor to his all-powerful British predecessor, felt

[21] Report on the Special Reference Made By His Excellency the Governor-General of Pakistan. Special Reference No. 1 of 1955. Reproduced in Sir Ivor Jennings, *Constitutional Problems in Pakistan* (Cambridge: Cambridge University Press, 1956), p. 283.

[22] *The Times* (London), October 30, 1954.

that just as the British civil servant had exercised untrammelled power and often kept the politicians under control, so should he be allowed to exercise his power without political interference. In Pakistan, particularly in East Bengal and in some areas of West Pakistan, a new group of politicians had emerged. They were eager to develop economically their respective areas or provinces as quickly as possible. They had come into conflict with the bureaucrats, but under Ghulam Muhammad, in addition to bureaucrats, army generals had also emerged powerful. East Bengali politicians and some of the politicians from the urban areas of West Pakistan had very little in common with the top oligarchs belonging to the army and the civil service. These two groups did not often meet socially and belonged to two different worlds. The army officers and civil servants got along well with the Punjabi and Sindhi landlords because they came from the same social background, had gone to the same schools, and belonged to the same social clubs. It was no wonder that Iskander Mirza, Minister for the Interior, expressed his complete contempt for the new group of politicians:

> They [illiterate peasants] elect crooks and scalawags who promise the moon. The scalawags make a mess of everything, and then I have to clean up the mess. Democracy required education, tradition, breeding, and pride in your ability to do something well.[23]

What were the objectives of the regime which sought to control democracy? We have already indicated that the Governor-General and the leading Punjabi members of the former Constituent Assembly desired the integration of West Pakistan as one unit. It has been reported that General Ayub had already prepared a plan for the integration of West Pakistan. Ayub argued that strategically and economically West Pakistan should be welded into one unit. The creation of such a united province, however, depended upon the large-heartedness of the biggest constituent, namely, Punjab. General Ayub suggested that Punjab should be persuaded into accepting 40 per cent representation in the West Pakistan legislature, which was less than what was due to it in proportion to its population, whereas other provinces should be accorded representation in proportion to their population.[24]

The technique used in integrating West Pakistan was spelled out in the famous documents which were drafted by the former Chief Min-

[23] *Reporter,* January 27, 1955, p. 32.

[24] General Ayub's plan embraced the whole of Pakistan. It was entitled "A Short Appreciation of Present and Future Problems of Pakistan." Colonel Mohammad Ahmed, *My Chief* (Lahore: Longmans, Green and Co., 1960), pp. 86–93.

ister of West Punjab, Daultana.[25] The combination of force and cunning that the documents recommended should be used in integrating West Pakistan suggests that the author must have modelled his plan on Machiavelli's *Discourses*. The documents referred to the fact that West Pakistan, in its confrontation with East Bengal, should speak as one entity because the politicians of East Bengal had often resorted to the " 'small brother's big brother' role of West disruption."[26] The course of action recommended was:

> The first necessity of the present context, therefore, is that we must clear the decks before we launch our political campaign. In other words, we must silence and render inoperative all opposition of which we are morally convinced that it is motivated by evil.[27]

The documents recommended the dismissal of the Chief Minister of Sind, Pirzada, a self-denying ordinance on Noon, the Chief Minister of West Punjab, "unreserved support to Rashid [Chief Minister of the N.-W. F. P.], stilling his suspicions, fortifying his nerve," and "no negotiations, no parleys" with Khan Abdul Ghaffar Khan, the leader of the Pakhtun movement in the Frontier. The author of the documents urged that propaganda in favor of integration should be organized in a highly skillful manner. Statements by prominent persons, a coordinated press campaign, pamphlets and tracts, an intensive political campaign designed to win the support of both the intelligentsia and the dispossessed (labor, tenants, small landowners), use of *mullahs,* etc., were all suggested. As to the role of the Punjab he wrote:

> At present we do not require too much noise in the Punjab. It will only put other people's backs up and cause suspicion.[28]
> At a later stage Punjab will have to take the lead. At that time I hope an effective intelligent Punjab leadership will have been put in place both at the Centre and at Lahore.[29]

[25] The Committee of the Constituent Assembly which examined the authenticity of these documents reported: "The views expressed by him (Daultana) were the views of the government and must have been written down by him after consultation with those interested in the One Unit Scheme." The One Unit Scheme refers to the scheme which was designed to integrate the various units of West Pakistan into one province or unit. Extracts from the documents were quoted in the Constituent Assembly when the Establishment of West Pakistan Bill was being discussed. *The Constituent Assembly of Pakistan Debates,* I (September 6, 1955), pp. 508–513, and (September 9, 1955), pp. 612–614.

[26] One Unit Documents. Document "X." Typescript, paras. 3 and 6. These documents were entitled Document "X," and Documents A, B, and C.

[27] One Unit Documents. Document B, para. 2.

[28] One Unit Documents. Document B, para. 6.

[29] One Unit Documents. Document "X," para. 7(biii).

After integration had been accomplished in this manner and the right kind of leadership was placed in power in West Pakistan, negotiations should be opened with the Bengali leaders, particularly with the ambitious and intelligent Suhrawardy, "on the basis of a four-subject Centre, two provinces, federal parity, complete provincial and cultural autonomy."[30]

As we have seen, the military leaders and the administrators were completely convinced that both military strategy and sound economics demanded that the provinces of West Pakistan should be integrated into one unit. They were aware that politicians, provincial civil servants, and the intelligentsia from the provinces of Sind and the North-West Frontier would offer resistance. The documents prepared by Daultana had suggested the use of skillful propaganda, but the army leaders and the bureaucrats were in a hurry. They knew that "the one real merit of the present regime is that it can hold a pistol to achieve political constitutional agreement," and they went about brandishing and using their weapons of arbitrary dismissals in Sind, the Frontier, and even in Punjab. In Sind, the Chief Minister, Pirzada Abdus Sattar, was able to produce a statement opposing the One Unit scheme signed by 74 of the 110 members of the Sind Assembly.[31] He was dismissed and replaced by Muhammad Ayub Khuhro. Khuhro was appointed Chief Minister on November 8, 1954, and by December 12, 1954, the same Assembly which had opposed One Unit under Pirzada reversed itself and passed a resolution approving the One Unit by 100 votes to 4.[32] Such quick and efficient methods of extracting the desired decisions from the Assembly or the electorate were characterized as "Khuhroism."

> It is very interesting to know what Khuhroism means! . . . that members of Legislative Assemblies shall be arrested; their relatives will be put under detention; officers will be transferred who will not carry out the behests against inconvenient persons; elections shall be interfered with and members of legislatures shall be terrorized.[33]

Even if a democratic regime had tried by gradual methods and by subtle and skillful propaganda to bring about the integration of West Pakistan, it would have encountered enormous resistance from the smaller provinces of Sind and the Frontier. Free and open use of force to eliminate opposition and impose integration further hardened the

---

[30] One Unit Documents. Document "X," para. 9.
[31] *Dawn*, October 24, 1954.
[32] *Dawn*, December 12, 1954.
[33] *Constituent Assembly of Pakistan Debates*, I (September 10, 1955), p. 656.

deep-seated opposition of Sindhi and Pathan leaders to what they regarded as Punjabi domination. What the dictatorial regime of Ghulam Muhammad sowed was reaped later by the revived democratic regimes at the Center and in West Pakistan. One of the causes of the breakdown of constitutional government in Pakistan was the holding of the pistol to enforce the One Unit plan. The Constituent Assembly was dissolved on October 4, 1954. Within five months of the dissolution, by appropriate dismissals and the installation of pliable regimes in the provinces, the Governor-General was all set to legalize the creation of West Pakistan. It may be noted that the legislature in East Bengal had not been allowed to meet and that the province had been under Governor's rule since May, 1954. On March 27, 1955, the Governor-General issued an ordinance to amend the Government of India Act, 1935, and invest himself with the power to establish the Province of West Pakistan. He made it clear that in issuing the ordinance his objective was not merely to create the Province of West Pakistan, but to arm himself with the power to provide a constitution for the entire country.[34]

The Governor-General was faced with another problem. The Federal Court in its judgment on the Constituent Assembly case had declared that no writs could be issued to the central government barring it from any action designed to obstruct the functioning of the Constituent Assembly, and that the act, which allowed the issuance of such writs was illegal because the Governor-General had not assented to it. This meant that a number of other acts, which had not received the assent of the Governor-General, were also illegal. The Governor-General, therefore, in his ordinance of March 27, 1955, declared that he was validating a number of acts invalidated by the judgment of the Federal Court. The reaction of the Court to such attempts was sharp and clear.

> The Governor-General can give or withhold his assent to the legislation of the Constituent Assembly but he himself is not the Constituent Assembly and on its disappearance he can neither claim powers which he never possessed nor claim to succeed to the powers of that assembly.

In the same judgment, the Federal Court declared:

> It might have been expected that, conformably with the attitude taken before us by responsible counsel for the Crown, the first

---

[34] The Emergency Powers Ordinance, 1955. Ordinance No. IX of 1955. See Sections 6(3) and 10. *A Collection of the Central Acts and Ordinances for the Year 1955* (Karachi: The Manager of Publications, Government of Pakistan, 1956), pp. 3–5.

concern of the Government would have been to bring into existence another representative body to exercise the powers of the Constituent Assembly so that all invalid legislation could have been immediately validated by the new body. Such a course would have been consistent with constitutional practice in relation to such a situation as has arisen. Events, however, show that other counsels have since prevailed. The Ordinance contains no reference to elections, and all that the learned Advocate-General can say is that they are intended to be held.[35]

Thus the Federal Court of Pakistan courageously raised its voice in defense of constitutional government while all others stood by as helpless spectators to the Governor-General's arbitrary use of power. In another judgment, the Governor-General was told that "he can only nominate the electorate and not members to the Constituent Assembly."[36] The course of action laid down for the government by the Federal Court was clear. They had to summon a new Assembly duly elected by the members of the provincial legislatures, and only the new Assembly could legalize the integration of West Pakistan and validate the invalid legislation. All that the Governor-General had been conceded was the right to validate the laws on a temporary basis until the meeting of the Assembly.

Why did the Governor-General decide to follow the ruling of the Federal Court and summon a new Constituent Assembly? Why did he not seize power and establish a dictatorship? It was obvious that besides being a sick man, he depended very largely upon the support of the army that he had received through the Commander-in-Chief, General Ayub Khan. General Ayub disclosed later that he "refused on several occasions the late Mr. Ghulam Mohammad's offer to take over the country."[37] Thus, without the army being willing to intervene directly at that time, the Governor-General had no other course available except to follow the ruling of the Federal Court and summon a new Constituent Assembly, which met on July 7, 1955.

The composition of the second Constituent Assembly was quite different from that of the first owing to the overwhelming defeat of the Muslim League in East Bengal in 1954. Indeed, Muslim League representation from that province was reduced to two. All the other Muslim Leaguers in the Assembly were from West Pakistan. As a result of this change, the East Bengali, Muhammad Ali Bogra, was replaced by Chaudhri Muhammad Ali, a West Pakistani, as Prime Minister in

[35] Usif Patel and Two Others v. The Crown. Reproduced in Jennings, pp. 245 and 255.

[36] Report on the Special Reference Made By His Excellency the Governor-General of Pakistan. Special Reference No. 1 of 1955. Jennings, p. 308.

[37] Field Marshal Mohammad Ayub Khan, *Speeches and Statements* (Karachi: Pakistan Publications, n.d.), II, 3.

August, 1955, and the Governor-General, Ghulam Muhammad, gave way to Iskander Mirza. The party composition in the second Constituent Assembly was:

Muslim League	26
United Front	16
Awami League	13
Congress	4
Scheduled Caste Federation	3
United Progressive Party	2
Others	16
Total	80

One of the important enactments of the new Constituent Assembly was the Establishment of West Pakistan Bill which was passed on September 30, 1955. The Assembly thus legalized the integration of West Pakistan as one province, a power which had been denied to the Governor-General by the Federal Court. The name of the eastern province was changed from that of East Bengal to East Pakistan in the 1956 Constitution; since then the two provinces have been referred to as West Pakistan and East Pakistan. The Constitution of 1956, which came into being on March 2, 1956, was largely the handiwork of the Prime Minister, Chaudhri Muhammad Ali, and had certain unique characteristics. In its desire to circumscribe the power of the President, it spelled out the mechanics of parliamentary government in all its essential details. In its attempt to accommodate the Bengali demand for autonomy and parity, and the demand of the orthodox elements for an Islamic state, it came halfway in making concessions to both of these groups.

The President who emerged in the constitution was not a mere figurehead. It was the duty of the Prime Minister to keep him informed about the entire administration and proposals for legislation. Above all, the President, according to Article 37 (3), was allowed to use his discretion in the appointment of the Prime Minister. This meant that when no party had a clear majority in the National Assembly, the President's discretionary power in the choice of the Prime Minister was bound to give him considerable influence over the National Assembly. Party loyalties in Pakistan were such that a majority often gravitated toward the man who was commissioned by the President to form a ministry. It was apparent that ever since 1951 Pakistan's political system had been plagued by the conflict between the head of state and the Prime Minister. The Governor-General or the President had not been willing to play the "dignified" role of a British monarch, letting his Prime Minister function as the "efficient" executive. Prior to 1956, the Governor-General could dismiss the Prime Minister and his Cabinet on the plea that the Ministers could hold office only "during his pleasure." Under the 1956 Constitution, Pakistan became a Republic, and the head of the state became known as President. After 1956, when there was no stable majority party in the Assembly, the President had his own political supporters in several parties, with the result that the conflict between the head of the state and the Prime Minister continued.

Article 31 of the Constitution was a concession towards the East Bengali demand that the gross underrepresentation of their province in the Defense Services should be rectified and that parity should be achieved between East and West Pakistan in other spheres of federal administration. As to whether elections should be conducted on the principle of joint electorates or separate electorates, it was suggested that parliament would resolve this issue after ascertaining the views of the Provincial Assemblies. On this question, it was clear that West Pakistan, because of the influence of the Muslim League, was in favor of separate electorates; whereas the East Pakistani position was that separate electorates would divide the East Pakistani representation into Hindus and Muslims and thus weaken the East Pakistani position in the National Assembly. [The Electorate (Amendment) Act, 1957, prescribed the principle of joint electorates for both national and provincial elections.] Similarly, under pressure from East Pakistan, the Provincial List of Powers was strengthened to include railways and industries, and matters like economic and social planning were placed on the Concurrent List. However, it could not be said that East Pakistanis were completely satisfied by these gestures. Their contention was that the province had suffered so much as a result of greater expenditure and industrial investment in West Pakistan that it would continue to lag behind even if parity were achieved in the allocation of resources between East and West Pakistan.

The orthodox elements were appeased by the declaration that Pakistan would be known as the Islamic Republic of Pakistan. As regards future laws, Article 198 laid down that no law would be enacted which was repugnant to the injunctions of Islam as laid down in the Holy Qur'an and Sunnah (Traditions of the Prophet). As regards the existing law, the President was to appoint a commission within a year of the inauguration of the Constitution to make recommendations as to how it could be brought into conformity with the injunctions of Islam.

Collapse of the Parliamentary System, 1956–58

Now that Pakistan had produced a constitution, one could see that the basic weakness of its political system was not the lack of a constitution but the absence of national political parties without which no democratic system could function. The Muslim League as a national movement under the charismatic leadership of Jinnah and Islam as a utopian ideology united the physically and culturally separate areas of northwest and eastern India and was able to achieve Pakistan in slightly over seven years after the Pakistan Resolution was passed in March, 1940. The fact that Pakistan could be achieved in such a short time misled Pakistanis into believing that Islamic unity and slogans like faith, unity, and discipline could do the same trick in building a modern state on stable foundations. For nearly seven years after Pakistan was achieved, the Muslim Leaguers thought that by invoking the name of Islam and characterizing all opponents of the Muslim League as traitors, they could maintain their party domination. They were rudely shocked when the East Bengali voters turned against the Muslim League in the elections of 1954, reducing the League from its overwhelming majority in the provincial legislature to a group of 10 in a house of 309 members. Even before this debacle, there were rumblings in Sind, the Frontier, and West Punjab. But in West Pakistan, the traditions of bureaucracy and feudal despotism were such that resistance to the existing government could be held in check by devices ranging from imprisonment of popular leaders like Khan Abdul Ghaffar Khan to rigged elections. The best training ground for a politician or a political party is an election, but Pakistani leaders did not get many opportunities to learn how the political process worked in a democratic society, for Pakistan never had a general election. As a result, Pakistani leaders did not get an opportunity to create or construct a national party which could aggregate the various regional and cultural groups at the national level.

The Muslim League, having played the role of a nationalist movement during the pre-independence period, could have emerged as a political party representing a constellation of interests both in East and West Pakistan. But it failed to transform itself into a political party with grass-roots support because of two factors. First of all, Muslim League leaders were not courageous enough to take a stand against the bureaucracy or the government of the day when some of their leaders were removed from office arbitrarily by the government. The image of the Muslim League in public eyes therefore was that of a party which rallied behind any leader that was foisted on a Provincial Assembly by the central government or on the National Assembly by the Governor-General or the President. The Muslim League, which at one time supported a Daultana in West Punjab or a Pirzada in Sind, was found to be equally loyal in supporting a Noon in Punjab or a Khuhro in Sind. Similarly, in the Center, the Muslim League supported Nazimuddin and after his dismissal was loyal to the new Prime Minister, Muhammad Ali Bogra, a nominee of the Governor-General and, at the time of his appointment, Pakistan's Ambassador to the United States. Secondly, the Muslim League was too much a prisoner of its past. Because it had been a principal advocate of separate electorates and had later supported Jinnah's two-nation theory, its leaders took the view that they would be betraying their principles if they were to accept joint electorates or a former Congressman as their leader. East Pakistani leaders were in favor of joint electorates because they thought that separate electorates would tend to divide the Bengali members of the National Assembly into Muslim and Hindu groups. In West Pakistan, after the integration of One Unit, it was felt that the best method of disarming opposition to the One Unit scheme in the North-West Frontier Province was to offer the chief ministership of West Pakistan to Dr. Khan Sahib, a former Congressman. The Muslim League, by taking a stand against this policy, lost power both in West Pakistan and in the Center in 1956. Thus by not adopting a flexible policy in order to attract maximum support from every important section of the country, the Muslim League failed to become a truly national party. Indeed, when it refused to support Dr. Khan Sahib as the Chief Minister of West Pakistan, Khan Sahib, backed by the Governor of West Pakistan and by the President, Iskander Mirza, successfully enticed nearly half of the Muslim League members in the Provincial Assembly into forming a new party called the Republican Party. The secretary-general of the new party revealed that its manifesto and constitution were written by Governor Gurmani of West Pakistan.

In Sind and the Frontier, the opposition to One Unit was deep and widespread. First of all, there was the traditional resentment of Sindhis and Pathans towards the Punjabis who controlled a major share of the West Pakistan administration. Indeed, their resentment was only reinforced by the inconveniences they experienced in travelling from their respective provinces to the distant capital of Lahore in order to obtain trade permits or redress for various injustices they might have suffered at the hands of the local administrators. The Republican Party manifesto put out for the expected elections was a document of pure opportunism so far as the question of One Unit was concerned. It enabled Republicans to oppose One Unit in Sind and the Frontier and to fight for its maintenance in Punjab.[38]

The Punjab group in the West Pakistan Assembly was hopelessly divided, and members from this group were leading both the Republican and Muslim League parties. In the Muslim League and in the Republican Party, it stood firmly in favor of retaining the existing, integrated West Pakistan Province. The National Awami Party, led

[38] *The Pakistan Times,* October 1, 1958.

by G. M. Sayed of Sind and a few supporters of Khan Abdul Ghaffar Khan of the Frontier, were prepared to support any party which would agree to split the West Pakistan province into its former constituent parts. Since it held the balance in the Assembly, it could bring about the defeat of any government in the house by supporting the opposition. Both the Muslim Leaguers and the Republicans were thus forced to woo the support of this group in order to command majority support in the house. The Republican government lost majority support when the Muslim Leaguers agreed in March, 1957, to support the demand of the National Awami Party that West Pakistan be broken up into its former constituent parts. It was saved, however, by the intervention of President Mirza, who imposed Governor's rule on the province. Later when the Republicans were restored to power, they, in their turn, were prepared to support the demand of the National Awami Party in order to save themselves from another defeat. The Assembly was thus reduced to a steady seesaw between the two rival groups, and Ministers were busier gathering support from members than in managing their departments. In order to get support, they had to bribe members with ministries or deputy ministerships, or resort to other corrupt practices, such as granting import licenses to members of the West Pakistan Assembly. A Chief Minister of West Pakistan admitted on the floor of the House that "now from top to bottom, there was hardly a person who was not corrupt."[39] Parliamentary government in West Pakistan was reduced to a farce, the administrative machinery paralyzed, and the Provincial Assembly was often in a state of pandemonium where it was difficult to determine on a particular day which party was in majority and where it stood on a particular issue.[40]

United as all Bengalis were in their bitterness against the Center and West Pakistan, politically they were divided into rival groups led by Suhrawardy and Fazlul Huq. These two leaders had combined to form the United Front Party in order to defeat the Muslim League in the spring of 1954, but as soon as the party assumed office, it split on the matter of distribution of offices, and the old rivalry for power in pre-Partition Bengal appeared in the form of the Awami League led by Suhrawardy and the Krishak Sramik (Peasants and Workers) Party

[39] *Ibid.*, August 26, 1958.

[40] Commenting on the trial of strength between the Republican Party and the Muslim League, a former Minister in the West Pakistan Government, wrote: "On May 31, the Budget was passed by a clear majority. At one stage of voting, when there was some confusion as to who had won, Mr. Daultana with some of his eminent colleagues staged a 'Bhangra' dance on the floor of the House, under the impression that his party had won. Ultimately it was established that they had lost." Syed Hassan Mahmud, *A Nation Is Born* (Lahore: 1958), p. 57.

(KSP) under Fazlul Huq. This was followed by Governor's rule in Bengal which lasted until August, 1955. After that, the Krishak Sramik Party was in office for a year.

The Awami League, when it was invited to form a government in September, 1956, enjoyed the support of about 200 members in a house of 309.[41] A great majority of the 72 Hindu members in the Assembly backed the League because of its support of joint electorates. In March, 1957, when Maulana Bhashani resigned as president of the Awami League because he disagreed with Suhrawardy's pro-Western foreign policy, a number of Awami League members in the Provincial Assembly also resigned in support of Maulana Bhashani's stand. Later, in July, 1957, these members joined the newly formed National Awami Party under Bhashani's leadership and their party strength in the Assembly was 28. The Krishak Sramik Party also enjoyed the support of the Nizam-i-Islam Party and the Muslim League. Their total strength hovered between 100 and 106.

The Awami League government soon ran into difficulties when it agreed with the central government to let the army seal the border districts to stop smuggling. It was well known that food, imported goods, and capital worth 800 million rupees were being drained away from East Pakistan's economy.[42] In December, 1957, the army launched its famous "operation close door." A number of Hindu members of the Assembly reacted sharply against this policy as it meant that a number of Hindu families, who were engaged in sending their capital and valuables out of Pakistan, would be adversely affected.[43] They threatened the Awami League with withdrawal of their support if the anti-smuggling drive by the army were not relaxed or abandoned altogether.

The tug-of-war between the Awami League and the KSP continued. On June 18, 1958, the Awami League was defeated because some of the Hindu members had withdrawn their support and also because the National Awami Party remained neutral when the ministry was faced with a division on the floor of the house. There was a KSP government for a few days, and the Awami League was back in power because the National Awami Party decided to support the Awami League Party when the latter had agreed to work for a neutral foreign policy and the disintegration of One Unit. This was sheer opportunism. In order to get back in power, the Awami League was prepared to agree to the

[41] *Dawn,* September 18, 1956.

[42] *Amrita Bazar Patrika,* September 9, 1958.

[43] The total smuggling of Hindu capital was Rs. 400 million. A. Sadeque *The Economic Emergence of Pakistan,* Part I (Dacca: East Bengal Government Press, 1954), pp. 23–24.

proposal of a neutral policy when its leader, H. S. Suhrawardy, was an ardent advocate of a pro-Western policy. However, Governor's rule was clamped on the province.

By the end of August, 1958, the Awami League government was again back in power when Governor's rule was lifted by the Center. On September 20, 1958, when the Assembly met, the Government moved a motion of no confidence in the Speaker mainly because the government suspected that the Speaker was supporting the opposition. Total disorder resulted when the Speaker was assaulted and government and opposition members exchanged blows.[44] On September 23, when the Deputy Speaker, who was a member of the Awami League, appeared to conduct the proceedings of the house, he was assaulted by the members of the opposition. The Inspector General of Police, on orders of the government, brought in policemen, and the members of the opposition were removed from the house. The government was thus able to have all its budget demands passed. A few days later the Deputy Speaker died as a result of the injuries received in the house. Parliamentary government had been reduced to a farce. East Pakistan at the time these tragic incidents took place was in the grip of acute food shortages, floods, and epidemics.

How does one explain the political fragmentation that had taken place in both parts of Pakistan? Politics in West Pakistan was by and large of a feudal nature. The West Pakistan Assembly was divided into two rival landlord factions. The Republican Party was supported by landowners like Qizilbash, Noons, Tiwanas, Gardezis, the Legharis, and the Gilanis from old Punjab. All of these families were sworn enemies of the Daultana group. They were also joined by Hasan Mahmood and the Lalekha family of Bahawalpur, Hoti from the Frontier, Talpur, Pirzada, and the supporters of the Pir of Pagaro from Sind. Daultana, who led the Muslim League, enjoyed support from landowners from Multan whence he came, Qureshis from Sargodha to whom he was related, and the Joya tribe, to which he belonged and which existed along both sides of the Sutlej River.[45] Some of these landlords were involved in feuds with each other dating back several decades. These disputes had originated in cases involving cattle stealing and claims against each other's landed property. Under parliamentary politics, they were forced into cooperating with one

[44] The author was present in the House when these events took place.

[45] The author is not aware of any study of Pakistan which throws any light on this highly important aspect of Pakistan's politics, namely, the support that politicians derive from their tenants and tribes. Even Chaudhri Muhammad Ali, who was not a landlord, was campaigning for support before Martial Law in areas where his tribe, Arains, were concentrated, such as Lyallpur and Bahawalpur.

another for the purpose of winning elections. Pacts like the Daultana-Gilani Pact (1949) and the Gardezi-Gilani Pact (1949) were formed.[46] In politics, however, they were not challenged by any group which threatened their interests as landowners. To them, politics with its competition for jobs and patronage became another outlet for pursuing their old feuds. Thus, the pacts failed to dissolve their age-old differences, and they started fighting their old battles in the provincial and central assemblies. It may also be noted that most of the civil servants and army officers in West Pakistan came from the landed gentry. The political groups that were formed were not organized against the government as such on the basis of an economic or social program. They were formed to win elections or topple a ministry, and they very often disintegrated after they had achieved their short-term objective. Landlords formed such groups or joined government-supported factions because they offered them protection against their enemies or rivals. If they did not join, they would lose their cattle, their lands might be raided, or irrigation water might be turned off their fields. The only group in West Pakistan which had a program was the National Awami Party, which stood for the breakup of the One Unit, and enjoyed the support of some of the progressive and leftish elements.

Outwardly the situation in East Pakistan, particularly when some of the members of the Assembly disgraced themselves by their disorderly conduct, was indistinguishable from that in West Pakistan on the eve of Martial Law. But many West Pakistanis conceded that East Pakistanis by and large were usually capable of displaying better political maturity and consciousness than their brethren in the West. It was true that the United Front, created at the time of the 1954 provincial elections, broke up into rival parties of the Awami League under Suhrawardy and the KSP under Fazlul Huq. However, there were clear signs in East Pakistan that the various factions would have crystallized into two major political groupings with the moderates and conservatives of the KSP and the Awami League and even the Nizam-i-Islam Party forming themselves as the majority party. The opposition would have been led by Bhashani's National Awami Party. The latter group consisted of socialists and other leftish elements who would have tried to build their movement on radical lines drawing support mainly from peasants and industrial workers. Unfortunately, such a realignment did not take place because of the Center's constant interference in East Pakistani politics, and above all, President Mirza's

[46] Photostatic copies of these pacts have been reproduced in Mahmud, pp. 20 and 21. These pacts were signed on a blank page facing the title page of the Qur'an and the signatories declared that they would support each other as God-fearing Muslims.

deliberate divisive tactics designed to dislodge the Awami League ministry and install another under the KSP.

President Iskander Mirza had one object in mind and that was to get himself elected as President after the next general election. Mirza had never outgrown the role of a Political Agent of the North-West Frontier. His training and experience had been such that he knew only one way of achieving his objects, namely, the old Frontier game of setting one tribe against another. There was nothing positive in the ends sought in this game, for by this policy one merely prevented the parties concerned from causing any damage to oneself and the government one represented. One of his colleagues, who had worked with him in the government of India, wrote that he "enjoyed getting the better of a man by a cunning trick, intercepting, for instance, a piece of intelligence that had been bought by the other side, buying it back before it was delivered, and substituting something else that would deceive the enemy and if possible mislead him to some mistake that would turn the laugh on him." People on the Frontier still relate with some relish the story of the Congress procession which Mirza, as Deputy Commissioner, thought would cause trouble, but which he managed to disperse. The processionists were entertained by a party of sympathizers and someone had laced the tea heavily with croton oil, "the swiftest and most violent of vegetable purges."[47] Mirza had great qualities for getting things done "by persuasion and finesse and bluff with just a hint of force in the background." This *hikmatamali* (judicious management) he demonstrated in abundant measure as Governor of East Bengal in 1954. But these qualities, derived from his innate drive and ambition, were out of tune with Pakistan's nationalism and particularly with the political aspirations of the urban classes.

Pakistani politicians were even more manageable tools than the Pathans for they lacked loyalty to the group or party to which they belonged. Having risen from the ranks of the civil service and played an influential role in improving the defense posture of Pakistan, Mirza had become fond of wielding enormous power. It was well known that a number of Republicans were "President's men," both in the Center and in West Pakistan; in East Pakistan, the President could depend upon several influential members of the KSP. The President would either bring about a change in the Center, and the new Prime Minister would try to place his supporting parties in the provinces, or the President would try to upset governments in the provinces with the result that this would disturb the coalition at the Center.

H. S. Suhrawardy, who became Prime Minister in September, 1956,

[47] Philip Woodruff, *The Men Who Ruled India. The Guardians.* (London: Jonathan Cape, 1954), p. 295.

formed a coalition Cabinet consisting of the Awami League and Republican Party Ministers. Suhrawardy's prime ministership lasted for slightly more than a year. By the beginning of October, 1957, it became clear that he had lost the support of some of the Republican Party members, particularly those from Sind and the Frontier. Matters came to a head over the question of One Unit when the Republicans in West Pakistan were trying to outdo the Muslim Leaguers in winning a majority in the Assembly by advocating the breakup of the One Unit. Suhrawardy, instead of depending upon the President to patch up his differences with the Republicans, decided to take a clear stand against the breakup of the One Unit and to campaign vigorously in West Pakistan for the preservation of the existing integrated West Pakistan province. He was taking certain calculated risks. He expected that Punjabi Republicans would stay with him and was prepared to lose the support of the Sindhi and Frontier Republicans. He also expected that even Muslim Leaguers like Daultana would support him on this issue. In October, 1957, however, faced with serious differences in the coalition with a number of Republicans withdrawing their support from his ministry, Suhrawardy advised the President to summon the National Assembly so that it might be known whether he enjoyed majority support in that body.[48] This aroused President Mirza's suspicions immediately. Had he agreed to Suhrawardy's request, it would have meant that the National Assembly, not the President, would have become the maker and unmaker of ministries. Secondly, Suhrawardy was trying to disrupt the Republican Party and this would have undermined the President's influence. Mirza asked Suhrawardy to resign at once or he would dismiss him. Suhrawardy resigned as Prime Minister on October 11, 1957.

When Firoz Khan Noon from Punjab became Prime Minister in December, 1957, the President found that his control over the Republicans was diminishing and that the new Prime Minister had come to an understanding with Suhrawardy. It was believed that Suhrawardy had assured Firoz Khan Noon that after the general elections, he would support Noon for the President's post. Suhrawardy also once disclosed that he had the names of a couple of candidates for the presidency in his pocket. President Mirza, perhaps rightly, suspected that Suhrawardy was planning to build an alliance between major groups in East and West Pakistan. The outlines of Suhrawardy's

[48] Suhrawardy expected support from 14 Awami Leaguers, 10 Republicans (Punjabis), 10 Muslim Leaguers, 4 Congress, 1 Azad Pakistan Party, 1 Ganatantri Dal. This would have given him the support of 40 members of a House of 80. The lure of office would have enticed a few more and thus ensured a sure majority for Suhrawardy.

strategy were broadly as follows: Using East Pakistan as its political base, the Awami League under his leadership would enter into an alliance mainly with Punjabi leaders who were in favor of preserving the province of West Pakistan as One Unit. Suhrawardy, by taking a firm stand over the issue of One Unit and thereby sacrificing his prime ministership, had won the support of Punjabi leaders. In addition to the support of Prime Minister Noon, it seemed that Suhrawardy could also expect support from Daultana.[49] Thus, Suhrawardy had embarked on a bold and brilliant plan of forging an alliance between Bengal and Punjab, something which had not been attempted before. Formerly, the Muslim League leaders from Bengal used to combine with Sind and the Frontier against Punjab. Suhrawardy, however, was shrewd enough to realize that political stability at the federal level was not possible without some kind of an understanding between the two major areas of Pakistan. It was also clear that such an alliance would help him to win a majority in the forthcoming elections and thus become the Prime Minister. The fatal flaw in Suhrawardy's plan was that the Punjabi leaders were hopelessly divided: it was difficult to foresee how Noon and Gurmani or Noon and Daultana could cooperate with each other.

President Mirza saw clearly that if Suhrawardy were to succeed in carrying out his plans, there was no possibility of his being re-elected as President. Mirza counteracted against Suhrawardy's strategy by first removing Governor Gurmani from office in West Pakistan and ensuring that his men were in power there. He then turned his attention to East Pakistan with a view to dislodging the Awami League ministry. The President's agents in East Pakistan were some of the leaders of the KSP. With the Awami Leaguers and KSP members coming to blows on the floor of the East Pakistan Assembly, these political machinations and intrigues had injected so much disorder into the political system that no government could function. The central government was also paralyzed by political instability. On the day Martial Law was declared, the President had sworn in two different Cabinets.[50] A caricature of the role of the President was presented in a cartoon in the *Lail-o-Nahar*. The tragic fighting in the East Pakistan Assembly in September, 1958, was pictured as a puppet show with the President pulling the strings.[51] The *New Statesman* correctly pointed out that

[49] A photostatic copy of Daultana's written assurance to Suhrawardy that he would support him if the Republican Party were to withdraw their support has been reproduced in Mahmud, p. 75. For Daultana-Suhrawardy negotiations, see *The Times of Karachi*, October 5, 1957.

[50] *The Gazette of Pakistan Extraordinary* (Karachi), October 7, 1958, pp. 1925–1928.

[51] *Lail-o-Nahar* (Lahore), September 28, 1958.

it was true that most of the politicians deserved to be stoned, but it was not for President Mirza to cast the stones.[52]

Why did President Iskander Mirza proclaim martial law on October 7, 1958? It was clear to him that there was not much prospect of his getting re-elected as President. He thought that if elections were held under this state of affairs, there was not much hope of stable and responsible governments emerging in the provinces and in the Center. The Muslim League was becoming popular in West Pakistan. In East Pakistan, with Suhrawardy's Awami League hanging on to power, the chances of the Awami League emerging as a majority party in that part of the country were good. In spite of the differences that existed among politicians in Pakistan, most of those who enjoyed popular support were agreed about one thing: Iskander Mirza should not be elected as President. In addition to these factors influencing the President, there was the Commander-in-Chief of the Pakistan army, General Muhammad Ayub Khan, whose counsel weighed more heavily with the President than that of anyone else. Ever since his appointment in January, 1951, the Commander-in-Chief had probably been in as close a contact with the political leaders as Iskander Mirza. Indeed, he was always in close touch with every Prime Minister, because the Prime Minister in Pakistan from the beginning was responsible for the Defense portfolio. In addition, the Commander-in-Chief could be regarded as one of the most important decision-makers in Pakistan since defense expenditure invariably constituted slightly more than half of the national budget. We have also seen how influential General Ayub was when Governor-General Ghulam Muhammad dissolved the Constituent Assembly and brought about the integration of West Pakistan. By way of comparison, it may be noted that during the years 1950–58, Pakistan had seven Prime Ministers and one Commander-in-Chief; whereas India had one Prime Minister and several Commanders-in-Chief. General Ayub had been Commander-in-Chief since January, 1951, and his tenure, which would have expired in January, 1959, had already been extended by President Mirza. Thus, it would not be fair to suggest that in seizing power, Ayub was motivated purely by personal considerations. We have seen that both the central and provincial governments had been rendered incapable of discharging their normal functions. Furthermore, there were signs that the younger officers might stage a coup.[53] Pressure was also being brought to bear upon Ayub by the senior generals that the time for drastic action had come. There is evidence to suggest that "a broad tactical outline" to

[52] *New Statesman* (London), September 18, 1958.
[53] L. F. Rushbrook Williams, *The State of Pakistan* (London: Faber and Faber, 1962), pp. 182–183.

impose Martial Law in the country was being prepared, and that it received the final approval of General Ayub Khan on the last day of September, 1958.[54] Later, even when Iskander Mirza was still the President, General Ayub disclosed that it was at his initiative that the President imposed Martial Law. "I said to the President: 'Are you going to act or are you not going to act? It is your responsibility to bring about change and if you do not, which heaven forbid, we shall force a change.' "[55]

Before Ayub could take action against what he considered the enemies of the country and tackle some of the basic problems, he thought he should first get rid of his friend, Iskander Mirza. Mirza was a serious political liability in the sense that in the eyes of the public he was responsible for most of the political intrigues. Ayub knew him as a man who believed in advancing his prospects by encouraging his rivals and foes to quarrel; indeed, now he was hearing reports that the President was determined to sow the seeds of discord in the army and other services as well. The result was that President Mirza was forced to resign on October 27, 1958, and the mantle of the presidency descended on Ayub's shoulders.

Martial Law, 1958–62

The constitutional changes brought about by the imposition of Martial Law were as follows: The Constitution of 1956 was abrogated, the central and provincial cabinets were dismissed, the National Assembly and the two Provincial Assemblies were dissolved, and all political parties were declared illegal.

General Ayub thought that he had to justify in two ways his seizure of power by unconstitutional means both to Pakistanis and to the outside world. First, he had to establish clearly that the previous regimes had brought Pakistan to the brink of disaster. Secondly, he had to show that he had not only saved Pakistan but could also get the country moving on the highroad of political stability and social and economic reform. In order to achieve the first objective, it was relatively easy for the President to pick the targets one by one and with the complete power that he had, he could shoot them with deadly accuracy.

Ayub announced that the country was riddled with "disruptionists, political opportunists, smugglers, black marketeers, and other such social vermin, sharks, and leeches."[56] The image that Ayub soon

[54] Major-General Fazal Muqeem Khan, *The Story of the Pakistan Army* (Dacca: Oxford University Press, 1963), p. 194.

[55] *The Pakistan Times*, October 10, 1958.

[56] Ayub Khan, I, 4.

created about himself was that he was a colossus of justice bestriding the corrupt world of Pakistan. The way the Martial Law regime proceeded against politicians, civil servants, business magnates, and smugglers confirmed the popular suspicion of corruption in high places. The dramatic arrest of M. A. Khuhro, a former Defense Minister, on a charge of selling a car on the black market, charges of corruption and misconduct against former Prime Ministers like Suhrawardy and Firoz Khan Noon and several Central Ministers and provincial Premiers, and the investigation of big firms for tax evasion — one and all created the impression that the regime was determined to cleanse the Augean stables.

The Director General, Anti-Corruption Department, West Pakistan, announced that cases of corruption or misconduct of nearly 150 former Ministers, Deputy Ministers and Parliamentary Secretaries, and about 600 members of the former central and Provincial Assemblies from West Pakistan were being investigated.[57] The Elective Bodies (Disqualification) Order, 1959, defined the term *misconduct* widely enough to include subversive activities, jobbery, and corruption. This meant that according to the Order, besides corrupt politicians, popular leaders like Khan Abdul Ghaffar Khan and others, who had been arrested earlier under the Security of Pakistan Act, 1952, would be disqualified from holding an elective office until December 31, 1966. Even the prestigious Civil Service of Pakistan was not spared. The Screening Committees, which were set up by the new regime to assess the integrity and efficiency of all civil servants, recommended that thirteen officers who belonged to the Civil Service of Pakistan, three to the Foreign Service, and fifteen to the Police Service, were to be removed from office or compulsorily retired. In all, as many as 1,662 civil servants belonging to the central and provincial services were dismissed or compulsorily retired.[58] Smuggling of all kinds was prohibited by Martial Law regulations, and maximum punishment was death. The Karachi Customs and Anti-Smuggling Police had been able to seize gold bullion and goods worth Rs. 30 million during the previous eleven years. But under Martial Law, the seizure of these items amounted to Rs. 20 million in a period of one month. One could see how effectively the borders had been sealed to stop smuggling by the fact that food prices rose sharply in the western districts of East Punjab, and Calcutta experienced a fish famine. Under a Martial Law regulation, persons who had filed false declarations of income for income tax purposes, were called upon to submit fresh declarations before January 15, 1959, in order to avoid punishment, which involved

[57] *The Pakistan Observer,* August 11, 1959.
[58] *Ibid.,* June 28, 1959.

rigorous imprisonment extending up to seven years. After fresh declarations had been filed, it was found that the total income concealed by taxpayers had been as high as Rs. 1,340 million. Foreign exchange surrendered locally was Rs. 40.6 million while unauthorized foreign exchange held abroad by Pakistani nationals and now declared to Pakistan authorities amounted to another Rs. 42 million.[59]

The Martial Law regime also created the image that it would act in the interests of the common man. Martial Law regulations fixed the prices of a number of commodities which appeared in the daily budget of the common man. Punishment ranging from fourteen years imprisonment to death could be decreed for contravention of regulations dealing with various kinds of hoarding. It may also be pointed out that special military courts were established all over the country for speedy trials of persons convicted under the ordinary law and Martial Law regulations. Under the dynamic leadership of General Azam Khan, Minister for Rehabilitation, the Korangi Township was set up outside Karachi and by 1960–61, 20,000 families or 100,000 refugees were settled in this colony. Thus Ayub, as the leader of the Martial Law regime, fitted admirably the image that a Muslim peasant or poor urban dweller had of a just and strong ruler. In the Islamic conception of obedience to God and His Commandments, there is a strong element of fear because again and again the Qur'an reminds the readers of the terrible punishment that awaits the sinners and unbelievers. In addition, the emergence of a strong military ruler was by no means a strange phenomenon in Muslim history. The Urdu magazine, *Mah-i-Nau,* pointed out that ever since 1250 A.D. in what constitutes Pakistan today, every time the nation was faced with a calamity, the savior of the nation arose from the ranks of the army.[60]

Several regimes, both central and West Pakistani, had promised land reforms. Looking at West Pakistan as a whole, 0.1 per cent of the landowners, or a little more than 6,000 landlords, possessed as much as 7.5 million acres (a little more than 15 per cent of the cultivated area) in properties of more than 500 acres each.[61] The First Five Year Plan impressed upon the government the introduction of land reforms as essential for economic development. But landowners in Sind and Punjab were so powerful that the matter was never pursued beyond verbal declarations. The Martial Law regime set up a Land Reforms Commission within a few weeks of its taking office. The Commission was headed by the Governor of West Pakistan, Akhter Husain, a civil

---

[59] *Pakistan Under the New Regime* (Karachi: Ferozsons, n.d.), p. 7.

[60] *Mah-i-Nau* (Karachi), February, 1959, p. 29.

[61] *Report of the Land Reforms Commission for West Pakistan* (Lahore: 1959), pp. 13–14.

servant, and the other seven members, including two co-opted members, were all civil servants. Three of the members represented landed interests, however; indeed, two of these three were themselves big landowners. Four members represented a progressive point of view, the most progressive being Ghulam Ishaque Khan, a Pathan from the Frontier. The Martial Law regime had banned political activities, but several civil servants and other members of the public appeared before the Commission to press their point of view. A senior civil servant, who later became the Establishment Secretary, submitted a memo-randum urging the Commission not to break up large holdings because only on large-scale farms could machinery and capital be profitably employed. Another memorandum was presented by a Sind landowner expressing the same point of view. University students and professors argued in favor of radical land reforms. Editorials in newspapers like *The Pakistan Times, The Civil & Military Gazette,* and the *Nawai-Waqt* supported land reforms. The chairman, Akhter Husain, perhaps repre-sented the President's point of view, for he thought the requirements of social justice and the interests of agricultural productivity were not identical and that therefore it would not be advisable on the part of the Commission to recommend radical measures.[62] The ceilings rec-ommended by the Land Reforms Commission were 500 acres for irrigated land and 1,000 acres for unirrigated land. The majority of the Commissioners were against a lower ceiling because the surplus land which would have become available for redistribution would have been too small to secure for each of the landless tenants a subsistence farm unit. They also argued that a lower ceiling would not have provided much of an incentive for higher agricultural productivity. The Martial Law regime immediately accepted the recommendation regarding ceilings and also announced that the old feudal land grants known as *jagirdari* were being abolished without compensation. Com-pensation was to be paid to landlords for their non-*jagirdari* holdings through non-negotiable but heritable bonds redeemable in twenty-five years. Ghulam Ishaque Khan, a member of the Commission, disagreed with the majority of the Commission and suggested that an individual holding should not exceed 150 acres of perennially irrigated land and that a family holding should be restricted to 300 acres of such land.[63] Some observers tried to interpret the recommendations of high ceilings as designed to protect the middle-sized landowners, from which class most of the army officers had been drawn. This was politically under-standable; having antagonized the big landowners by introducing land

[62] Ayub Khan, I, 48.
[63] *Report of the Land Reforms Commission for West Pakistan,* p. 32.

reforms, which no previous government had the courage to undertake, General Ayub could not afford to alienate his own army officers as well.

What was the net effect of these land reforms? The total area of land resumed by the state from the big landowners was 2.2 million acres and this was to be distributed among 150,000 tenants. The land-lords were allowed to retain about 6.4 million acres. This goes to show that the land retained by about 6,000 landlords was about three times the area given to 150,000 tenants.[64] One could also argue that as a result of high ceilings the feudal system with its social inequalities would not be eliminated in the near future.

A major objective of the Martial Law regime was to restore health and vigor in an economy which had been suffering from acute inflation, increasing deficits in the balance of payments, and mounting food shortages. The policy of deficit financing was severely curbed. The supply of money was regulated according to the requirements of the economy; whereas under the previous regimes it was allowed to increase far in excess of the growth of national income. As the government budget was brought into equilibrium with the support of foreign aid, it became possible for the monetary authorities to make available to the private sector an increasing supply of commercial credit. The aggregate increase in commercial credit during 1959–62 exceeded by over 60 per cent the total expansion of commercial credit recorded during 1949–59.[65] The government claimed that there was a distinct shift in its industrial policy in favor of private enterprise. The President and the Finance Minister constantly emphasized that the government was determined to give greater scope to private enterprise. New industries were allowed a tax holiday, which ranged from four years in developed areas to eight years in the less developed areas, and substantial reduction was offered in the business profits tax on existing industries up to certain limits. A policy of gradually transferring industries which were operated by the Pakistan Industrial Development Corporation to the private sector was pursued. In order to boost exports, two schemes were launched — the export bonus scheme, under which exporters were given the option to import raw materials or a host of consumer items or to sell their bonus vouchers on the open

[64] Mushtaq Ahmad, *Government and Politics in Pakistan,* 2nd ed. (Karachi: Pakistan Publishing House, 1963), p. 199.

[65] For this information, see Chapter 2, Mohammed Shoaib, *Pakistan's Economic Growth Since 1958* (Karachi: Ministry of Finance, n.d.) and Parvez Hasan, *Deficit Financing and Capital Formation. The Pakistan Experience 1951–1959* (Karachi: The Institute of Development Economics, 1962), pp. 65–67.

market, and an export credit guarantee scheme whereby exporters were covered against financial risks not normally covered by insurance companies. The government claimed that as a result of its economic and liberal commercial policies, the index of industrial production registered an increase of 66.5 points during 1959–62 (three-and-a-half years) as compared to a corresponding increase of 35.8 points during the years 1955–58.[66] It was equally painstaking in improving agricultural productivity. Attempts to arrest waterlogging and salinity, launching of crash programs, and extension of credit to farmers through the Agricultural Development Bank indicated that the government was making every effort to increase agricultural output. The index of agricultural production of all crops rose from 108 in 1958–59 to 131 in 1961–62.

The Martial Law regime also claimed that the economy of East Pakistan, which was stagnant under the previous regimes, made rapid strides. East Pakistan's economy had shown some improvement soon after Suhrawardy became Prime Minister during 1956–57, but the pace of progress was even greater during the Martial Law period. The revenue receipts of the provincial government also indicated marked increase. Formerly, the loans that were sanctioned were seldom adequately utilized. The government claimed that the allocation of foreign aid and assistance to East Pakistan, prior to Martial Law, was undoubtedly far below the level of the needs of the province. During 1958–61, however, the annual rate of such allocation increased by at least three times that of 1957–58.[67]

The seizure of power by the Commander-in-Chief of the Pakistan army has sometimes been described as the October Revolution in Pakistan. Was this a revolution? Did it bring into being a new social and political philosophy? Did the reforms introduced by the Martial Law regime constitute a new set of ideas or disturb the existing social order? Did these reforms originate in the minds of young army or civil officers who were disgusted with the existing system of social and economic inequalities? The simple fact of the matter is that the Martial Law was not intended to be a revolution. General Ayub Khan and his other military colleagues had all started their careers in the British army and were contemporaries of the senior civil servants in the Pakistani government. It was well known that the former Indian Civil Service and not the British Indian army had attracted the cream of Muslim intelligentsia. It was also true that the civil servants had spent most of their lives in an organization where decision-making

[66] Shoaib, Chapters 4 and 5.

[67] *Years of Progress 1958–1962. East Pakistan.* (Dacca: Information Department, Government of East Pakistan, 1962), p. 3.

was woefully slow and where the files moved at a steady, solemn, and measured pace from desk to desk. The army administrators could claim that they could take quicker decisions. But the Civil Service of Pakistan had also produced a few dynamic administrators who could claim credit for the impressive industrial progress that the country had made during the initial years. The great contribution that General Ayub Khan made was that he removed a number of legal and political obstacles so that civil servants could carry on the day-to-day administration efficiently and implement policies designed to bring about social and economic development of the country.

In his very first speech General Ayub made it clear that Martial Law would in the main be operated by civilian agencies.[68] A number of senior army generals and officers were brought into the civilian administration, but they had come in mostly to speed up and rationalize the existing administrative procedure. We have seen in the case of land reforms that most of the Commissioners were civil servants and the recommendations that were accepted were those of the conservative majority. The national economy was put on an even keel and industrial productivity increased largely because the government followed an anti-inflationary policy and extended greater encouragement to private enterprise than the previous regimes had done. There was nothing revolutionary in these reforms. One could say that the ideas behind them originated mostly from civil servants or industrial and commercial interests. Thus, unlike the political regimes — because it was backed by the coercive power of the army — the Martial Law regime was successful in removing some of the glaring social inequalities, in pursuing a more efficient and rational economic policy, in housing refugees, in curbing corrupt practices, and in weeding out some of the inefficient and corrupt civil servants. The political leaders, on the other hand, could not accomplish these objectives because they did not have the support of well-organized and national political parties. There were no national elections held; consequently the political leaders did not get an opportunity to build national coalitions. As a result, political leaders like Suhrawardy and Chaudhri Muhammad Ali, who had certain national objectives, had to spend all their time in humoring Assemblies which were riddled with factions, intrigues, and the shifting loyalties of politicians who once bought did not stay bought.

The Martial Law regime could justifiably take credit for establishing Basic Democracies and in introducing the Muslim Family Laws Ordinance, 1961. The system of Basic Democracies, under which tiers of local government were created reaching right down to the village level, was designed to make the governmental process more meaningful to

[68] Ayub Khan, I, 4.

the peasant, thus making him a more active and responsible citizen. This subject is more fully discussed in Chapter 10. The attempt of the Muslim Family Laws Ordinance in curbing polygamy is discussed in Chapter 7.

However, the Martial Law regime soon discovered that the fundamental problems of Pakistan could not be settled by merely setting up a more efficient and honest administration.[69] The basic problem was one of political and national integration. General Ayub was fully aware that as long as he derived his power mainly from the army and used it with the cooperation of the civil service, his regime would continue to rest on insecure foundations. Both the military and the civil service in its upper strata were predominantly West Pakistani institutions. Earlier we noted that the demand of East Pakistanis for a full-fledged parliamentary system was motivated by their desire to correct the imbalance that existed in the political and governmental structure of Pakistan due to West Pakistan's domination of the army and the senior ranks of the civil service. Even after the Martial Law regime had channelled funds to East Pakistan for its economic development, sent the energetic Azam Khan as Governor, and placed East Pakistani civil servants in a number of key positions in the East Pakistan administrative structure, one could not say that most of the province's basic grievances had been removed. There was smouldering restlessness beneath the surface. Thus, Suhrawardy's arrest in early 1962 was followed by widespread student demonstrations in which the target of attack was President Ayub himself.

Indeed, Ayub could not always be sure that the civil service and the army would continue to remain loyal to a regime which did not derive its authority from any constitution. Thus, the only course open to him was to carry out the promise he had made when he had seized power — "to restore democracy, but of the type that people can understand and work." In what ways the Martial Law regime has been altered into a diluted form of democracy is the theme of the next chapter.

[69] Publications put out by the Bureau of National Reconstruction talked of provincialism, antisocial forces, lack of national outlook. See *The Challenge and the Response* (Karachi: Ferozsons, n.d.), pp. 4 and 19. A conference of psychologists referred to "factionalism, egocentricity, sectarianism and other narrow and parochial loyalties." The same conference discussed the inadequacies of Islamic ideology in terms of Muslim intolerance and authoritarianism in Islam. Q. M. Aslam and M. A. Ansari, eds., *Observations and Recommendations Made by a Conference of Psychologists* (Karachi: Bureau of National Reconstruction, n.d.), pp. 6 and 37–44.

5

Constitutional Autocracy

The British often take pride in having trained several Asian and African nations in the art of responsible government. But it is seldom realized that the bureaucratic and army machines that they left behind in these countries had been far better trained than the political leaders, who had had only a smattering of, and often interrupted, political experience. The result was that when these political leaders inherited the task of governing politically and culturally heterogeneous communities, they found they did not have the requisite political machinery like disciplined political parties to bring about political integration and economic development.

During the initial period when there was popular excitement over independence, it looked as if alliances between landowning or urban politicians and the army and the bureaucracy would work smoothly. But the more the politicians got into difficulties over regional tensions and rising economic expectations, the more it became apparent to the bureaucracy and the army that the politicians could not function without the support of the coercive power of the police and the army. Indeed, the army soon realized that power was there merely for the asking and that political leaders were in no position to bring about political stability in the country.

It is clear that the central executive of the post-Martial Law period was not the same as the central executive that existed between 1947 and 1951 under Jinnah and Liaquat. During the latter period it was primarily an executive based on popular support but which functioned with the loyal cooperation of the bureaucracy. President Ayub's regime can be compared to the British viceregal system which existed in India during the thirties and forties of this century. The Viceroys, like Ayub, also had a legislative assembly, which they could control through their powers of certification of the budget and other legislative measures essential for the safety, tranquillity, or interests of British India. Like Ayub, they were also faced with opposition from political forces, but like Ayub they could often keep them under control with the help of military and police power.

However, since the introduction of the new Constitution in June, 1962, and the politicization of the regime through the revival of political parties and the holding of elections, is the political process in Pakistan now set on a different course? An answer to this question may be attempted in three parts. In the first, we shall discuss the political philosophy of the regime; in the second, we shall analyze the political process; and in the third we shall consider the role of the judiciary and the press.

Political Ideas of the New Regime

One can easily criticize Ayub's views on parliamentary democracy and Islamic ideology, but the fact remains that he (more than any of his predecessors, including Jinnah) has initiated in Pakistan a public discussion of some of these fundamental ideas. Ever since he seized power, he has consistently argued that parliamentary democracy is not likely to work in Pakistan where literacy is so low and where the people are not informed or mature enough to use their votes to support certain national policies or programs. This does not mean that he has a thinly concealed contempt for the people. His view of the masses is that of an army leader who thinks that the rank and file, if properly led, can bring about victory. He has often said that the "heart of our people is still sound. The malaise which afflicted the body politic has not touched their soul which is still noble, true and pure as ever."[1] This, in short, is the theory of man-management on which the army lays so much stress. It is argued that it was the politicians who exploited the ignorance and credulity of the people; they had every opportunity to serve their country, but they misused the trust placed in them.

Ayub attributes this failure and lack of character to the sort of education and the atmosphere which prevailed under foreign rule, and he has singled out the lawyer-politicians, followed by traders and industrialists, for this serious breach of trust and responsibility. Their devotion to the parliamentary form of government he has characterized as a suicidal activity which would bring about instability in government "for the sake of satisfying some requirements of foreign theoreticians applicable to their own conditions."[2] This is again the sort of distrust and resentment that most army officers have towards

[1] Field Marshal Mohammad Ayub Khan, *Speeches and Statements* (Karachi: Pakistan Publications, n.d.), II, 25.
[2] *Ibid.*, III, 30.

politicians, lawyers, and industrialists. It has been heightened by the fact that the Pakistan army in its upper ranks consists of a large number of officers drawn largely from the rural areas of Punjab and the Frontier Province.

Ayub's arguments that parliamentary democracy is not suitable to Pakistan cannot be brushed aside lightly. He feels that parliamentary democracy through its party system tends to divide people into majorities and minorities when a developing country needs unity and singleness of purpose. This disintegrating process causes further havoc in a country which is already divided into tribes, religious sects, and regional and linguistic groups. All this may be true, but the real criticism of Pakistan's political leaders would be that democracy failed in Pakistan because the leaders did not properly follow the democratic process — that is, they did not establish viable political parties which could construct working majorities out of diverse linguistic and regional groups. Politicians would argue that this might have happened if democracy had been given enough time and elections. Army generals, supported by cohesive modern military machines, can seldom resist the temptation to seize power when their governments, faced by rising expectations, are struggling hopelessly to raise living standards with extremely limited resources. In contrast to the united military apparatus that the generals possess, the politicians have to depend upon the ever-shifting loyalties of factions and groups.

The army, on the other hand, is a monolithic organization and also regards itself as a powerful embodiment of national unity. General Von Seeckt in his *Thoughts of a Soldier* wrote: "Hands off the army is my cry to all parties. The army serves the state and the state alone, for it is the state." This discipline and sense of unity is such that armies even in new countries maintain their unity in spite of the fact that they are drawn from different classes, races, or regions. Political parties in new countries, on the other hand, except when they are waging a struggle for independence, are often hopelessly split into religious groups or linguistic factions. The logic of the democratic process is such that the more a group or party appeals to parochial or clannish interests, the greater the chances of an electoral success. Such victories have turned out to be pyrrhic when the army has seized power in the name of national unity and patriotism.

Like other Pakistani leaders, Ayub has constantly asserted that the *sine qua non* of Pakistan's establishment as a state was to give shape and reality to Islamic ideology. And like any other Pakistani political leader, he is also aware that Islam provides the only stable bond of unity between the two disparate wings of the country. Arab and other Muslim states could embark on a territorial and secular nationalism, but not Pakistan. Again, it is obvious to Ayub, as it was to several other Pakistani leaders, that the Islamic system is dynamic enough to provide an ideology which is consistent with the requirements of a modern state. However, the difference between Ayub and other leaders lies in the fact that because he is a soldier, and above all, because he is backed by the coercive power of the army, he has been able to express his thoughts more bluntly.

Ayub has taken a firm stand against those orthodox *ulama* who "have reduced our religion to a fairy tale of *jins* [spirits] and angels, hedging it with superstition" and who constantly preach against modern science and technology in their Friday sermons. The Bureau of National Reconstruction and the Auqaf Departments (Religious Trusts) have put pressure on the *imams* (those who lead prayers) of mosques to acquaint themselves with modern subjects and with science.[3] Ayub has also tried to popularize birth control in spite of the expected religious opposition. Above all, by instituting the Muslim Family Laws Ordinance, 1961, he has tried to put effective checks on polygamy, even though it is permitted by Islam.

Ayub has shrewdly used Islam to support the kind of authoritarian system that he has envisaged for Pakistan. Islam believes in a well-knit community of believers for whom clear injunctions have been laid down in the Qur'an. The Commander of the Faithful merely needs an Advisory Council to assist him in the matter of interpretation of these principles. Ayub has poured scorn on Western-educated intellectuals and lawyers who "make lofty professions about Islamic Constitution but when the time for putting them into practice comes we take resort to philosophies of Aristotle, Socrates, and Plato by jettisoning our own traditions."[4] According to Ayub, "without centralization, unity, and solidarity no system can claim to be an Islamic system."[5] For him, the Islamic type of constitution envisages a presidential system under which the President is advised by an assembly or parliament whose members express their opinions on national problems according to their free judgment and are not influenced by party or group considerations.[6]

Ayub, in referring to the Advisory Council set up by the Caliph Omar (634–644) as the proper Islamic type of parliament, suggests the kind of role that he would like to assign to the parliament in Pakistan. Just as the Advisory Council during the time of Caliph Omar advised

---

[3] *Report of the Activities of the Bureau of National Reconstruction* (Dacca: East Pakistan Government Press, 1962), pp. 3–4.

[4] Ayub Khan, II, 144.

[5] *Ibid.*, II, 144–145.

[6] *Ibid.*, II, 145–146.

the Caliph on the interpretation of Muslim law as laid down in the Qur'an and the traditions of the Prophet, Ayub would perhaps also like the parliament merely to advise the President as to how his blueprint for reforms should be implemented. Yet it would be difficult to see how any elected assembly could confine itself to such a tame role. Ayub has reinforced these arguments by pointing out that the needs of economic development are such that the new countries cannot progress under the "strains and stresses of the western democratic system. Their development, if you study their history carefully, took place under almost a totalitarian system. . . ."[7]

The New Constitution and the Political Process

Ayub's argument is that he seized power, mobilized, accumulated, and increased it under the Martial Law regime. He has used it for certain social purposes, and he has no intention of abdicating it to satisfy the constitutional standards of either domestic or foreign critics. His constant argument has been that an emerging country needs stability and firm government for its economic and social development. He has certainly no intention of going back to the 1956 parliamentary Constitution which, according to him, was an "unholy wedlock of the executive, legislative, and judicial functions of the state in which the ultimate power for good government remained illusive, undefined, and therefore, inoperative."[8] He is prepared to soften the language of the Martial Law regulations, but the purpose that lay behind them and the presidential power to enforce them would remain intact. He has made it clear that his intention is to convert the Martial Law "into a document which will form the basis of running the country."[9]

Thus, in the new Constitution (which was brought into being on June 8, 1962) the government of Pakistan has emerged, as Chaudhri Muhammad Ali has described it, as a government of the President, by the President, and for the President.[10] This is borne out by the powers that the President has compared with those of the National Assembly and the provinces. So far as nonfinancial legislation is concerned, the President's veto cannot be overridden even by a two-thirds majority, for he can refer the bill in question to a referendum. In an assembly elected under the system of Basic Democracies, which, as we suggest in later chapters, obviously favors the government, it is difficult to imagine that the government will be faced with the opposition of a two-thirds majority. On the other hand, given the coercive and patron-

[7] *Ibid.*, III, 51.

[8] *Ibid.*, I, 96.

[9] *Ibid.*, I, 58.

[10] *Dawn*, April 2, 1963.

age powers of the government, it is easier for it to mobilize a two-thirds majority for amendment bills. In the first National Assembly (1962–65), the government group did not command the support of the two-thirds majority necessary for amendment bills. Therefore, the government had to resort to coercive tactics to mobilize the necessary two-thirds majority. It was made clear to certain opposition members, who were landlords, that they would have to face the prospect of irrigation water being turned off their land or that some of their valuable lands could be acquired by the government for public use if they did not support it. Members representing urban constituencies could, should they not support the government, lose their import permits or permits which gave them route monopolies to ply their buses and trucks.[11] For these reasons, as many as nine members crossed the floor and thus allowed the passage of the Constitution (Second Amendment) Bill in June, 1964.[12] This bill advancing the President's election by five months was bitterly fought by the opposition who argued that the early election of the President would enable him to influence the subsequent elections for the National Assembly in favor of his party. Similarly, the government was able to obtain a two-thirds majority for the Constitution (First Amendment) Act passed in December, 1963. This Act made the Fundamental Rights justiciable and laid down that the state "shall not make any law which takes away or abridges the rights so conferred." At the same time, however, it was made absolutely clear that the Fundamental Rights guaranteed by the Act did not imply that certain Presidential Orders, Martial Law Regulations, Ordinances promulgated by the President, Central Acts, Ordinances promulgated by the Governor of West Pakistan, and a West Pakistan Act — altogether 31 laws — would become null and void because they were in contravention of the Fundamental Rights. The government claimed that these 31 laws included progressive reforms like the West Pakistan Land Reforms Regulation, the Muslim Family Laws Ordinance, 1961, the Basic Democracies Order, 1959, etc. Similarly, laws like Public Offices (Disqualification) Order, 1959, and the Public and Representative Offices (Disqualification) Act Declaration Order, 1960, which barred certain civil servants and politicians from holding public offices because they had been found guilty of corrupt or other illegal practices, and the West Pakistan Criminal Law Amendment Act, 1963, under which accused persons could be tried by Government-appointed Councils of Elders instead of the courts, were all consistent with public

[11] For instances of such coercive tactics, see "The Second Amendment Story," *Outlook*, II, No. 35 (July 4, 1964), p. 9.
[12] *Dawn*, June 9, 10, and 12, 1964.

interest and therefore could not be declared null and void because they denied or abridged the Fundamental Rights enjoyed by the citizens.

The National Assembly under the Constitution of 1962 has 156 members, 6 of whom are women (3 seats each from West and East Pakistan have been reserved for women). The Assembly was elected by an electorate consisting of 80,000 Basic Democrats. Since the elections were held at a time when parties were banned, the groups that emerged in the first National Assembly were either factions led by certain leaders or formed on the basis of provincial loyalties. After the passage of the Political Parties Act, 1962, these groups crystallized into government groups and opposition groups. The government group consisted of about 78 members and its components were the Conventionist Muslim League, (46), Democratic Group and others (32). The opposition groups were Pakistan Independent Group (24) and Pakistan People's Group (36) which together had 60 members. The remaining members were Independents belonging to no groups. It was significant that the bulk of the government support came from West Pakistan and the majority of opposition members were from East Pakistan. The leader of the government coalition was from East Pakistan, and the opposition, which derived the bulk of its support from East Pakistan, was led by a West Pakistani. If the government's weapons were coercion and patronage, the opposition resorted to their normal weapons like violent and biting speeches in denouncing government policy and action, adjournment motions and a strenuous use of the question hour to extract information or embarrass the government. The government introduced 40 bills, of which 39 were passed; whereas out of the 232 private members' bills, 35 were introduced and only one was passed. Over 900 resolutions were offered by members, of which 696 were admitted, but hardly a score could be discussed, with three being adopted. There were 68 divisions. About 3,800 questions were offered, including over 300 short notice questions, and over 75 per cent of them were admitted and answered in the house.[13]

The present National Assembly (1965–   ), like the first, has also been elected by 80,000 Basic Democrats, but unlike its predecessor has been elected on a party basis. The position of the government party, which is called the Pakistan Muslim League, in the present National Assembly, in contrast to its predecessor, is so strong that the government may not have to resort to very much pressure or persuasion. The government claims the support of well over 130 members, including the 6 women members. The opposition consists of no more than 17

[13] *The Pakistan Times,* January 23, 1965.

to 18 members and is divided into parties like the National Democratic Front (5), Awami League (5), Council Muslim League (4), National Awami Party (3). Out of these groups, a party called the United Parliamentary Party consisting of about 13 persons, has emerged under the leadership of Nurul Amin, a former Chief Minister of East Pakistan. So far, the National Awami Party, has refused to become an integral part of the opposition because of its support for the Government's independent foreign policy.

The Constitution arms the government with enormous powers, of which a good example is the President's powers in the matter of the budget. Control of the purse is a power which every legislature in both the presidential and parliamentary systems is supposed to exercise in an unfettered fashion. The National Assembly of Pakistan can control only that part of the annual budget statement which represents new expenditure. The term new expenditure has been carefully defined in the Constitution (Articles 40 and 42). First, in a developing country like Pakistan, the government is very likely to include projects in the annual budget statement or a supplementary budget statement which cannot be financed in their entirety from a given year's resources. Thus, it may present cost estimates of a given project for a period of years and may ask the National Assembly to approve in advance the total phased cost of that project as specified against individual years. Once the Assembly approves the phased cost of a particular project, its cost estimates, which have been approved in advance, may no longer be regarded as new expenditure in future years, and the Assembly has no control over such expenditures. If the government presents revised estimates for a project, the phased cost of which has been approved by the Assembly, only that portion of the revised estimate which exceeds the expenditure approved for that year by more than 10 per cent of the approved expenditure is regarded as new expenditure and votable by the Assembly. Secondly, any other nonrecurring expenditure is considered new expenditure. Third, only those recurring expenditures come under the category of new which are for new purposes or for those purposes for which provision had been made in previous years and which exceed the authorized expenditure for the previous financial year by more than 10 per cent. It is true, as several critics have remarked, that since new expenditure represents a smaller proportion of the budget each year, the President can regard himself as independent of the National Assembly in incurring the bulk of government expenditure. In order to understand the degree of control which the National Assembly can exercise over the budget in terms of new expenditure, we may take, for example, total expenditure and new expenditure for each year of the Ministry of Defense over a period of three years. One can say that proportionately new expenditure in the Ministry of Defense has risen by a greater margin than total expenditure. There may be instances in the budget, as in the case of capital outlay on defense services during the year 1964–65, when the entire expenditure may be new. Government spokesmen may argue that in a developing country like Pakistan, new expenditure sometimes may constitute a substantial proportion of the budget. Since these expenditures have been placed under the control of the Assembly, it cannot be said that the financial powers given to the Assembly are insignificant.

Table 2

Defense Expenditure
(Rs in millions)

	Total Expenditure	New Expenditure
1962–63	1,168.88	45.29
1963–64	1,292.81	129.19
1964–65	1,426.10	220.87

Source: Ministry of Finance, *Budget of the Central Government for 1962–63. Demands for Grants and Appropriations* (As laid before the National Assembly) (Karachi: Ministry of Finance, 1962). *Ibid.*, 1963–64 and 1964–1965.

The fact remains that the financial powers given to the National Assembly of Pakistan under the present presidential system are much less than those its predecessors enjoyed during the parliamentary regimes. In a parliamentary system like that of Britain, because of the control exercised by the Cabinet over the Parliament, the financial powers enjoyed by a legislature are not as great as those enjoyed by the American Congress. The National Assembly of Pakistan, which functions under a presidential system, seems to enjoy financial powers which are far inferior to legislatures of either the presidential or parliamentary variety. It is obvious that it is not these Western models of government that have influenced the thinking of the makers of the Pakistan Constitution. The fear implied in restricting the financial powers of the Assembly is that it may be so obstructive as to refuse to pass the government's budget and thus paralyze the government machinery. The American Congress, despite occasional evidence to the contrary, has developed sufficient maturity to refrain from exercising its absolute power. But the National Assembly of Pakistan, according to the government view, is still inexperienced and immature, and needs to be protected against its own inclination towards folly by being swaddled in this manner. President Ayub and other spokesmen of the government believe that the great majority of the people of

Pakistan, who are illiterate, are not yet ready for a full-fledged demo-cratic system and that there should be an indirect system of election whereby 80,000 Basic Democrats elect a President, a National Assem-bly, and the two Provincial Assemblies. Indeed, by restricting the powers of the Assembly in this way, the government seems to suggest that even the educated few, who have been elected to the National Assembly, are not yet mature and responsible enough to control the executive.

The President can exercise as effective a control over the provinces as he does at the Center. So far as the constitutional position is con-cerned, it is clear that the Center's control over the provinces has been stated in unmistakable terms. Pakistan is to be only "a form of federa-tion with the Provinces enjoying such autonomy as is consistent with the unity and interests of Pakistan as a whole."[14] In the name of national interest — which has been stretched to include the security of the country, planning or coordination, or the achievement of uniformity — the central legislature can ignore the Third Schedule (which includes central powers like defense, external affairs, currency, etc.) and legislate on any matter not stated in that Schedule.[15] The Constitution (Article 133) clearly restricts the power of the courts to decide whether a legislature in framing laws has overstepped the central or provincial domain. However, this article has been designed only to restrict the power of the courts and not that of the central legislature. It is clearly not intended to create confusion and let the central and provincial legislatures invade each others' fields. Article 134 clearly lays down that if a provincial law is inconsistent with a central law, it is the central law which shall prevail. In addition, it may be noted that the central laws, as compared to the provincial laws, enjoy another advantage in the sense that the central government can declare in the name of national interest that the central laws are necessary (Article 131, clause 2). This matter came up before the East Pakistan High Court when the President's authority to issue an ordinance governing the settlement of industrial disputes was chal-lenged on the plea that it encroached upon the provincial sphere. The argument was that since labor and industrial relations had not been clearly listed among the forty-nine powers allotted to the Center in the Third Schedule, the matter clearly belonged to the provincial sphere. But since the preamble to the President's ordinance clearly stated that it had been issued "in the national interest of Pakistan," in accordance with Article 131 (2), the Dacca High Court ruled that

[14] See the Preamble of *The Constitution of the Republic of Pakistan* (Karachi: Manager, Government of Pakistan Press, 1962).

[15] Article 131 of *The Constitution of the Republic of Pakistan*.

in the light of such a clear declaration by the government, "It is therefore, futile to argue that the ordinance is *ultra vires* the President."[16]

To convey clearly the bias of the present regime toward centralization, one may cite the *Report of the Standing Organisation Committee* which was set up to look into the reorganization of the functions and structure of the central government in the light of the new Constitution. The Committee suggested that since the central legislature has been armed to interfere even in normal provincial matters where the national interest of Pakistan is concerned, the central government should maintain administrative units to deal with education, health, food and agriculture, labor, social welfare, railways, industries, and fuel and power. The Committee, though set up under the Minister for Economic Coordination, presumably consisted of mainly central civil servants because the Report was brought out by the Establishment Division of the Secretariat. The recommendations of the Committee reveal the mind of the central administrators and how the Constitution is likely to be interpreted and implemented.

> The Committee, therefore, has aimed at an administrative framework which should maintain in essence the strong character of the Central Government, but only by vesting the Centre with broad policy functions, as opposed to operational or executive functions which must remain the sole responsibility of the Provincial Governments.[17]

Thus, it would be difficult to describe Pakistani federalism as even quasi-federal because one can see that the central government is not only strong in its own right but can lay down policy even in matters which have been allotted to the provinces. The provinces are expected to function as mere administrative agencies very much like local governments in a unitary state. The Governors are mere agents of the President in the sense that they are appointed directly by him. In the matter of appointment of Ministers and in their relationship with their Provincial Assemblies, they have to function under the instructions of the President. According to the Rules of Business, if there is any disagreement between a Secretary and his Minister, the matter has to be placed before the Governor for final orders.[18]

[16] Chittagong Mercantile Employees' Association *v.* Chairman, Industrial Court of East Pakistan. *All-Pakistan Legal Decisions* (PLD) 1963 (Dacca) Vol. XV, p. 860.

[17] *Report of the Standing Organisation Committee on the Reorganisation of the Functions and Structure of the Central Government in the Light of the New Constitution* (President's Secretariat, Establishment Division, April, 1962) (typescript), pp. 3–4.

[18] *The Civil and Military Gazette,* July 13, 1962.

In spite of this centralization, Ayub can claim that under his regime there has been an increasing amount of administrative delegation to the provinces. This is borne out by the greater resources that have been placed at their disposal as a result of the recommendations of the National Finance Commission made in 1962 and later in 1964–65. It was recommended by the National Finance Commission of 1964–65 that out of the net proceds of taxes like income tax, corporation tax, sales tax, excise duties on jute and cotton, 65 per cent should be assigned to the provinces and 35 per cent retained by the Center.[19] Table 3 illustrates that the percentage of total revenue available to the provinces as compared to that available to the Center has been increasing since 1960–61.

Table 3

Revenue Receipts of the
Central and Provincial Governments
(in millions of rupees)

	Central Govt.	*East Pakistan*	*West Pakistan*	*Total*	*Percentage of Provincial Receipts*
1956–57	1,331.4	303.8	613.1	2,248.3	40.8
1957–58	1,525.0	314.1	610.7	2,449.8	37.7
1958–59	1,958.7	522.8	880.9	3,362.4	41.7
1959–60	1,977.5	397.9	804.9	3,180.3	37.8
1960–61	2,094.7	447.7	823.2	3,365.6	37.8
1961–62	2,198.5	706.1	933.2	3,837.8	42.7
1962–63	2,138.5	738.7	1,251.3	4,128.5	48.2
1963–64 (Revised)	2,662.2	1,003.5	1,528.0	5,193.7	48.7
1964–65 (Budget)	2,973.7	1,063.0	1,647.3	5,684.0	47.7

Source: These figures have been worked out from information supplied by the Planning Board, East Pakistan, and that available in *Pakistan Economic Survey 1963–64* (Rawalpindi: Ministry of Finance, 1964).

The key to this administrative delegation in East Pakistan is the growing number of East Pakistani civil servants who are taking over most of the important positions in the province formerly held by West Pakistani civil servants posted in East Pakistan. For a long time East Pakistan groaned under the rule of West Pakistani civil servants. The central government formerly depended upon West Pakistani civil servants who were unpopular in East Pakistan. Now the central govern-

[19] *Report of the National Finance Commission 1964–65* (Rawalpindi: Government of Pakistan Press, 1965), p. 11.

ment depends upon East Pakistani civil servants for the implementation of its policies and mobilization of political support.

East Pakistani Ministers in the central government have been pointing out to the people in East Pakistan that the disparity in economic development between East and West Pakistan must be largely attributed to the former politicians from East Pakistan who failed to protect the interests of their province. They have asserted that the Martial Law regime and the present government have been generous in pouring money into East Pakistan. During the Second Plan period, development expenditure in East Pakistan has increased at a rapid pace and we shall see in Chapter 8 that the disparity in per capita income between East and West Pakistan has started declining. The government claims that by 1985, when the Twenty Year Perspective Plan (1965–85) will have ended, there should be no disparity between per capita income of East and West Pakistan. Government supporters may also point out that in the Constitution among the Principles of Policy, it has been laid down that "parity between the provinces in all spheres of the central government should, as nearly as is practicable, be achieved." In addition, the Railways, the Pakistan Industrial Development Corporation, Water and Power Development Authority, the Small Scale Industries Corporation, and the Forest Development Corporation have all been bifurcated and made provincial responsibilities.

In East Pakistan, Ayub was able to win majority support in the 1965 presidential election, with 53.1 per cent of the vote as compared to 46.6 per cent obtained by Miss Jinnah. It is true that his support in West Pakistan was as high as 73.5 per cent. It is also true that the system of indirect elections under which he obtained this support favored the government candidate in the sense that the Basic Democrats elected to local councils, being dependent upon the support and good will of government officials in the districts, could not easily vote against the government candidate. But it was not merely the bureaucratic influence which won political support for Ayub, because in spite of this influence, the opposition candidate obtained as much as 46.6 per cent of the votes in East Pakistan. A considerable part of the support accorded to Ayub, therefore, must be due to the fact that he has been able to persuade the East Pakistani voters that the interests of East Pakistan have been looked after better under his regime than they were under his predecessors. But the presidential election (1964–65), the National Assembly elections (March, 1965), and the East Pakistan Provincial Assembly elections (May, 1965) have all demonstrated two things. First, the voters feel that the central and provincial governments have not done enough to satisfy the grievances of East Pakistanis, and the wide economic gap that exists between the two provinces has yet to be removed. By casting their votes for the Independent and opposition candidates, East Pakistani voters have shown that they would like to have spokesmen in the Assemblies who would put across vigorously the point of view and interests of East Pakistan. In the National Assembly election in East Pakistan, the government party, the Pakistan Muslim League, captured approximately 72 per cent (52 seats) of the province's seats, but it polled slightly less than 50 per cent of the total votes cast. Were it not for splitting of the opposition vote by the Independent candidates, the opposition parties would have won over 30 seats instead of the 13 which they did win. In the provincial elections, the government party won barely 50 per cent of the 148 seats which it contested. It is true that the government has not been able to win much more than 50 per cent of the East Pakistani votes in the three elections because Ayub's regime in East Pakistani eyes is by and large dominated by West Pakistanis. But the government's failure to win considerable majority support is also due to the fact that the government party has not yet built a strong grass-roots party organization.

So far as the President's political support from West Pakistan is concerned, it rests on some of the well-known landowning families, some of the Punjabi and Sindhi *pirs* (spiritual guides), and several *maliks* (tribal chiefs) from the Tribal Agencies of the Frontier. The President exercises his control over these landlords through the Governor of West Pakistan. The Governor, in his turn, operates through the Deputy Commissioners without whose good will and support it would be difficult for many landlords to carry on their activities and control their tenants. It is often said that many of the Punjabi and Sindhi landlords still carry on their activities in a semifeudal fashion, but it may be pointed out that the sort of feudal control they exercise over their tenants largely exists because successive governments have found it convenient to exercise their control over the rural society of West Pakistan through such feudal intermediaries. (We shall explore how these relationships exist and work in Chapter 9.) According to the Election Commission figures, there were 40 landlords (33 from West Pakistan and 7 from East Pakistan) in the National Assembly of 1962–65 which consisted of 156 members.[20] Another source estimated the number of landlords as 70 (58 from West and 12 from East Pakistan).[21] In the West Pakistan Assembly there were 76 landlords

[20] These figures are derived from reference papers prepared by the Election Commission.

[21] Mushtaq Ahmad, *Government and Politics in Pakistan,* 2nd ed. (Karachi: Pakistan Publishing House, 1963), p. 273.

out of 155 members (1962–65) according to the Election Commission. They can all be regarded as President's men because their support in the Assembly can be effectively controlled through Governors and the Deputy Commissioners who are central civil servants and in whose charge are placed vital matters like land revenue and irrigation dues of the districts concerned.

It is obvious that in the present West Pakistan Provincial Assembly (1965–   ) hard-core opposition consists of less than 10 members in a house of 155, but it is significant that this opposition is confined to members from cities like Karachi, Peshawar, Sialkot, Lahore, etc. The former Governor, the Nawab of Kalabagh, drew his political support mostly from the rural areas and was a vigorous champion of rural interests. He felt that tribes and communities belonging to the rural areas had not been given their due share in government services and that city lawyers and business interests monopolized governmental and commercial power. In December, 1964, the West Pakistan Council of Ministers, meeting under the chairmanship of the Governor, announced that 75 per cent of those posts that were filled by direct recruitment in departments like Irrigation, Agriculture, Excise and Taxation, Basic Democracies, Health, etc., should be reserved for persons who belonged to the rural areas.[22]

The most important and powerful element among the supporters of the President is the army. It has been laid down in Article 238 of the Constitution that for the next twenty years the Defense Minister must be a senior officer from the Defense Services of Pakistan. The present Defense Minister is a former Commander-in-Chief of the Pakistan navy. In addition, several senior diplomatic posts and appointments in various government and economic corporations have sometimes been given to military officers. Similarly, since 1960 several young army officers have been admitted into the Civil Service of Pakistan.

One should mention the new entrepreneurial class that has risen in Pakistan and that supports Ayub's regime because it has provided stability and strong government. This class is dominated by four small communities — the Memons, the Chiniotis, the Bohras, and the Khojas — who constitute about one-half per cent of the population but control over half of Pakistan's industrial wealth.[23] It is well known that Pakistan has been making remarkably rapid strides in industrial development. Indeed, the Second Plan (1960–65) has demonstrated that growth rates of higher than 5 per cent per annum have been achieved in both East and West Pakistan. As a result, the rate of economic

[22] *The Pakistan Times,* December 15, 1964.
[23] Gustav F. Papanek, "The Development of Entrepreneurship," *The American Economic Review Papers and Proceedings,* Vol. 52 (1962), p. 54.

growth is almost double the population growth. The private sector has made an outstanding contribution towards this economic growth. When there was a shortfall of about 4 per cent in the government-financed sector, the privately financed sector exceeded the Plan targets by about 37 per cent. There has been constant criticism of the government because its economic policy has concentrated the economic wealth in the hands of some twenty-two families. Criticism of this kind has been particularly strong in East Pakistan where it is probably felt that all this increase in prosperity is confined to mostly West Pakistan industrialists. An East Pakistani economist has said:

> The present economic policy of the country has given rise to some lucky sponsored capitalists who are making a high rate of profit thriving under the protection of State and helped in turn by means of tariff walls, indirect taxation, and tax holidays.[24]

It may also be pointed out that according to the Second Five Year Plan (1960–65):

> On 31 March, 1959, 63 per cent of the total bank credit went to only 222 accounts in the form of advances of Rs. 1 million and above; advances to borrowers of small means did not exceed 6 per cent of the total credit spread over more than 37,275 accounts.[25]

The reaction of the government to the criticism that its policy has resulted in the enrichment of the big industrial families is that since the country does not have an abundant supply of capital or private initiative, "the policy of the government is neither to liquidate the big industrial families nor to deny them participation in the future growth of the country but only to ensure that opportunities are created for newcomers and for investors with modest means to participate in industrial ventures and to safeguard competition and to avoid the growth of monopolies."[26] The government also claims that it has taken steps to provide better and easier credit facilities to smaller entrepreneurs; that it has refused permission to holders of large industrial undertakings to open financial institutions like banks and insurance companies; and that it has imposed new taxes like the wealth tax, capital gains tax, and gift tax to reduce the concentration of wealth. It is also considering enactment of a law to regulate vertical integration and interlocking of industrial and financial capital which have arisen

[24] A. N. M. Mahmood of Dacca University in *The Dacca Times,* October 18, 1963.

[25] *The Second Five Year Plan, 1960–65* (Government of Pakistan, 1960), p. 71.

[26] *The Budget 1965-66. Speech of Mr. Mohammad Shoaib, Finance Minister.* June 14, 1965. (Government of Pakistan, Ministry of Finance, 1965), p. 15.

in certain industries. However, the basic economic creed of the government seems to center around private enterprise. The President has made it clear that "there have been no grand experiments in nationalisation, no fancy slogans about socialism, no undue intervention in the private sector. It has been the constant endeavour of the Government to mobilize the creative energies of the nation and to give all possible incentives for the stimulation of private initiative."[27]

The Federation of Pakistan Chambers of Commerce and Industry (FPCCI), which represents fourteen chambers of commerce and about forty-six different industries in Pakistan, has been extremely influential and successful in persuading the government to adopt some of its recommendations as government legislation. It recommended to the government that the Industrial Disputes Ordinance, 1959, should be amended in such a way that there should be appeals from the tripartite labor courts (i.e., industrial courts) to the High Courts and the Supreme Court. The President amended this ordinance, and a new ordinance entitled the Industrial Disputes (Amendment) Ordinance, 1962, was issued which incorporated the Federation's recommendation. The National Assembly approved this ordinance in December, 1962, even though it had not been given prior consideration by the Tripartite Labor Conference and was strongly opposed by labor and opposition leaders in the Assembly. Opposition leaders argued that trade unions in Pakistan were financially weak; therefore, appeals from decisions of tripartite courts, where representatives of the workers were present, to High Courts and the Supreme Court would involve delay and expense and would place them at a serious disadvantage.

The Federation made another recommendation. In a memorandum on taxation dated January, 1962, it urged the government to liberalize its income tax exemption regulations applicable to foreign technicians, and it also demanded that the government pay interest at 6 per cent on tax refunds whenever payment of these refunds was delayed beyond a period of 3 months.

Both of these recommendations were accepted by the Finance Minister in his budget speech in 1964; and a resolution of the West Pakistan Zonal Committee of the Federation for extending the tax holiday to new industries in the entire area north of the River Jhelum was also accepted, but with modifications.[28]

[27] Cited in *ibid.*, p. 14.

[28] For the Federation demands and recommendations regarding labor legislation, liberalization of income tax regulations, and tax holiday, see The Federation of Pakistan Chambers of Commerce and Industry, *Brief Report of Activities 1961-62* (Karachi: n.d.), pp. 94, 124–125, and 50. See also R. J. W. Leishman, *The Interest Group Approach to the Study of Political Systems of Transitional Societies* (B.A. thesis, Queen's University, December, 1964).

In spite of the tremendous constitutional and political power that Ayub has mobilized, his regime can be shaken by several forces. Muslims all over the world are often spellbound by great orations delivered in a grand style. In Pakistan, too, the masses can be spurred into hasty action or violence by the orations of politicians. This fascination for the power and majesty of the spoken word can be ascribed to their illiteracy, and also to the influence of the Qur'an which as the most important religious work and as a literary master-piece has profoundly influenced the style and structure of Muslim languages like Arabic, Persian, and Urdu. Ayub has remarked, "The biggest weapon of the politician is his tongue, which we have con-trolled."[29] In addition, there are explosive issues, such as the modern-ization of Islam attempted under Ayub's regime and the continued absorption of former provinces like the Frontier Province, Sind, Baluchistan, etc., into the integrated province of West Pakistan. Thus, Qayyum Khan can draw thousands of people to his mass rallies and hurl frontal assaults at Ayub's regime by characterizing it as a military dictatorship. These outbursts may be reinforced by the *maulanas* who may denounce the Muslim Family Laws Ordinance (designed to curb polygamy) as totally un-Islamic. Khan Abdul Ghaffar Khan, if allowed, could use his prestige and persuasive tongue to set many a Pathan heart on fire on the issue of the Pakhtun Province.[30] The late H. S. Suhrawardy enjoyed support both from the people of East Pakistan at large and also from most of its leaders.

Ayub has been able to disarm such opposition by having these and many other political leaders disqualified from holding any elective or public office until the end of 1966. When he feared they still might cause him trouble by organizing or reviving political parties, he promul-gated an ordinance which barred these disqualified politicians from holding office or from belonging to political parties as well. This ordinance was approved by the National Assembly in April, 1963, but one could see that the former politicians enjoyed considerable support even in the National Assembly for the ordinance was approved by only 71 votes to 62.[31]

Ayub feels that if powerful politicians were given the freedom to organize political parties and criticize his regime they would not only present a serious danger to it but might also cause political instability in the country. The logical outcome of Qayyum Khan's campaigning

---

[29] *The New York Times,* October 19, 1958.

[30] Khan Abdul Ghaffar Khan had often been in prison since the estab-lishment of Pakistan. In 1964 he was released on medical grounds. He i now residing in Afghanistan.

[31] *Dawn,* April 18, 1963.

for example, might be the undoing of Ayub's reforms and the unleashing of mob and religious hysteria in West Pakistan.

It is true that, besides these national objectives, Ayub is interested in exercising personal power and leadership. But one must also give him credit for maintaining political stability and economic progress. When he was Commander-in-Chief of the Pakistan army, he was criticized for having elbowed out some of the competent generals. Nevertheless, he did succeed in building the army into a fine fighting machine. It must also be borne in mind that politicians who are united in opposing Ayub are hopelessly divided against one another on a number of issues. In addition to the cultural and political differences that exist between West Pakistani and East Pakistani leaders, there are personal and political differences among West Pakistani leaders themselves. It is difficult, therefore, to foresee how the politicians can offer a united or stable government if they should succeed in ousting Ayub's regime.

The basic political problem still remains to be solved. If Pakistan were a country consisting merely of illiterate masses and a few hundred highly competent bureaucrats and army officers, at least the political problem of governing would not be very difficult. But Pakistan has (according to the Census of 1961) 728,986 matriculates and 268,701 people with a college education.[32] This means that out of a population of 93.8 million there are nearly a million people with education ranging from matriculation to the college level. It is these educated people — traders, school teachers, clerical workers, lawyers, politicians, engineers, doctors, and other professional persons — who would identify themselves more closely with a regime which offers both economic development and political freedom. In order to bring about a sense of identification between his regime and this influential educated group, Ayub offered a Constitution. But their pressure has been such that Ayub has been forced to bring about increasing politicization of his regime.

The Role of the Judiciary and the Press

One of the great legacies of British rule in former colonial areas is considered to be the respect for the rule of law and the role of an impartial and independent judiciary. Lord Keynes once referred to the United States as "this lawyer-ridden land," and said that "the May-

---

[32] Matriculates correspond to high school graduates in the United States. The figures of 268,701 people with college education is a total of Intermediate, 155,162; Degree, 82,069; and Higher Degree, 31,470. Those with Oriental education, 3,803, are excluded from these figures. *Literary and Education. Population Census of Pakistan 1961.* Census Bulletin No. 4 (Karachi: 1962), p. 161.

flower, when she sailed from Plymouth, must have been entirely filled with lawyers." President Ayub has also chafed under the enormous influence that lawyers exercise in Pakistan. There are about 40,000 legally trained people in Pakistan, and lawyers take pride that its founder was a lawyer, and that some of the Ministers and Prime Ministers have belonged to this profession. In the first National Assembly (1962–65), there were 38 lawyers, and, if educationists and social workers were included, about 73 members out of 156 would constitute an influential group which would favor restoration of some form of parliamentary rule, and above all, the justiciability of the Fundamental Rights. Particularly in East Pakistan has the campaign for parliamentary democracy and the restoration of Fundamental Rights been led primarily by lawyers. Indeed, Islam itself with its emphasis on Shariah (Islamic law), provided the underpinning for rule of law in Pakistan. Significantly, some of the active opposition to Ayub's regime has come from a religious-cum-political organization called the Jamaat-i-Islami.

The government's reaction to the campaign for making the Fundamental Rights justiciable was that such a campaign was deliberately designed to strengthen the judiciary and cripple the executive. The President, however, was prepared to settle for a compromise. He felt that the constitutional amendment designed to guarantee Fundamental Rights to citizens should make it clear that certain laws and ordinances introduced by his regime — such as land reforms, Basic Democracies, and the disqualification from holding office of certain politicians declared to be corrupt — could not be nullified on the score that they were inconsistent with the Fundamental Rights of citizens conferred by the Constitution. The President declared: "If you make everything justiciable, well, then you might as well pack up."[33] This view was fully incorporated in the Constitution (First Amendment) Act, 1963, which became law in January, 1964. As noted earlier in this chapter, according to this amendment, altogether thirty-one laws and ordinances were placed beyond the purview of the Fundamental Rights.

The government probably hoped that since the Fundamental Rights were so constricted, it would not be easy for the courts to place restrictions on executive action banning certain political activities or detaining certain persons in the name of national interest or the security of the state. It must be said to the credit of the courts that they have given a liberal interpretation to the Fundamental Rights in order to protect some of the safeguards and freedoms guaranteed in the Constitution.

In early January, 1964, the Governor of West Pakistan, exercising his powers under the Criminal Law Amendment Act, 1908, declared

[33] Ayub Khan, VI, 8.

the Jamaat-i-Islami to be an unlawful association. Its leader, Maulana Maudoodi, and some of his associates were arrested under the West Pakistan Maintenance of Public Order Ordinance. The government of East Pakistan also took similar action against the Jamaat and its leaders in that province. According to the two provincial governments, the Jamaat was engaged in a number of subversive activities and was receiving financial support from foreign sources hostile to Pakistan. When the matter came before the Supreme Court of Pakistan, the Court in a majority opinion declared that the action of the government in de-legalizing the Jamaat-i-Islami under the Criminal Law Amendment Act was not proper, as the Jamaat was a political party and therefore came under the purview of the Political Parties Act, 1962. The Court also pointed out that the government action denied to the Jamaat the fundamental right of freedom of association that every citizen was entitled to. Justice S. A. Rahman wrote:

> To place an instrument in the hands of the party in power by which they can effectually eliminate from the political scene any opposition, without let or hindrance, cannot be held to be consistent with healthy functioning of the body-politic on democratic lines. Under the Constitution, the executive powers in the Provinces vest in the Governors, who are not popular representatives, and who hold office at the President's pleasure and are subject to his directions. The Head of the State himself is not supposed to be above politics in so far as he is also the head of a political party.[34]

In October, 1964, the West Pakistan High Court ordered the immediate release of Maulana Maudoodi and forty-three other leaders of the Jamaat-i-Islami on the ground that the West Pakistan Maintenance of Public Order Ordinance, under which they had been detained, was void, as it did not conform to the requirements laid down in the Fundamental Right No. 2 of the Constitution for such detention. (These leaders had originally been arrested in January, 1964, and their detention had been extended for a period of two months. Later, by a series of orders, the period had been extended up to March 6, 1965. The government had extended the period of detention under the Ordinance, which provided that the government could detain a person in preventive custody for a period beyond two months and could also extend that period from time to time as it saw fit if the Detenus [Detainees] Review Board was satisfied that sufficient grounds existed for such a detention.) First, there was discrepancy between the Ordinance and the Fundamental Right No. 2 with regard to the initial period of detention: the former referred to a period of two months and the latter to a period of three months. This meant that

[34] PLD 1964 (SC), 734.

the government could authorize the detention of a person for a period exceeding three months if the appropriate advisory board had reported before the expiration of that period that there was sufficient cause for such detention. The West Pakistan government, not having brought the ordinance into conformity with the Fundamental Right No. 2, had extended the period of detention on the basis of the report of the Detenus Review Board beyond a period of two months. The judges found that the review board constituted under the West Pakistan Maintenance of Public Law Ordinance was not proper, because the Home Secretary, who had produced the charges against the detenus, was himself a member of the advisory board and had thus functioned as a judge in his own cause. Finally, the court held that the charges levelled against the Jamaat — that it had created dissatisfaction among the armed forces and had attacked Iran and its royal family — were matters of defense and external affairs over which the provincial legislature had no legislative competence; the legislature therefore could not make laws for preventive detention since it had no jurisdiction in defense and external affairs.[35]

In another judgment, the West Pakistan High Court declared that Section 8 of the West Pakistan Maintenance of Public Order Ordinance was *ultra vires* the Fundamental Rights guaranteed by the Constitution. The decision was given on a writ petition filed by Nawabzada Nasrullah Khan, a former member of the National Assembly, who complained that the District Magistrate had sent two police officers to a meeting of the National Democratic Front's Central Executive, which was being held at a private residence. The District Magistrate had taken this action under Section 8 of the West Pakistan Maintenance of Public Order Ordinance. The court observed: "There is no provision in Section 8 to regulate the exercise of this naked power enjoyed by the District Magistrate and keep it under check within reasonable limits in the interest of public order."[36] Thus, in the eyes of the court, this section was *ultra vires* the Fundamental Rights Nos. 6 and 7 of the Constitution. These rights referred to the freedoms that every citizen enjoyed to assemble peacefully and to form associations subject to any reasonable restrictions imposed by law in the interest of morality or public order.

After lifting Martial Law and introducing the Constitution in June, 1962, the President was faced with the task of creating political support for his regime. It was true that during the period of Martial Law he had been able to have as many as seventy-eight politicians disqualified from holding public office until the end of 1966 under the Elective

[35] *The Pakistan Times,* October 10, 1964.
[36] *Dawn,* July 20, 1965.

Bodies (Disqualification) Order, 1959. These politicians were often known as "EBDOed," the letters E, B, D, O being derived from the Elective Bodies (Disqualification) Order. After the revival of political parties, these EBDOed politicians were further disqualified from associating themselves in any manner with the political parties. It was well known that some of them during the pre-Martial Law days had not only organized political parties, but they or their associates had also started a number of newspapers to propagate their respective points of view. Thus, even though a politician like the late H. S. Suhrawardy could be EBDOed, a Bengali newspaper like the *Ittefaq* or an English weekly, *The Dacca Times,* both of which supported him and the Awami League, continued to criticize the government strongly for having suppressed political freedom and abolished the parliamentary system. Therefore, the government had to take the next logical step, and that was to prevent the press from doing what the EBDOed politicians had been forbidden to do, namely, launch bitter denunciations of government policy. This was done through the two provincial ordinances known as the West Pakistan Press and Publications Ordinance of 1963 and the Press and Publications (East Pakistan Second Amendment) Ordinance, 1963. Under these ordinances, the government was given power to close down the presses where the offending publications were printed and to take over the newspapers or journals. It could take these steps if a publication contained "any words, signs, or visible representations" which tended "directly or indirectly to bring into hatred or contempt the Government" or which were "likely to create or excite feelings of enmity, ill will or hatred between the population of the two provinces."[37] The government proceeded against several newspapers in East and West Pakistan, charging that by publishing certain news items and editorials they had violated these ordinances.[38] The government also felt that suppression of criticism was not enough; there should be a number of newspapers in Pakistan which would put forward the government point of view and create public opinion in its favor. Consequently, the government-backed National Press Trust, sponsored and financed by twenty-four

[37] Article 23 of The Press and Publications Ordinance (XV of 1960). (As modified up to the 1st September, 1964.)

[38] Some of the newspapers proceeded against were the *Ittefaq,* the *Sangbad, The Dacca Times* (weekly), all from East Pakistan, and an English weekly like *Outlook* from West Pakistan, which was forced to abandon publication in August, 1964. The courts set aside some of these orders on the plea that the paper concerned was entitled to create public opinion by healthy and even forceful criticism of the Government in power. See particularly High Court Judgment in *The Dacca Times* case, *The Dacca Times,* August 9, 1963.

well-known industrialists, was set up to establish and publish new newspapers and to acquire some of the existing newspapers and periodicals.[39] In this way, what *Outlook,* a former English weekly from Karachi, called "a class of paid pipers" was brought into being.

These press restrictions so blunted the critical attitude of the press that the government felt confident enough in July, 1965, to announce a twelve-month moratorium on press laws, leaving the press free to regulate its conduct on a voluntary basis through its own court of honor. A Code of Press Ethics was formulated. According to this code, it was agreed that the press would not publish anything which was likely to create ill will between different sections of the people. But it was made clear that this restraint would not preclude "legitimate airing of grievances and views in matters of disparity between regions and groups." Similarly, the press would restrict itself to factual reporting of events without trying thereby to encourage or provoke labor strikes or student agitation. If the press court of honor, set up by the Council of Pakistan Newspaper Editors, found that a particular newspaper had committed a serious breach of press ethics, the maximum punishment awarded in such cases would be the expulsion of the offending newspaper from the Council of Newspaper Editors. All this meant that the government would watch the functioning of the press under its own Code of Press Ethics for a year to see whether it had become unnecessary to invoke its own press laws.

The regimes which preceded Martial Law had to operate within the framework of a parliamentary system. The result was that the system often reached a breaking point because there were no national parties to aggregate the various regional forces and produce a workable constitution and national policies. The Martial Law regime started off by discrediting the parliamentary system and suspending all political activity. However, it merely succeeded in carrying out certain obvious and long-felt economic and social reforms, soon ran out of new ideas, and lost momentum. It found it needed political support to build a sense of partnership between East and West Pakistan as well as to bring about a more stable integration of West Pakistan itself. In order to mobilize this political support, the Constitution of 1962 was introduced. The fact that President Ayub had no clear notion as to how he should mobilize political support was indicated by the stand he took on the question of reviving political parties. At first he was against the revival of political parties; later he agreed that "he had been trying to lay down the rules for a game which was now too old for any change and had finally decided to play the game according to the people's rules."[40]

[39] *Morning News,* March 28, 1964.
[40] *Ibid.,* May 30, 1963.

It is obvious that under the present political system, the traditional roles of the parliament, the judiciary, the parties, etc., have been so modified that they have lost their vigor and liveliness. Ayub has defended his system on the plea that Pakistan's executive, if hamstrung by the irresponsible criticisms of the parliament or the agitational activities of the political parties and regional movements, would neither be able to maintain national unity nor bring about economic development. Thus, faced with such a situation, what has been his *modus operandi?* In the first place, both under and after the Martial Law, he has consistently tried to deactivate political forces opposed to his regime. The methods he has used — namely, the Elective Bodies (Disqualification) Order, 1959, the Press and Publications ordinances, and the 1962 Constitution itself — have been discussed in this chapter. In the second place, he has tried to mobilize political support for his regime by manipulating West Pakistani landlords, certain conservative politicians of East Pakistan, business interests, and also religious influentials like the *pirs,* the *maulanas,* and the *mullahs.*

To a large number of educated Pakistanis, both in East and West Pakistan, the Constitution of 1962 is like a strait-jacket which has been put on the country in the name of political stability. It is clear that there is an excessively strong executive, an extremely weak parliament, a system of elections which clearly favors the government, and restrictions on the activities of certain politicians popular and strong enough to challenge the government. Indeed, Ayub may have acquired powers which are probably in excess of his needs. But there is no doubt that Pakistan is still beset with the problem of political and economic discontent in East Pakistan as well as in parts of West Pakistan like Baluchistan and the former North-West Frontier Province. After acquiring considerable reserve power, Ayub could have easily given more powers to the parliament so that some of these regional demands might be articulated through that institution. He also could have encouraged the political parties to form broad coalitions of regional interests so that a united opposition might emerge. The present government seems to be efficient in curbing opposition forces but not skillful in creating political support.

The viceregal system, which we have characterized as constitutional autocracy, is by no means totalitarian in the controls it imposes upon the people. It does not seek to remove all pluralistic barriers between itself and the people as a totalitarian system does. In Pakistan, a formal institutional check to the President's power like the National Assembly has been rendered effete. But the judiciary, though assigned a circumscribed role in the Constitution, has acted as a check. In addition, there are other countervailing economic and political forces which are still active. There is Bengali regionalism which has constantly reasserted itself against the centripetal forces of the federal government. Politicians and political parties often have to operate under a host of disabilities; nevertheless they do continue to oppose the government. Business groups have also emerged as a counter-vailing force to bureaucratic dominance in the government.

6

Bureaucracy and Political and Economic Development

There has often been a tendency to judge or evaluate the role of bureaucracy in developing countries in the light of Western norms. As a professional organization, the bureaucracy in any system is often expected to conform to the characteristics noted by Max Weber. The functions it performs are specialized and highly differentiated. Recruitment takes place on the basis of achievement rather than on ascription. Similarly, placements, transfers, and promotions are made on the basis of universalistic rather than on particularistic criteria. Finally, even though bureaucracy is a hierarchical organization, its chain of command and decision-making follow certain rational and functional lines. Such an organization has emerged mostly in highly industrialized societies of the West.

However rationalized and functional the role and organization of bureaucracy may be, the fact remains that it has to operate within the norms of the Western political system. In such a system, policy-making is largely in the hands of the elected political leaders, and the bureaucracy is assigned the execution of that policy. It is true that no Western model works in such a neat fashion that the different parts of the system carry out these respective allotted functions. But there is no such "rough-and-ready" demarcation of functions in the political system in developing societies. We may have political leaders who not only formulate policies, but who also interfere in the operations of their bureaucracies. On the other hand, we have powerful bureaucracies, as in Pakistan, where, due to the lack of political stability, national consensus, and a body of trained political leaders, civil servants often play a decisive and dual role in policy formulation and its execution.

The most powerful and elitist administrative service in Pakistan is the Civil Service of Pakistan, the successor to the former Indian Civil Service, which was organized at a time when the colonial power was interested in maintaining law and order and not much concerned with welfare administration. The Civil Service of Pakistan finds itself so well entrenched that even though the country is trying to grapple with the problems of economic development, the elitist civil service has been able to resist functional reorganization of the bureaucracy and the deconcentration of the power that it holds. It may be argued that when the country was faced with political instability and lack of national consensus, a generalist civil service like the Civil Service of Pakistan was fortunately available to fill the vacuum created by the lack of political leadership and to act as an instrument of national unity. A highly specialized and functionally organized bureaucracy might not have been able to fulfill these tasks.

It is also unrealistic to expect that recruitment to the bureaucracy in Pakistan would be on the basis of merit rather than on ascriptive criteria. The former British practice of giving special consideration to minorities in India has been continued in Pakistan where 80 per cent of the Central Superior Service posts each year are recruited on the basis of quotas assigned to various regions, and 20 per cent on the basis of merit.

Structure

There are three kinds of central services in Pakistan. There is the generalist-administrative service, the Civil Service of Pakistan. There are functional services like Audit and Accounts Service, Taxation Service, Military Accounts Service, Customs and Excise Service, Railway Accounts Service, etc. The third kind consists of the specialized services like the Central Engineering Service and the Geological Survey. Another way of classifying Pakistan's central bureaucracy would be to divide each of the services into four classes — Class I, Class II, Class III, and Class IV. Class I and Class II services are the better-paid gazetted services in the sense that the names of these officers appear in the official gazette and they also enjoy higher powers and responsibilities in the hierarchy. The minimum academic qualification for members of Class I and Class II services is a B.A. or an equivalent degree. Class III civil servants are mainly secretarial and others who carry on routine work under the supervision of Class I and Class II officers. Class IV employees consist of manual workers. In this chapter we shall consider the Central Superior Services and other specialist services generally; and we shall take a close look at the elitist Civil Service of Pakistan, which plays a highly influential and powerful role in the economic and political development of the country.

Table 4

Central Services of Pakistan

Category of Service	Number of Officers*
Civil Service of Pakistan	434
Pakistan Foreign Service	138
Police Service of Pakistan (East Pakistan)	79
Police Service of Pakistan (West Pakistan)	110
Pakistan Audit and Accounts Service	94
Pakistan Taxation Service	205
Pakistan Military Accounts Service	62
Pakistan Customs and Excise Services	44**
Pakistan Railway Accounts Service	46
Central Engineering Service Class I	69**
Telegraph Engineering Service Class I	105
Telegraph Traffic Service Class I	3
Pakistan Postal Service Class I	50
Post and Telegraph Traffic Service Class I	23
Pakistan Military Lands and Cantonments Service	46
Geological Survey of Pakistan	60

* These figures have been taken from *Civil List of Class I Officers Serving Under Government of Pakistan,* 1st January, 1964 (Rawalpindi: The President's Secretariat, Establishment Division, Government of Pakistan, 1964), pp. 315–428, and 100–104.

** As these figures were not available in the 1964 Civil List, they have been taken from *Civil List of Class I Officers Serving Under Government of Pakistan,* 1st January, 1963 (Rawalpindi: The President's Secretariat, Establishment Division, Government of Pakistan, 1963), pp. 338–340, and 348–352.

It may be noted that a considerable number of key appointments in the Central Secretariat, the two Provincial Secretariats, and at the district level have been reserved for the officers of the CSP. The authorized strength of the CSP in 1954 was set at 470. On the basis of the latest requirements, the authorized strength of the CSP cadre is likely to increase to about 546.[1] The strength (in 1965) of the CSP is 461. CSP officers, who are the decision-makers in these matters, have maintained that the quality of this elitist service should be

[1] *Report of the Administrative Reorganisation Committee* (Karachi: Efficiency & O & M Wing, Establishment Division, President's Secretariat, 1963), pp. 340–341.

maintained; therefore, the intake should be so regulated that the standards of the service do not decline.

Table 5

The Strength of the CSP During 1960–64

	Total Strength	Civil Intake	Military Intake	Total Intake
1960	358	25	5	30
1961	383	21	5	26
1962	410	27	3	30
1963	434	30	1	31
1964	461	33	0	33

These figures have been derived from *Civil Lists of Class 1 Officers Serving Under Government of Pakistan* and *Gradation Lists of the Civil Service of Pakistan* which are published each year on the first of January. For accuracy regarding the total strength or the total intake of a given year, one cannot depend upon either the *Civil List of Class I Officers* or *Gradation List of the Civil Service of Pakistan* of that year. Therefore, one has to work out a more accurate figure from the *Civil Lists* and *Gradation Lists* of subsequent years. For example, according to the *Civil List of Class I Officers* of 1961, the total strength of the CSP in 1960 was 357 and the total intake was 29, but according to the *Civil List of Class I Officers* of 1962, the total intake in 1960 was 30. The discrepancy arose because of the fact that in the 1961 List, the civil intake was shown as 24 when it should have been 25. In this way, we have corrected the total strength for 1960, showing it as 358 instead of 357, the civil intake as 25 instead of 24, and the total intake as 30 instead of 29. Similarly, the 1964 *Gradation List of the Civil Service of Pakistan* shows the total strength to be 432, civil intake to be 28, and total intake to be 29, but *Gradation List of the CSP* of 1965 shows that the civil intake was 30 because 2 officers are included in it who were not mentioned in 1964 Gradation List of the CSP. Thus, we have shown the total strength to be 434, civil intake to be 30, and total intake to be 31.

One cannot assume that the total number of officers in the CSP in a given year is equal to the total number of officers in the previous year plus the total intake in that year because some officers may have retired or left the service during the year.

It may be noted that the average annual intake during the last five years in the CSP is about 30. This includes military officers. The practice of taking military officers into the civil service dates back to the British days when army officers were taken into the Indian Political Service, and such officers were posted mostly in the Indian states and the border areas of the Frontier. The practice was revived in Pakistan after the emergence of the Martial Law regime, and five military officers were admitted into the CSP in 1960.

Recruitment and Training

Every October the Central Public Service Commission conducts a common examination for the recruitment of the CSP, the Foreign Service, the Police Services, the various financial and taxation services like Audit and Accounts, Taxation, Customs, etc., and for the Pakistan Postal Service and Pakistan Military Lands and Cantonments Service. A degree from a recognized university is the minimum qualification, and the candidates have to be between the ages of twenty-one to twenty-five. The competitive examination is divided into written, oral, and psychological tests. Written tests consist of compulsory and optional papers. Compulsory subjects are essay, English, general knowledge, and current affairs, and the optional list offers a wide variety ranging from pure mathematics and statistics to American history, social sciences, and the various natural and physical sciences, of which the candidates have to select three. In order to qualify for entrance into the Superior Services a candidate has to secure at least 25 per cent marks in the compulsory subjects, and his average should be at least 50 per cent in all the written tests. For a large number of the young men of Pakistan, the highest ambition of their lives is to get into the prestigious Civil Service of Pakistan. The following table, showing what services the candidates list as their first choice, indicates that the Civil Service of Pakistan is the most preferred service among the candidates appearing for the Central Superior Services examination.[2]

Percentage of Candidates Listing a Service as Their First Choice

Year	Civil Service of Pakistan	Pakistan Foreign Service	Police Service of Pakistan	Pakistan Audit and Accounts Service	All Others
1961	78.3	15.3	2.7	1.6	2.1
1962	79.7	14.2	2.8	1.6	1.7

It is also clear that the number of vacancies in all the Superior Services is so limited that the great majority of those who qualify are not taken into any of the Superior Services. Thus, in October, 1963, 1,242 candidates appeared for the Central Superior Services examination, of

[2] The table is derived from *Central Public Service Commission Annual Report For the Year 1963* (Karachi: Manager of Publications, 1964), p. 105.

whom 266 were declared qualified; of this number, however, there were vacancies for only 88 in all the services.[3]

At the time of Partition, there were in all 1,157 officers in the Indian Civil Service and the Indian Political Service, of whom 608 were British, 448 were Hindus and others, and 101 were Muslims. Out of 101 Muslims, 95 opted for service in Pakistan (83 ICS and 12 IPS).[4] It is well known that most of the Muslim ICS officers were not taken into the ICS strictly on the basis of their standing in the competitive examination but because of the British policy of giving special consideration to an important minority. However, it could be argued that the Muslims selected for the ICS were the best from among the Muslim candidates. At the time of Partition it was also clear that a large number of Muslim officers who opted for service in Pakistan came from Muslim-minority provinces in India and spoke Urdu. A third or more of the Muslim officers who opted for Pakistan were from the Punjab, and only one or two were from Bengal.[5] Since the Central Service officers occupied key positions both in the central and provincial governments, Bengalis openly expressed their bitterness by suggesting that East Pakistan was being ruled by West Pakistan. This explains the quota system according to which the various Central Superior Services recruit their candidates. Twenty per cent of the vacancies are filled on the basis of merit, while the remaining 80 per cent are divided equally between East and West Pakistan. The West Pakistan quota is further divided, with Punjab and Bahawalpur being allotted 23 per cent, Sind, the N.-W.F.P., Tribal Areas and Baluchistan 15 per cent, and Karachi 2 per cent.[6]

[3] *The Pakistan Times,* June 1, 1964.

[4] Ralph Braibanti, "Public Bureaucracy and Judiciary in Pakistan," in Joseph La Palombara, ed., *Bureaucracy and Political Development* (Princeton: Princeton University Press, 1963), pp. 365–367.

[5] According to figures cited by Braibanti, *ibid.,* there were 27 Muslim officers in Punjab in 1947. It is well known that a few of these officers were not originally from Punjab, though they were placed on the Punjab cadre. Similarly, according to the same source, there were 18 Muslim officers in Bengal, some of whom were originally from Punjab. In all, 83 Muslim ICS officers opted for Pakistan in 1947. This explains the author's caution in stating that: "A third or more of the Muslim officers who opted for Pakistan were from the Punjab. . . ." As regards the number of ICS officers from Bengal at the time of Partition, figures vary. Shahabuddin, Minister for Information, speaking in the National Assembly, said there was only one ICS officer from East Pakistan in 1947 (*Dawn,* June 27, 1965). According to the Parliamentary Secretary to the Establishment Division, there were two ICS officers from East Pakistan at the time of Partition. This is based on the *Gradation List* of 1951. *National Assembly of Pakistan Debates,* II, No. 6 (June 11, 1963), p. 241.

[6] *Dawn,* April 7, 1963.

It seems that the performance of the candidates from Punjab seems to be the best in terms of the ranks achieved in the competitive examination. The performance of candidates from East Pakistan seems to be improving, particularly since East Pakistani candidates have stood first during the last two years.[7] It is obvious that because of the quota system all officers are not admitted into the CSP on the basis of their ranks achieved in the competitive examination. It often happens that in a given year, when 25 to 30 officers may be taken, several Punjabi candidates who were placed among the first thirty are not admitted into the CSP. In 1963, the civilian intake of 30 consisted of candidates from the following areas: Punjab, 11; East Pakistan, 13; Sind, 2; North-West Frontier Province, 2; and Karachi, 2. Among those taken in, three East Pakistanis were admitted into the CSP even though they were placed 33rd, 37th, and 42nd in the competitive examination. The two candidates from the Frontier who were included in the CSP were placed 32nd and 41st in the order of merit. In 1964, among the 33 officers taken into the CSP, there were 13 each from Punjab and East Pakistan, 5 from Sind, and 2 from the Frontier. Among the Sindhi officers, there were 4 who were placed 50th, 53rd, 59th, and 86th. The two officers from the Frontier were placed 40th and 90th in the order of merit. It may be argued that even in this method of selection of 80 per cent of the officers on the basis of quotas allotted to each region, the principle of merit is not being abandoned because the officers selected are those who have obtained the highest rank among the candidates appearing from a particular region.

After their selection the officers are trained at the Civil Service Academy for a period of eight months. The subjects taught at the Academy include public administration, development economics, Pakistan's legal system, including revenue laws, and current affairs. It is supposed to be a well-rounded program in which the day starts early in the morning with riding and physical training followed by classes in

---

[7] The first thirty places secured by candidates from various areas in the 1962, 1963, and 1964 examinations were:

	Punjab and Bahawalpur	N.-W.F.P.	Sind	Other Areas In West Pakistan	East Pakistan
1962	16	0	2	2	10
1963	18	0	1	0	11
1964	19	1	1	0	8

This table has been derived from the Central Superior Services examination results published in *Dawn*, June 15, 1963, *The Pakistan Times*, June 1, 1964, and *The Pakistan Times*, June 5, 1965.

the forenoon and sports in the afternoon. The officers, who are called probationers during their period of training, are constantly reminded that they are not "mere students but are members of the CSP" and are enjoined to follow and uphold the traditions of this illustrious service, which include strength of character and strict impartiality in judging issues and taking decisions. They are also required to appear in appropriate and prescribed attire for riding, physical training, small arms training, and for attending classes and dinners.[8]

The CSP has been under attack for maintaining traditions of the old colonial service and for not being well trained as administrators of a modern welfare state and particularly of a developing country like Pakistan. In the training program at the Civil Service Academy a greater stress is being placed on subjects like public administration and development economics, and the study of law is being relegated to a position of secondary importance in the curriculum.[9] The training at the Academy is followed by one-and-a-half-year's practical training when the probationers are appointed as Assistant Commissioners in various districts.

There is a separate Finance Services Academy in Lahore where officers of the Audit and Accounts, Military and Railway Accounts, and Customs and Taxation Services are trained for the first nine months of the total probationary period of two years. Subjects taught are economics, public finance, public administration, financial organization, etc. Unlike the Civil Service Academy, where a broad comprehensive training both in administration and economics is given, the training at the Finance Services Academy is of a more specialized nature and is related mostly to fields of finance and accounts. The training is followed by departmental training in the particular finance and revenue departments to which the probationers belong, and finally the probationers are attached to business firms, commercial banks, the State Bank, and the Pakistan Industrial Development Corporation.[10]

District Administration

For administrative purposes, West Pakistan and East Pakistan are divided into divisions and districts. West Pakistan with its population of 42.9 million (1961 census) and an area which is over five times that of East Pakistan, has 12 divisions and 53 districts. East Pakistan

[8] *Standing Orders Regulating Probationers' Conduct in the Civil Service Academy* (mimeographed), pp. 1–2.

[9] M. R. Inayat, ed., *Perspectives in Public Administration* (Lahore: Civil Service Academy, 1962), p. 102.

[10] Government of Pakistan, Ministry of Finance, *Finance Service Academy Brochure 1963–64* (mimeographed), pp. 21–22.

with its population of 50.8 million (1961 census) has 4 divisions and 17 districts. Divisions are under Commissioners and districts are under Deputy Commissioners. Most of these district posts are reserved for CSP officers, but since there is a gap between the authorized strength and the existing strength of the CSP, a large number of the posts of Deputy Commissioner and Additional Deputy Commissioner are held by provincial civil service officers. For example, in 1961, the number of reserved posts in the districts for CSP officers in West Pakistan was 52, but of these, the CSP held only 32. Districts vary both in population and area. In West Pakistan, districts range in area from 887 to 30,931 square miles. In East Pakistan, the range in area is from 1,371 to 6,361 square miles. Twelve districts in East Pakistan and four in West Pakistan have populations of over two million, which means that they are more populous than 21 states in the United States. All of the districts in East Pakistan, except the Chittagong Hill Tracts, and 18 districts in West Pakistan have a population of over one million. East Pakistan has more populous districts; whereas districts in West Pakistan are considerably larger in area.[11]

In East Pakistan, each district is subdivided into subdivisions and below the subdivision the administrative unit is the *thana,* each of which has a police station. In West Pakistan, about 40 out of 53 districts have subdivisions. A more common administrative unit built around revenue administration in West Pakistan is the *tehsil.*[12] The district, however, is the most important unit of administration and in its headquarters are located the district offices of the Departments of Police, Revenue, Judiciary, Agriculture, Transport, Education, Taxation, and Food.

The responsibilities of the Deputy Commissioner have been defined as (a) development and coordination of governmental activities, (b) revenue, (c) law and order.[13] This means that every conceivable activity, political or economic, taking place within a district has been placed under the purview of the Deputy Commissioner. It may be noted that economic development has been described as his first responsibility, indicating the importance attached to it. But the collection of land revenue and the maintenance of law and order still form important parts of the district administration, and a question has often been raised as to whether the Deputy Commissioner has enough

---

[11] For facts regarding the population and areas of districts, see *Population Census of Pakistan 1961,* Census Bulletin No. 2 (Karachi: Office of the Census Commissioner, 1961).

[12] This revenue administrative unit is called *taluka* in Sind.

[13] *Decisions of the Cabinet on the Report of the Provincial Administration Commission* (Rawalpindi: President's Secretariat, 1962), p. 24.

time available to devote to developmental work when his normal duties pertaining to collection of revenue and maintenance of law and order absorb so much of his time. However, the question why so much power is concentrated in the hands of a young officer, particularly a CSP officer who has had no more than six to ten years of service, may be answered by the simple fact that to a peasant or rural mind a representative of the government should answer or attend to all his needs. He does not see government as a collection of specialized agencies, each attending to a specific function. A peasant still thinks in terms of the government offering him relief by postponing the collection of land revenue when his harvest has failed or meting out speedy justice when his property has been trespassed or kith and kin attacked. Thus, a Deputy Commissioner is described in the petitions that people bring to him as "Incarnation of Justice," "Cherisher of the Poor," *"Ma Bap* [Mother and Father] of the People." Those who defend the existing system of public administration in Pakistan would also argue that there has to be coordination of the various government activities if economic and social development are to take place in a balanced manner.

There is no such thing as the theory of separation of powers so far as the powers of the Deputy Commissioner are concerned. He controls the police organization and is responsible for the maintenance of law and order. In matters of criminal law, he is the Chief Magistrate of the district. Under him is placed the entire machinery of land revenue collection. The collection of land revenue dates back to Mughal times and is a sort of land tax based on the principle that the state is entitled to a share of the produce realized by a peasant in cultivating his land. The system of land revenue administration, particularly in West Pakistan, descends right down to the village and involves elaborate and detailed records of the land holdings of each proprietor. The Deputy Commissioner also acts as the highest revenue judge in the district in appeals arising out of disputes regarding rents, mutation and partition of land, etc.

In matters of criminal law, enormous power has been placed in the hands of the Deputy Commissioner. Criminal cases involving thefts, murders, or those causing public disturbance, may be tried in the first instance by magistrates who are under the administrative control of the Deputy Commissioner. One may argue that these magistrates cannot decide these cases fearlessly and impartially when matters like their promotion, leave, etc., depend upon the recommendations and the confidential reports the Deputy Commissioner sends to the government. Though there are police officers in the district, the police organization normally functions under the supervision of the Deputy

Commissioner who has the power to sanction the prosecution of a particular person and send the case to one of his own subordinates or even try it himself. Most of the serious criminal cases in the district are state cases. If the Deputy Commissioner were to acquit the accused, the prestige of the police officers who work under his supervision and who have taken much trouble in apprehending and prosecuting the accused, would be undermined. It is possible to file an appeal against the orders of the District Magistrate to a higher court where the District Judge presides, but most of the people in the district cannot afford the expenses involved in this procedure. Furthermore, the present government has taken the view that the elaborate procedure of taking evidence developed during the British days does not promote justice, as both sides in a case produce false and tutored witnesses. Thus, according to this view, simple and illiterate villagers can often get "rough-and-ready" justice from courts working under the supervision of the Deputy Commissioner rather than from a higher court where, besides delay and expense, the villager has to face clever lawyers and sometimes false witnesses.

The West Pakistan Criminal Law Amendment Act, 1963, is designed to provide for the "more speedy trial and most effective punishment of certain heinous offenses," i.e., murder, kidnapping, dacoity, trespass, illegal import of goods, corrupt practices, etc. This means the government in West Pakistan thinks that the magisterial courts in the districts do not provide for speedy trial and condign punishment for heinous offenses. Therefore, these offenses should be adjudicated by a tribunal constituted under the Act by the Deputy Commissioner and presided over by a magistrate with four other persons appointed by the Deputy Commissioner out of a panel approved by the Commissioner. Lawyers may appear before the tribunal, but the tribunal has been empowered to rely on any evidence, including hearsay evidence and private inquiries. According to the Chief Justice of the Supreme Court of Pakistan, the procedure followed in these tribunals is "rigorously kept free of every kind of rule or regulation that might savour of due process."[14] The Deputy Commissioner either upholds or rejects the findings of the tribunal. The Deputy Commissioner may sentence the convicted person up to fourteen years imprisonment and

[14] Muhammad Akram and others v. the State. *All-Pakistan Legal Decisions* (PLD) 1963 (SC) Vol. XV, p. 376. The Chief Justice was referring to *jirga* (council of tribal leaders) trials under the Frontier Crimes Regulation, 1901, under which the *jirgas* follow a similar procedure as the tribunals do under the West Pakistan Criminal Law Amendment Act. The Frontier Crimes Regulation applies to some of the Tribal Areas in West Pakistan; whereas the West Pakistan Criminal Law Amendment Act applies to the whole of West Pakistan except the Tribal Areas.

impose a fine. There is no appeal from any of the orders of a Deputy Commissioner to any superior court except that the Commissioner of a Division may revise the orders of a Deputy Commissioner. It may be noted that, on the whole, district administration in West Pakistan ever since the British days has operated under more authoritarian traditions than its counterpart in East Pakistan. There, all the districts, except the district of Sylhet, which originally belonged to the province of Assam, have inherited traditions of regulated provinces. These provinces came under British control earlier than the nonregulated provinces and were governed by what are known as the Bengal Regulations. On the other hand, in West Pakistan, all the areas except the former province of Sind, inherited the authoritarian traditions of nonregulated provinces where the administration was overcentralized in the hands of the DC and the Superintendent of Police. Instead of the detailed Bengal Regulations, it was said that the nonregulated provinces were governed "by the light of a clear conscience and a clear head" of the DC. It may also be pointed out that according to the Constitution (First Amendment) Act, 1963, which makes Fundamental Rights justiciable, the West Pakistan Criminal Law Amendment Act, 1963, cannot be held null and void on the basis that it is inconsistent with the Fundamental Rights. Thus, one may argue that East Pakistanis in this sense enjoy more unrestricted Fundamental Rights than their fellow citizens in West Pakistan.

Under the Pakistan Essential Services Maintenance (Amendment) Ordinance, trade union leaders accused of having created industrial unrest or of being responsible for starting strikes can be given a summary trial by the First Class Magistrates, who function under the supervision of Deputy Commissioners.[15] Similarly, magistrates working under the control of the Deputy Commissioner can also take measures under the Code of Criminal Procedure to prevent breaches of the peace by demanding security from persons likely to disturb law and order. All this violates the general principle of separation of the judiciary from the executive because magistrates who try these cases are in direct administrative subordination to Deputy Commissioners who are interested in prosecuting offenders or other persons likely to commit breach of the peace. Furthermore, through these powers of the Deputy Commissioners, the central or provincial governments can take action against their political opponents. There have been cases where Deputy Commissioners under the West Pakistan Maintenance of Public Order Ordinance have ordered certain persons to leave their districts and when they have moved to other districts, the Deputy

[15] See a discussion of the Pakistan Essential Services (Amendment) Ordinance in the National Assembly, *Dawn*, July 9, 1965.

Commissioners of those districts have been asked to exclude them from those districts as well.[16] All this suggests that the Deputy Commissioner is performing the same kind of political role that his predecessor played during the British days. One of his primary responsibilities is not only to maintain law and order in the district but also to keep his area safe and free from political unrest and agitation.

The Deputy Commissioner is important in economic development. First, he is the administrative head of the district, which means that he supervises and coordinates the activities of departments like Agriculture, Food, Irrigation, Transport, Roads, Health, and Cooperatives. He writes annual reports regarding the conduct and efficiency of the officers of these departments to the Divisional Commissioner, and it has been laid down as a decision of the Cabinet that "the recommendations of the commissioner in respect of transfer or posting of any particular officer of divisional or regional rank serving in his division should not be disregarded except with the approval of the Governor."[17] This suggests that the Deputy Commissioner, who works under the Divisional Commissioner, is expected to keep a close watch over the activities of officers connected with the welfare departments. Obviously, the officers connected with technical departments resent the control that a generalist DC, who often does not have more than five to eight years seniority in his service, exercises over them. Moreover, it is often pointed out that in development administration the coordinating officer is expected to provide dynamic leadership and not to curb the enthusiasm of technical officers by excessive controls and authoritarian attitudes. Technical specialists in welfare departments resent the great prestige and power that the generalist officers enjoy in the administrative hierarchy in modern India and Pakistan where economic development is supposed to be of paramount importance. They argue that the pace of economic development depends very much upon the efficiency and specialized knowledge of experts on agriculture, irrigation, public health, and industries.

It is not likely that this controversy between the generalist and the specialist will be resolved for some time to come. But it is obvious that the needs of developmental administration are being realized, and the DC's are urged to create popular enthusiasm for the overall economic development of their respective areas. This is clearly the

[16] The West Pakistan High Court has ruled such orders as illegal because, according to the ordinance, the government could exclude persons from a province or a district but could not order the removal of a person from a province or district of which he was an ordinary resident. *The Pakistan Times*, January 22, 1965.

[17] *Decisions of the Cabinet on the Report of the Provincial Administration Commission*, p. 9.

intention of the scheme of Basic Democracies wherein, "It is intended that Government operation should be discussed in the councils, so as to make the administration accountable to the people and responsive to their actual needs and aspirations."[18] The District Council, which functions under the chairmanship of the DC, consists of an equal number of official members drawn from various departments and unofficial members chosen from among the chairmen of the Union Councils and of the Town and Union Committees in the district. In the Basic Democracies Order, 1959, the District Councils have been empowered to review the progress in various branches of administration in the district and also to formulate and recommend development schemes of the district to the Divisional Council. This means that both the DC's and the officers of various departments have to take into confidence and consultation the chairmen of Union Councils and of the Town and Union Committees who are elected representatives of the people in their respective Councils. Some of the compulsory functions allotted to the District Councils include agricultural development, promotion of sanitation and public health, maintenance and improvement of public roads, water works, primary schools, etc.[19]

In the synthesis that is being attempted of local public opinion and administrative power it is likely that for some time to come the administrative power will overwhelm the public representatives, and economic development in the district will take place only if the DC, through his coordinating role, can generate enough cooperative effort and enthusiasm among the welfare departments. It is true that compared to the technical departments it is the DC alone who can evaluate developmental activity in its totality. The design, estimates of cost, location, etc., of a bridge to be constructed in a district are problems which can best be tackled by an engineer. But the problem of public protest resulting from the particular location of a bridge can perhaps best be resolved by the DC because of his dealings with the public. Those who do not seem to appreciate the need for a coordinator in the district administration think the DC is not likely to be a go-getter compared to a technical officer, simply because the DC is immersed in a host of other activities and is fond of giving balanced judgments in the light of his knowledge of the working of the entire administration.[20] If the DC is overworked and does not have time

[18] President Ayub's letter to Chairmen of District Councils. *The Pakistan Times,* March 19, 1960.

[19] For functions of District Councils, see *The Basic Democracies Order, 1959* (Karachi: Government of Pakistan Press, 1959). Sections 33 and 34.

[20] For the point of view that the DC is not a "go-getter," see *Report of the Food and Agriculture Commission* (Karachi: Food and Agriculture Commission, Government of Pakistan, 1960), pp. 200-201.

for a proper performance of his coordinating role, he should be given more staff officers who can relieve him of some of his responsibilities with regard to the supervision of police, revenue, and judicial departments. However, a more cogent criticism of the role of the DC would be that he is a part of an administrative system which relies far too much on coercion rather than on education and persuasion of the public. Development can take place only if the creative faculties of the people are released and energized, and if the Union, the Thana or Tehsil, and District Councils start pulsating with new life and vigor.

Secretariat — Its Organization and Functions

The central and the two provincial Secretariats in Pakistan constitute the hubs of their respective administrative organizations. Just as the Deputy Commissioner is the chief coordinator in the district so is the Secretary with regard to his ministry, where he is the supreme coordinator of the activities of Divisions, Attached Departments or Directorates and Subordinate Offices under his ministry. But the main difference between the Secretary and the Deputy Commissioner is that the Secretary is the principal adviser of his ministry with regard to policy-making; whereas the Deputy Commissioner is the principal source of information from his district and the implementor of the government policy within his area. A book written more than fifty years ago described the roles of the Secretariat and the district administration admirably: "The Government of every Indian province is an automaton plus the mirror of consciousness. The Secretariat is consciousness and the Collectors form the automaton. The Collector works and the Secretariat observes and registers."[21]

The Secretary, who is usually in charge of a ministry, functions under a Minister, or the President, who may be in charge of certain ministries. The Secretary controls several divisions under his ministry. He deals with all cases, summaries, and reports called for by the President, or the Minister, or the Cabinet, cases of appointments or promotions of senior officers in his ministry, and all important cases relating to development plans, annual budget, and foreign exchange requirements. Usually a ministry has several divisions under it. For example, the Ministry of Finance has under it the Budget Division, Expenditure Division, Internal Finance Division, and External Finance Division. A Joint Secretary, unless he is in charge of a ministry, is usually entrusted with a division in a ministry. One can say that most

---

[21] George R. Aberigh-Mackay, *Twenty-One Days in India* (Calcutta and Simla: Thacker Spink & Co., 1914), p. 65. A Deputy Commissioner has been known as District Magistrate or Collector in certain provinces of India.

The Central Secretariat

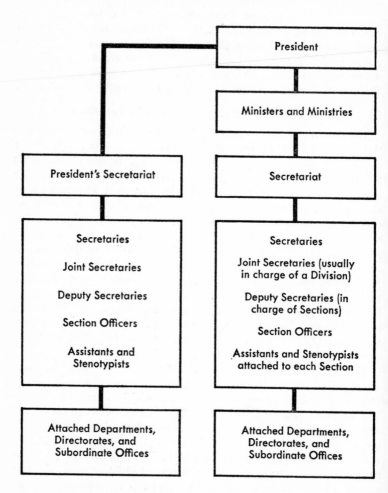

of the work that the Secretary deals with is with regard to policy-making; whereas the functions of the Joint Secretaries may roughly be divided into two halves, those of being an advisor to the Secretary with regard to policy-making and administering his division. There are usually two or three Deputy Secretaries under a Joint Secretary. Deputy Secretaries provide data and information to the Joint Secretary and are expected to dispose of on their own responsibility cases in which no major questions of policy are involved. Deputy Secretaries are in charge of sections which function under their respective Section Officers.[22]

CSP officers hold a large number of the positions in the Secretariat ranging from those of Section Officers at the lowest tier to those of Secretaries at the highest. How dominant is the position of this elitist service, particularly at the policy-making level, may be seen from the fact that in 1963, out of the seven highest positions in the President's Secretariat, all were held by CSP officers. In the ministries and divisions other than those of the President's Secretariat, out of 21 such senior positions, fourteen were in the hands of the CSP in 1963.[23]

In terms of hierarchy, the Attached Departments, Directorates, and Subordinate Offices function below the ministries and divisions in the Secretariat. These Departments or Directorates are attached to the ministry concerned. For example, the Ministry of Food and Agriculture has under it Attached Departments like Agriculture Census; Food and Agriculture Council, Karachi; Department of Marketing Intelligence and Agricultural Statistics, Rawalpindi; and Department of Plant Protection. Some of the Subordinate Offices attached to the Ministry of Food and Agriculture are Pakistan Animal Husbandry Research Institute, Comilla; Soil Survey Project of Pakistan, Lahore; and Marine Fisheries Department. Heads of these Attached Departments and Directorates have often complained that in the civil service hierarchy they occupy a subordinate position to the generalist CSP officers, who man most of the key positions in the Secretariat. Under the existing system, they have to submit their technical proposals to the Secretariat officer, who, even though he is a layman, sits in judgment on the technical proposals submitted by the Attached Department. The fact that there has been friction between the Secretariat officials and the technical officers of the Attached Departments is indicated by the decision of the government, which reads: "Heads of Departments should be responsible for the technical soundness of their proposals, which, as a rule, should not be subjected to any technical examination by the Ministry concerned."[24] Nevertheless, the government has made it clear that the Secretary of a ministry is responsible for policy-making

[22] For additional information regarding functional and structural organization of the Secretariat, see *Report of the Administration Reorganisation Committee*, pp. 255–274.

[23] *Civil List of Class I Officers Serving Under Government of Pakistan.* Up to 1st January, 1963. (Rawalpindi: The President's Secretariat, Establishment Division, 1963.)

[24] *Report of the Administration Reorganisation Committee*, p. 271.

and the Attached Department should be concerned primarily with the implementation of that policy. "There should be no confusion of staff and line functions."[25]

The CSP officers in the Secretariat have defended the present system by pointing out that a technical expert, impressed by the technical soundness of his proposals or by his specialist enthusiasm, may see no flaw in his proposal; whereas the Government policy has to take into account a host of other factors like the financial implications of the technical proposal concerned. The Secretariat officer also has to see whether the policy that he is recommending on behalf of his ministry after receiving the necessary technical advice is consistent with the overall economic or industrial policy of the government. Technical officers, representing the point of view of the Attached Departments, have argued that, "The imposition of 'administrative' judgment over technical proposals simply results in the substitution of an unqualified technical judgment for an informed one."[26] However, the battle between the technical experts and the generalist CSP Secretariat officials continues. Technical departments have recently won two significant victories. First, there should be no bar on the technicians being appointed as Secretaries of ministries. Secondly, in cases of disagreement between the heads of technical departments and Secretariat officers, the technical officers would be allowed direct access to the Ministers.[27] The process of technicalization of certain ministries has already started. The Secretariat of the Ministry of Health and the Railway Wing of the Ministry of Communications are manned exclusively by members of their respective technical services. Similarly, a large number of educationists have been appointed to hold senior positions in the Ministry of Education.

The functional and structural organization of the Secretariat has been inherited from the British days when, in the words of Lord Curzon, "Round and round like the diurnal revolutions of the earth went the file, stately, solemn, sure and slow; and now, in due season, it has completed its orbit and I am invited to register the concluding stage." American experts, Rowland Egger and Bernard Gladieux, felt that the position in Pakistan had hardly undergone any change since

[25] *Ibid.*, p. 264.

[26] Bernard L. Gladieux, *Reorientation of Pakistan Government for National Development* (mimeographed) (Karachi: May, 1955), p. 69.

[27] *Report of the Standing Organisation Committee on the Reorganisation of the Functions and Structure of the Central Government in the Light of the New Constitution* (typescript) (President's Secretariat, Establishment Division, April, 1962).

the British days.[28] Administrative pace could be leisurely during the British days when it was said that the basic unit in the administrative system consisted of one expensive officer and ten cheap clerks.[29] But in Pakistan, when the supreme objective was rapid economic development, it was pointed out that the practice of writing longer and longer marginal notes on files, congestion at the top, overcentralization, overcoordination, and excessive cross-referencing could bring the machine to a grinding halt.[30] Foreign experts also cited a few outrageous and ludicrous cases when money sanctioned by foreign governments or foundations for a given year lapsed because the officers in the Secretariat were busy writing marginal notes, citing precedents, and referring the matters back and forth to the Ministry of Finance with the ultimate result of files being lost in the process. The administrative machinery since Martial Law has been considerably streamlined and improved. Routine matters are being dealt with by Section Officers under the supervision of Deputy Secretaries, and Joint Secretaries and Secretaries are supposed to be concerned primarily with matters involving policy-making.

The system of financial control exercised by the Finance Ministry over other ministries obstructed economic development and paralyzed the normal operations of the ministry. Under this system, the Ministry of Finance scrutinized not only the proposals submitted by various ministries at the time a budget was formulated but continued to exercise further controls over the administrative ministries after the budget had been passed. These ministries were required to seek concurrence of the Ministry of Finance to incur expenditure for proposals which had already been included in the budget and against funds which had already been appropriated. The latter control was known as the "expenditure sanction" method. The argument of the Ministry of Finance was that at the time of the formulation of the budget, ministries were inclined to include all kinds of proposals in their budget submissions partly because they did not have time to examine and scrutinize the new proposals and partly because they wanted to inflate the budgets of their particular ministries. Their strategy was

[28] Rowland Egger, *The Improvement of Public Administration in Pakistan* (Karachi: 1953), and Bernard L. Gladieux, *Reorientation of Pakistan Government for National Development* (Karachi: 1955).

[29] Philip Woodruff, *The Men Who Ruled India: The Guardians* (London: Jonathan Cape, 1954), p. 197.

[30] For frustrating experiences of technicians when Secretariat officers held up or delayed schemes already scrutinized by expert technicians in the departments concerned, see *Report of the Food and Agriculture Commission,* p. 202.

to ask for more than they actually needed because they were always afraid that the Ministry of Finance might give them less than their actual needs. This meant that budgetary procedure was creating administrative indiscipline among the Ministries, and at the same time was undermining the implementation of the proposals sanctioned in the budget. The "expenditure sanction" method with its additional scrutiny of sanctioned proposals created such delays that proposals could not be implemented within the given fiscal year. This delay proved particularly costly and cumbersome to East Pakistan because in addition to being far away from the capital, it needed early sanctions from the Ministry of Finance for its construction projects. The building season in East Pakistan was governed by the monsoons and could last only from September through May. In February, 1960, the government introduced the scheme of financial advisers which meant that a financial adviser was appointed to assist each ministry in the preparation of its budget. Under the new budgetary system, the preparation of the budget was to begin twelve months ahead of the financial year to which the budget related. The Secretary of the ministry was made the Principal Accounting Officer and given the power to ensure that funds allotted to his ministry or its Attached Departments or Subordinate Offices were spent for the purposes for which they were allocated.[31] In this way the "expenditure sanction" method was eliminated. In drawing up the budget and maintaining accounts, the Secretary of a ministry was to rely on the advice of the financial adviser of his ministry; consequently, the Ministry of Finance could relax its controls. Nevertheless, the financial advisers were to be under the control of the Ministry of Finance in the sense that they were placed under the administrative control of that ministry and were to be paid from its budget.[32]

Since the emergence of Martial Law, the tempo of economic development has been increasing, and even though the administrative machinery has improved one wonders whether it can cope with the pace of economic development. The government may have found in S. M. Yusuf a brilliant successor as Secretary of Industries to his illustrious predecessors, Ghulam Faruque and Abbas Khaleeli, but like his predecessors he finds that he almost singlehandedly has to deal with the development of a variety of industries which include petroleum, gas, minerals, steel, jute, textiles, etc.[33] Thus, even some of the CSP

[31] *Report of the Administrative Reorganisation Committee*, pp. 292–296.

[32] *Budget-Making in Pakistan* (Karachi: Pakistan Publications, 1964), p. 6.

[33] Some of the industrialists interviewed by the author said that after years of experience they could master all the details of a particular industry

generalists, through experience, are finding that it is a waste of talent to expose a bright CSP officer through all the necessary tiers of district, divisional, and provincial administration before promoting him to the rank of a Joint Secretary or Secretary in ministries like Finance, Commerce, and Industries. The old idea that an officer, once selected for an elitist service like the ICS or the CSP, can bring his intelligence, common sense, and vast experience to any job and make a success of it is steadily losing ground. The government has formed a pool of officers known as the Economic Pool for the Ministries of Finance, Commerce, and Industries, and the Economic Affairs Division of the President's Secretariat. These officers are to be recruited from the Civil Service of Pakistan, the Pakistan Audit and Accounts Service, the Pakistan Military Accounts Service, the Pakistan Railway Accounts Service, the Pakistan Customs Service, Class I, the Income Tax Service, Class I, the Central Excise Service, Class I, and the Commercial Secretaries and Attachés and Trade Commissioners (when constituted into a separate service.) CSP officers will form 60 per cent of the pool with all other services comprising the remaining 40 per cent. Officers who are not older than thirty-five years of age and who are in their sixth or seventh year of service will be recruited to the pool and promotions will be strictly on the basis of merit. This means that there is no quota system in the recruitment to the pool. Sixty-four CSP officers were admitted into the Economic Pool by January 1, 1965.

Thus, it is clear that the role of a generalist service like the CSP cannot be dispensed with. But it is equally clear that the CSP cannot continue to occupy the citadel of power without broadening their horizons in order to equip themselves with the knowledge and training necessary for development administration. It may also be pointed out, however, that it is not only the CSP who have been found lacking in knowledge of development administration; officers of the Audit and Accounts, and various other Accounts and Taxation services, who man key positions in the ministries of Finance and Commerce, have been found to be equally deficient in development economics and administration. In order to provide in-service training for all these officers, several institutions have been established by the government. The Pakistan Administrative Staff College, established in 1960, provides training to senior officers of the ranks of Joint Secretaries and senior Deputy Secretaries, Commissioners, and Deputy Commissioners whose service record ranges from fifteen to twenty-five years. During 1960–

---

and they wondered how a government officer could grapple with the problems of a host of industries at the same time.

63, the college had trained 89 officers. In addition, officers from government corporations and executives from private corporations have also been provided training in the college. The National Institutes of Public Administration set up in Karachi, Lahore, and Dacca provide training for middle-range officers of the central and provincial governments, autonomous agencies, and private firms. Trainees from government departments in these Institutes are Deputy Secretaries, Deputy Commissioners, and officers of equivalent status, possessing seven to fourteen years of experience in government service. Under the United States AID (Agency for International Development) participant program, 81 Pakistani officers have been trained in public administration in the United States during 1963–65. In addition, during 1962–65, AID has sponsored and financed the training of 250 to 300 Pakistani officers in specialized fields like agriculture, education, public health, etc.

Economic Development

According to Max Weber, "The expert, not the cultivated man, is the educational ideal of a bureaucratic age."[34] The Civil Service of Pakistan, inheriting its traditions from the Indian Civil Service, looked mostly for a cultivated liberal arts graduate. Under pressures of the developmental needs of the country, the CSP have agreed to broaden the horizons of their officers by including and emphasizing development economics and administration in their training programs, but the end product is still intended to be a generalist. The growing power and influence of the Planning Commission suggests that this institution will continue to make steady inroads into the citadel of decision-making power that the CSP has held unchallenged so far. The growing importance of the Planning Commission can best be gauged by the growing size of Pakistan's Five Year Plans. The developmental outlay of the First Plan (1955–60) was Rs. 10.8 billion. The target for the developmental outlay of the Second Plan (1960–65) was Rs. 23 billion, but when the plan ended in June, 1965, it was found that the total expenditure was Rs. 26.3 billion.[35] It is estimated that in the Third Plan (1965–70), the developmental outlay will amount to Rs. 52 billion. It is from the Planning Commission that a number of creative and constructive ideas have originated. The First Five Year Plan came out strongly in favor of the introduction of land reforms in West Pakistan and a better and more functional organiza-

[34] Reinhard Bendix, *Max Weber, An Intellectual Portrait* (New York: Doubleday, 1962), p. 430.

[35] Economic Adviser to the Government of Pakistan, *Pakistan Economic Survey 1964–65* (Rawalpindi: Ministry of Finance, 1965), p. xxviii.

tion of the bureaucracy for promoting economic development.[36] Later, the Planning Commission strongly recommended family planning and the Rural Public Works Program to energize the rural society. East Pakistani economists, by first persuading the Planning Commission, were able to put across to the government their point of view regarding the removal of economic disparity between East and West Pakistan. The Planning Commission also came out in favor of the government using indirect rather than direct controls in its economic policy and successfully urged it to adopt an import liberalization program. It may also be pointed out that the presence of Harvard economists in an advisory capacity in the Planning Commission and the strong backing that some of these proposals received from the United States administration were important factors which facilitated the adoption of these ideas. Moreover, the long-term objectives of government policy have been stated in what is known as the Perspective Plan covering a twenty-year period from 1965 to 1985. These consist of more than doubling the per capita income, full employment, universal literacy, elimination of economic disparities between East and West Pakistan, and a steady diminution in Pakistan's dependence on foreign assistance.[37] Thus, the Planning Commission's long-term goals, with the exception of Basic Democracies, include nearly all the major social and economic policies adopted by the government of Pakistan since 1958.

One of the main reasons why the First Five Year Plan (1955–60) could not be implemented properly was the fact that the Planning Board (which was later renamed the Planning Commission) did not receive adequate political backing. Indeed, the Plan was not published until April, 1957, that is, nearly two years after the First Plan period began. The Second Five Year Plan, on the other hand, has been much more successful because the Planning Commission has become a part of the administrative hierarchy; it is a Division in the President's Secretariat. In addition, the President is the chairman of the Planning Commission, and the Deputy Chairman, the operational head of the Commission, has been given the ex-officio status of a Minister. The main functions of the Planning Commission are: formulation of the Five Year Plan and the annual development program within the framework of the Five Year Plan, advice on economic policy, evaluation of economic progress, and stimulation and planning of the private sector. The Commission has a staff of over one hundred technical and economic experts, which means that in terms of numbers and

[36] National Planning Board, Government of Pakistan, *The First Five Year Plan 1955–60* (Karachi: 1958), pp. 308–310, and 93–95.

[37] Planning Commission, Government of Pakistan, *The Third Five Year Plan 1965–70* (Karachi: May, 1965), p. 17.

quality of expertness it is vastly superior to any other government department. Not only is it represented in various important decision-making bodies, but it has within its administrative hierarchy seven CSP officers who hold important positions ranging from Secretary and Joint Secretary of the Planning Division to Deputy Chief of the Planning Division.[38]

Significantly, the Planning Commission has steadily penetrated the bureaucratic structure and is represented on every important economic decision-making body of the government. Under its influence, the two provincial governments have set up their Planning Departments, and the various ministries and departments of the central and provincial governments have created Planning Cells. All development projects in the public sector above certain minimum financial limits, including those submitted by autonomous bodies such as the two Provincial Water and Power Development Authorities and Industrial Development Corporations, are scrutinized by the Central Development Working Party, which functions under the chairmanship of the Secretary to the Planning Commission. The National Economic Council, the highest decision-making body in economic matters, meets from time to time to make major decisions concerning Pakistan's Five Year Plans and lays down guidelines regarding the country's economic and commercial policies. According to the Constitution, its primary object is to formulate economic policies and plans in such a way that disparities between the provinces and between the different areas within a province may be removed. The Deputy Chairman of the Planning Commission is a member of the National Economic Council. Other members are the Governors of the two provinces, all the important Ministers of the central Cabinet, provincial Finance Ministers, and senior officials of the central and provincial governments. The Planning Commission also provides the Secretariat for the Executive Committee of the National Economic Council, which sanctions major provincial and central developmental schemes costing more than certain prescribed limits. The Executive Committee also considers specific problems of economic policy like granting protection to indigenous industries and consideration of the Industrial Investment Schedule. The Industrial Investment Schedule, which lists for the private sector broad targets for each industry within the framework of the Five Year Plan, is formulated by the Ministry of Industries in consultation with the Planning Commission.

---

[38] The positions held by CSP officers in 1965 in the Planning Division are: 1 Secretary; 1 Joint Secretary; 1 Chief, Economic Section; 3 Deputy Secretaries; 1 Deputy Chief. *The Gradation List of the Civil Service of Pakistan.* Corrected up to 1st January, 1965 (Karachi: Establishment Division, President's Secretariat, 1965).

Based on the earlier set target of Rs. 23 billion as the total developmental outlay in the Second Plan,[39] the total expenditure in the public sector was set at Rs. 12.4 billion. In addition, there was the semi-public sector which consisted of government-sponsored corporations drawing their finances from both public and private sources. These corporations were set up in different fields of development like water and power, industry, fuel and minerals, transport and communications, and housing and settlements. The idea was that since private enterprise was not likely to be forthcoming in the initial stages to develop these areas or resources, the government should take the initiative and set up public corporations with financial resources drawn from both the government and private investment. Notable examples of such corporations are the West Pakistan Industrial Development Corporation, the East Pakistan Industrial Development Corporation, West Pakistan Water and Power Authority, and East Pakistan Water and Power Authority. In the Second Plan, it was estimated that the corporations would undertake a total investment program of Rs. 3.8 billion with the government contributing Rs. 2.2 billion through loans and grants and the remaining share of Rs. 1.6 billion coming from private investment. In addition to the public and the semipublic sectors, there was the private sector in which the total investment would amount to Rs. 6.8 billion. Thus, Pakistan could regard its economy as mixed in the sense that the government was investing its resources in the public and the semipublic sectors, and private enterprise was contributing its resources both to the private sector and the semipublic sector. In terms of financial investment, the private sector controlled 36.4 per cent of the total outlay in the Second Five Year Plan, and in terms of area of development given to its exclusive charge, the private sector controlled 29.6 per cent of total development. These are target figures. In terms of actual achievement, it has been estimated that the private sector in Pakistan has exceeded the Second Plan targets assigned to it by 37 per cent and its share constitutes 43 per cent of the total investment.[40]

In Pakistan's mixed economy, one may say that it is the private sector which provides the forward-moving thrust; the role of the public sector has been confined to the creation of necessary facilities like transport, power, and communications, to enable the private sector to play its dynamic role. Unlike other developing countries, Pakistan has thus decided to give maximum encouragement to the private sector and to restrict the role of the public sector.

[39] As stated earlier, the actual developmental outlay when the Plan ended in June, 1965 was Rs. 26.3 billion.

[40] President's Secretariat, Planning Commission, *Preliminary Evaluation of Progress During the Second Five Year Plan* (Karachi: 1965), p. 26.

During the earlier phase of planning, the government set up an elaborate machinery of administrative controls to regulate prices, profits, production, investment credit, and so on. This policy of direct controls pursued during the 1950's made the government realize that economic development could perhaps best be stimulated through indirect controls. The Planning Commission, a vigorous advocate of controls through fiscal and monetary means, persuaded the government to agree to a progressive dismantling of the apparatus of direct controls. Since 1960, the government has been trying to liberalize imports as much as possible by extending the scope of the free import list to include all the important raw materials, books, drugs, and scientific instruments. Even in relying on monetary and fiscal controls, the basic approach of the government has been to stimulate and not repress private enterprise.

For certain projects involving large capital outlay — such as paper, steel, and shipbuilding — government permission is necessary. With the exception of these projects, the Industrial Investment Schedule lists all the industries which private industrialists can establish without any further permission from the government. But as far as financial assistance and foreign exchange is concerned, industrialists have to rely upon the government-sponsored Pakistan Industrial Credit and Investment Corporation (PICIC) and the Industrial Development Bank of Pakistan (IDBP). The PICIC looks after the financial needs of projects which involve over Rs. 2.5 million, and projects below that amount fall within the scope of the IDBP. These two institutions are vital in the industrial development of Pakistan because their permission is necessary for obtaining the foreign exchange and financial assistance to initiate new projects or to modernize existing plants.

We have shown the influence of the Planning Commission and also pointed out how a number of new ideas and policies have originated in it. But the key decision-makers so far as the actual establishment and promotion of industries are concerned are the civil servants like the central Secretaries of Industries, Finance, Commerce, and Communication, officials in charge of investment promotion and supplies, and export promotion, Chief Controller of Import and Exports, and Provincial Directors of Industries. These officials, as their titles suggest, make vital decisions regarding allocation of foreign exchange, the licensing of imports, controls over the location of industries, and the allocation of scarce materials. Private industrial development has been taking place at such a rapid pace that the Industrial Investment Schedules have had to be periodically revised, and sometimes the targets set even in the Revised Schedule are exceeded by over 40 per cent. Manufacturing industries constituted 5.8 per cent of the

GNP during 1949–50; during 1964–65, their share was 11 per cent. All this means that even though the Planning Commission is responsible for laying down the broad lines for industrial development, a civil servant like the provincial Director of Industries may have to make a decision or send his recommendations to the higher authorities after hearing conflicting demands made by two or more groups of industrialists. For example, a group of industrialists who manufacture spare parts of bicycles may demand that the import of such spare parts should be prohibited. On the other hand, representatives of firms which assemble bicycles may demand that import of spare parts should be facilitated because the quality of local manufactures is inferior. In another case, the civil servant concerned may have to advise an industrialist against setting up any additional units in an industry in which several other plants have already been established, but have not yet utilized their full capacity.

This suggests that the civil servants and particularly the CSP officers have become powerful in both spheres, that of law and order where they exercise power as Deputy Commissioners or Commissioners and in the industrial and commercial sphere where they, as Secretaries of the government or controllers of imports and exports or as directors of industries, wield formidable economic power. Their power over law and order has caused continuous concern to citizens in general and politicians in particular, and their economic power has created new concern among all classes of people in Pakistan. Technical officers complain that the generalist CSP is not trained to make decisions which pertain to technical aspects of industrial development. Industrialists and other business interests complain that civil servants do not make quick decisions and do not realize that time is vital in industrial development. Members of the National Assembly, lawyers, journalists, and others have expressed concern over the fact that civil servants in their decision-making on industrial and commercial matters have become exposed to a host of corruptive influences. Some of these reports are exaggerated. However, it is true that lately, retired civil servants and military officers have made full use of their talents and the connections they built up during their careers and thus have become leading industrialists in fields like insurance, assembly of automobiles, oil, sugar, etc.

National Integration and Political Development

The British often described the Indian Civil Service as the steel frame of the whole structure which constituted the government of India. This has been the boast of the CSP officers in Pakistan, for every time the country was faced with political instability or unrest, the head of the state or the province, as the case may be, has had to turn to the civil service as the last resort. The claim of the CSP to be the most cohesive instrument of national integration rests on two factors. First, they have a tremendous *esprit de corps* as members of an elitist civil service in the country. Secondly, members of this service are placed in commanding positions in the districts, in the provincial Secretariats, in the central Secretariats, and in a number of other agencies and corporations of the government.

Until the emergence of Martial Law, the CSP could claim that they were a more centralized civil service than even the old Indian Civil Service. In the former ICS, civil servants were allotted to the various provincial cadres. They were brought to the Center for short periods, but they belonged to the provincial cadres to which they were originally assigned. The founders of Pakistan, and particularly the first Secretary-General of the Civil Service, Chaudhri Muhammad Ali, centralized the Civil Service of Pakistan. The newly recruited CSP officers had to spend five out of the first ten years in a province to which they did not belong. They were told that they were members of the central service and did not remain on any provincial cadres but could be moved from province to province or from a province to the Center. This policy was not implemented rigorously. First of all, there was a shortage of East Pakistani CSP officers; this meant that most of the CSP officers coming from East Pakistan could not be posted in West Pakistan. The number of West Pakistanis in the civil service cadre being considerably larger than East Pakistanis, it meant that many more West Pakistanis would be posted in East Pakistan than the number of East Pakistanis who could be assigned to West Pakistan. In 1954, it was said, "If one went to the East Bengal Secretariat one was surprised not to find a single Bengali Secretary in the whole of the Bengali Secretariat."[41] In June, 1961, the policy of posting the CSP officers in provinces other than their own was reversed to the extent that the central government announced that henceforth East Pakistani officers would be posted in East Pakistan. As a result of the introduction of provincial cadres and the increase in the number of East Pakistanis in the CSP, most of the senior positions in the district administration and the provincial Secretariat in East Pakistan could be held by East Pakistanis. In early 1964, there were 15 East Pakistani Secretaries out of a total of 19 Secretaries in the East Pakistan Secretariat. In the district administration, out of 61 positions of Commissioners, Additional Commissioners, Deputy Commissioners, and Addi-

[41] *Constituent Assembly (Legislature) of Pakistan Debates,* I, No. 26 (July 17, 1954), p. 1474.

tional Deputy Commissioners, 53 were occupied by East Pakistanis.[42]

This goes to show that regional or provincial groups in Pakistan do not believe that a CSP officer, irrespective of the region he belongs to or the language he speaks, will be fair and impartial in his administration. They feel that their interests can be looked after best by an officer who comes from their area and speaks their language. One of the constant and bitter complaints of East Pakistanis has been that in spite of their larger numbers and the greater foreign exchange earnings of their province, East Pakistan's economic development has been much slower than that of West Pakistan largely because of their underrepresentation in the central services. The government has been at pains to show that this disparity in services is being rectified and that East Pakistan, according to figures disclosed in 1965 in the National Assembly, had 151 CSP officers.[43] This would mean that based on the total strength of the CSP of 461 in 1965, East Pakistani CSP officers would constitute 34.6 per cent of the total. But the fact that East Pakistanis have come a long way since Partition, when they had no more than one or two officers in the entire CSP, has not by any means satisfied their grievances. Their political leaders are aware that the Secretaries of the central government occupy key positions in the decision-making hierarchy of Pakistan. During 1964–65, there were no more than two East Pakistani officers in the central Secretariat who were holding the rank of acting central Secretaries.[44] An East Pakistan economist would complain that unless he had an East Pakistani Secretary negotiating loans with foreign governments, he would not be confident of the loan being obtained on the best terms for a project in East Pakistan. East Pakistanis are not the only ones who are concerned about the representation of their Province in the total CSP cadre. Members of the National Assembly from Sind and the North-West Frontier Province in West Pakistan are concerned about the representation of their regions in the CSP cadre too.[45]

As an elitist group in Pakistani bureaucracy the CSP wields tre-

[42] This information was furnished to the author by the Deputy Secretary, Home Department, of the government of East Pakistan.

[43] *Dawn*, June 27, 1965.

[44] This means that they were not full Secretaries but Acting Secretaries. This information was disclosed in the National Assembly, *The Pakistan Observer*, April 17, 1964.

[45] Questions concerning representation of Sind and the North-West Frontier Province in the CSP and the Police Service of Pakistan have been asked in the National Assembly. *National Assembly of Pakistan Debates*, I, No. 3 (March 11, 1963), pp. 156–157. *Ibid.*, I, No. 15 (March 29, 1963), p. 934. *Ibid.*, II, No. 9 (June 14, 1963), pp. 449–451.

mendous power and influence. Indeed, during the parliamentary regimes (prior to Martial Law), it was able to prevent the publication of two reports which were adverse in their comments on its role and efficiency.[46] Under the present regime, another report entitled *Report of Pay and Services Commission 1959–1962,* prepared by a group of officers under the chairmanship of Chief Justice Cornelius, has not yet been published. It is common knowledge that one of the reasons this report is treated as a classified document is because of the strong criticisms that it contains. It recommends, for example, that the post of Deputy Commissioner should not be monopolized by the CSP but should be thrown open to officers of other services. Another recommendation is that the status of the Secretary be lowered as compared to that of the executive head of a department. Since the economic development of the country is of paramount importance, it is essential that "the utmost progress in the Service will be ensured to the practical man whose interest lies in the execution of the larger tasks pertaining to his speciality, and not to the man whose aptitudes are for criticism of the work of practical men and for policy-making under the shadow of a Minister." However, even though it is true that the CSP has resisted deconcentration of power and has been highly skeptical about the functional reorganization of Pakistan's bureaucracy, to their credit they have displayed remarkable adaptability to the changing needs and circumstances of the country. We have noted that economic development has been spearheaded by some of the CSP officers. In addition, by introducing necessary changes in the training of officers and in the creation of the Economic Pool, the CSP has been both willing and eager to help in the economic development of the country.

It is undoubtedly true that the senior CSP officers (who belonged to the former Indian Civil Service) represent a group who are on the whole conservative in outlook and upper class in background. At the time of Partition, 83 Muslim ICS officers came over to Pakistan. Of these, only 49 remained in active service in 1965, two of whom belonged to the judicial service; this means that altogether there are 47 CSP administrative officers who belonged to the former ICS. All these 47 are Urdu-speaking and non-Bengali.[47] They not only occupy key positions in the civil service hierarchy — twelve of them occupy the highest positions in the Secretariat as Secretaries of various ministries — but some of them are related to each other. For example, the

[46] Rowland Egger and Bernard L. Gladieux.

[47] In addition to the 49 Muslim CSP officers, there are 4 non-Muslim officers of whom 3 are British and one a Pakistani Christian. Of these 4 non-Muslim CSP officers, 2 are in the judicial service and 2 are in the administrative service.

two brothers-in-law of the Secretary of External Affairs are Secretary of Economic Affairs and Secretary, Home and Kashmir Affairs. In addition, the brother of the Secretary of External Affairs is Pakistan's Ambassador in Washington. Other examples could be cited to show that a number of senior civil servants, diplomats, and army and air force officers are related. It is not being suggested that these persons have acquired these jobs through nepotism. They have come from a small number of educated and well-placed families, which in the course of time have established relationships through marriage with each other.

Another fact to be noted is that the CSP officers from West Pakistan by and large come from conservative, wealthy, and landowning families. A large number of them have been educated at Government College, Lahore. Of the 11 officers from Punjab who were taken into the CSP in 1963, 8 had been educated at Government College, Lahore, where the tuition fee is twice as high as other colleges in West Pakistan.[48] Thus, one begins to wonder whether a great majority of West Pakistan officers, who come from an upper-class, conservative background have much in common with their East Pakistani counterparts whose background is usually low middle class and who are inclined to be more liberal in their social philosophy.

What has been the impact of the enormous power that Pakistan's bureaucracy wields upon the political development of the country? We have already suggested that at the central Secretariat and provincial Secretariat levels, the generalist CSP officer has not merely confined his role to that of being an adviser to his Minister in matters of policy formulation. Political instability and the lack of well-trained and experienced political leaders drawing their support from organized political parties have forced the CSP officer to combine within himself the roles of adviser, policy-formulator, and policy-implementor. But perhaps more serious than all this is the way the civil servants in the districts have prevented the politicans from functioning as representatives of their constituents. The essence of democracy lies in the ability and the opportunities that a public representative has in articulating and aggregating the demands of various interests in his constituency. In Pakistan, the Deputy Commissioner is the spokesman of the government's policy in his district; at the same time he brings to the attention of the government the needs and grievances of the people placed in

[48] This is based on the author's findings. According to another source, 71 per cent of the CSP officers in Lahore attended colleges which were held high in public esteem. Obviously the reference is to colleges where students from well-to-do families are educated. Muneer Ahmad, *The Civil Servant in Pakistan* (Karachi: Oxford University Press, 1964), p. 62.

his charge. This is something similar to the role of the prefect in France. It is clear that the Deputy Commissioner, by keeping the district under his close supervision, has greatly disabled the politician from performing his representative role.

Emerging Trends

We have already seen that the CSP has been under steady attack for resisting functional deconcentration of authority by technical officers and thus standing in the way of economic development. But at the same time we have noted that the CSP has displayed considerable resilience by adapting itself to the requirements of development administration and also by introducing appropriate changes in the training of young officers in the Civil Service Academy. In spite of all this, it is somewhat doubtful whether the CSP will continue to be the elite service with all the levers of bureaucratic power under its control. It has been seen that the Planning Commission with its staff of over one hundred technical and economic experts has emerged as a highly influential body which is represented in the economic decision-making process. There are a few CSP officers in the Planning Division, but most of the officers known as Chiefs, Deputy Chiefs, and Assistant Chiefs, in areas like Economics, Agriculture, Engineering, etc., in the Planning Division, are technical experts who do not belong to the CSP. Nor are there many CSP officers in the more than twenty government-sponsored corporations which include financial institutions like the National Bank of Pakistan, Industrial Development Bank of Pakistan, Pakistan Industrial Credit and Investment Corporation (PICIC), and Agricultural Development Corporation, and other corporations like National Shipping Corporation and Pakistan International Airlines Corporation. And although several CSP officers have been placed in key positions in the two well-known provincial industrial development corporations and the Water and Power Development Authorities, which play a vital role in the economic development of the country, the great majority of the officers in these corporations are non-CSP officers. Even in the Secretariat in the Ministry of Finance, a majority of the influential positions are occupied by officers belonging to services like Audit and Accounts, Railway Accounts, Military Accounts, and Pakistan Taxation Service. We may conclude, therefore, that even though the CSP continues to be the most powerful service in the central and provincial secretariats and in district administration, the demands of economic development are such that the non-CSP technical and financial services are emerging as influential as the CSP in matters of economic decision-making.

❖ *7* ❖

Islam, Political Culture and National Unity

Political scientists have often suggested that the political culture of a developed polity like the United States is by and large secular and homogeneous, whereas a developing polity is often characterized by its fragmented political culture. In this chapter we are concerned primarily with two related questions: What is the impact of Islam on Pakistan's political culture? How effective is Islam as an instrument of national integration?

Political culture has been defined broadly as that sector of the national or general culture which consists of values, beliefs, and attitudes pertaining to politics as a whole. It is only when we have some knowledge of these values, beliefs, and attitudes in a given country that we can predict or understand the behavior and reaction of its people to certain political events. Values, beliefs, and attitudes can be analyzed in both procedural and substantive terms. For example, procedural values are concerned with the procedures or the manner in which a policy or decision is made and implemented; that is, they tell us something about the conceptions of authority that a people may have. Thus, the democratic conception of authority is that by and large decisions should be made only after free and open debate and discussion. Substantive values are concerned with conceptions of purpose for which authority is delegated or exercised. In the American system, such values are said to be the preservation of private property, freedom of speech, defense against external enemies, etc. Indeed, these values are enumerated in the preamble to the Constitution of the United States.[1]

[1] For discussion of the term *political culture,* see Gabriel Almond, "Comparative Political Systems," *Journal of Politics,* 18 (1956), 391–409; Samuel

In Pakistan, on the other hand, it is worth noting that the preamble to every constitution has emphasized the commitment to the setting up of a political system in which Islam will be the guiding force.[2] In what way does Islam contribute to the uniqueness of Pakistan's political system? The preambles to all these constitutions, including the present one, state that the "sovereignty over the entire Universe belongs to Almighty Allah alone, and the authority exercisable by the people within the limits prescribed by Him is a sacred trust." Further, "the Muslims of Pakistan should be enabled, individually and collectively, to order their lives in accordance with the teachings and requirements of Islam as set out in the Holy Qur'an and Sunnah [traditions of the Prophet]."[3] The preamble also states that Pakistan will adhere to the principles of democracy, freedom, equality, and social justice, but makes it clear that Pakistan is not merely following Western practice in this fashion, for such principles have been enunciated by Islam.[4]

Islam and Political Orientations of Modernist and Orthodox Groups

Can one say that appropriate ingredients from traditional and Western ideas have been mixed in the preamble to produce a soothing syrup of compromise? The Islamic idea that it is Allah who is the ultimate sovereign of the universe has been combined with the democratic idea of the popular sovereignty of the people to produce the formula that the sovereignty of the universe, which belongs to Allah alone, is to be exercised by the people but within the limits prescribed by Allah. Pakistan is to be a democratic state, but Muslims have been assured that Pakistan is not imitating Western secular democracy and

---

Beer and Adam Ulam, eds., *Patterns of Government* (New York: Random House, 1962), pp. 32–45; and Lucian W. Pye and Sydney Verba, eds., *Political Culture and Political Development* (Princeton: Princeton University Press, 1965), pp. 3–26, 512–560.

[2] This preamble can be traced back to the Objectives Resolution which was passed in the Constituent Assembly in March, 1949. Most of the clauses of the Objectives Resolution have been successively reproduced in the following constitutions: Draft Constitution of the Islamic Republic of Pakistan of 1954; The Constitution of the Islamic Republic of Pakistan (1956); The Constitution of the Islamic Republic of Pakistan, 1962 (as modified up to the 12th October, 1964).

[3] The exact citations are from the 1962 constitution, as modified up to October 12, 1964.

[4] Liaquat Ali Khan, the first Prime Minister, moving the Objectives Resolution in the Constituent Assembly in March, 1949, suggested that Islam had "a distinct contribution to make," for its concept of social justice "meant neither charity nor regimentation." *Constituent Assembly of Pakistan Debates,* V, No. 1 (March 7, 1949), p. 4.

is committed to the establishment of an Islamic democracy and Islamic social justice. Perhaps the most reassuring provision so far as orthodox Muslims are concerned is the declaration that necessary facilities should be created for the Muslims of Pakistan to order their lives in accordance with the teachings and requirements of Islam.

It is not surprising that the Constitution Commission appointed by President Ayub found that 96.6 per cent of the people whose opinions it consulted through questionnaires or interviews were in favor of adopting a preamble with Islamic provisions to the Constitution.[5] As we have pointed out earlier, all constitutions from 1954 onward have had almost identical preambles. This goes to show that the great majority of influential people consisting of both the modernist elements like lawyers, civil servants, educationists, and a number of professional classes, on the one hand, and the *ulama* (the learned in Islamic religion) and other orthodox and fundamentalist elements, on the other, are in favor of such a preamble. But there are sharp and wide differences between the modernist elements and the orthodox and fundamentalist groups with regard to the interpretation and enforcement of the preamble. The modernist elements, who have read and admired the writings of Ameer Ali[6] and Iqbal, believe that Islam is a dynamic and progressive religion. They think that in addition to the Qur'an and the Sunnah, legislation in an Islamic community can take place through *ijma* (consensus) and *ijtihad* (exercise of judgment). Indeed, Iqbal had clearly stated that *ijtihad* could be exercised by a National Assembly.[7] They often cite the tradition of the Prophet — "My people will never agree in error," — to show that a duly elected parliament, representing the great majority of Muslims, can decide which of the interpretations proposed by the *ulama* and others regarding an injunction of the Shariah (Islamic law) should be accepted for purposes of legislation.[8] Thus, the modernists would like to invest the Assembly both with *ijma* and *ijtihad*. They point out that the *ulama* should not be confused with priests, for the term is applied merely to those who have received training in theology. Islam has no ordained priesthood. The *ulama* have never been included in any department of administration in Pakistan. Thus, modernist leaders argue that if the Islamic character of Pakistan's polity is incorporated in the pre-

[5] *Report of the Constitution Commission, Pakistan, 1961* (Karachi: 1962), p. 114. The Constitution Commission reported that 6,269 questionnaires were answered, and in addition 565 persons were interviewed.

[6] Author of *The Spirit of Islam* (London: Christophers, 1922).

[7] Sir Muhammad Iqbal, *The Reconstruction of Religious Thought in Islam* (Lahore: Sh. Muhammad Ashraf, 1960), p. 157.

[8] I. H. Qureshi, *Pakistan An Islamic Democracy* (Lahore: n.d.), pp. 25–26.

amble to the Constitution, there need be no fear of the country's becoming a theocratic state dominated by the *ulama.*

It is true that the *ulama* are not powerful or influential in the administrative hierarchy, but they exercise considerable sway over the masses who venerate them and other religious leaders like the *pirs* (spiritual guides) for their Islamic fervor and piety. As we have pointed out in earlier chapters, the Muslim League, while waging its campaign for the establishment of Pakistan, depended heavily on religious leaders to mobilize mass support for its cause. After the establishment of Pakistan, the Muslim League did not build a strong grass-roots organization, nor did the leaders try to put forward a liberal or modern interpretation of Islam before the masses. As a result, the *ulama* and particularly the *pirs* have been able to maintain their influence over a great majority of the people in rural areas. The *ulama,* and especially those religious leaders belonging to the fundamentalist school of thought like Maulana Maudoodi, have often been successful in impressing upon the people the fact that the promised Islamic state has not been established and that political leaders merely invoke the name of Islam to win political support. This explains why all governments have had to pay some heed to the demand of the *ulama* that the Constitution should clearly declare that one of the objectives of state policy is to create the necessary conditions for the establishment of an Islamic way of life in Pakistan.

The *ulama* and the fundamentalists like Maulana Maudoodi, the head of the Jamaat-i-Islami movement, however, differ in their views as to what the government or political institutions should do to establish the Islamic way of life. The intellectual horizons of the orthodox *ulama* have remained confined within the bounds of the Shariah as found in the Qur'an and the Sunnah and certain schools of Islamic law developed during the classical period of Muslim history. They have hardly any knowledge of how the administrative apparatus of a modern state functions or of the kind and tempo of social changes that are taking place in Muslim countries. This has been realized by Maulana Maudoodi, and this is why he claims that a new group of religious leaders like himself and others in the Jamaat-i-Islami are needed. He believes that all true Muslims should not only profess and practice the principles of their faith, but should also seek guidance from the Qur'an and the traditions of the Prophet for reconstructing their polity. The government itself has admitted that the Jamaat has been able to infiltrate government offices and labor organizations.[9] Its followers are concentrated among those lower middle-class, urban

[9] *Dawn,* January 7, 1964.

elements who have had Western education, but who have not been deeply influenced by it; they occupy medium or lower positions in the official hierarchy.

For the orthodox *ulama*, Islam is a perfect and eternal religion from which laws can be derived for all time to come. Such laws can be discovered for particular purposes within Islam only by the learned *ulama*, and in this sense *ijma* or *ijtihad* for purposes of legislation have to be vested only in the *ulama*. "Our law is complete and merely requires interpretation by those who are experts in it. According to my belief no question can arise the law [*sic*] relating to which cannot be discovered from the Qur'an or the *hadith* [report or compilation of the Prophet's Sunnah or traditions]".[10]

The Jamaat-i-Islami, on the other hand, argues that though Islam has laid down clear and rigid principles regarding certain matters, it does not cover every aspect of modern legislation. Thus, it classifies legislation into three categories — the mandatory, the recommendatory, and the permissible. The mandatory elements of Islamic law as classified by Maudoodi are broadly those laws laid down in clear terms in the Qur'an or the authentic traditions of the Prophet, such as the prohibition of alcoholic drinks, interest and gambling, the punishments (stoning and cutting off of hands) prescribed for adultery and theft, and the rules for inheritance.[11] The recommendatory provisions are those which the Shariah desires Muslim society to observe and practice. "Some of them have been very clearly demanded of us, while others have been recommended by implication and deduction by the sayings of the Holy Prophet."[12] The remaining sphere, permissible legislation, is "exactly the sphere where we have been given freedom and where we can legislate according to our discretion to suit the requirements of our age." It is flexible and "has thus the potentialities of meeting the ever-increasing requirements of every age."[13]

The Jamaat has antagonized a considerable section of the modernist elements by putting forward a rigid interpretation of Islamic doctrines. The Jamaat's view that punishments like severance of hands for thefts is a part of the mandatory legislation which cannot be set aside by a modern legislature is not likely to be accepted by most of Pakistan's

[10] *Report of the Court of Inquiry Constituted Under Punjab Act II of 1954 to Enquire Into the Punjab Disturbances of 1953* (Lahore: Government Printing, 1954), p. 211. This Report is commonly known as the Munir Report.

[11] Syed Abul Ala Maudoodi, *Islamic Law and Constitution* (Karachi: Jamaat-e-Islami Publications, 1955), p. 25.

[12] *Ibid.*

[13] *Ibid.*, pp. 25–26.

bureaucrats or industrialists on the plea that this may be a strict interpretation of the letter of the Shariah, but not its spirit. But obviously this does not disturb the Jamaat and its founder, for their firm view is that in any case the modernist elements are not qualified to be the principal lawmakers or innovators in an Islamic state. Maudoodi has made it clear that only those who have complete and sincere faith in the Shariah, thorough knowledge of the contributions of earlier Islamic jurists and thinkers, and an adequate grasp of the Arabic language can measure up to the qualifications which he considers essential for those who propose to undertake *ijtihad* (exercise of judgment leading to innovation or new interpretation) in Islamic law.[14]

It must be said to the credit of all governments in Pakistan that they have not surrendered themselves to the demands of the orthodox *ulama* or even the fundamentalists like Maulana Maudoodi and the Jamaat-i-Islami. Even when the *ulama* were at the height of their influence in 1952, the most that was conceded to them by the Basic Principles Committee[15] was the setting up by the head of the state of a board of not more than five persons well versed in Islamic laws. Any bill challenged in the legislature on the grounds of "repugnancy" to the Qur'an and Sunnah would be referred to the board for advice. After consulting the board, if the head of the state found that the board was divided in its opinion, it was up to him to give his assent to or withhold his assent from the bill. It was only when the board was found to be unanimous against the bill in question that it was to go back to the legislature for reconsideration. If the legislature passed the bill again with a majority of Muslim members being present and voting, the bill would become law. This meant that on a particular bill the majority opinion of the Muslim members in the legislature could override the unanimous opinion of a board of five or more persons well versed in Islamic laws, some of whom might be *ulama*.

The Constitution of 1956 provided that no law would be enacted which was repugnant to the injunctions of Islam; presumably the matter of repugnancy was to be determined by the legislature itself. However, if the legislature had erred in this matter, this error could perhaps be rectified by the commission, which was to be appointed

[14] Abul Ala Maudoodi, "The Role of Ijtehad and the Scope of Legislation in Islam." Paper read before the International Islamic Colloquium, Lahore, on January 3, 1958.

[15] The Basic Principles Committee was set up by the Constituent Assembly in March, 1949 to recommend the main principles on which the future constitution of Pakistan should be framed. It published its report in 1952. Khwaja Nazimuddin, who was then the Prime Minister, was said to be under the influence of the *ulama*.

by the President to make recommendations for bringing existing law into conformity with Islamic injunctions.

After the emergence of the Martial Law regime, it looked as if the Sandhurst-trained President Ayub was determined to keep both the orthodox and fundamentalist leaders under firm control. The military leaders had not forgotten that the first Martial Law in Pakistan had been imposed in Lahore in March, 1953, to quell lawlessness arising out of religious disturbances. It was during the Martial Law regime (1958–62) that the Family Laws Ordinance, 1961, imposing curbs on polygamy and other matters was promulgated by the President.

Under the Constitution of 1962, there is provision for an Advisory Council of Islamic Ideology, consisting of not less than five and not more than twelve members, to be appointed by the President. The functions of the Council are recommendatory and advisory. It can make recommendations to the central and provincial governments regarding the facilities they should create to enable Muslims to order their lives in accordance with Islamic injunctions. It can also examine the laws in force before the commencement of the Constitution (First Amendment) Act, 1963, which deals with Fundamental Rights, with a view to making recommendations as to how they should be brought into conformity with Islamic injunctions. Another function of the Advisory Council of Islamic Ideology is to advise the National Assembly, a Provincial Assembly, the President or a Governor as to whether a proposed law is or is not repugnant to Islamic injunctions.

It is obvious that the Advisory Council of Islamic Ideology has not been assigned an independent role; that is, it can only make recommendations and offer advice to the government and the Assemblies. In addition, the government, through some of its measures like the Family Laws Ordinance and other policy declarations and the kind of appointments it has made to the membership of the Council, has created the impression that the Council may be used as an instrument to modernize Islam. The membership of the Council set up soon after the inauguration of the Constitution in 1962 consisted of a judge of the Supreme Court as the chairman, one educationist who was also at that time head of the Islamic Research Institute, three well-known religious figures bearing the honorific of *Maulana* (an honorific applied to a learned man in Islamic religion), and a former political leader who at the time of his appointment was the head of the Islamic Academy at Dacca.[16] The Jamaat-i-Islami in a resolution demanded that a new Council be constituted in which due representation be given to the *ulama,* who were considered the best authorities on

[16] *Dawn,* July 31, 1962.

Islamic law. According to the resolution, the Council, as it stood then, "would be used as a platform for subverting the fundamental principles of Islam."[17] Later the membership was altered — there were only two religious leaders known as *Maulana* — but educationists and political leaders were still dominant in the Council.[18] In addition to the Council, the Central Institute of Islamic Research was set up to undertake Islamic research for the purpose of "assisting in the reconstruction of Muslim society on a truly Islamic basis." Its director has taken a clear and firm stand against the anachronistic views of the orthodox *ulama* on matters like the rate of interest charged in commercial transactions.[19]

The annual report of the Advisory Council for the year 1964 indicates how the government has been able to influence the recommendations of the Council by appointing certain members with pronounced modernist views on it. The Council reports that it is in disagreement as to whether interest charged or paid by commercial or other institutions would be covered by the *riba* (usury), which is forbidden in Islam. In response to another reference, there is a note of dissent by a member which records that consumption of alcohol, if it does not produce actual intoxication, is not prohibited by Islam.[20] All this must have aroused alarm among the *ulama* and particularly in the Jamaat-i-Islami whose leader, Maulana Maudoodi, during the presidential election said that he would prefer committing one sin by supporting the woman candidate, Miss Jinnah, to committing ten sins by supporting the candidacy of President Ayub.

All this goes to show that President Ayub has no intention of letting the *ulama* make use of the Islamic provisions in the Constitution in demanding that the government should take steps to bring into being the kind of Islamic society that it would like to see established in Pakistan. But apart from this preventive action, what positive steps has the President taken to reform some of the Islamic institutions so that Muslims may play a creative role in speeding up the pace of social change in Pakistan?[21] The President has been hailed as a great social reformer and is classed with those few innovators in the Muslim world who have been bold enough to introduce progressive changes

[17] *Dawn,* August 4, 1962.

[18] *Dawn,* May 16, 1964.

[19] Fazlur Rahman, "Sunnah and Hadith," *Islamic Studies,* I (Karachi: 1962), p. 33.

[20] *Annual Report of the Proceedings of the Advisory Council of Islamic Ideology for the Year 1964* (1965), pp. 5–6.

[21] The President has been accused of trying to modernize Islam by conservative political leaders like the late Khwaja Nazimuddin. *Dawn,* December 14, 1962.

in Muslim personal law. The Muslim Family Laws Ordinance of 1961 has been designed to regulate certain aspects of the family life of Muslims like divorce, polygamy, minimum age of marriage, and registration of marriages. In order to bring about these changes in the rural sector where they are needed most, the Ordinance has empowered the Union Councils to become the main instruments of change. In order to regulate polygamy, the Ordinance requires that any person desiring to have a second wife must seek the permission of an Arbitration Council set up by the chairman of the Union Council. Similarly, in matters of divorce, an Arbitration Council set up for this purpose by the chairman of the Union Council is first expected to bring about a conciliation; in the event of a failure, the divorce becomes effective after ninety days. An Arbitration Council is also set up if a wife lodges a complaint against her husband about his failure to maintain her adequately. Considerable opposition to this Ordinance has been reported in certain districts of West Pakistan, where the hold of the *ulama* is strong and the chairmen of Union Councils are not cooperating in implementing the Ordinance. In certain other districts, compromises have been effected by the Arbitration Councils in a great majority of divorce cases, but it seems that 80 to 90 per cent of the applications for second marriages have been approved by some of the Union Councils.[22]

One of the great weapons that the *ulama* and other orthodox elements have is the institution of the mosque. There are mosques in every village and in almost every locality of a city. It is in the mosque that the congregational prayers are held and sermons delivered, often in denunciation of modern innovations. In addition, there are schools known as *madrasahs* or *maktabs* where education with a heavy religious emphasis is imparted. The government has become increasingly aware of the great potentialities which exist in the institution of the mosque for initiating changes in the social and religious outlook of the people in the rural areas and among the poorer sections of the urban areas. But as long as the sermons are given by *imams* who have been educated only in Islamic theology and as long as the prayers and sometimes the sermons are delivered in Arabic, which an overwhelming majority of Muslims in Pakistan do not understand, mosques will continue to be the main bulwarks of resistance to social change. The West Pakistan Auqaf (religious trusts) Department created in January, 1960, has been taking over properties bequeathed to mosques with an

[22] For these cases regarding divorce and second marriage applications, see Inayutullah, ed., *Basic Democracies District Administration and Development* (Peshawar: Pakistan Academy for Rural Development, 1964), pp. 168–169.

estimated income of about Rs. 6 million. It has set up Jamia Islamia at Bahawalpur, which is intended to function as an Islamic seminary and provide postgraduate courses to *imams* and others who are planning to become teachers. Besides traditional subjects relating to theology, other subjects like Urdu, the history of Pakistan, and geography have been included. The *Madrasah* system in West Pakistan has also been reorganized so that at all stages — primary, middle, and matriculation levels — in addition to religious subjects, general subjects have been included. For example, at the matriculation level, there are six religious subjects and three general which include English, social science and Persian. It is significant that *madrasahs,* where education with an emphasis on Islamic studies is imparted, were reformed as early as 1915–16 in Bengal and even during this early phase the course of study given in these *madrasahs* included instruction in not only the Qur'an, Arabic, Urdu, and Bengali, but in subjects like arithmetic, geography, history, and English as well. During 1947–48, there were as many as 1,074 High and Junior *Madrasahs* in East Bengal of which only five were government-managed; the rest were private institutions. In all, there were 85,629 pupils in these *madrasahs* during 1947–48.[23] *Madrasah* education is linked through the Government Islamic Intermediate colleges to the Department of Islamic Studies of Dacca University. Perhaps it is because of the existence of this reformed *Madrasah* system of education in East Bengal that the *ulama* and other religious leaders in East Pakistan are not so thoroughly imbued with Islamic conservatism and rigidity as their counterparts in West Pakistan. It may also be noted that in West Pakistan religious leaders like *pirs* and *mashaikh* have functioned as parts of the semifeudal system that has existed there.

It is apparent that most of the modernists and all the traditional forces in Pakistan agree that the establishment of an Islamic society is the goal which the state should pursue. We have indicated that the two forces are not in agreement as to what kind of Islamic society should be established in Pakistan. We should now like to show how the respective interpretations of Islam influence or color attitudes toward democratic values. It seems that the more orthodox a person's orientation toward Islam, the less democratic he tends to be in his attitudes and beliefs. Democracy implies that there should be a free discussion or debate between opposing forces and that a matter may be resolved finally when the majority recommends a certain course of action. Lasswell speaks of the democratic character as "multi-valued,

[23] For details regarding the East Bengal Madrasah system, see *Report of the East Bengal Educational System Reconstruction Committee* (Dacca: Government of East Bengal, 1952), pp. 228–235.

rather than single valued, and as disposed to share rather than to hoard or to monopolize."[24] A rigid belief in a religion, on the other hand, implies that the particular religion possesses the only truth, and that all opposing views are false or misguided. Some of the orthodox *ulama* seem to take the view that Islamic law is complete and merely requires interpretation by experts. Such a rigid approach obviously colors the attitude of these *ulama* toward those who offer different or opposing interpretations of Islam. For example, Maulana Shabbir Ahmad Usmani was of the view that Ahmadis were apostates and that the appropriate penalty in Islam for apostasy was death.[25] In his view, members of a minority community like the Hindus could hold positions in the administrative machinery of the state, but they could not form a part of the higher decision-making bodies entrusted with formulating general policy for the state or dealing with matters vital to its safety and integrity.[26] A fundamentalist like Maulana Maudoodi has argued that an Islamic state is not theocratic in the Western sense because it is not ruled by a particular religious class, but by the whole community of Muslims. However, it is not democratic in the Western sense because the people in an Islamic state are not completely sovereign, their sovereignty being limited by the divine law of Islam and the suzerainty of God. He suggests, therefore, that an Islamic state is a "theo-democracy" or a divine democratic government.[27] It may be noted that Maudoodi and the Jamaat have expressed themselves in favor of a democratic regime in their opposition to Ayub's system of government. Their opponents have often characterized this stand as one motivated by a desire to dislodge Ayub's government without any intention of according a similar right to their opponents if and when the Jamaat are in power.

There is a greater degree of ambivalence in modernists like the poet Iqbal, President Ayub, and a former Prime Minister, Chaudhri Muhammad Ali. As indicated earlier Iqbal believed that *ijtihad* in Islam could be exercised by a modern assembly. He also argued that an attempt in a Muslim country to establish social democracy was "not a revolution but a return to the original purity of Islam."[28] At

[24] Harold D. Lasswell, "Democratic Character," in *The Political Writings of Harold D. Lasswell* (New York: The Free Press of Glencoe, 1951), pp. 497–498.

[25] See the Munir Report, p. 18.

[26] *Constituent Assembly of Pakistan Debates*, V, No. 3 (March 9, 1949), p. 45.

[27] Syed Abul Ala Maudoodi, *Political Theory of Islam* (Pathankot: n.d.), pp. 31–32.

[28] Letters of Iqbal to Jinnah, reproduced in Mohammed Noman, ed., *Our Struggle 1857–1957* (Karachi: Pakistan Publications, n.d.), p. 27.

the same time he often admired dictatorial regimes and poured scorn on popular sovereignty as popular stupidity. President Ayub, who has consistently put forward the view that the people of Pakistan are not yet ready for a Western type of democracy, has reinforced his pleas in favor of a centralized or even authoritarian system by pointing out that such a system was not only sanctioned by Islam but also was necessary if a program of rapid economic development was to be implemented.[29] Chaudhri Muhammad Ali is a better example of the kind of ambivalence that exists in the mind of a modern Muslim in Pakistan. He is the architect of the 1956 parliamentary Constitution and both during and after the Martial Law period advocated the restoration of a full-fledged parliamentary democratic system.[30] At other times, however, he has suggested that a Muslim country like Pakistan can develop merely by acquiring the technical know-how from the West without setting up its social and political institutions on Western lines. He believes the phenomenal Western industrial progress is not explained by Western political institutions or social doctrines because such progress has occurred in both the democratic United States and the totalitarian Soviet Union. What Chaudhri Muhammad Ali recommends, therefore, is not Western rationalism or democracy but a recapturing on the part of Muslims of total faith in Islam. He does not explain how this can be done, and he admits that the existing Muslim society in Pakistan is decadent and inegalitarian. "The equality of opportunity that our society provides is not even a hundredth part of that provided by many non-Muslim countries."[31]

We have seen that the *ulama* in their total adherence to Islam reject modern secular and democratic ideas. The late H. S. Suhrawardy, a former Prime Minister of Pakistan, stood on the opposite side and his commitment to secular, democratic politics was such that he regarded the oft-repeated Islamic bond between East and West Pakistan as "fatuous." In his view, what kept the two parts of the country together was "the realization that neither part of Pakistan can live without the other."[32] Furthermore, when he was Prime Minister, he advocated a joint electorate on the plea that the Pakistani nation consisted of both Hindus and Muslims as members with equal rights, and he suggested that the concept of an Islamic nation was universal

---

[29] Field Marshal Mohammad Ayub Khan, *Speeches and Statements* (Karachi: Pakistan Publications, n.d.), I, 3.

[30] See his reply to the questionnaire of the Constitution Commission, *The Pakistan Times,* June 13, 1960.

[31] Mohammad Ali, *The Task Before Us. Iqbal Day Address* (Karachi: Pakistan Publications, 1952), p. 39.

[32] *Constituent Assembly of Pakistan Debates,* I (January 31, 1956), p. 2231.

and embraced Muslims living throughout the world. The two-nation theory, which led to the creation of Pakistan, he suggested, ceased to be valid as soon as Pakistan was established.[33] Most of the *ulama,* on the other hand, had advocated separate electorates or segregation of Muslim and non-Muslim voters into separate constituencies.

It is true that Suhrawardy's stand on the question of the electorate was also influenced by political considerations. As a Bengali leader, he wanted to maximize his political support among the Bengali representatives by getting as many of his party supporters as possible elected from joint constituencies instead of relying mostly on Muslim representatives elected under separate electorates and leaving the representatives elected by separate Hindu or non-Muslim constituencies to plow their separate furrows. It may be noted that in 1961 Hindus constituted 18.4 per cent of the population in East Pakistan; whereas they comprised only 1.5 per cent of the population in West Pakistan. Jinnah also expressed liberal views in his very first pronouncement before the Constituent Assembly when he declared that, "in course of time Hindus would cease to be Hindus, and Muslims would cease to be Muslims, not in the religious sense . . . but in the political sense as citizens of the State."[34] But Jinnah, faced with the problem of provincial conflicts and jealousies, had to stress the common bond of Islam, and it seemed that the liberal principles he recommended remained a distant ideal.

Pakistan's modernist leaders are on the horns of a dilemma which is both political and psychological. They know that the great majority of Muslims supported the Pakistan Movement in the hope that Pakistan would bring into being an Islamic society. They are also aware that without the rallying bond of Islam the country would have found it extremely difficult to survive the challenges and difficulties it faced soon after its establishment. But they feel that the kind of Islamic state that the orthodox *ulama* recommend cannot and should not be established; yet they do not know how to modernize Islam without stretching the meaning and interpretation of some of the injunctions laid down in the Qur'an. They cannot embark on a secular course much as Kemal Pasha did in Turkey because they need Islam to keep the two wings together and united against what they regard as their inveterate enemy, India.

How does one explain the persistent attempts that some of Pakistan's intellectual leaders have been making to build bridges between Islamic

[33] H. S. Suhrawardy, *The Principle of Electorate.* Speech in the National Assembly of Pakistan, Dacca, October 10, 1956, pp. 3–5.
[34] *Constituent Assembly of Pakistan Debates,* I, No. 2 (August 11, 1947), p. 20.

traditions and modernity? The psychological dilemma of the modernists is similar to what Erikson has called the "identity crisis."[35] One has to explore the different or conflicting elements that exist in the political or social behavior of Pakistan's modernists. To begin with, they are brought up as Muslims and the residual influence of Islamic principles which they have imbibed from the Qur'an, theology, and Muslim history is to a varying degree in all groups of modernists. Islamic training is followed by exposure to Western education, which tends to make them wonder whether Islam in its complete form can ever become a political or social reality. It is, however, by no means easy for them to turn away from Islam, not only because Islam has been a part and parcel of their lives and way of thinking but also because they fear that in some mysterious way God will punish them. Brought up by semimodern or traditional families, modernist Muslims still cling to certain superstitious practices and beliefs which they cannot shake off in spite of their predominantly modern outlook. Thus, one sees the Sandhurst-trained President visiting shrines of saints to offer his prayers or seeking spiritual comfort and guidance from living *pirs*.[36] Some of the modernists have tried to model their lives on Western patterns, but have found that apart from a few intellectuals, the West has not treated them as equals, and practices racial discrimination of one kind or the other. Their bitter response is often in the form of a return to their cultural moorings, but in a halfhearted way.

Muslims in general, and particularly the orthodox group, conceive of the world in hostile terms. Islam has set up a wall between believers and unbelievers. The word *kafir* (infidel) is repeatedly used in the Qur'an. Similarly, *jihad* (holy war for the spread of Islam) is recommended, though there are several other verses which stress tolerance and generous treatment of minorities. Then, there are others which suggest that Islam should be preached by peaceful means, and if unbelievers persist in their beliefs, they should be left unmolested. But the overall impression is that a community of believers is surrounded by a hostile world which will not leave Muslims alone unless unbelievers are converted or overcome. It seems that this attitude is not confined to Muslims alone, for its counterpart is Western antagonism towards Islam which may be unconscious but can often be traced back

[35] Erik H. Erikson, *Young Man Luther* (New York: W. W. Norton & Co., 1962), p. 14. Lucian Pye has used this concept to explain the behavior of Burmese political leaders. Lucian W. Pye, *Politics, Personality and Nation Building. Burma's Search for Identity* (New Haven: Yale University Press, 1962), Chapter 14.

[36] It is well known that President Ayub visits shrines of saints while hunting in the countryside or while paying official visits to a city like Lahore. *Dawn*, October 19, 1964. It has also been reported that he consults Pir of Deval Sharif.

to the bitter memories of the Crusades and of Islam as a proselytizing faith.[37] At the elite level, however, it is significant that the modernist leaders in Pakistan often argue that liberals both in Britain and the United States tend to be unsympathetic towards Pakistan because of their liberal bias against the idea of a religion being used as an ideology to create a state.[38]

Earlier we commented that the modernists are faced with a kind of identity crisis. Their native hue of Islamic resolution seems to be sicklied over with the pale cast of Western thought or the spirit of inquiry. This may partly account for the lack of decisive leadership or a clear set of goals that has plagued Pakistan now and again. But the fact that the modernists have not been able to use Islam in formulating a rigid ideology perhaps augurs well for the future working of Pakistan's political system. Absence of a rigid Islamic ideology has provided Pakistan's political system with a considerable element of flexibility. V. O. Key remarked that over the past seventy-five years the United States has been able to cope with social problems because of the absence of a "rigid and powerfully held consensus on substantive fundamentals."[39] Similarly, since Pakistani leaders have not been able to construct an Islamic ideology which gives clear answers on problems like secular democracy, socialism, and the rights of property, it gives them and their successors sufficient flexibility to cope with such problems in a pragmatic fashion.

Islam and Mass Political Culture

What kind of a Muslim is a rural East Bengali? How strictly or sincerely does he practice his faith? These same questions may be asked about the state of Muslim consciousness in the rural areas of West Pakistan. A. F. A. Husain has made a revealing study on East Pakistan entitled *Human and Social Impact of Technological Change in Pakistan*. Unfortunately, the number of persons interviewed is very few when one considers the nature of the conclusions the author has drawn from his interviews. This study suggests that Muslims from the districts of Noakhali, Chittagong, Tipperah, and Sylhet are more religious than Muslims from other districts,[40] for here the influence of

[37] Western attitudes of unconscious hostility towards Islam have been commented upon by Ian Stephens, *Pakistan* (London: Ernest Benn Limited, 1963), pp. 17–18.

[38] See Khalid B. Sayeed, "Pakistan's Foreign Policy: An Analysis of Pakistani Fears and Interests," *Asian Survey*, IV, No. 3 (March, 1964).

[39] V. O. Key, *Public Opinion and American Democracy* (New York: Alfred A. Knopf, 1961), p. 41.

[40] A. F. A. Husain, *Human and Social Impact of Technological Change in Pakistan* (Dacca: Oxford University Press, 1956), II, 14–15, 23–24, 41–42, 51–52.

the *pirs* and the *maulanas* (term of respect applied to the *ulama*) is strong. Indeed, 50 to 60 per cent of the interviewees say their daily prayers regularly, and perhaps more keep their fasts during the month of Ramadan.[41] But Muslims who leave their villages and start working in the cities do not adhere to the rituals as rigorously.[42] It is equally significant that not as many Muslims in the rural areas of other districts like Bogra, Khulna, Mymensingh, and Dinajpur practice their faith strictly.[43] The findings of my own survey, though based so far only on interviews of students at Dacca University, suggest that the educated groups when separated from their rural homes become either indifferent or lax in the observance of the rituals.

What is striking about West Pakistan is the enormous influence that the *pirs* (spiritual guides) and *mullahs* (preachers) wield in the rural areas. People in rural areas believe that the *pirs* have miraculous powers. *Pirs* offer charms and undertake to pray on behalf of their followers so that God may confer blessings like offspring or wealth on them.[44] The two leading *pirs* of Sind, the Pir of Pagaro and the Makhdum of Hala, can count their followers in the hundreds of thousands.[45] Similarly, there are *pirs* with comparable followings in the Frontier and parts of Punjab.

Muslims often claim with pride that there is no ordained priesthood in Islam. Islamic injunctions are laid down so clearly in the Qur'an for all time to come that Muslims do not need priests to guide them or lead their prayers in mosques. But the fact remains that a great majority of Muslims, particularly in the rural areas, have placed themselves under the spiritual guidance of the *pirs*. This has occurred in part because Muslims belonging to the poorer classes are not only illiterate, but cannot follow the Qur'an or the sermons given in the mosques. An overwhelming majority of these Muslims do not understand Arabic. In East Pakistan, out of a population of 40.8 million Muslims, only 263,017 people can read and write Arabic. In West Pakistan, out of a population of 41.6 million Muslims, the number of people who can read and write Arabic is 158,909 or 0.48 per cent

[41] *Ibid.*

[42] *Ibid.*, II, 148, 184, 268, 305, 311.

[43] *Ibid.*, II, 27–28, 32, 37, 46.

[44] Malcolm Lyle Darling, *Rusticus Loquitur* (London: Oxford University Press, 1933), p. 245. Also see W. L. Slocum, Jamila Akhtar, and Abrar Fatima Sahi, *Village Life in Lahore District* (Lahore: University of Panjab, 1959), p. 41.

[45] The Makhdum of Hala claims that he is the spiritual leader of over one million followers. *Dawn,* December 30, 1964. Hazrat Badshah Gul and others of the Tribal Areas in the Frontier claim that they have about 5 million followers all over West Pakistan. *The Pakistan Times,* December 10, 1964.

of the population.[46] Large numbers of urban Muslims who can read and write Arabic have been included in these figures, however. This means that an ordinary rural Muslim has to depend on *pirs* or *mullahs* for guidance in religious matters. Indeed, since the number of Muslims who can read and write Arabic both in urban and rural areas is so small, Muslims by and large tend to take their religion itself on trust without understanding the very words they utter in their prayers. They thus do not develop inquiring or creative minds. It is noteworthy that the Pakistan government has issued a directive to the two provincial governments that *imams* in mosques should be requested to explain in the local languages the meaning of the Qur'anic verses recited during congregational prayers.[47]

A number of Muslim intellectuals, among whom Iqbal is an outstanding example, have often asserted with considerable conviction that classical Christianity is spiritual but that it is entirely other-worldly and thus devoid of creative and dynamic vigor as an historical force. These intellectuals claim that Islam, because of its intense concern for human welfare, has urged Muslims to follow the Qur'anic injunctions regarding *zakat* (charity) and the disposition of inherited property. But at the same time, Muslims are aware that the great majority of their people are steeped in ignorance, poverty and despair. It would not be fair to say that Islam by itself has influenced the people to adopt a fatalistic attitude toward their environment and living conditions. However, a survey conducted by Dacca University in East Pakistan discloses that most of the people are strongly fatalistic, that concerted action for building dams, embankments, or roads is rare, that nothing can be done to check the growing numbers of people because religion stands against birth control, and that calamities are often sent by God to punish people for their sins.[48] Some of the surveys conducted in West Pakistan have come up with similar findings. In answers to questions regarding their belief in *qismat* (fate), all the interviewees seem to believe in it, and two-thirds (or 67 per cent) of those interviewed, seem to think that whatever has been ordained for them would be fulfilled and that personal efforts would be of no avail.[49] A study made of a village which is within the urban orbit of Lahore also seems to indicate that in their complete faith in the will of God the villagers find comfort and solace for their poverty.

[46] Figures of persons able to read and write Arabic are from *Census of Pakistan Population 1961*, Vol. I (Karachi: Ministry of Home and Kashmir Affairs, 1961), Table 40, p. IV–19.
[47] *Morning News,* July 28, 1964.
[48] Husain, II, 10, 15, 24, 28–29, 33, 36–37, 42, 51–52, 149, 184, 270.
[49] Slocum, Akhtar, and Sahi, p. 39.

Such a fatalistic attitude enables them to accept negligence or lack of action on the part of government in opening schools or providing other services. When they are told that other villages have made rapid progress, their reply is that it is God who has given them a better share of food and shelter. "One must not question the will of God who may give much to some and little to others."[50]

Grinding poverty, religious fatalism, and a strong government with its layers of authority reaching down to the village level through revenue and police officials have together instilled in the villager an attitude of utter helplessness and servility. Thus, when the government sets up Union Councils under its scheme of Basic Democracies and holds elections, he does not understand how he can better his lot by using his vote. In West Pakistan he is a member of his *baradari* (group of families with blood relations with one another living in a village or villages) which enforces strict endogamy and other social controls relating to his occupation; he is a follower of a *pir* and a tenant of his landlord, who in areas like Sind can evict him from his land without much difficulty. Living under these conditions and disabilities, it is obvious that he will vote for the nominees of the *pir* or the landlord, for basically he feels that God has set certain people in authority and that he must resign himself to his fate. The idea of Basic Democracies — that Union Councillors are elected by the free choice of the people and will sit in concert to solve their problems — still seems unreal and fanciful to most of the villagers in West Pakistan.

In East Pakistan, on the other hand, it is true that the landlords are not powerful in the rural areas and that the *pirs* do not exercise as much influence as they do in West Pakistan. We have already indicated that East Pakistan has been ahead of West Pakistan in so far as religious education imparted through *madrasahs* is concerned. It is significant that in 1951 the number of people who could read and write Arabic in West Pakistan was 28,369, whereas in East Pakistan the number of such people in 1951 was over five times that of West Pakistan, namely, 142,739.[51] The difference became narrower by 1961. However, *pirs* and *maulanas* are powerful in certain areas of East Pakistan. It has been reported that during the presidential election of 1964–65, the Pir Sahib of Sarsena exercised his influence in obtaining votes for Ayub in Barisal. And the influence of religious leaders in the district of Noakhali is well known. Presidents of political parties like the Muslim League and the Awami League have sometimes been *maulanas*, and the leader of the National Awami Party is the well-known Maulana Bhashani, a socialist with pro-Chinese sympathies.

[50] Agha Sajjad Haider, *Village in a Rural Orbit* (Lahore: University of Panjab, 1960), pp. 7–8.
[51] *Census of Pakistan Population 1961*, Vol. 1, Table 40, p. IV–19.

There are certain changes afoot in Pakistan. In East Pakistan claims have been made that the Rural Public Works Program launched through Basic Democracies has encouraged the people to believe that roads, embankments, and other public works can improve their economic life. Even in West Pakistan, the bureaucratic leadership is attempting to make the people development-conscious. The *pirs* are realizing that they cannot remain merely as spiritual guides and that the future prosperity of their followers depends upon whether they can influence the government into opening new industries in their areas.[52]

In contrast to the mass apathy of the rural areas, some of the urban areas in Pakistan have had to face mass violence from time to time. During the early part of 1953, there was widespread lawlessness in some of the cities of Punjab when the Central government refused to concede the demand of the *ulama* and other religious leaders that the Ahmadi sect be declared a minority and officers belonging to that sect be dismissed. During the spring of 1954, some of the industrial areas in East Pakistan were faced with riots between Bengali and non-Bengali Muslims. In June, 1963, Lahore witnessed Shiah-Sunni riots. And in the city of Khulna, East Pakistan, in 1964 the local Muslim workers attacked Muslim workers from Noakhali so that they would return to their district and not compete with the local people for jobs in factories. How does one explain this anomic violence in cities, and particularly the fact that it is directed against fellow Muslims who may belong to a minority group or sect?

An enormous increase in population has taken place as a result of industrialization and expansion in governmental activities in some of the urban areas of West and East Pakistan. (See Table 6 on page 178.) It is obvious that a considerable part of the increase in this urban population has been caused by an exodus of people from the rural areas in search of employment and better opportunities. In addition, in cities like Karachi, Hyderabad, Dacca, Chittagong, and Khulna there are concentrations of refugees from India. In the rural areas, a person knows his place by the tribe or *baradari* he belongs to. He does not protest too much because he fears the landlord or the police official. But when he comes to a city, he suffers loss of identity in both a personal and social sense. He finds as a mill hand or as a rickshaw puller that he cannot pray regularly or keep his fasts during the Holy Month. He finds that in some of the wealthier areas there is no segregation of sexes, and when he casts his eyes at the richly dressed women or dancing halls, he thinks that the ruling circles are given to dissipation, sexual laxity, and drinking, all of which are

[52] It is well known that the Pir of Pagaro finances an English weekly in Karachi, *The Statesman*.

Table 6

Percentage Increase in Population of Urban Areas Between 1951–61

West Pakistan	Percentage increase or decrease
Peshawar City	44
Rawalpindi City	43
Lyallpur City	137
Lahore City	53
Sialkot City	−2
Multan City	99
Hyderabad City	80
Karachi City	79
East Pakistan	
Khulna City	203
Dacca City	64
Narayanganj City	123
Chittagong City	24

Source: *Population Census of Pakistan, 1961. Final Tables of Population.* Census Bulletin No. 2. (Karachi: Ministry of Home Affairs, 1961), pp. 68–94.

forbidden by Islam. In the cities, he is also haunted by the problem of unemployment and rising prices. To questions like "What is wrong with the Government of Pakistan", "Do you like the present Prime Minister or the President", the answers invariably given by such people to the author are, "What can we tell you? We are ignorant and poor people. Who listens to us? There is a lot of corruption and police tyranny. Prices are rising, and we can't make both ends meet." And when asked, "Why don't you do something about all this?", the answer again is, "Only you who are educated and probably a government officer can do something. We are poor and helpless people. Who listens to us? All that we pray to God is for two square meals a day."[53]

As Erich Fromm points out, even though this type of alienation produces in a man apathy and withdrawal, he becomes an easy prey for manipulation.[54]

As is well known, the loss of identity and the consequent potential for violence which exists occurs not only in developing areas; it has also arisen in the metropolitan centers of the advanced countries.

[53] The author was in Pakistan during May-November, 1958, May-September, 1960, June-August, 1962, December, 1963-January, 1964, and December, 1964-January, 1965.

[54] Erich Fromm, *The Sane Society* (New York: Fawcett World Library, 1965). See pp. 111, 128–129, and 164–170.

In a Muslim country like Pakistan there is in addition the problem of the *ulama* and other religious leaders who exploit the religious susceptibilities of the people and who cite Islamic injunctions to justify acts of violence against Ahmadis, whom they regard as apostates. Furthermore, a large number of Muslims in cities consider their rulers corrupt since they deviate from Islamic principles by imitating Western ways, i.e., by permitting drinking, gambling, and dancing. Moreover, they themselves feel guilty because they cannot adhere to Islamic rituals and practices and because they have become fascinated by movies and advertisements. At the same time they feel frustrated that they have neither the education nor the wherewithal to enjoy life as the wealthy and powerful do.

The community which provoked an intensely hostile attitude of the orthodox *ulama* during early 1953 was that of the Ahmadis, who number about 200,000. They believe that their prophet, Mirza Ghulam Ahmad (1835–1908), had appeared to reform and renovate the original religion of Islam. Ever since Mirza Ghulam Ahmad proclaimed his faith towards the end of the nineteenth century, Muslims felt outraged that one of the cardinal doctrines of Islam, namely, the finality of the Prophethood under Muhammad, who had brought the best and the most perfect faith, was being challenged. It was well known that a few Ahmadis had been stoned to death in Afghanistan. Intense feelings of hostility towards Ahmadis existed even before Partition. But after Pakistan, when Sir Muhammad Zafrullah Khan became its Foreign Minister, it was felt that he and other Ahmadis were not only propagating their faith but also establishing themselves in positions of importance in the administrative and political structure of Pakistan. The campaign against the Ahmadis started soon after the establishment of Pakistan. According to the Munir Report, the campaign against the Ahmadis from 1948 onwards had assumed a clear pattern. Religious leaders would describe Zafrullah as an apostate and a traitor and often justify the killing of Ahmadis. Many incidents are described in the Report that show that enraged individuals would leave these meetings in such a state of fury that they would search out Ahmadis and kill them. This campaign gained steady momentum, and several religious leaders demanded that Ahmadis be declared a minority and that Sir Zafrullah and other Ahmadis be dismissed from their offices. It was significant that both the central and provincial Muslim League governments were aware that this campaign was gathering momentum and watched it with mounting alarm, but took no clear and firm action against the movement until the very end.

The movement against the Ahmadis assumed its most violent form in Lahore, Sialkot, Gujranwala, Rawalpindi, Lyallpur, and Montgomery in late February and early March, 1953. The pattern of violence was similar: crowds numbering between five to ten thousand would attack the police, burn public property and shops. Every time the police tried to take action against the demonstrators, they would seek shelter in mosques where sermons would be preached against the Ahmadis and the people would be urged to demonstrate against the government. It is noteworthy that the movement had the moral support of lower division clerks working in the government Secretariat and other employees working in telegraph and postal offices. Even when certain police officers had been killed and the main police stations besieged by angry crowds, some of the police officers recommended public appeasement and the issuing of a statement by the Chief Minister declaring that the demands of the public should be conceded. On March 6, 1953, the Chief Minister Daultana did issue a statement that the provincial government would support the demands of the anti-Ahmadi movement and would recommend strongly to the central government that Foreign Minister Zafrullah should be forced to resign.[55] It may be noted that the Prime Minister, Khwaja Nazimuddin, the Governor of West Punjab, Chundrigar, and the Chief Minister of West Punjab, Daultana, were not clear in their minds as to whether they should take drastic action against the agitators. The Prime Minister, who was a devoutly religious man, held long discussions with the *ulama*. It has been suggested that he was faced with a "troublesome conflict between his own religious convictions and the implications resulting from the acceptance of the demands."[56] Eventually he rejected the *ulama*'s demands. The Chief Minister of West Punjab, Daultana, guided probably by his political interests, accepted the *ulama*'s demands on March 6, 1953, but he changed his position when Martial Law was declared in Lahore on the same day and the military had brought the situation under control. He issued a statement on March 10, 1953, declaring that the movement launched for the preservation of the doctrine of the finality of the Prophethood of Muhammad had been exploited by disruptive groups and appealed to the people to cooperate with the central and provincial governments in their determination to suppress lawlessness.

It is true that Islam in times of stress is a great unifying force, but in ordinary times one notices that there are deep conflicts between one *pir* and another and between one sect and another. According to the Munir Report, no two *ulama* could agree on the definition of a Muslim.[57] The antagonism between the Sunnis and the Shiahs, for

---

[55] The Munir Report, pp. 165–166. For a complete account of the disturbances, see pp. 151–182.

[56] *Ibid.*, p. 234.

[57] *Ibid.*, p. 218.

example, sometimes manifesting itself in violent clashes between the two sects, is about thirteen-and-a-half centuries old. The Sunnis claim that the Shiahs abuse three of the four Caliphs who followed the Prophet Muhammad and who are held in great veneration by Sunni Muslims. The Shiahs, on the other hand, complain that the Sunni preachers have often attacked the Shiah beliefs and injured their religious feelings. In June, 1963, when the Shiahs were marching through the streets of Lahore, violent clashes took place between the two sects. A curfew had to be imposed and the army called in.[58] It has been suggested that some of the serious differences between the sects could be resolved if a high-powered committee or conciliation board were to examine the religious literature of the two sects in order to eliminate the material which is likely to injure the feelings of each. This is very unlikely because such a conciliation board would probably consist of Sunni and Shiah divines who take rigid positions. "It is difficult to persuade a Shiah or a Sunni to ignore in his religious books what he rightly believes to be a part of his faith as long as he professes that faith."[59] The government officer who was called upon by the Governor to hold an inquiry into sectarian disturbances came to the conclusion that such disturbances could be avoided only if the government took strong preventive measures during the month of Moharram when processions were held and if it created an atmosphere of mutual tolerance.[60]

All this suggests that if Pakistani leaders were to allow the various groups in the country to articulate their demands in a democratic fashion, the mass political culture is such that violent conflicts would likely occur. President Ayub's solution is to consolidate enormous power in the hands of the President and the bureaucracy and not unduly expose himself to democratic pressures. The government believes that the reactionary *ulama,* who often try to exploit the religious beliefs of the people, should be held in check. Indeed, the government, through education and its propaganda machinery, should try to change the religious attitudes of the people in such a way that Islam does not stand in the way of economic progress or the unity of the country. But all this is based on the assumption that the elite are clear in their minds about how to modernize Islam and understand their people well enough to bring about the necessary changes in their attitudes.

[58] Abdur Rashid Khan, *Report of Enquiry Into Sectarian Trouble in Lahore During Moharram, 1963* (Lahore: Superintendent, Government Printing, 1964), pp. 4–21.

[59] *Ibid.,* p. 37.

[60] *Ibid.,* see pp. 37–43.

Islam and National Unity

One may go so far as to say that Pakistan was not entirely a creation of Jinnah and the Muslim League. Pathans in the North-West Frontier Province, who had refused to return a Muslim League government in the provincial election of 1946, voted in favor of Pakistan in the Referendum of 1947. In the Referendum, the choice offered to them was whether they would like their province to join a predominantly Hindu India or Muslim Pakistan. We have also seen in Chapter 3 that the Muslim League appealed for electoral support in the elections in 1945 and 1946 in the name of Islamic solidarity. The Muslim League also sought the support of *ulama* and other religious leaders in its election campaign.[61]

All Muslims are brought up from childhood to turn to God in times of dire personal crises. This applies to educated Muslims as well and there is a particular verse in the Qur'an which they recite in order to invoke God's blessing and his support when faced with any anxiety or danger.[62] It is significant that in moments of national crises Muslims seem to turn to Islam in order to reassure themselves that God will not abandon the faithful. During the war with India, the front page of *Dawn* carried verses from the Qur'an; the message that was being conveyed to Muslims through these verses was to have faith in God, to be confident of their ultimate victory, and to remain united under the banner of Islam. For example, *Dawn* on September 13, 1965, carried this verse on its front page:

> O Prophet! urge the believer to fight. If there be of you twenty steadfast, they shall overcome two hundred — and if there be of you a hundred, they shall overcome a thousand of those who disbelieve, because they are a people who do not understand. Qur'an, Chapter 8, verses 65–66.

David E. Apter has pointed out: "In the new developing areas consensus is low, primordial loyalties high."[63] When faced with a threat from India or separatist tendencies from East Pakistan, Paki-

---

[61] The Muslim League thought that its appeal for electoral support would become more effective so far as the rural masses were concerned if this were made through *pirs* and *mashaikh*. The need for the services of *pirs* was so great that even some of the highly Westernized landowners, who were often seen in the Lahore Gymkhana Club or Lahore race tracks, were presented as venerable *pirs* to the masses. The Munir Report, p. 255.

[62] The verses which are recited are those from Chapter 67 of the Qur'an entitled "The Kingdom."

[63] David E. Apter, ed., *Ideology and Discontent* (New York: The Free Press of Glencoe, 1964), p. 22.

stanis have found in Islam an admirable symbol or rallying cry for national solidarity. But they have not been very successful in using Islam to build a national consensus on more mundane issues like equitable allocation of economic resources between various parts of the country. Indeed, some of the East Pakistani leaders are so bitter about the economic disparity between their province and West Pakistan that they think Islam is being used by West Pakistani leaders to lull them into accepting their inferior economic position. They complain that Islam cannot be the only bond of unity between East and West Pakistan and that the two parts can remain together only so long as both feel that the economic advantages that accrue to each one of them from a united country outweigh those they may derive from being separated.

A survey of Pakistani university students undertaken by the author indicates that unity between the two provinces cannot be built on the Islamic factor alone. These students were selected by their instructors because in the opinion of the latter they were considered not only above average but were also expected to be cooperative in filling out a fairly long questionnaire of twenty-six questions. These questions were designed to bring out the educational background of both the students and their parents. There were other questions which sought information regarding how and at what age a student came under the influence of political and social ideas. Finally, the questionnaire probed into the religious background of a student and what his views were regarding the degree of compatibility between religion and modern science, his views concerning Islam's attitude to non-Muslims, and the effectiveness of Islam as a bond of unity between East and West Pakistan. (See Table 7 on p. 184.)

It is apparent that West Pakistanis who think that Islam is an effective bond of unity constitute a far greater proportion of the total than East Pakistanis who hold the same view. Eighty-seven out of 100 West Pakistanis, or 87 per cent, think that Islam is an effective bond; whereas only 28 out of 42 East Pakistanis, or 66.7 per cent, regard Islam as an effective bond of unity between East and West Pakistan. It is true that the number of East Pakistani students who have answered the questionnaire is much smaller, but this defect was partially corrected by the interviews in depth of another 40 East Pakistanis. These 40 East Pakistanis included students, teachers, civil servants, other professional men, and housewives. It is significant that they have all had religious instruction during their childhood, which included the reading of the Qur'an in Arabic, which they do not understand. Some of them have read the Qur'an in Bengali or in English translations. Most of them are frank enough to admit that the Qur'an

Table 7

Islam as an Effective Bond of Unity Between East and West Pakistan

	Yes	No	Not Answered	Total
East Pakistan	28[a]	13[b]	1	42
West Pakistan	87[c]	5[d]	8	100

[a] Out of the 28 students in East Pakistan who said that Islam was an effective bond, 3 were of the opinion that it was not the only bond and mentioned fear of India as an additional bond. Three said that the Islamic bond between the two wings would be broken if West Pakistan continued to exploit East Pakistan.

[b] Out of the 13 students in East Pakistan who said that Islam was not a unifying bond, 2 felt there was no unifying bond, while one said fear of India was the unifying bond.

[c] Out of the 87 students in West Pakistan who said that Islam was an effective bond, 23 were of the opinion that Islam was not the only bond. Sixteen said fear of India was an additional bond and other bonds cited were economic advantages, common history, and nationalism.

[d] Out of the 5 students in West Pakistan who said Islam was not an effective bond, 3 felt fear of India was the bond between the two wings. The economic advantages of unification were also mentioned.

does not exercise much influence on their day-to-day activities, but nevertheless they all have deep reverence for the Qur'an as a sacred book. A great majority also are of the view that Islam as a unifying force between the two regions is gradually losing its strength. In these interviews, East Pakistanis displayed a sense of loneliness and isolation and pointed out that East Pakistanis would like to continue their union with West Pakistan because of economic and geographical reasons. Again, the binding force is the fear of India. Resentment towards West Pakistan may be considerable, but their fear and suspicion of India is greater.

8

Politics of Regionalism

In Pakistan it may be said that the two most culturally cohesive groups are the Bengalis[1] and the Pathans. Punjabis and Sindhis may also be regarded as linguistically and culturally identifiable groups, but they are not as culturally cohesive as the Bengalis and the Pathans. Bengalis are deeply conscious of belonging to a distinct cultural group. They regard their language as one of the most beautiful and constantly speak of the heights of literary excellence it has reached. Bengalis feel that the land in which they live and the language they speak have together given them a uniqueness which is neither shared by the descendants of Aryans who live in northern India nor by some of the descendants of the Arabs or Mughals who live in West Pakistan. An East Pakistani has written of his people:

> They are neither Aryans nor Arabs. Their body and their mind have been formed by the soft soil of East Pakistan, by its wide blue sky, its murmuring rivers, its warm benevolent sun, its pleasant breezes and its splendid seasons. Nature has given their mind and body a distinctive stamp.[2]

It is significant that the emergence of regionalism in the Indian subcontinent has been contemporaneous with the rise of middle-class groups who are interested in creating administrative and political units

[1] In this chapter the term *Bengalis* is synonymous with East Pakistanis. The term *Bengali* is better suited for describing the culture and language of East Pakistan. Slightly over 50 million people, out of a total population of 50.8 million in East Pakistan, regard Bengali as their mother tongue. Some 310,628 people claim Urdu as their mother tongue in the province, though 679,163 can speak Urdu.

[2] Shamsuddin Abul Kalam, "Social Questions in Bengali Fiction," in S. Sajjad Husain, ed., *Dacca University Seminars On Contemporary Writing in East Pakistan*, (Dacca: 1958), p. 60.

185

which they can dominate. In East Pakistan, this process has been further facilitated by the fact that the dominant middle class or the intelligentsia can claim to speak on behalf of the whole region; whereas in West Pakistan, Punjabis and Sindhis, with their tribal and caste or community divisions, have found it difficult to weld their societies into cohesive regional entities. In addition, a group like the Punjabis, with their established predominance in Pakistan's civil and military forces, would be interested in playing their role in an all-Pakistan setting rather than limiting it within regional confines. The Pathans, on the other hand, are different from the Punjabis and the Sindhis, although they too live divided among tribes. They are more egalitarian than the Punjabis and the Sindhis and, above all, more conscious of belonging to a separate race and possessing a separate culture symbolized by *Pakhtun Wali* (tribal code of honor). Indeed, some Pathan leaders have demanded the creation of a separate state called Pakhtunistan, to include all the Pushtu-speaking areas, namely, the Tribal Areas in the northwest, the former North-West Frontier Province, and parts of Baluchistan.[3]

It is noteworthy that despite the poverty of the great masses of people in developing areas Communists have not been able to mobilize much support among the people and have had to build their strength by aligning themselves with regional or caste groups.[4] Thus, regional movements both in India and in Pakistan seem to be stronger and more popular than Communist party organizations. The strength of regionalism in developing countries is in sharp contrast to the situation in developed countries — for example, the United States; there group identification built around ethnic and religious differences has been undergoing a steady process of erosion as a result of social mobility, religious tolerance, and ethnic assimilation. This phenomenon has been characterized as the diffusion of social identity.[5]

East Pakistan's Political Culture

When one looks at East Pakistan, one is struck by the more than one thousand miles of distance that separates it from West Pakistan, and also by its geographical proximity to and cultural affinity with West Bengal in India. It is true that before Partition Muslims living in

[3] This demand for a separate state of Pakhtunistan has been supported by Afghanistan; whereas most of the Pathan leaders in Pakistan would rather settle for a separate province called Pakhtunistan within Pakistan. See Khalid B. Sayeed, "Pathan Regionalism," Reprint No. 13, Duke University Commonwealth Studies Center (1964).

[4] Selig S. Harrison, "Caste and the Andhra Communists," *American Political Science Review, L,* No. 2 (June 1956).

[5] See Robert E. Lane, *Political Ideology* (New York: The Free Press of Glencoe, 1962), pp. 388–399.

Punjab and Bengal were profoundly influenced by Hindu culture and social practices. But Bengali Hindus, particularly after the emergence of British rule, produced a culture which left a far greater impact on the Muslims of Bengal than did the contributions of Punjabi Hindus and Sikhs on Punjabi Muslims. Bengali Hindus, from their positions of vantage in the new social and administrative structure that the British had created, could obviously influence Bengali culture to a far greater degree than the Muslims could. In Bengal, the term *bhadralok* (higher status people) was applied almost exclusively to Hindus because by birth, education or occupation, they considered themselves above manual toil. It was significant that throughout East Bengal, where Muslims heavily outnumbered Hindus, the Hindus, both in rural and in urban areas, controlled most of the key positions in land revenue administration as well as those in professions like law, education, medicine, trade, etc.[6] It has been estimated that 75 per cent of the landlords in East Bengal were Hindus.[7]

The famous Bengali poet, Rabindranath Tagore, is widely read throughout East Pakistan, and Hindu ideas and concepts in Bengali literature have had a profound effect on the minds of Bengali Muslims in East Pakistan. The catholic and eclectic spirit of Hinduism has had, perhaps, as much impact as the austere and uncompromising tone of Arabic Islam on the thinking of some of the writers and political leaders of East Pakistan. Thus, Abul Mansur Ahmad, a well-known writer and former Central Minister from East Pakistan, advocating the separation of religion from politics, has written:

> Let him then, in proper time in a proper mood, come to religion as a blissful retirement from the humdrums of active social life. Let religion succeed where politics fails. Let religion begin where politics ends. The two must not meet.[8]

In contrast, Iqbal denounced the Western secular outlook based on a clear and rigid divorce of politics from religion because, according to him, politics of this kind, uninspired by religious principles, has led to imperialism and exploitation.

[6] See, for example, *Eastern Bengal District Gazetteers Dacca* (Allahabad: The Pioneer Press, 1912), pp. 62 and 64, and J. C. Jack, *Final Report on the Survey and Settlement Operations in the Bakarganj District 1900 to 1908* (Calcutta: Bengal Secretariat Book Depot, 1915), p. 59.

[7] This figure, given by Firoz Khan Noon, was disputed in the Constituent Assembly. See *Constituent Assembly of Pakistan Debates,* I (February 14, 1956), p. 3056. However, according to information furnished to the author by Additional Collector of Revenue, Dacca, on November 4, 1958, out of the nine landlords in the Dacca District with an annual rental demand of Rs. 40,000 and above, six were Hindus and three were Muslims.

[8] Abul Mansur Ahmad, "Secularism Versus Religion In Politics," *The Concept of Pakistan,* No. 4 (November, 1964), p. 42.

Bengali culture, even though molded by the dominant influence of Bengali Hindus, had certain clear secular strands in it. Bengali writers had been influenced by British and European ideas of liberalism and humanitarianism. It was because of its secular and liberal features that it could influence both Hindu and Muslim leaders. Even though the Muslim League demand for a separate state of Pakistan had won over the great bulk of Muslim leaders in Bengal, one could see that during the time of Partition in 1947, there were a few influential Bengali Muslim leaders like Suhrawardy who seriously considered the establishment of a united and separate Bengal state. This proposal, at a time when Hindu-Muslim hostility had degenerated into mass killing and carnage, was seriously discussed by both Hindu and Muslim leaders as an alternative to the partition of Bengal into West Bengal and East Bengal, with West Bengal joining the Indian union and East Bengal becoming a part of Pakistan. Later, in 1954, Fazlul Huq, the Chief Minister of East Pakistan, said he "would not take notice of the fact that there was a political division of the Province of Bengal into East and West Bengal."[9] For this he was denounced by the Prime Minister of Pakistan as "a self-confessed traitor to Pakistan."

In spite of this cultural affinity between Bengali Muslims and Bengali Hindus, the fact remains that Islamic fervor, particularly among the Muslim masses of East and West Pakistan, was largely responsible for the realization of the Pakistan state. Islam continues to be a unifying force between the two parts: the masses may be super-stitious or fatalistic, but their desire to become better and purer Muslims continues. However, as we have noted in the chapter on Islam, at the elite level, leaders like Suhrawardy from East Pakistan and East Pakistani university students do not attach as great an importance to Islam as a bond of unity between East and West Pakistan as West Pakistani leaders and university students do. This suggests that the elite political culture in East Pakistan differs from that of West Pakistan. *The Pakistan Observer* has repeatedly pointed out that although Islam was the main source of inspiration that unified East and West Pakistani Muslims in the forties, in the sixties this integrating force had been replaced by the utilitarian or economic force.[10] The Finance Minister of East Pakistan has pointed out that if economic disparity between the two wings continues to widen, "it would be unfair to expect that our spiritual bond through Islam will be so strong . . . that we shall forget all our economic disparities and will still remain united and unified as a nation."[11] It is significant that

[9] *The Statesman* (Calcutta), May 10, 1954.
[10] *The Pakistan Observer*, November 10 and 13, 1961.
[11] *Morning News*, July 1, 1965.

during the September, 1965, war between India and Pakistan, newspapers in West Pakistan repeatedly exhorted their readers to be ready to defend the cause of Islam by fighting for Pakistan against Hindu India. Throughout the war, *Dawn* carried verses from the Qur'an on its front page which urged the Muslims to fight because their true and just cause would ultimately triumph even though Muslims might be heavily outnumbered by the infidels.[12] An East Pakistani newspaper, *The Pakistan Observer,* in its thirty-two editorials written between September 5 and October 30, 1965, referred once to "the dichotomy of the Hindu mind" and another time to "the new Asian bugbear, Hindu India."[13] In response to Turkish and Iranian help during the war, it wrote that the new consciousness of the Muslim bond should provide a "beginning for the Muslims to bestir themselves towards the reassertion of their identity and stance in history."[14] But in other editorials, *The Pakistan Observer* emphasized secular concepts like freedom or called upon the government to enable all citizens of Pakistan "without distinction of caste, creed or politics" to offer their services to the country.[15]

Almost from the very beginning, the central government has been aware of the centrifugal force of Bengali regionalism. Leaders like Jinnah and Liaquat were aware that East Pakistan, in addition to being so distant from the central government, was also the home of Bengali culture. They stressed the bonds of Islamic unity and suggested that Urdu, which was written in the Arabic script and had a strong admixture of Arabic and Persian words, should be the state language of Pakistan. The central government tended to rely upon those Bengali Muslim League leaders like Khwaja Nazimuddin who were themselves apprehensive of Hindu influence on Bengali culture and life and wanted to mold Bengali culture on Islamic lines. However, the attempt of the central government to adopt Urdu as the official language failed when there were widespread demonstrations by students in East Pakistan in February, 1952. As a result of the police firing on the crowd in Dacca on February 21, 1952, several people were killed and a large number injured. One of the persons killed was a student. Since then, February 21 has been observed as the "Shaheed (martyrs) Day" in East Pakistan when meetings and processions are held. The whole tone of the meetings and speeches are clear in the sense that the audience are reminded that it was the central government dominated

---

[12] See, for example, *Dawn,* September 13, 1965. The Qur'anic verses quoted are from Chapter 8 (65–66).

[13] *The Pakistan Observer,* October 12 and 13, 1965.

[14] *Ibid.,* October 13, 1965.

[15] *Ibid.,* September 7, 1965.

by West Pakistanis which tried to impose the Urdu language on East Pakistan and in resisting this policy successfully, East Pakistanis had to face death. Some of the emotional symbols used in speeches and on posters read, "Those who defied death to defend their language," "Remember them, remember them today," and "The Mother Bangla weeps."[16] The growing unpopularity of the central government and of the Muslim League Provincial government in East Pakistan resulted in the crushing defeat of the Muslim League in the March, 1954, provincial elections. In May, 1954, an amendment to the Basic Principles Committee Report to the effect that Urdu and Bengali should be recognized as state languages was adopted by the Constituent Assembly. Since that time, all constitutions have accepted Urdu and Bengali as two official languages.

There are two schools of thought regarding the future development of the Bengali language and culture among East Pakistanis. The majority of the elite groups consisting of university and school teachers, lawyers, traders, other professional groups, and university students, who are concentrated in cities like Dacca and Chittagong, believe that the composite character of Bengali culture should continue. Thus, in clubs, theaters, and other cultural meetings, songs and dances drawn from both Hindu and Muslim writers are presented.[17] There is some resentment among this group that Muslim refugees from India, concentrated in some of the cities of East Pakistan, are against the continuation of this composite Bengali culture. Indeed, this school of East Pakistanis thinks the outbreak of communal violence between Hindus and Muslims in East Pakistan is inspired by vested interests and that Bengali-speaking Hindus and Muslims in East Pakistan have so much in common that they can live in peace and harmony.[18]

The second school consists of those Muslim League leaders, some of the orthodox *ulama,* and some officials who hold the view that Hindu influence should be eliminated from the Bengali language and literature. This group is supported by the central government. An academy called the Bangla Academy has been established. The chairman of the Bangla Academy in his presidential address pointed out that the early form of Bengali, particularly under the patronage of Muslim kings during the 14th to 16th centuries, was not influenced by Hindu ideas. He conceded, however, that the language in its present

---

[16] *The Dacca Times,* February 28, 1964. "Mother Bangla" suggests deification of the land, Bengal. Such a concept and symbolic representation would be regarded as un-Islamic by the orthodox *ulama.*

[17] *The Pakistan Observer,* August 9, 1963.

[18] Serajul Hussain Khan, "Our Society and Communal Harmony," *The Dacca Times,* February 28, 1964.

form had been influenced considerably by the Hindus.[19] In the annual meetings of the Bangla Academy, the chairman of the Academy and the Governor of East Pakistan have condemned the continuing influence of West Bengal Hindus on East Pakistani Muslims through the export of Bengali books. They have pointed out that such alien cultural influences, "howsoever may be the artistic perfection," should be stopped. The Governor also suggested that the syllabi of the universities should also be revised to remove alien influences and emphasize Islamic cultural values.[20] But *The Dacca Times,* representing the point of view of perhaps the majority of the Bengali elites in East Pakistan, has condemned the Governor's remarks and suggested that Bengali language and literature have been enriched by both Hindu and Muslim influences. "Similarly any suggestion to eliminate Rabindranath Tagore or Nazrul Islam from the natural course of Bengali language and literature would be unsound, improper and impracticable."[21] One can detect a definite secular trend in current Bengali literature. The group which treats social questions from an Islamic point of view is small and their point of view sometimes dismissed by most Bengali writers as medieval. There are others who try to show how the simple, common peasantry of East Pakistan is being exploited in the name of religion.[22]

Political Demands

East Pakistan's regional movement differs from other regional movements, for example, like that of the French-speaking Canadians in Quebec, in the sense that East Pakistanis do not seem to be apprehensive about losing their cultural identity in a growing Pakistani nationalism. Physical separation from West Pakistan, their larger numbers as compared to West Pakistanis, and above all, a sense of pride in their distinct cultural tradition have given them confidence in their future identity. What concerns them most is the fact that despite their larger numbers (East Pakistan's population is 50.8 million; West Pakistan's population is 42.9 million, according to the 1961 census) and their greater contribution towards Pakistan's foreign exchange earnings, they have been dominated politically by West Pakistan's bureaucracy and the army, and their region has lagged behind West Pakistan in economic development.

Although East Pakistani representatives in the Constituent Assembly always took a firm stand on the question of provincial autonomy, the

19 *The Pakistan Observer,* August 5, 1963.
20 *Morning News,* December 6, 1965.
21 Cited in *The Statesman,* December 27, 1965.
22 Shamsuddin Abul Kalam, pp. 61–62.

first concrete demand on this question was put forward in the 21-Point Program of the Combined Opposition Parties during the provincial election campaign of 1954 when the Muslim League suffered an overwhelming defeat. The two principal components of the opposition were the Awami League Party led by H. S. Suhrawardy and the Krishak Sramik (peasants and workers) Party led by Fazlul Huq. The 21-Point Program stated that the province of East Pakistan should enjoy full autonomy with regard to all subjects with the exception of defense, foreign affairs, and currency, which belonged to the central sphere.[23]

It was clear that East Pakistan's political leaders, by demanding maximum autonomy, were trying to establish a new balance of political and economic power between the Center and the provinces in such a way that economic development in their province would move at a much faster pace. They felt that the central government, dominated by bureaucrats from West Pakistan, had extended their power over an area like industrial development and diverted most of the resources of the country to West Pakistan's industrial development, thereby neglecting East Pakistan. But East Pakistan's regional governments soon found out that East Pakistan was handicapped by several factors. In the first place, the economy of East Pakistan was handicapped by high density of population, constant recurrence of floods and food deficits, and lack of skilled manpower and industrial know-how. In addition, industrial entrepreneurs favored West Pakistan for the investment of their capital and the setting up of new industries. It was difficult, therefore, to match the promises put forward in the 21-Point Program by performance.

It must be said to the credit of Suhrawardy's ministry in the Center (1956–57) that for the first time an attempt was made to allocate foreign exchange on a parity basis to East Pakistani traders. The ministry was not only led by an East Pakistani Prime Minister, but the Commerce and Industries Minister was also an East Pakistani. In response to demands made by East Pakistani commercial interests, the Commerce Minister in November, 1956, announced that separate offices of the Controller of Imports and Exports would be set up for the two provinces under the central Ministry of Commerce. By issuing licenses and foreign exchange for imports, the two provincial governments would be able to look after the interests of their respective provinces through their representatives on committees set up by the central government. In addition, the principle of parity in the alloca-

---

[23] For text, see *One Year of Popular Government in Pakistan* (Dacca: Government of East Pakistan, 1957), p. 15.

tion of foreign exchange would be maintained. Since the import trade was concentrated largely in the hands of certain West Pakistani importers, the Commerce and Industries Minister announced that the government would encourage new traders, particularly from East Pakistan and other commercially backward areas of West Pakistan. It was significant that the new policy was attacked by West Pakistan's business interests and particularly by the Federation of Chambers of Commerce and Industries as one which was designed to foment provincialism and party politics.[24] However, Suhrawardy was out of office by October, 1957, and the policy initiated by his government was reversed by the succeeding Muslim League government. But Noon's ministry (December, 1957–October, 1958), which drew its support from Suhrawardy's East Pakistani-based party, the Awami League, tried to restore the policy based on parity formulas in imports and allocation of foreign exchange.

We have shown in Chapter 4 how democratic governments, both in the Center and the provinces, broke down and Martial Law was established in 1958. Politicians in East Pakistan do not accept the thesis of President Ayub that the entire responsibility for this breakdown must be borne by politicians who, through their machinations and corrupt practices, brought about political instability and retarded the overall progress of the country. East Pakistani politicians in particular point out that President Mirza, supported by a large number of West Pakistani civil servants with entrenched positions both in the Center and in East Pakistan, constantly interfered with the normal functioning of parliamentary governments. Thus, the East Pakistanis feel that parliamentary government did not fail in East Pakistan; it simply was never allowed to work there.

In the light of all this, East Pakistani politicians are highly critical of the 1962 Constitution. It is natural that East Pakistani politicians would be against such a constitution for the simple reason that the National Assembly is the only institution where they can try to redress the balance of power in favor of their province against a government which is dominated by West Pakistanis. They seem to think that there has been a conspiracy to concentrate power in the hands of certain West Pakistani circles. First, the East Pakistani majority was reduced to equality so far as representation in the National Assembly was concerned. Secondly, under the 1962 Constitution the National Assembly has been given extremely limited powers; whereas the President, who

[24] See *Dawn*, November 21 and December 11, 1956, and March 5, 1957. See also T. Maniruzzaman, *Political Development in Pakistan 1955–58* (Ph.D. thesis, Queen's University, 1966).

is from West Pakistan, enjoys enormous powers. Thirdly, the electorate for the National Assembly and the President has been restricted to 80,000 Basic Democrats.[25]

In East Pakistan, there has been a consistent campaign against the 1962 Constitution over the issues of civil rights and direct elections. The agitation often takes the form of complete *hartal* (strike), which involves the closing of shops, schools, colleges, etc. A particular day is picked when big processions, consisting of students, workers, rickshaw drivers, and other groups march through the main streets of a town raising slogans and demanding direct elections, the release of political prisoners, freedom of the press, etc. Finally, they assemble in a meeting where they are exhorted by the politicians to continue their agitation for their democratic rights.[26] It is apparent that there is a difference between the political culture of the two provinces. East Pakistan's public opinion seems to get stirred up very easily on political and linguistic issues; whereas West Pakistanis seem to react strongly only when religious or ideological issues are raised. In East Pakistan, the power of the landlords or officials is not as strong as it is in West Pakistan. This means that the masses in West Pakistan can be stirred out of their apathy only when strong religious and ideological issues are raised. We have seen in Chapter 7 that Martial Law had to be imposed in Lahore in 1953 when the anti-Ahmadi agitation led to lawlessness. Similarly, politicians can more easily arouse public opinion in West Pakistan than they can in East over the question of the right of self-determination of Kashmiris.

Apart from economic disparity, the other disparities that have concerned East Pakistanis most are those in the civil and armed services. It is well known that in Pakistan and India, central civil servants occupy most of the important positions both in the district administrations and provincial secretariats. Provincial leaders have often felt, therefore, that they are not complete masters of their own provinces. We have seen in Chapter 6 that in East Pakistan this problem was further accentuated because for a long time most of the central civil servants working in the provincial administration were from West Pakistan. This imbalance was corrected, for beginning in June, 1961, East Pakistani CSP officers were posted in East Pakistan instead of spending the first few years of their careers in a province other than

[25] Sixty out of 75 East Pakistani members of the National Assembly opposed the 1962 Constitution. *The Economist,* February 8, 1964, p. 494. For detailed criticisms of the Constitution, see the statements of the three former Chief Ministers of East Pakistan, *Dawn,* June 25, 1962.

[26] March 19, 1964, was celebrated throughout East Pakistan as the Direct Election and Franchise Day. For reports from various districts, see *The Pakistan Observer,* March 22, 1964.

their own. Furthermore, the number of East Pakistani officers in the CSP has also increased, and by 1964, most of the key positions in the province were being held by East Pakistanis. But the disparity in the central Secretariat during 1964–65 was so great that out of seventeen central Secretaries, only two East Pakistani officers had attained the rank of Acting Secretary.[27] Therefore, East Pakistani politicians continued to complain that since the civil servants were so influential in the decision-making process in Pakistan, economic disparity between the two provinces could not be corrected unless a greater number of East Pakistanis were placed in senior positions in the Secretariat. To the central government's plea that such appointments could not be made in view of the fact that a sufficient number of senior East Pakistani CSP officers was not available, East Pakistani politicians have suggested that the central government could recruit East Pakistanis to the CSP on an *ad hoc* basis. Through such *ad hoc* appointments, parity should be brought about in the senior posts of Secretaries and Joint Secretaries in the central Secretariat.[28]

Another major grievance of the East Pakistanis concerns the disparity in the armed services where they are even less equally represented than they are in the civil services. In 1965, of the seventeen highest officers in the Pakistan army — one general, two lieutenant-generals, and fourteen major-generals — only one East Pakistani held the rank of major-general. Indeed, according to government figures, East Pakistanis constitute no more than 5 per cent of the officers in the Pakistan army. In the navy, East Pakistanis constitute 19 per cent of the technical officers and 9 per cent of the nontechnical officers. Their proportion in the naval ranks on the technical side is 28.4 per cent and 28.5 on the nontechnical side. Among air force officers, East Pakistanis constitute 11 per cent of pilots, 27 per cent of navigators, 17 per cent of the technical officers, 31 per cent of administrative officers, and 13 per cent of education officers.[29] The Ministry of Defense has argued that the defense departments cannot be blamed for existing disparities. East Pakistanis do not seem to respond to their persistent recruitment efforts. However, the East Pakistani complaint is that military authorities, by maintaining certain high physical qualifications, have kept East Pakistanis out of the armed services. They point out that this policy is a continuation of the British policy

[27] *The Pakistan Observer,* April 17, 1964. The number of central Secretaries keeps changing as new departments are created or old ones merged with others.

[28] *Ibid.,* August 30, 1962.

[29] *National Assembly of Pakistan Debates,* I, No. 1 (March 8, 1963), pp. 29–31. Information regarding other positions in the army, navy and air force may also be obtained from the same source.

of restricting recruitment to certain martial races, most of whom were to be found in northwest India. They complain that as long as such physical requirements are maintained, Pakistan's armed forces will not become a national institution. It may be noted that India has adopted a more flexible policy in order to draw the personnel of the armed forces from a national base rather than from a few provinces.

Even though the percentage of literate persons is higher (17.6) in East Pakistan than in West (13.6), the number of matriculates, graduates, and postgraduates is much lower in East Pakistan than in West Pakistan. It may be noted in Table 8 that in the case of graduates and postgraduates, East Pakistani numbers have actually registered an appreciable decline between the years 1951 and 1961; whereas the percentage of variation between 1951 and 1961 in West Pakistan has been as high as 143.7, in the case of matriculates, and 68.6 in the case of postgraduates. All such figures have been cited by East Pakistani politicians to show that their province is not only being kept behind West Pakistan, but that the disparity between the two wings is actually widening, with West Pakistan forging ahead.

Articulation of Economic Demands

In a political system dominated by a bureaucracy, politicians may be vociferous, and the bureaucracy may be responsive to their demands to the extent that they do not want to use coercive power more than is necessary to prevent anomic protests from getting out of hand. In such a system, politicians do not have the information necessary to articulate concrete demands; nor do they occupy positions of power in the decision-making process to convert inputs (demands) into outputs (government decisions). In a system of bureaucratic dominance like that of Pakistan, East Pakistani bureaucrats, economists, and other experts have been more successful than politicians in articulating the demands of their region and in persuading and pressuring the governmental machinery to meet these demands, at least halfway, through appropriate government decisions. One should also note that the President and his civil service advisers, most of whom are from West Pakistan, are also in a position to control West Pakistan's political forces in such a way that they do not protest the central government's concessions to the demands of East Pakistanis. Under political regimes prior to the Martial Law regime, East Pakistan's regional demands were resisted not only by West Pakistan's bureaucrats, but also by its political forces.

We have seen that under Ayub's regime, civil servants from East Pakistan have been given most of the key positions in the East Pakistan administration. In addition, the regime has also appointed East Pakistanis to important institutions and decision-making bodies like

Table 8

Number of Matriculates, Graduates and Postgraduates in 1951 and 1961 and Their Variation, Pakistan and Provinces

(−) denotes decrease

	Matriculates			Graduates			Postgraduates		
	1951	1961	Per cent of Variation 1951–1961	1951	1961	Per cent of Variation 1951–1961	1951	1961	Per cent of Variation 1951–1961
PAKISTAN	521,856	884,148	69.4	85,988	82,069	(−) 4.6	22,546	31,470	39.6
East Pakistan	282,158	299,967	6.3	41,484	28,069	(−) 32.3	8,117	7,146	(−) 12.0
West Pakistan	239,698	584,181	143.7	44,504	54,000	21.3	14,429	24,324	68.6

Source: *Population Census of Pakistan 1961*, I (Karachi: The Manager of Publications, Government of Pakistan, n.d.), p. IV–26.

the National Economic Council, Planning Commission, Tariff Commission, Industrial Development Bank (the Managing Director is from East Pakistan). The Province of East Pakistan also has its own Planning Board, and former central corporations and agencies like the Pakistan Industrial Development Corporation (PIDC), Water and Power Development Authority (WAPDA), the Railways, the Small Scale Industries Corporation, etc., have all been bifurcated into the two provincial corporations and agencies. East Pakistani civil servants and economists, moreover, are well represented on bodies like the National Finance Commission. East Pakistan has had the advantage of its case being represented by a number of highly trained and competent economists. It may be noted that Dacca University and the East Pakistan Planning Board have had more highly trained economists on the whole than universities or similar institutions in West Pakistan. The director of the Institute of Development Economics in Karachi is also an East Pakistani, and the Finance Minister of East Pakistan is a former head of the Department of Economics, Dacca University.

These experts have been able to put forward a very impressive and cogent case for East Pakistan and have effectively shown that the reason its economy has lagged is due to the kinds of policies followed by the central government. The basic premise on which all their arguments rest is that Pakistan does not have a single economy, but that it consists of two economies.[30] East and West Pakistan are two separate geographic and economic regions. West Pakistan has been a beneficiary of the bulk of central government expenditure, particularly defense expenditure and the expenditure incurred first for the capital at Karachi and now the new capital at Islamabad. In addition, industrial development has been much greater in the West than in the East. But the physical separation of the two provinces is such that there is practically no mobility of labor, and the multiplier effect of central expenditure and industrial development in West Pakistan is confined to that province. Mobility of goods is extremely difficult because it takes seven days to move goods from one province to the other. It has been estimated that it is cheaper to import cement to East Pakistan from Egypt or Yugoslavia than from Karachi. Because

[30] The term "two economies" was first used by A. Sadeque, *The Economic Emergence of Pakistan*, Part II (Dacca: Provincial Statistical Board and Bureau of Commercial and Industrial Intelligence, Planning Department, 1956). See Chapters I and II. For more recent usages, see Rahman Sobhan, "The Meaning and Significance of the Two Economies Thesis," *New Values*, XII, No. 3 (1961), and the Finance Minister, East Pakistan, Speech on the Budget in the East Pakistan Assembly, *Morning News*, June 30, 1965, and July 1, 2, and 3, 1965.

of all these factors, East Pakistani economists have argued that it would be most unfair to continue with the earlier system of one national economic policy in which resources are invested in those areas which yield the highest returns. They have argued that there should be two separate economic policies for the two wings of the country and that the government, in planning investment of national resources, should not compare an industry in East Pakistan with the same industry in West Pakistan. A proper comparison would be between one industry in East Pakistan with other industries in East Pakistan itself.

In order to show how former economic policies of the Central Government have had an adverse impact on the economy of East Pakistan, East Pakistani economists have produced an impressive array of figures. These are to be found in Tables 9, 10, and 11.

It may be seen from Table 10 that in terms of the contribution of manufacturing to gross domestic product, East and West Pakistan both started from about the same level, but after independence, the rate of industrial growth in West Pakistan far outpaced that in East Pakistan. How does one explain West Pakistan's higher rate of growth? There are several explanations. The first in order of importance, according to East Pakistanis, would be the fact that East Pakistan's foreign exchange earnings were utilized for the import of capital and other goods into West Pakistan thereby facilitating the industrialization of that province. Total exports of East Pakistan during the years 1947 to 1962 amounted to Rs. 13.08 billion; whereas those of West Pakistan during the same period amounted to Rs. 9.9 billion. In contrast, total imports into East Pakistan during that period amounted to 7.9 billion while those for West Pakistan amounted to 18.7 billion.[31] Thus West Pakistan, which had exported much less than the eastern province, imported much more from 1947 to 1962. The argument runs that East Pakistan's industrial backwardness has forced that region to purchase goods and services from West Pakistan, and that in order to do this, it has had to surrender a substantial portion of its foreign exchange earnings. Moreover, since West Pakistan's industries have been operating behind protective tariff walls, East Pakistan has been purchasing West Pakistani goods at higher prices than it would have paid for the same goods if they had been purchased abroad.[32]

East Pakistan has complained bitterly that the responsibility for this inter-provincial disparity should be borne by the central government,

[31] These figures have been taken from Government of East Pakistan, Planning Department, *Economic Disparities Between East and West Pakistan* (Dacca: East Pakistan Government Press, 1963), pp. 28–29.

[32] *Ibid.* See also editorial, "The Perils of Industrialization — I," *The Pakistan Observer,* April 30, 1965.

Table 9

Per Capita Incomes

(GNP at Factor Cost of 1959/60)

	1959–60	1960–61	1961–62	1962–63	1963–64*
East Pakistan	269	278	287	280	305
West Pakistan	355	359	368	382	388
Pakistan	318	325	334	336	353
Extent of Disparity (Pakistan = 100) †	28%	26%	25%	31%	24%

* Provisional

† The Pakistan figures cover 97 per cent of the GNP. The remaining unallocated 3 per cent has been excluded.

Source: Planning Commission, Government of Pakistan, *The Third Five Year Plan 1965–70* (Karachi: May, 1965), p. 127.

Table 10

Contribution of Manufacturing to Gross Domestic Product (in 1949–53 Prices)

(Rs. in crores)

Years	East Pakistan	West Pakistan	Index for West Pakistan with East Pakistan = 100
1949–50	59	60	102
1954–55	78	114	147
1959–60	109	169	155

Source: Planning Department, Government of East Pakistan, *Economic Disparities Between East and West Pakistan* (Dacca: East Pakistan Government Press, 1963), p. 8.

Table 11

Per Capita Electricity Generating Capacity

	Power Generating Capacity (in K.W.)	
Years	East Pakistan	West Pakistan
1947–48	0.2	4.0
1954–55	1.6	7.3
1959–60	3.5	17.4
1961–62	5.6	19.2

Source: Planning Department, Government of East Pakistan, *Economic Disparities Between East and West Pakistan* (Dacca: East Pakistan Government Press, 1963), p. 9.

who have handled the development of industries since 1948. The Center has shown preferential treatment to West Pakistani industrialists by granting them foreign exchange, by issuing licenses and permits for the establishment of new industries, and by making bigger allocations, loans and grants, both from its own resources as well as from foreign aid. Dollar development loans from the United States made available to East Pakistan by the central government between 1959–65 amount to $100.3 million; whereas those made available to West Pakistan during the same period amount to $282.8 million.[33]

As noted earlier, there are several able civil servants and highly trained economists in East Pakistan who can not only demonstrate clearly and convincingly that East Pakistan has been denied a fair deal in the matter of allocation of resources, but can also suggest positive and concrete remedies for the removal of inter-provincial disparities to decision-making or fact-gathering bodies or commissions. This is precisely what five East Pakistani members (three CSP officers, one professor of economics, and one managing director, Industrial Development Bank) of the ten-member Finance Commission, did. The Finance Commission, appointed in 1961, was split evenly between the five East Pakistani and the five West Pakistani members over the question of what steps the central government should take to eliminate disparity. The five East Pakistani members filed a separate report in which they pointed out that by allocating equal resources to East and West Pakistan, the central government would never be able to eliminate the disparity between the two provinces, as the western province was already far ahead of the eastern one. They then suggested: "there must clearly be accelerated growth in East Pakistan as compared with West; in other words, West Pakistan's economy, although it will undoubtedly still continue to grow, will grow at a slower pace than that of East Pakistan."[34] In evolving a formula of allocation of resources, they considered various possibilities. If allocation of resources were made only on the basis of population, the gap, though tending to become proportionately smaller, would not be eliminated because of the lead that West Pakistan's economy enjoyed in development. They pointed out, therefore, that it was necessary for resources

[33] Figures obtained from the U.S. AID Office in Washington. It may be noted that West Pakistan received a dollar development loan of $12.8 million during the fiscal year 1958, whereas East Pakistan received none. All these figures do not include technical assistance. In addition, development loans were given on an all-Pakistan basis, which are also not included in these figures.

[34] *Report of Five Members of the Finance Commission* (Dacca: January 18, 1962), p. 11.

to be allocated not only on the basis of population "but of population weighted by the inverse ratio of per capita income." The precise formula they suggested was as follows:

> . . . if the population ratio between the two wings is taken to be 54:46 in favour of East Pakistan, while the per capita income ratio is taken as 1.25:1 in favour of West Pakistan, then the percentage of developmental resources to be made available to East Pakistan should be 54 x 1.25 = 67½.[35]

It was obvious that if 67½% of the resources were allotted to East Pakistan, West Pakistan would strongly object. Indeed, the Finance Commission's West Pakistani members did object, maintaining that if the suggested formula were applied, East Pakistan would be deluged with resources which it could not absorb, whereas West Pakistan, being denied adequate resources, would face economic stagnation and decay. But the absorptive capacity of East Pakistan did not present a difficult problem to the East Pakistani members of the Commission. They argued that if the social overheads like the provision of power, communication, and education and technical training were provided soon in East Pakistan, its capacity to absorb other forms of investment would automatically and speedily increase. They also argued that there would not be an economic decline in West Pakistan and that the province's rate of growth would continue, although it might slow down. "We are confident that in the interest of the prosperity and solidarity of the Pakistani nation the people of West Pakistan would be willing to make this contribution to the uplift of their brothers in the Eastern Province."[36] The five East Pakistanis strongly recommended that the new constitution which was being drafted not only contain the objective that disparity between the two provinces would be eliminated within a maximum period of 25 years, but also the formula which they had suggested in their report for allocation of developmental resources.

In another report, prepared by the Planning Department of East Pakistan, it was recommended that the President of Pakistan declare the intention of the government to remove all interprovincial disparities by 1980–85. In order to achieve this objective, it was necessary to create adequate infrastructure and social overheads in East Pakistan to make up for past deficiencies. "The Government of East Pakistan is of the view that the share of East Pakistan in future investments should be of the order of 60 per cent till disparity is removed. . . ."[37]

[35] *Ibid.,* p. 12.
[36] *Ibid.,* p. 14.
[37] *Economic Disparities Between East and West Pakistan,* p. 25.

East Pakistani economists and civil servants were able to convince the East Pakistan government to such an extent that it was prepared to urge the central government to divert developmental resources from West Pakistan to East Pakistan. Their actions clearly prove: first, East Pakistani regional demands, that had earlier been put forward by politicians, were now being put forward, perhaps in a more rigorous and convincing manner, by East Pakistani bureaucrats and economists. Secondly, regionalism was such a strong force that it could infect the bureaucrats as well as the politicians. Third, articulation of demands is so important in a political system that when politicians are no longer in a position to articulate their demands, this function has to be performed by bureaucrats.

Policy Response to Regional Demands

Even those West Pakistanis who agree that East Pakistan has not received its share in the allocation of resources, insist that the central government or West Pakistan cannot be blamed entirely for the fact that East Pakistan's economic development has lagged behind. There are several other explanations. East Pakistan is one of the most densely populated areas in the world: the average density is 922 per square mile, unequalled anywhere except in parts of Indonesia and China. And in several districts the density is well over 1,200; indeed, in some of the subdivisions of Dacca District, it is between 2,500 to 3,000 per square mile. Its roads and other means of communications are relatively much less developed than those in West Pakistan which, because of its strategic importance, inherited from the British a fairly advanced network of roads and communications. In addition, as is well known, in the subcontinent of India and Pakistan business and entrepreneurial acumen is a quality which is not widely shared or acquired; rather, it has remained concentrated in certain castes and communities. Thus, the industrial development of Pakistan was almost entirely spearheaded by the Memons, the Bohras, and the Khojas, most of whom came from Bombay or their ancestral homes in Gujarat, Kathiawar, and Kutch, places which are all fairly close to Karachi. These communities and the local Chiniotis from Punjab control over half of Pakistan's industrial wealth.

Bengalis by temperament are more imaginative and artistic than pragmatic. It is true that they were one of the first communities to profit from British education, a system which emphasized liberal arts to such an extent that when the British left there were over one hundred colleges and universities in Pakistan, but only one agricultural and one engineering college. Upper-class Bengalis, most of whom were Hindus, took full advantage of British liberal education and occupied a large number of the available government positions, both in Bengal and in the central government. But when industrial development started in India people from other provinces poured into Bengal, and particularly into Calcutta, searching for new opportunities in commercial and industrial life. In West Bengal, which was much more advanced than East Bengal, commercial and industrial life came to be dominated by Marwaris and Gujaratis. In East Bengal, where Muslims were much less advanced than the Hindus in West Bengal, industry and commerce came under the domination of the Marwaris and later, after the outflow of Hindu refugees, by West Pakistan's business classes. Earlier we noted that East Pakistan was politically more conscious than West Pakistan and that this political awareness when intensified by political dissatisfaction, has sometimes resulted in labor unrest. Labor agitation has also taken the form of Bengali Muslim workers rioting against non-Bengali management.

The Martial Law regime, untrammelled by political pulls and pressures, was prepared to get to the source of the political and economic malaise that afflicted Pakistan. And in certain cases, if the diagnosis disclosed unpleasant facts, it was ready to tackle them as best it could. One of these unpleasant facts was that more than any other group of West Pakistanis, Punjabis had become very unpopular in East Pakistan; because of their dominant position both in the civil service and in the army they had provoked jealousies and fears, both in East Pakistan and among the Sindhis and Pathans in West Pakistan. We have already seen that in June, 1961, the central government decided to post East Pakistani CSP officers in East Pakistan instead of requiring them to serve the first few years in a province other than their own. This policy soon resulted in East Pakistanis occupying most of the key positions in the provincial administration. In April, 1960, General Azam Khan, a Pathan, was appointed as Governor of East Pakistan. During the two years of his governorship, he endeared himself to a large number of East Pakistanis not only because of the new vigor and dynamism he injected into the administration, but because East Pakistanis found in him an outspoken champion of their demands and rights in his dealings with the central government. In May, 1961, President Ayub in a press conference, while pledging that his regime would make every effort to develop the economy of East Pakistan, admitted that in the past some of East Pakistan's foreign exchange earnings from jute exports had been utilized in West Pakistan. But he attacked the concept of two economies as one which might lead to the disintegration of the country. What was important, the President said, was that disparity in development between the two wings be narrowed down.[38] In October, 1961, he announced that he would appoint a

[38] *The Pakistan Observer,* May 24 and 25, 1961.

Finance Commission to examine the question of equitable allocation of resources between the two provinces. Since then, under the Constitution of 1962 (Article 144), the President has appointed several Finance Commissions, which have recommended the transfer of certain proportions of taxes collected by the Center to the provinces. The provinces are getting 65 per cent of the divisible pool of central taxes and the Center receives 35 per cent.

For the first time, the 1962 Constitution stated clearly that the government of Pakistan was determined to ensure that economic disparities between the provinces, as well as those between different areas within a province, would be removed in the shortest possible time.[39] What are the steps the government has taken since the inauguration of the 1962 Constitution to eliminate economic disparity between the provinces? Under the Second Five Year Plan (1960–65), an increasing amount of public sector resources were diverted to East Pakistan. East Pakistan's share of public sector resources rose from 36 per cent in 1959–60 to 47 per cent in 1963–64. For the first time in the gross budgeted allocations for 1964–65, East Pakistan was given a higher share than that allotted to West — Rs. 2.05 billion (EP) and Rs. 1.9 billion (WP). East Pakistan was also allotted a higher share in the Rural Public Works Program — Rs. 250 million (EP) and Rs. 150 million (WP). Public development expenditure in East Pakistan has increased at a rate which is more than twice as high as that in West Pakistan. During 1960–61, public development expenditures in East Pakistan, including the allocation of central expenditures, amounted to Rs. 810 million. During 1964–65, these expenditures are projected at nearly Rs. 2 billion, which means an increase of nearly 150 per cent. Compared to this, West Pakistan's public development expenditure during 1960–61 was Rs. 1.17 billion, rising to nearly Rs. 2 billion in 1964–65. This represents an increase of only about 70 per cent.[40]

The Third Five Year Plan (1965–70) envisages a total expenditure of Rs. 52 billion out of which Rs. 27 billion have been allocated to East Pakistan and Rs. 25 billion to West. Under the Third Plan, the

[39] The 1962 Constitution states that one of the principles of policy would be that "parity between the Provinces in all spheres of the Central Government should, as nearly as is practicable, be achieved." (Clause 16). Article 145(4) refers to the removal of disparities in relation to per capita income in the shortest possible time. As compared to this, the 1956 Constitution merely states that steps would be taken to bring about parity in all spheres of federal administration and that people from all parts of Pakistan would be given an opportunity to participate in the defense services. (Article 31)

[40] Planning Commission, Government of Pakistan, *The Third Five Year Plan 1965–70* (Karachi: May, 1965), pp. 127–129. However, East Pakistanis complain that West Pakistan's public development expenditure far exceeds that of East Pakistan if the expenditure of Rs. 9.05 billion for the Indus Basin projects located in West Pakistan is taken into account.

regional income of East Pakistan is expected to increase by 40 per cent and that of West Pakistan by 35 per cent. During the Second Plan, the actual increases in regional incomes for East and West Pakistan were 30 and 28 per cent respectively. Expected sector-wise rates of growth during the Third Plan for the two regions may be seen in Table 12.

Table 12

Rates of Growth

	East Pakistan	West Pakistan	All Pakistan
Agriculture	4.5	5.5	5.0
Manufacturing	15.5	6.6	10.0
Large-scale	(21.0)	(8.3)	(13.2)
Small-scale	(3.0)	(3.0)	(3.0)
Other Sectors	8.4	6.4	7.2
Totals	7.0	6.0	6.5

Source: Planning Commission, Government of Pakistan, *The Third Five Year Plan 1965–70* (Karachi: May, 1965), p. 129.

There has been a progressive narrowing of the gap in per capita incomes between East and West Pakistan. One can see in Table 9 (p. 200) that disparity in per capita income has been brought down from 28 per cent in 1959–60 to 24 per cent during 1963–64. (In 1962–63 a sudden rise in the extent of disparity — 31 per cent — resulted from cyclones and other natural calamities.) It is frankly stated, however, in the Third Five Year Plan that disparities in income between East and West Pakistan cannot be eliminated either during the Third or even the Fourth Plan. "Given a dedicated effort, it should be feasible, however, to eliminate disparities completely within the period of the Perspective Plan."[41] The Perspective Plan deals with Pakistan's long-term growth over a period of twenty years, 1965–85.

East Pakistan has lagged behind more in the private sector than in the public sector. In the Third Five Year Plan, it is proposed that in the private sector Rs. 22 billion should be allocated equally to East and West Pakistan. This represents, so far as East Pakistan is concerned, an increase from an estimated level of private sector expenditure of Rs. 3.3 billion during the Second Plan to Rs. 11 billion during the Third Plan or an increase of about 233 per cent. In West Pakistan, on the other hand, private sector expenditure during the Second Plan

[41] *Ibid.*, p. 129. For details and growth rates regarding long-term perspectives, see pp. 18–30.

was in the order of Rs. 6.3 billion, which means that the proposed Rs. 11 billion expenditure in the Third Plan represents an increase of about 75 per cent.[42]

In East Pakistan a variety of measures — such as lower customs duties for import of machinery and spare parts than those charged in West Pakistan and a tax holiday during a maximum period of eight years for the establishment of new industries — have been adopted to accelerate development, and the provincial government has made it clear that maximum encouragement will be given to East Pakistan's entrepreneurs. As a result, a small but influential class of East Pakistani entrepreneurs and traders has arisen. They resent the fact that West Pakistan's entrepreneurs continue to set up new industries in the private sector in East Pakistan. East Pakistani traders and entrepreneurs have also complained that West Pakistani industrialists transfer their profits from East Pakistan to West Pakistan, and the East Pakistan Provincial Government has promised to take steps to prevent the transfer of such profits.[43]

Another major source of grievance of East Pakistani industrialists and political leaders has been the way the Pakistan Industrial Development Corporation (PIDC) has disinvested certain big industries in East Pakistan. The PIDC took the initiative in floating certain basic industries both in West and East Pakistan when private capital was reluctant to embark on such ventures. As soon as these ventures became profitable enterprises, the PIDC sold them to a few big industrialists from West Pakistan. This created resentment in East Pakistan. Now that the PIDC has been bifurcated and industries have been placed under provincial control, the East Pakistan government has formulated a policy for future disinvestments by the East Pakistan Industrial Development Corporation (EPIDC) which will transfer industrial ownership by gradual stages to groups of small owners every year. Through this method of gradual disinvestment, the EPIDC expects to avoid the purchase of these industries by a few big industrialists. Secondly, the provincial government is also of the view that the EPIDC would not disinvest certain basic industries such as public utilities, but would retain permanent interest in or control of such industries.[44]

It is significant that because there are only six or seven big East Pakistani industrialists, Chambers of Commerce in East Pakistan tend to represent the interests of small or medium-size traders. Conse-

[42] *Ibid.,* pp. 128–129.

[43] See the Finance Minister, East Pakistan, Speech on the Budget in the East Pakistan Assembly, *Morning News,* July 3, 1965.

[44] *Ibid.*

quently, they are often at variance with representations made by the Federation of Pakistan Chambers of Commerce and Industry (FPCCI), which is dominated by West Pakistan's big industrialists. The president of the Chittagong Chamber of Commerce and Industry has advocated the introduction of anticartel and antitrust laws similar to those in the United States; imposition of taxes like the wealth tax, or the death duty; and the nationalization of all basic and heavy industries. The Chittagong Chamber has also demanded the bifurcation of the FPCCI and the setting up of a separate organization in East Pakistan.[45] In addition, it has informed the Planning Commission it strongly opposes the suggestion of the FPCCI that economic controls should be removed in the interests of free economy. According to the president of the Chittagong Chamber, free economy is synonymous with cartels and combines. In his protest note, he told the Planning Commission that since East Pakistan's representation is only one-third in the Managing Committee of the FPCCI, the latter body is in a position to disregard the interests of East Pakistan.[46]

Emerging Trends

The most fundamental question that has challenged the constitution-makers and other political leaders in Pakistan is how to keep the two physically and culturally separated regions of the country linked together as one nation and one state. The two major integrating forces in Pakistan have been ideological or religious and utilitarian or economic. We have seen that the ideological or religious factor as an integrating force was somewhat overestimated when Pakistan came into being. As long as the Muslim League was a nationalist movement, waging its struggle for Pakistan against the Congress and the British, Islam as a unifying factor was strong enough to overcome divisive forces like language, distance, culture, etc. But after the formation of Pakistan, politics, so far as the elites were concerned, became problem-oriented. During this phase, the central government has had to rely on the economic factor and, above all, the fear of India as a common enemy of both East and West Pakistan. We have seen that the economic factor, instead of unifying the country, can also generate interregional bitterness over the allocation of resources. To a certain extent, there has been a diminution in economic grievances of East Pakistanis with the increasing efforts of the central government to reduce disparities. Partial or complete satisfaction of grievances may lower the tension between the regions, but by itself does not bind them

[45] Aminul Islam Chowdhury, "Cartels," *The Dacca Times,* April 10, 1964, pp. 5 and 13.

[46] *The Pakistan Observer,* March 3, 1965.

into a united nation. Thus, positive bonds are needed. And this partly explains why Islam as an integrating factor has been constantly stressed.

There is, however, a secular trend afoot, not only among the elites but even among the masses: as people leave villages and flock to cities in search of jobs, religion ceases to have as compulsive or strong an influence as it did on their lives in rural areas. In addition, we have seen how strong is the pull of Bengali language and culture. This is likely to increase even more as Bengali becomes the medium of instruction in schools, colleges, and universities.[47] But some East Pakistanis emphasize the fact that Bengali in East Pakistan is developing in an Islamic mold in the sense that a large number of Arabic and Persian words are being used.[48] Others are fearful of increasing Hindu influence from across the border in West Bengal through a constant inflow of Bengali literature into East Pakistan. However, one has to consider the fact that Bengali as a language, in response to the needs of science and modern technology, will have to move away both from its Islamic moorings as well as from the purely literary influences of Bengali Hindu poets and playwrights. All this means that eventually Bengali dialects of both West Bengal and East Pakistan must emerge as one regional language if Bengali is to function as a vehicle of scientific thought. Thus, so far as the language factor is concerned, it is likely to reinforce the existing regionalism and may in the long run turn out to be a disintegrating force.

In the foreseeable future, however, fear of India and the economic advantages of remaining linked with West Pakistan as one state provide greater hope for the unity of the country. East Pakistani elites may be dissatisfied or bitter because the central government has not been fair towards their province's demands or interests, but they know that the other extreme alternative, namely, separation, would result in loss of independence and absorption by India. Above all, it would also mean that they would have far fewer opportunities for economic advancement as Bengali Muslims in a united India. Some of them remember, and others have been told, how much worse off Bengali Muslims were in a united Bengal during pre-independence days.

We have seen how skillfully East Pakistan's bureaucrats and economists have articulated the regional demand for the removal of economic disparity between the two wings and how, in a system of bureau-

[47] Dacca University is taking steps to introduce Bengali as the medium of instruction in the first year of the graduate classes for the academic year 1968–69.

[48] "Poetry in East Bengal," *Pakistan Quarterly,* IV, No. 1 (Spring, 1954), 35.

cratic dominance, these demands have been converted into governmental outputs. This system of bureaucratic dominance can remain in a state of equilibrium as long as the demands emanate from bureaucrats and economists who are aware of the scarcity of economic resources and who thus formulate their demands in such a way that the existing system is not thrown into a state of fundamental disequilibrium. But as we have noted earlier, political forces in East Pakistan are stronger than they are in West; therefore, it seems that East Pakistani politicians cannot be persuaded to operate under self-imposed restraints so that the country may make uninterrupted economic progress. The wide intellectual and political gulf existing between East Pakistani politicians and the central government's decision-makers is evident. Sheikh Mujibur Rahman, the leader of the Awami League in East Pakistan, has demanded that the central government should be converted from its present unitary form to a confederal form with its jurisdiction confined to defense and foreign affairs. It should be stripped of all tax-levying power. Taxes would be collected by the two federating units, and the federal government would be given a share from state taxes to meet its obligations. Foreign trade would also be within the provincial sphere. He has demanded that there be a parliamentary form of government where the legislature is supreme and elected on the basis of universal adult franchise and direct voting. This six-point demand for regional autonomy[49] by the East Pakistan Awami League has been opposed by the Awami League in West Pakistan as well as by other parties.[50] What is significant, however, is the way President Ayub has reacted to these demands. In his view, they have hardly anything to do with the major problems facing the country: "What the people needed was stability and unity in the country, more educational facilities, economic development, stronger military defence, and general development in the country." The President has also dubbed the six-point program as the demand for a "Greater Bengal," which means that East Bengal and West Bengal would combine to form an independent state. This is bound to result in East Pakistan's Muslims being enslaved by Caste Hindus of West Bengal.[51] The President has also threatened that if necessary, the "language of weapon" would have to be used and the country might have to go through a civil war as the United States did.[52]

All this clearly suggests that the President admits that even though he has tried to satisfy East Pakistan's economic demands, he has

[49] *Dawn,* February 12, 1966.
[50] *Ibid.,* February 12 and 18, 1966.
[51] *The Pakistan Times,* March 20, 1966.
[52] *Ibid.,* March 21, 1966.

failed to create sufficient political support there for his regime. And unfortunately, having failed to defeat East Pakistani separatism by political means, which East Pakistan politicians respect and understand, he is threatening to use military means thereby reminding the East Pakistanis that West Pakistani arms can triumph over East Pakistan's political resistance. The tragedy is that President Ayub means well, but does not seem to have a sympathetic understanding of the political aspirations of East Pakistan's political and urban elites.[53] To these classes, the bonds of Islamic religion and the fear of India become meaningful if East Pakistan's political leaders are allowed an effective voice and political role in the shaping and sharing of power in Pakistan. They are not satisfied with mere economic concessions. They are painfully aware that the country's bureaucracy and the army, which are the two major influential elements in the decision-making process, are predominantly West Pakistani. Under Suhrawardy, East Pakistan did not receive as much share in economic allocations as it has under the present regime. But there was much less political alienation under Suhrawardy for the simple reason that under his regime, East Pakistani politicians were politically more effective.

[53] It is noteworthy that President Ayub ever since he became President in 1958 has carefully avoided including any of the Awami League or National Awami Party leaders from East Pakistan in his Cabinet. He has taken several Muslim League leaders from East Pakistan into his Cabinet, but the Muslim League suffered a crushing defeat in the 1954 provincial elections in East Pakistan. It is apparent that with the exception of a few leaders, most of the popular leaders in East Pakistan are either from the Awami League or the National Awami Party (NAP) or the National Democratic Front (NDF formed in 1962). The NDF consists of former Muslim Leaguers, former NAP members, and former Krishak Sramik Party members, who demand restoration of a parliamentary form of government.

9

Parties and Elections

It is difficult to classify the party system in Pakistan. It neither belongs to the Indian variety of one-party dominance, nor can it be placed under the rubric of single-party states either in Asia or in Africa.[1] If one were to apply the Weberian analysis to the political development of Pakistan, one could see that the country was brought into being by a charismatic leader like Jinnah, who overwhelmed the rural and semifeudal social structure, particularly of West Pakistan. But it has been noted that the charisma of Jinnah was not as potent a factor as Islam in overcoming opposition from the rural gentry. The active workers of the Muslim League very largely came from the urban areas. They hoped that Pakistan would be a Muslim state in which there would be no fear of Hindu competition. After the death of Jinnah in 1948, the only way the Muslim League could maintain its power was to follow the same *modus operandi* that Jinnah had initiated, namely, to keep the urban areas united and to dominate the rural areas through active urban political workers. But it was difficult even for Jinnah's lieutenant and first Prime Minister, Liaquat Ali Khan, to keep the urban wing of the Muslim League united. First of all, the urban areas of Karachi, Hyderabad, and, to some extent, Lahore, were dominated by refugees who were all newcomers and who could not easily get together and establish their leadership. Large

[1] For the Indian system of one-party dominance, see W. H. Morris-Jones, "Parliament and Dominant Party. Indian Experience," *Parliamentary Affairs,* vol. 17, no. 3 (Summer, 1964); W. H. Morris-Jones, *The Government and Politics of India* (London: Hutchinson University Library, 1964), pp. 148–154; and Rajni Kothari, "The Congress System in India," *Asian Survey* (December, 1964), 1162–1172. For the single-party systems in Africa, see Ruth Schacter, "Single-Party Systems in West Africa," *American Political Science Review,* LV (June, 1961), 294–307.

numbers of these refugees had not been successfully rehabilitated by the government and their demand that they should be allotted lands, houses, and shops left by Hindus in Pakistan provoked opposition from the landowners of Sind and Punjab. In addition, the Muslim League found it increasingly difficult to satisfy the demands of Bengali politicians who felt that the economic interests of East Pakistan were not safe under the bureaucratic domination of West Pakistan. This splintering and ineffectiveness of the Muslim League urban organization produced different results in East and West Pakistan. In East Pakistan, the dissidents from the Muslim League formed a coalition known as the United Front, moved into the rural areas, and swept the Muslim League from power in 1954. In West Pakistan, political power gravitated towards Punjabi feudal landowners. The overall result was political fragmentation bordering on chaos because neither the new coalition in East Pakistan could stay together and form stable governments nor could the Punjabi feudal and rural gentry rally support from the different areas of West Pakistan to maintain political stability.

Ayub's diagnosis of this political fragmentation is that the politicians, who are no better than demagogues, in their scramble for power have gone to extreme lengths in pandering to the parochial and regional loyalties of a people who are predominantly illiterate. This kind of political process tends to divide and disrupt society when the national interests of the country demand that there should be a sense of strong unity throughout the country to preserve national independence and promote speedy economic development. The vocal opposition to the government has mainly come from politicians and students of the urban centers of Karachi, Lahore, Peshawar, Dacca, and Chittagong.

Ayub's approach to Pakistan's politics is similar to that of the British regime in India. The British felt that the demand for representative government and political independence was largely confined to urban groups, particularly the city lawyers, and therefore, if they were held in check, it would be relatively easy to control the rural areas.[2] Ayub has followed the same strategy in controlling political activity in the urban areas through measures like the Elective Bodies (Disqualification) Order, the University Ordinances, and the Press and Publications Ordinances. His system of Basic Democracy has been designed to mobilize political support in the rural areas. The present regime is similar to the British regime which also tried to manipulate various interests in order to maintain power and bring about certain limited political and economic changes. We shall see

[2] Sir Michael O'Dwyer, *India As I Knew It 1885–1925* (London: Constable & Company Ltd., 1925), pp. 408–410.

how Ayub has tried to manipulate the rural interests and even certain urban interests so that his regime may carry on its task of economic development.

Politics at the Urban Level

Refugees in the cities of Karachi and Hyderabad constitute about half the population of these cities. Most of them have come from parts of India like the United Provinces, Hyderabad, Bihar, which are regarded as non-agreed areas in the sense that the government of Pakistan has not been able to come to any clear understanding with the government of India as to how the properties and assets left by these people should be exchanged for properties and assets left by Hindu refugees in Pakistan. The present government of Pakistan has taken the view that the claims for compensation made by these refugees are too high and that they should be scaled down. Furthermore, these refugees were not compelled to leave their homes, but came to Pakistan voluntarily, perhaps for better opportunities, compared to refugees from the adjoining areas of Punjab who fled because of communal killing and carnage. This policy has alienated the refugees in Karachi and Hyderabad with the result that in the January, 1965, presidential election, Ayub obtained 837 votes in Karachi as compared to 1,049 for Miss Jinnah, and in Hyderabad both candidates obtained 201 votes each. In contrast to this, a great majority of refugees living in East Pakistan supported Ayub in the presidential election because to them a strong central government offers protection against regional or separatist tendencies of East Pakistanis.

In addition to the refugees, there is the larger group of people belonging to the middle class who are by and large antagonistic towards the present regime. In the cities of West Pakistan, they feel that the rewards of economic development are largely being monopolized by a few families belonging to certain exclusive business communities like the Memons, the Bohras, the Khojas, and the Chiniotis. In East Pakistan, middle-class Bengalis feel that most of the industries are being run by entrepreneurs from West Pakistan.

The leadership of the middle class in Pakistan is largely in the hands of lawyers and journalists. Pakistani lawyers have been brought up on norms and concepts of British law and are strong advocates of the British parliamentary system. They regard Ayub's regime as an autocracy which governs largely through ordinances. They are also bitter that by restricting the electorate to 80,000 Basic Democrats or Union Councillors, a great majority of whom come from rural areas, the present regime has ensured the exclusion of most of those politicians who oppose it. The government has gone a step further in its attempts to prevent the election of members who are strongly opposed to the present regime by resorting to what the opposition critics would term gerrymandering tactics.[3] Secondly, Ayub has not only barred a large number of former political leaders from contesting for political offices, but has also set up a Constitution under which the National Assembly has neither the power of removing a government in which it has no confidence, as under the parliamentary system, nor the power of withholding supplies which is available under the American presidential system.

Another group which has often tried to lead forces of opposition is that of university students. In the universities of Karachi, Panjab (Lahore), and Dacca, in all 75,310 students appeared for university examinations in 1959–60.[4] The education that they receive has by and large a Western and liberal bias and they feel that in a country where the great majority of people are illiterate, the university students have to be both intellectual and political leaders. The student movements in East Pakistan reflect the political alertness of Bengalis and their regional demands for better representation in industry, commerce, and government services. Students have become increasingly restive in West Pakistan as well, with demonstrations in Karachi, the urban areas of Sind, and particularly in Peshawar, where they represent Pathan regionalism. Indeed, students all over Pakistan have been agitating against the University Ordinances which have empowered the university authorities to take action against students and university teachers. In certain cases, the government in East Pakistan has withdrawn degrees from students who have participated in student demonstrations and which sometimes have resulted in violence.

Ayub has tried to insulate the emerging political parties from the influence of the former politicians by disqualifying the politicians from becoming members or officeholders of a political party or even associating with the activities of a political party.[5] The government has armed itself with so much power that it can legally prevent any news-

[3] The leader of the opposition in the last National Assembly filed a writ petition alleging that in his constituency of Kohat votes of Tribal Areas were included. *Dawn,* March 12, 1965. Basic Democrats from Tribal Areas are nominated by government officers, unlike other areas where they are elected. There are several other cases of governmental gerrymandering.

[4] This figure has been derived from *The Pakistan Statistical Yearbook 1962* (Karachi: Central Statistical Office, 1962), p. 357.

[5] First, certain politicians were disqualified from holding any public office on charges of misconduct or corruption under the Elective Bodies (Disqualification) Order, 1959. These EBDOed politicians were further disqualified from becoming members or officeholders of a political party by the Political Parties Act, 1962, Act III of 1962, Gazette of Pakistan Extraordinary, July 16, 1962, printed in *The All-Pakistan Legal Decisions* (PLD), December, 1962, pp. 698–700. Later they were barred even from associating with the activities of a political party under the Political Parties (Amend-

16 PARTIES AND ELECTIONS

paper from voicing criticism of the Government. According to the
Press and Publications Ordinances of the two provinces, a newspaper
cannot print reports or editorials which are either criticisms of the
government policy in general or its policy towards certain provinces or
regions. In East Pakistan, criticism of the government, despite such
restrictions, has continued. Thus, citizens are not likely to become
law-abiding in a country where the government itself is not in a
position to enforce its laws. The government's policy has incurred
the implacable hostility of all opposition forces and the dangers to
Pakistan's political stability arise from this attitude. Normally, the
opposition forces through their criticisms either hope to extract certain
concessions from the government or to persuade the electorate to
support them in the next election so that the existing government may
be removed. The present regime does not seem to tolerate either of
the roles of the opposition.

Under the new system of elections in Pakistan, 80,000 Basic
Democrats or Union Councillors, 40,000 from each province, are
elected by adult franchise, and these 80,000 Basic Democrats then
elect a President, the National Assembly, and the two Provincial
Assemblies.[6] In the October-November, 1964, elections for Basic
Democrats the pro-government Muslim League, called the Pakistan
Muslim League, very shrewdly did not nominate any government
candidates because the government was perhaps confident that it
would be able through patronage and pressure to win over a large
number of Basic Democrats to their side. In addition, by deciding to
hold the presidential elections prior to the National Assembly elections,
the President ensured maximum support for himself. If the National
Assembly elections had been held earlier, the government, by giving
its support to one of the faction leaders in a rural area, would automatically antagonize others. This could be avoided by holding the
presidential elections first.[7]

---

ment) Ordinance, 1963, Ordinance I of 1963, Gazette of Pakistan Extraordinary, January 7, 1963, printed in *The All-Pakistan Legal Decisions* (PLD),
February, 1963, pp. 11–12.

[6] Election at the primary level is on an adult franchise basis. There are
about 1,000 to 1,500 voters in each constituency who elect a Basic Democrat.
The 80,000 Basic Democrats elect a President, but for the election of the
National Assembly and the Provincial Assemblies, they are grouped into
constituencies. Thus, for the National Assembly, each constituency has on
an average 533 voters.

[7] In order to hold the presidential election prior to the National Assembly
elections, the Constitution had to be amended and this was done through
the Constitution (Second) Amendment Act, 1964, Act VI of 1964. Text
given in Government of Pakistan, Ministry of Law and Parliamentary

The five parties which formed the Combined Opposition Party (COP) with Miss Jinnah as their presidential candidate tended to nominate their candidates in the elections for Basic Democrats. Each party had its own pockets of strength, and since the government was expected to use pressure and patronage, they hoped to counteract these weapons by nominating the party faithfuls. To nominate candidates for 80,000 seats, however, would strain the resources of any organized party and particularly parties in Pakistan, which had drawn most of their party workers from urban areas, were grossly inequipped for this task, for their organizations had been practically inactive ever since Martial Law. In addition, the Awami League and the National Awami Party in East Pakistan in their competition for political support, nominated rival candidates in the elections for Basic Democrats.[8]

The Combined Opposition Party (COP) consisted of the Muslim League, otherwise known as the Council Muslim League, (the Muslim League had splintered into two factions, the government faction known as the Conventionist Muslim League, but which called itself the Pakistan Muslim League, and the anti-government faction known as the Council Muslim League), the Awami League, the National Awami Party, the Jamaat-i-Islami, and the Nizam-i-Islam Party. The Council Muslim League was strong only in West Pakistan, particularly in several areas of Punjab, refugee areas of Karachi, Hyderabad City, and other scattered areas in Sind. With the exception of a few refugee leaders in urban areas, most of its influential leaders were those landowners of West Pakistan who had often cooperated with Daultana and who were mildly progressive and modernist in their outlook on social issues such as land reforms, foreign policy, social justice, etc.

The Awami League was strong in East Pakistan. It had been originally organized by Suhrawardy and had built up support through patronage when it was in office in East Pakistan with interrupted intervals from 1956–58 and by championing the cause of autonomy for East Pakistan. In addition to its support from middle-class groups in East Pakistan, the Awami League was financially supported by the small but growing number of capitalists in East Pakistan who were interested in keeping the East Pakistan economy free from the domination of West Pakistan capitalists. The National Awami Party in East Pakistan, which stood to the left of the Awami League in matters

---

Affairs, *The Constitution of the Islamic Republic of Pakistan* (As modified up to the 12th October, 1964). (Karachi: The Manager of Publications, 1964), pp. 165–168.

[8] "Dissensions in COP Inevitable," *The Pakistan Times,* November 27, 1964.

of foreign and economic policy, was led by Maulana Bhashani, who had tried to organize a strong wing of peasants in the party with varying success.

The National Awami Party in West Pakistan was led by Khan Abdul Ghaffar Khan and his lieutenants in the Frontier and other Sindhi and Baluch leaders who all stood for the breakup of the integrated province of West Pakistan into the former provinces of Sind, the North-West Frontier Province, and West Punjab. (Baluch leaders also wanted a separate province for Baluchistan, which was formerly a centrally administered area.) The fourth component was the Jamaat-i-Islami, led by Maulana Maudoodi, consisting of no more than 1,500 card-carrying members, but claiming the support of thousands of citizens, particularly in urban centers of Karachi, Lahore, and other smaller towns of Punjab. It drew its support from those lower middle-class Muslims who felt alienated from the government. The lower middle class had acquired education recently and was neither sufficiently Westernized nor privileged enough to be included in the upper-class Muslims who were either industrial and commercial entrepreneurs or civil servants belonging to the superior cadres of the bureaucracy. This group found their psychological anchor in the program of the Jamaat-i-Islami with its uncompromising stress on the revival of Islamic values and the establishment of an Islamic state. The Jamaat, consisting of this band of dedicated workers, was the envy of every political party.[9] Even after political parties had been allowed to revive under the Political Parties Act, 1962, the Jamaat was banned by the two provincial governments in January, 1964. The government of West Pakistan, explaining its decision, pointed out that the Jamaat was making efforts "to create cells in government administration and the workers of the Jamaat infiltrated into various governmental, labour, and student organizations" with the real purpose of suborning the loyalty of government services.[10] This ban was finally removed by the Supreme Court on September 26, 1964.[11] Thus, the Jamaat had barely a month to get reorganized for the elections of Basic Democrats held

[9] Membership of the Jamaat is restricted to about 1,500 persons and there are said to be only one hundred paid workers. The support of the Jamaat is not confined to members alone, for there are supposed to be thousands of initiates, sympathizers and supporters. "Jama'at-i-Islami — A Mixture of Opposites," *Morning News*, March 7, 1965.

[10] Press note of the government of West Pakistan cited in *The All-Pakistan Legal Decisions* (PLD), October, 1964, p. 780.

[11] Saiyyid Abdul A'la Maudoodi, Misbahul Islam Faruqi and Umar Farooq *v*. The Government of West Pakistan and The Government of East Pakistan, and The Province of East Pakistan *v*. Tamizuddin Ahmad and The Government of Pakistan. *The All-Pakistan Legal Decisions* (PLD), October, 1964, pp. 673–792.

in November, 1964. After the elections were over, the Jamaat produced a report in which it alleged that the government had resorted to corrupt malpractices involving inflation of electoral registers by bogus voters, delimiting constituencies in favor of its own candidates, rejecting nomination papers of opposition candidates, etc. This report went into minute details to produce evidence in support of these charges,[12] indicating that the Jamaat had an extremely well organized machinery of party workers who could produce such detailed evidence.

The Nizam-i-Islam Party also had a religious orientation, though its fundamentalism was not as rigid as that of the Jamaat. Its followers in East Pakistan were mostly people educated in religious institutions known as *madrasahs*. Its leader in East Pakistan was a young lawyer and vigorous spokesman of the opposition in the National Assembly, Farid Ahmad. In West Pakistan, it was led by Chaudhri Muhammad Ali, a former Prime Minister and a civil servant who, being a member of the Arain community, enjoyed considerable support in a city like Lyallpur and in certain areas of the district of Montgomery.

The Combined Opposition Party (COP) produced a Nine-Point Program, which included the restoration of the parliamentary system of government with complete legislative and budgetary powers to be vested in the National and Provincial Assemblies, removal of economic disparity between the two wings within a period of ten years, a number of economic measures to help the common man and reverse the trend towards concentration of wealth in the hands of a few families, and amendment of the Family Laws Ordinance to bring it in accord with Islamic law.[13] It was obvious that parties like the Jamaat-i-Islami in accepting a woman, Fatima Jinnah, as a presidential candidate, and the Awami League, in agreeing to take a moderate stand on the question of economic disparity and Bengali regionalism, were willing to modify some of their rigid approaches, presumably because they were eager to produce a united front against Ayub's regime. It may also be noted that the National Awami Party in West Pakistan was willing for the sake of unity in the COP to forego its insistence on the breakup of the integrated West Pakistan province into its former cultural and linguistic units.[14]

Miss Jinnah's great advantage was that she was the sister of the founder of Pakistan and had been detached from the political conflicts that had plagued Pakistan after the founder's death. The sight of this venerable but dynamic lady moving about in the streets of big cities and even in the rural areas of a Muslim country was both moving and

---

[12] "White Paper of the Jamaat-i-Islami — Ten Days of Karachi Elections" (Urdu), *Aain,* December 5, 1964.

[13] For a text of the COP Nine-Point program, see *Dawn,* October 31, 1964.

[14] *Ibid.*

unique. People referred to her as *Madar-i-Millat*, mother of the nation. She attacked the President as a power-hungry dictator who had conspired for years to seize power. Her campaign generated such tremendous public enthusiasm that most of the press people agreed that if the contest were by direct election, she would win against Ayub. The campaign that Miss Jinnah conducted was in the old style, intended to create such a massive public upsurge in the urban areas that it would soon spread into the rural areas. The mistake she made, however, was that in her repeated pledges to restore parliamentary democracy, she created a clear impression that under the system of adult franchise, Basic Democrats would lose their importance and particularly their right to vote in the presidential and National Assembly elections. Miss Jinnah tried to retract, but the impression had been created that the Basic Democrats would perhaps be relegated to the position of local councillors and the rural areas would lose the funds and the attention that they had received under Ayub.

Ayub enjoyed certain clear advantages which his opponent could not counteract effectively. For example, he held the urban areas under control. He had not only prevented the old politicians from campaigning against him by placing legal bars on their political activities, but his provincial governments also frustrated the campaign activities of others by placing them under frequent arrests during the election campaign. He could claim that the country had made steady economic progress under his regime. But he was aware that a politician with a gifted tongue could arouse public indignation against him. All politicians with such gifts had been silenced, and it came as a surprise to everyone that Miss Jinnah could mount such a vigorous campaign. She capitalized on Ayub's weaknesses. Ayub, in spite of all his achievements, was not a charismatic leader like Nasser. Miss Jinnah in her campaign tried to tarnish his image by accusing him of having helped his relatives to establish the Ghandhara Industries, a car assembly plant and the successor of General Motors of Pakistan. Above all, in a poor country like Pakistan, there is always a fund of ill will or resentment against the government because no government could in a short time do more than a modicum to alleviate poverty and suffering among the vast majority. Thus, wherever Miss Jinnah went, she was greeted by vast crowds. Even government party workers conceded after the presidential election that the government had won the election, but lost the people. One of the Awami League leaders told the author, "When we saw so much upsurge, we felt that we did not have to do much canvassing."

It was this simple fact that did not enter the optimistic calculations of the opposition, namely, that the Basic Democrats could resist the tide of public opinion. Thus, the general secretary of the National Awami Party and a member of the steering committee of the Combined Opposition Party, giving district-wise figures of East and West Pakistan to show how the Combined Opposition Party had been successful in electing Basic Democrats, claimed that 63,000 out of 80,000 Basic Democrats would vote for Miss Jinnah.[15]

When the results were announced, it was found that President Ayub had polled 49,951 votes (63.3 per cent of the total vote).[16] The COP was confident that East Pakistan would stand solidly behind Miss Jinnah. The general secretary of the East Pakistan Awami League claimed a week before the polling date that she was likely to win 80 per cent of the votes in there, but the actual results indicated that she obtained only 46.6 per cent of the vote in that province.[17]

The percentage of votes polled by Miss Jinnah in the large urban areas was higher than what she polled throughout the country. Her showing in large urban centers of East and West Pakistan was about the same as the strength she displayed in East Pakistan. Some political observers in East Pakistan felt that if the urban electorate in East Pakistan had been polled on an adult franchise basis, Miss Jinnah would have obtained support from a great majority of the voters. Her support in the large urban centers may be seen in Table 13. (See page 222.)

It is often said that East Pakistanis by and large have greater political consciousness than the people of West Pakistan and that they tend to vote against every government in power. It was expected that their sense of grievance against Ayub's government would be even greater because he had put an end to the parliamentary system through which East Pakistanis, who constituted a majority, could exert their political influence against the bureaucratic domination of West Pakistan. Furthermore, in the eyes of a number of East Pakistanis, Ayub's government depended on the support of the Pakistan army, which was predominantly a West Pakistan institution. Ayub upset all such calculations when he won majority support in East Pakistan. (He obtained 53.1 per cent of the vote in East Pakistan as compared to 73.6 per cent in West Pakistan.) This helped his national image and the problem of national integration loomed less dangerously. It was quite possible that if Ayub had lost the East Pakistan vote and won the election on the basis of his considerable majority in West Pakistan, separatist forces in East Pakistan would have been sufficiently encouraged to start thinking in terms of secession.

[15] *The Pakistan Times,* November 21, 1964.

[16] *Presidential Election Result 1965* (Rawalpindi: Election Commission Pakistan), p. 24.

[17] *The Dacca Times,* December 20, 1964.

Table 13

Voting in Some of the Urban Centers in the Presidential Election of 1965

Cities in West Pakistan	Total Votes	Ayub	Jinnah	Other Two Candidates	Invalid	Total Votes Cast
Karachi	1907	837	1049	4	13	1903
Hyderabad	406	201	201	0	3	405
Lahore	1210	819	371	1	17	1208
Lyallpur	397	274	123	0	0	397
Rawalpindi	318	202	106	2	8	318
Peshawar	521	299	215	0	6	520
Cities in East Pakistan						
Dacca	558	199	352	1	3	555
Chittagong	334	181	151	0	2	334
Khulna	283	167	113	2	0	282
Comilla	287	156	128	0	2	286
Totals	6221	3335	2809	10	54	6208

Ayub won 53.7 per cent of the vote in these urban areas.
Miss Jinnah won 45.2 per cent of the vote in these urban areas.

East Pakistan can roughly be divided into two areas. The eastern part of this province consists of Dacca and Chittagong divisions. These are economically and politically more advanced areas because, besides Dacca and Chittagong, which are educational and industrial centers of the province, districts like Mymensingh, Sylhet, and Noakhali have often displayed a high degree of political consciousness. Compared to this eastern part of the province, the northern and western areas consisting of Rajshahi and Khulna divisions have been industrially less developed and politically less advanced. Now and again political leaders of these areas complained that the provincial government neglected them and that most of the industrial and commercial development was largely confined to Chittagong and Dacca divisions. In 1955, a group of legislators from these areas issued a statement that a separate province consisting of the northern districts should be created. When the Constitution Commission was interviewing political leaders in East Pakistan during 1960, it was reported that most of the leaders from the northern districts who came to testify before the Commission said that they were not in favor of parliamentary democracy and that they preferred the presidential system under which a strong President could allocate larger resources to the northern areas than the parliamentary regimes had done. The present regime, by encouraging the economic development of these areas, created the distinct feeling that they could expect a better deal from a strong government like that of Ayub than from political regimes which would be more under the influence of political forces and economic interests concentrated in Dacca and Chittagong. It can be said that by and large the western part of East Pakistan voted solidly for Ayub, whereas the eastern part of East Pakistan voted for Miss Jinnah. Miss Jinnah did make a few inroads in Ayub's areas of support, like the Nilphamari subdivision in the Rangpur district and two other subdivisions, Magura and Narail, in the Jessore district. But Ayub penetrated areas of the eastern areas of East Pakistan: the Chittagong district and subdivisions in Comilla and Sylhet districts. Several other factors helped Ayub's impressive election returns in the western half of East Pakistan. There was a concentration of refugees in Khulna and Rajshahi divisions who tended to support Ayub. With the exception of the small Rajshahi University, there were not many university students who could spread out and activate the countryside against Ayub. Maulana Bhashani, leader of the National Awami Party, who had considerable influence in the Rajshahi division, did not campaign actively for Miss Jinnah, probably because he did not want to upset Ayub's foreign policy which was veering steadily towards increasing friendship with China. Politicians opposed to Ayub concentrated their electioneering activities mostly in areas which they knew best and did not pay much attention to the northern

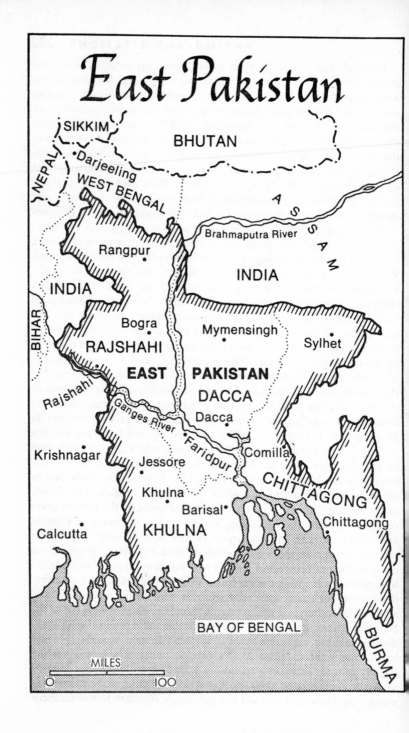

East Pakistan

SIKKIM

BHUTAN

NEPAL

•Darjeeling

WEST BENGAL

ASSAM

Brahmaputra River

Rangpur

INDIA

INDIA

BIHAR

Bogra

Mymensingh

Sylhet

RAJSHAHI

EAST PAKISTAN

Rajshahi

DACCA

Ganges River

Dacca

Krishnagar

Faridpur

Jessore

Comilla

Khulna

CHITTAGONG

Barisal•

Calcutta

KHULNA

Chittagong

BAY OF BENGAL

BURMA

MILES

0   100

districts. Pakistani politicians, not being used to much campaigning, tended to campaign only in areas where they expected large and enthusiastic crowds. This is a part of the style of Pakistani politics which is largely dominated by fiery orators who like to declaim and denounce before crowds who wish to be entertained in this fashion. Both sides therefore concentrated on areas where they were already strong.

Politics — Old Style and New Style

This brings us to a characteristic of Pakistani politics which has been present ever since the creation of Pakistan. During the pre-Martial Law regime, in some of the large cities like Karachi, Lahore and Dacca, political meetings were dominated by what might roughly be described as Roman mobs. These consisted mostly of refugees and industrial workers who for a small remuneration and transportation would assemble at meetings to cheer or heckle speakers. As pointed out earlier, political parties, in order to build support throughout the country, first needed vast crowds at their public meetings in the urban areas. Once this was obtained, they thought it was relatively easy to move into the rural areas for additional support. In order to organize such public meetings, they needed speakers with oratorical gifts and the financial support of big industrialists and merchants so that crowds might be assembled and meetings organized.

Under the new style of politics which came into being after the lifting of Martial Law, adult franchise had disappeared and the electors were the Basic Democrats. This meant that orators were not needed so much as political workers who would approach the Basic Democrats on a person-to-person basis and canvass for their support by promising them material advantages of various kinds or by reminding them of political and other debts that they owed to them individually or to the party. In this kind of politics, there could not be any constant party or personal loyalties. These shifted almost from day to day and only the government with its enormous resources of patronage and coercion had a distinct advantage. The president of the West Pakistan Muslim League, who was also the provincial Finance Minister, said that at first only 54 per cent of the elected Basic Democrats from Karachi were behind President Ayub. Still later this figure was raised to 58 per cent.

Today 66 per cent of the Karachi MECs [Members of the Electoral College] are behind President Ayub. By the time the nation goes to polls for the Presidential election this support from Karachi will rise to 70 per cent. We are gaining as the time is passing.[18]

[18] *The Pakistan Times,* December 4, 1964.

It was significant that the President placed Muhammad Shoaib, the Central Finance Minister, in charge of the Muslim League organization in Karachi to maximize his electoral support there. It was alleged that the government Muslim League was willing to spend any amount of money to win over the Basic Democrats to the President's side. This was denied by the Finance Minister, but it was obvious that the principal supporters of the President in Karachi were the business magnates and, as we shall see later, that a large number of the government Muslim League candidates in cities like Karachi, Lahore, Lyallpur, and Rawalpindi were business magnates. Election results were not in doubt, and these industrialists were dependent upon government support for import of raw materials and other products.

As for the crowds that flocked to Miss Jinnah's meetings, Ayub knew that this did not necessarily mean that Basic Democrats were behind her. Nevertheless, he was deeply disturbed that the vast crowds at her meetings would create the impression that the people at large were behind her and that Ayub had won the election by merely pressuring the pliable Basic Democrats. If Miss Jinnah could attract crowds, so should he in order to maintain his political prestige. Unfortunately, his party, the Muslim League, mostly consisted of pro-government "hangers-on" and not active political workers. Therefore, he was forced to rely upon the services of police and other officers for collecting crowds for his meetings. A photostatic copy of a letter issued by the Deputy Commissioner to about one hundred bus and truck owners in Rangpur town in East Pakistan asking them to place their buses and trucks at the disposal of the government so that crowds might be brought to the President's meeting was published.[19]

The senior police officers in Pakistan were intelligent, university graduates who had been trained in political intelligence work. In selecting the proper stadium or grounds for the President's meetings, in distributing pamphlets, in having posters put up and in using ingenious methods for drawing crowds to meetings, these officers functioned as the President's political workers. They were far more useful to him than the officeholders of the moribund Muslim League organization, and their task of pressuring the Basic Democrats in town and cities into voting for the President was even less difficult: the senior police officer would speak to the more influential BDs and his subordinate and junior officers would speak to subleaders and individual BDs. The author was assured that these BDs came to the officers for guidance and that no coercive methods were used. This political role of the civil servants is not unique to Pakistan. The governments of

---

[19] *The Dacca Times,* November 6, 1964.

both India and Pakistan have inherited their existing systems of bureaucracy in which civil servants exercise political and administrative control over every sphere of activity in the districts. Even in India, where more elections have been held, it is well known that in a state like West Bengal, for example, the Subdivisional Officers expect promotions if Congress candidates are elected.

The present regime, working under the influence of bureaucrats and an army officer like Ayub, has tried to inject into the political system a considerable degree of orderliness. It does not regard political activity or campaigning as merely consisting of mass meetings where people gather partly to be entertained and partly to hear some of their own prejudices or beliefs being expressed in grand style by the orators. The Election Commission organized ten Confrontation meetings, six in West Pakistan and four in East Pakistan, in which the four presidential candidates[20] were called upon first to put forward their views and their programs before the Basic Democrats and later answer questions. These meetings were presided over by a former judge of the High Court, who was also a member of the Election Commission. In some of the meetings, particularly in Karachi and in East Pakistan, there was considerable heckling.[21] The Election Commission also organized Projection meetings during the National Assembly elections in which the rival candidates were called upon to present their views and answer questions. These meetings were usually presided over by Session Judges.

Issues and Interests

The present regime has taken pride in the fact that under the system of indirect elections, the electors, namely, the Basic Democrats, over 80 per cent of whom are literate, are vastly superior to the general population, of whom over 80 per cent are illiterate. Could it be said that under this system of indirect elections, the quality of political debate would be much higher than it would be in the case of mass meetings under adult franchise? In the Confrontation meetings, the presidential candidates did concentrate on issues and their respective programs, but the two candidates, Ayub and Jinnah, often indulged in bitter broadsides against each other. Miss Jinnah denounced her oppo-

[20] The four presidential candidates were Field Marshal Muhammad Ayub Khan, K. M. Kamal, Mian Bashir Ahmad, and Mohtarama Miss Fatima Jinnah.

[21] In Karachi, the Basic Democrats, who were raising slogans against President Ayub, were warned by the Presiding Justice that they would be prosecuted if they continued to disturb the meeting. *The Times of India,* December 18, 1964.

nent as a dictator and denied his claims regarding economic development of the country under his regime. Ayub's usual attack was that his opponent was supported by five political parties, three of which were not loyal to Pakistan. But Ayub did try to link stable prices and economic development to political stability and a strong presidential government. His supporters and even some of the newspapers have claimed that he did emerge as a superior candidate in the Confrontation meetings because of his amazing and detailed mastery of the economic problems of different areas and the way his government had tried to tackle or solve them.

However, both candidates tried to exploit the most potent issue, namely, the threat of India. Miss Jinnah's line of attack was that Ayub, by coming to terms with India over the Indus Waters dispute, had surrendered control over the rivers to India. Ayub pointed out that political instability resulting from Miss Jinnah's election would encourage India to attack and enslave Pakistan. In one of the meetings organized by the President's supporters in an area where most of the BDs were refugees, the author found that the President's supporters tried to drive home the point that a weak government in Pakistan under Miss Jinnah would either embolden India to attack Pakistan, or the Hindus in India to slaughter the Muslims there. "Muslims in Delhi are praying with tears in their eyes and saying, 'Oh, God, give victory to Ayub so that we may be saved.'"

What kind of issues and interests emerged in the Projection meetings held during the National Assembly elections? Three of the four government Muslim League candidates in Karachi were representatives of big industrial interests who tended to concentrate on economic development as the main issue of the campaign. Their opponents attacked the regime for having allowed concentration of wealth in the hands of a few wealthy families and for having subjected the people to the heavy burden of taxation. In cities like Karachi, Lyallpur, and Rawalpindi, some of the government candidates were also representatives of big industrial interests, who made promises regarding the improvements in health and education that they would try to bring about in their cities.

Even though a number of candidates in urban areas, both from the government and the opposition parties, were supported by relatively modern associational groups like political parties, business associations, or trade unions, the community and kinship loyalties which some of these candidates invoked and which were important factors in influencing the votes of the Basic Democrats should be taken into account. In Lahore, candidates belonging to the Arain and Kashmiri communities would expect support from Basic Democrats belonging to these communities. In one of the constituencies of Karachi (NW 4), appeals were made by the prominent Baluch Basic Democrats, presumably to those members of the Electoral College who belonged to the Baluch community, to vote for the government candidate who came from a wealthy industrial family, but did not belong to the Baluch community.[22] The government candidate knew that since his opponent came from the Baluch community, a large number of Baluch Basic Democrats might vote for the opposition candidate unless the influence of other prominent Baluch leaders was brought to bear against his Baluch rival. This indicates that a candidate who was supported by the government and had adequate financial resources could still obtain the support of a community to which he did not belong if he could enlist the support of prominent leaders of that community. In Rawalpindi, an opposition candidate was confident that he would be successful in winning the seat "which includes areas where he and his family have deep-rooted relationships with the people."[23] The government candidate, who was a wealthy businessman, overcame such factors, for he won the election.

It is clear that under the present regime even at the urban level there is not much wheeling and dealing among the interest groups, both traditional and associational, and the political leaders or parties mainly because the National Assembly in Pakistan has not been given any effective power either in legislation or over the budget. Political contests under such a system are largely mock fights in which both the contestants know that in most of the cases the government is going to emerge as the winner. This leads to frustration and sometimes anomic violence. Contests between political parties in Pakistan have often been presented to the Pakistani citizen in highly emotional or affective terms so that there are only triumphs with their heroes and national tragedies brought about by traitors. The creation of Pakistan was a triumph of Jinnah against overwhelming odds — all political parties agree on this phase of Pakistan's political development. But a difference arises over the interpretation of later developments, for these, according to the supporters of the present regime, were a series of acts perpetrated by the villainous politicians who brought the country to the verge of political chaos and economic bankruptcy. It was only the heroic and timely seizure of power by Ayub which transformed this tragedy into a triumph.

When one asks an industrial worker or a government clerk what his views are regarding the political issues and the presidential contest, unless he is a partisan, he complains in bitter terms that no matter

[22] *Dawn,* March 8 and 10, 1965.
[23] *Ibid.,* March 15, 1965.

what happens, he is not likely to derive any tangible benefits. Cheaper housing, cheaper food, better schools for his children, salaries and wages which can keep him at or above subsistence level are not things which he can either demand or extract from the government; they are gifts which he may get if there is political stability in the country. In this kind of politics, therefore, it is difficult to detect any clear issues related to identifiable interests. But economic development cannot arrest political change; often it leads to political changes. As a result of economic development and urbanization, certain regional groups, economic interests, and students are getting restless. If they cannot obtain redress by pressuring political parties in the parliament, they resort to violence, and they have found from experience that violence can extract certain concessions even from an autocratic government. The arrest of the late H. S. Suhrawardy in January, 1962, led to violent student demonstrations in East Pakistan, which in turn persuaded Ayub to make tangible concessions in the form of greater allocations to East Pakistan and to insert a clause in the Constitution declaring that every effort would be made to bring about parity between the provinces in all spheres of the central government. Similarly, student violence against the University Ordinances resulted in the government appointing a Commission to look into the grievances of students.[24]

Politics at the Rural Level

Political scientists, borrowing from the vocabulary of sociologists, have pointed out that the political system in agricultural or rural societies of developing nations is characterized by "particularistic, ascriptive, and functionally diffuse norms and structures." To translate this into Pakistani terms, the social structure of rural areas in West Pakistan consists of *baradaris* (groups of families with blood relations with one another living in a village or villages) and tribes with their feudal and religious leaders or spiritual guides. To all this, we must add two more characteristics. Rural society in each of the areas of Pakistan is fragmented so that there are conflicts between communities or tribes, between rival landlords, and between rival *pirs* (spiritual guides). Secondly, powerful as the landlords and the *pirs* may be in their respective areas, they can hold or exercise this power only with the support or connivance of district officials.

In countries like India and Pakistan the problem is how to make the local social structures conform with political systems which have been

[24] Student demonstrations in Karachi against the University Ordinance during early December, 1964, resulted in violence and police firing. The government appointed a commission to look into the problems and grievances of students.

introduced under foreign influence. In India, the Congress Party has tried to bridge the gap between the two so that members of castes and tribes have been joining the Congress Party and at the same time extracting concessions from the government by using the Congress machinery. In Pakistan the present regime can claim that the new political system of Basic Democracies accommodates the kind of social structure which exists in the countryside. Under this system, an attempt is made to include the rural influentials in the Union Councils, which operate at the lowest level, and the Union Councillors (80,000 throughout Pakistan) serve as electoral colleges for the election of the President and the three legislatures. Since Union Councillors are under the influence of landlords, *pirs*, and government officers, it would be interesting to see what new patterns of political relationships are emerging in Pakistan and how free or controlled are elections in that country.

West Pakistan

It is well known that the Sindhi peasant, the *hari*, is the most dependent and servile person in Pakistan.

> Whenever the hari is in serious trouble, be it on account of his lack of finance, his social relations with his fellowmen, his implication in police cases, the ill-health of members of his family, the abduction of his women, the loss of his bullocks, the procurement of his bare necessities in consumer's goods, the recruitment of casual labour to aid him in harvesting and weeding his crops or for other reasons, it is to his zamindar that he first appeals for help.[25]

In spite of Ayub's land reforms, the Sindhi peasant is still utterly dependent upon the landlord, for he can be evicted. However, it may be noted that the landlord can help or cause trouble for a peasant only with the support of revenue and police officials.

Another influential in the social structure of Sind is the *pir*. The two biggest *pirs* are the Pir of Pagaro and the Makhdum of Hala, who is also a member of the National Assembly. It is said that the Pir of Pagaro exercises complete hold over his followers, who are known as the Hurs. They worship him as a man endowed with miraculous powers. If they suspect anyone of being disrespectful towards the Pir, they would go to the extent of killing him. In one of the meetings that the President addressed in the interior, it was reported that 250,000 Hurs were present.[26] The total following of the Pir is reported to consist of over 900,000. The two *pirs*, the Pir of Pagaro and the

[25] *Report of the Government Hari Enquiry Committee 1947–48* (Government of Sind, n.d.), p. 7.
[26] *The Pakistan Times,* December 6, 1964.

Makhdum of Hala, who are opposed to each other, support the President. Thus, often the President, after speaking to an enthusiastic crowd in the Pir of Pagaro's areas of support, would move to the adjoining areas where he would be feted by the Makhdum of Hala and his supporters.

The bigger landlords in Sind, who are known as the *mirs,* belong to the Baluch tribe, which constitutes about 23 per cent of the Muslim population of Sind.[27] There are several other smaller tribes. Several tribal chieftains announced the support of their tribes for the President during the presidential election.[28]

One of the main characteristics of this social structure is that in a district or a village one *mir* is in conflict with another *mir*. This conflict may have originated generations ago over land disputes or cattle thefts, etc. Among other reasons, it was because of this conflict-ridden social structure that the President decided to hold the presidential elections first so that all the *pirs* and *mirs* might support him: it would not hurt his interests too much if these people fought against each other for seats of the National Assembly as long as the winner finally joined the government party. It is clear why they all support the government. First of all, because of the disappearance of the provincial government of Sind after the integration of West Pakistan, they are not in a strong position to bargain with a government like that of West Pakistan which sits far away in Lahore and which does not depend exclusively upon their support. On the other hand, the landlords need government support because in order to evict troublesome peasants, they need the support of the revenue and police officials. If they take a stand against the government on any issue, the Deputy Commissioner or the police officials can start cases against them. Even if such cases are false and the landlords seek the protection of the courts, they will still be involved in expense and worry. Besides trying not to displease the government, landlords have to make every effort to keep it on their side for positive benefits like the allotment of a sugar mill in their area. The government, under the present circumstances, would lend support only to that landlord who impressed them through the number of Basic Democrats he controlled in an area or a district. This means that the government did not have to use the government machinery too openly or excessively in the presidential elections. The Deputy Commissioner merely had

[27] *Report of the Government Hari Enquiry Committee 1947–48, op. cit.,* p. 4.

[28] For a statement of the chiefs of Gabole and Chandio tribes, see *The Pakistan Times,* December 3, 1964. For the statement of the Chief of Khoso tribe, see *The Pakistan Times,* December 28, 1964. For that of the Chief of Maher tribe, see *Morning News,* January 2, 1965.

to watch that some of the potential malcontents (because they expected that they might not get government support in the National Assembly elections) did not work against the President and endanger his election in the district.

Once the presidential election was over, it was clear that the opposition felt disheartened and was in no position to offer any strong candidates of their own in the National Assembly elections except in a few constituencies. Since the President enjoyed support from both rival landlords or *pirs* in an area, he did not want to alienate either by taking sides in the National Assembly elections. The government did offer the Muslim League endorsement to certain candidates, but election returns indicated that government machinery was not used against the Independent candidates. The following election figures show that the margin of difference between Ayub and Miss Jinnah was greater (which may suggest the use of government machinery) than that between rival landlords in the National Assembly elections.[29]

Jacobabad

Presidential	Ayub	Jinnah
	341	135
National Assembly	PML	Independent
	290	194

Nawabshah

Presidential	Ayub	Jinnah
	454	189
National Assembly	PML	Independent
	376	264

Tharparkar

Presidential	Ayub	Jinnah
	466	203
National Assembly	PML	Independent
	234 (defeated)	277

Thatta

Presidential	Ayub	Jinnah
	264	71
National Assembly	PML	Independent
	150 (defeated)	186

The opposition must have felt frustrated in its futile attempts to make a dent in the rural areas when the government with all the patronage and coercive power it had at its command was manipulating

[29] Presidential election results are from *Presidential Election Result 1965*, pp. 1–25, and the National Assembly election results are from *Morning News*, March 22, 1965.

the social structure to maximize its political support. An organization like the National Awami Party would use Sindhi nationalism against the government by pointing out that Ayub and his government stood solidly behind the integrated West Pakistan province and would not allow the Sindhis to re-establish their separate province of Sind. But the National Awami Party had to work in cooperation with parties like the Council Muslim League and leaders like Chaudhri Muhammad Ali, who would not favor the disintegration of the integrated West Pakistan province. Thus, the only support that the opposition could mobilize was through the influence of certain landlords who were daring and tenacious enough to oppose the government. The COP could put up only two candidates in Sind, and both of them were for the two Hyderabad division seats, NW 70 and NW 71.

In his interview with the National Awami party workers in Sind, the author was told that the NAP workers had to be shrewd and skillful in trying to build up their party organization among the peasants. At this stage they were trying to articulate only those interests of the peasants which did not run counter to those of the big landlords. However, they felt encouraged by the fact that transistor radios had come into villages, that Ayub's land reforms were at least designed against the big landlords, and that the influence of the *pirs* was on the decline for they had ceased to be mere pious, spiritual guides and were taking part in elections which involved corruption and the use of money. In addition, the NAP workers detected the emergence of certain economic conflicts between the middle-size landowners, who were Basic Democrats, and their leaders and patrons, the *mirs* and the *pirs*. Under the Basic Democracy system, the chairmen of Union Councils may be elected to *Tehsil* and District Councils and thus become aware of the business or commercial opportunities that exist in towns or cities. They would also like to buy cash crops like rice or cotton in the countryside and make a profit by selling them in the town markets. This brings them into conflict with the big landlord who has so far monopolized this business.[30]

[30] The author was told that the BDs from rural areas had become sufficiently exposed to towns and cities and were trying to buy cash crops in the countryside with a view to selling them in the town market. In this way, they came into conflict with the big landlord who was interested in buying the entire stock in the country and selling it in the city. Correspondence columns in *Dawn* include letters written by aggrieved farmers over questions like government discrimination in banning rice cultivation around certain towns to prevent water logging. One of the correspondents alleged that the ban was not uniformly imposed all around the towns and the ban limits were reduced in certain areas because "the farmers on the other side were more resourceful." *Dawn*, April 9, 1965. See also editorial, "A Complaint from Shikarpur," *Dawn*, March 29, 1965.

In the Punjab, the peasant was not as servile an instrument in the hands of the landlord or the *pir* as his counterpart in Sind. Here he enjoyed not only proprietory rights; he was also a member of an endogamous group of families known as the *baradari*. These communities were supposed to be descendants of Hindu castes who had been converted to Islam. Islamic egalitarianism had not allowed the excessive caste rigidity of Hinduism to develop. There were no Untouchables or Scheduled Castes, but communities could be identified like the Jats, who were scattered all over the Punjab; Rajputs and Awans with their martial traditions who lived between the Indus and the Jhelum; and the Arains, who were concentrated in Lyallpur, Montgomery, and parts of Lahore City. These communities had built up associations of their own which decided disputes within the community. They had constitutions with objectives like the promotion of solidarity within the community and protection and furtherance of the educational and economic interests of the community.[31] Unlike Sind, the Punjab also had a number of enlightened landlords. The best known among these was Daultana, a former Chief Minister of Punjab and a former Central Minister. There were others in Jhang, Campbellpur, Muzaffargarh, who were all COP candidates and who went down to defeat in the National Assembly elections. In Jhang, for example, the leading landlord was also a spiritual leader and belonged to the Shiah community. In the primary election for Basic Democrats, the supporters of this landlord were returned in a large majority. Politicians belonging to the COP and some of the landlords in Jhang alleged that coercion could overcome spiritual and political allegiance in the presidential election. A few days before the presidential polls, the secretary-general of the West Pakistan National Awami Party claimed that all the tribal chiefs of the Dera Ghazi Khan district, with the exception of two, had joined the COP, but the COP leaders found out on January 2, 1965, that the government had enough power to undermine the tribal loyalties of the BDs, for the President won 449 votes against Miss Jinnah's 268.[32] A young landlord from Dera Ghazi Khan alleged that he saw

---

[31] *Objectives and Rules and Regulations of the Jat Association of Pakistan* (Urdu), July, 1956. Organizing Committee, *Constitution of Central Awan Conference, Punjab* (Urdu) (Lahore: Chaudhri Muhammad Husain, General Secretary, n.d.). *Rules and Regulations of the Pakistan Awan Conference* (Urdu) (Lahore: n.d.). The author also has a copy of a circular issued on April 11, 1950, on behalf of the Muslim Rajput Association which states that the meeting of the Association was being called to consider ways and means by which Rajputs could protect their interests as a community in the forthcoming elections for the Punjab Assembly. Minutes of a meeting held on April 28, 1950, state that the Rajput community should try to capture all the main positions in the government.

[32] For statement of the secretary-general of the National Awami Party, see *Dawn,* December 30, 1964.

only *thanadars* (lower police officials) canvassing for the government, but he never saw Muslim League party workers working for the government. One way to explain all this is that the landlords themselves had created the feeling among their followers that they should always be on the government side with the result that when the landlords themselves went against the government, they lost support in their areas.

A scion of a leading landowning family in the district of Sargodha, home of the famous Noons and the Tiwanas, explained to the author how the Basic Democrats had to support the government:

> In our society, the arm of the law is removed from where you live. It may be twenty or thirty miles away. I may be dead before I get to law. The tendency, therefore, is to gang up . . . If somebody stole my friend's cattle, my friend is right when he bashes him up. I support my friend irrespective of whether he is right or wrong. This is a sort of insurance policy for the whole group. Living in that kind of society, you naturally vote with the group. And you vote for a leader who helps in getting one's nephew released from police lock-up.

There were certain pockets in Punjab where the landlords or the *pirs,* some of whom are known as *makhdums,* held unchallenged sway and in ten out of the forty-four constituencies in the Punjab, the government candidates were declared elected without any contests.[33] All this destroyed the myth that a landlord in West Pakistan by himself could literally command his tenants or supporters to vote according to his instructions.

In the Pathan areas or the former North-West Frontier Province, the President had won most of the Tribal Area votes long before the campaign started. These were his "pocket boroughs" because in the Tribal Areas the Basic Democrats had not been elected but nominated by the government officers known as Political Agents. Out of 2,544 votes in the Tribal Areas, Miss Jinnah could win only 66. In the Malakand Agency, she won 2 out of 1,431 votes. One of the well-known Pathan leaders of the COP pointed out to the author that these Tribal Areas were so remote that it would have taken at least two days for the Polling Officer to get to the nearest telephone, and yet Radio Pakistan was announcing results from these areas soon after the polling finished, that is, early in the evening of January 2, 1965.

In the Settled Districts, the President could not hope to walk away with the election without campaigning and making a skillful use of patronage and pressure. Particularly in the districts of Mardan, Pesha-

---

[33] *The Gazette of Pakistan Extraordinary,* April 2, 1965, p. 117f.

war, and Kohat, the COP could rely upon the grass-roots organization that the former Red Shirts of Khan Abdul Ghaffar Khan had built and who were now in the National Awami Party. This grass-roots organization of the National Awami Party in the Pathan rural areas was strong for two reasons. First, the prestige of the Red Shirts for having performed social work in the villages was high. They had become known as *Khudai Khidmatgar* (servants of God). Secondly, they had also built their organization around factions led by the *khans* (landlord leaders) in the villages. But the government enjoyed two advantages: frequent imprisonment of Red Shirt leaders after 1947 had weakened their organization; and the coercive, and patronage machinery of the government was so overwhelming that the tribal and factional loyalties of the Union Councillors could be overcome. In a by-election for the National Assembly seat from Bannu in the Frontier held in May, 1964, the government candidate belonged to one of the rival factions of the Marwat tribe. The opposition candidate not only enjoyed the support of the other rival faction of the Marwat tribe, but was also backed by another major tribe of the district, the Banuchis. It was reported that the government snatched its victory from the jaws of defeat by resorting to methods ranging from promises to distribute thousands of acres of land and outright purchases of votes to holding Basic Democrats in safe custody until the polling day.[34]

During the presidential election, it was well known that the National Awami Party was well entrenched in the district of Mardan and parts of Peshawar. The party workers reported to the secretary of the NAP that in Charsadda in the Peshawar district, out of 340 BDs, 284 had signed the pledge to support Miss Jinnah. But when the results were announced it was found that Miss Jinnah had obtained only 157 votes. It was well known that a Red Shirt could seldom be bribed into voting against his party. Apart from charges of coercion, the only explanation that the author could reach was that the NAP party workers had given the party endorsement to the prosperous *khans* who were by no means loyal followers of the NAP and who did not think that it was in their interests to vote according to their pledges.

On the other hand, those tribal and aristocratic leaders who worked for the President suggested that their organization rested on what they called *parajamba* and which they regarded as the main principle of party organization. One of the leaders said that *parajamba* meant that a leader reminded his followers of the services he had rendered to them and the services they and their ancestors had rendered to the leader and his ancestors. "If you do not help, the old *parajamba* will break

[34] "Verdict from Bannu," *Outlook,* May 30, 1964, p. 6.

and I will have to fall at the feet of Abdul Ghaffar Khan." But he admitted that this feeling of tribal and other loyalties was declining, and people were becoming more amenable to monetary and other considerations.

East Pakistan

It may be said that as East Pakistan is lagging behind West Pakistan in economic development, in terms of political development it is West Pakistan which is backward as compared to East Pakistan. There are 8.9 million literates (17.6 per cent of the population) in East Pakistan as compared to 5.4 million literates (12.7 per cent of the population) in West Pakistan. It cannot be said that these literates are more concentrated in urban areas of East Pakistan, for the urban population of the province constitutes only 5.2 per cent of the population as compared to West Pakistan where the urban population constitutes 22.5 per cent. This means that a large number of literates are to be found among the rural population in East Pakistan.

As compared to the semifeudal and tribal social structure of large areas of West Pakistan, the social structure in East Pakistan, particularly after the disappearance of Hindu landlords, has developed in an egalitarian direction. Choudhuries in East Pakistan claim to have once been the feudal chiefs of the village, and Khundakars claim their lineage from the priestly class.[35] But these are mostly claims; indeed, power and influence in the village society have gravitated towards the *mullah* or *imam* or the village school teacher or *bhuyans* (wealthy peasant proprietors).

Ayub must have been aware that the noisy demonstrations against him in the cities did not necessarily mean that he could never hope to win political victory in East Pakistan. The total urban population in the province was only 5.2 per cent. Therefore, he paid more attention to rural areas and particularly, as we have seen, to those areas of the western half of East Pakistan which were far away from the politically conscious Dacca and Chittagong divisions. The system of Basic Democracies was an admirable instrument for this purpose and through a program of Rural Public Works, Ayub started pouring money into the rural areas. It was significant that he was allocating more money for rural public works in East Pakistan (Rs. 200 million in 1963–64) than for the same program in West Pakistan (Rs. 100 million).

In East Pakistan, the politicians found that it was not the CSP Deputy Commissioner with his office in the district town who used his power to support the President. The lower officers and particularly the Circle

[35] Nazmul Karim, *Changing Society in India and Pakistan* (Dacca: Oxford University Press, 1956), p. 153.

Officer (Development), who was responsible for the allocation of development funds, emerged as the main force who could pressure and persuade the BDs to vote for the government party.[36] Another instrument to do the government's bidding was the local police officer. In such an environment, it was natural that the Basic Democrats could not look beyond their village interests and think of the larger issues of East versus West Pakistan or presidential autocracy versus parliamentary government on which the politicians concentrated in their campaign.

The politicians went through all the stages of the 1954 election campaign when they trounced the former Muslim League. They thought that the ground swell created by Miss Jinnah's mass meetings in cities would flood the rural areas. They were perhaps aware that they had no organization below the subdivisional level, but they thought that the students of Dacca University and the political workers would fill this gap. They soon found out that Miss Jinnah could attract hundreds of thousands of people to her meetings, but it was the Circle Officers (Development) and police officers who could collect the Basic Democrats for the meetings addressed by government Ministers. It was reported that when it became clear that the COP was going to lose the election, some of the political leaders tried to create their own coercive machinery to counteract the government pressure. One of the politicians is reported to have said that the Basic Democrats would be treated either with sticks or with garlands depending upon how they voted in the presidential election.[37] The government was fearful that Miss Jinnah's mass meetings and the pressure tactics of the opposition might frighten the BDs into voting for the opposition candidate. A few days before the polling day, therefore, the government called upon the army to start patrolling the country, perhaps as a reassuring device and for the maintenance of law and order. Another unfair practice the opposition thought that the government had resorted to was to have a counterfoil of the ballot paper. In the polling station, the voter had to first sign his name or give his thumb impression on the counterfoil of the ballot paper. The opposition charged that when the voter obtained his ballot paper after signing his name on the counterfoil, he might fear

[36] The East Pakistan Election Tribunal in their judgment on the Comilla by-election case unanimously held that along with the Central Minister for Communications, Khan A. Sabur, a subdivisional officer, a circle officer and other government officers had canvassed in favor of the Muslim League candidate in a by-election to the Provincial Assembly. *The Pakistan Observer,* November 17, 1964.

[37] It was reported that the COP in East Pakistan had set up "Dhurmush Committees" (Hammer Committees) and "Dhulai Committees" (Washing Committees). *The Pakistan Times,* December 30, 1964.

the government would be able to find out how he had voted by checking the counterfoil. According to the opposition, this was a device to create fear in the mind of the voter who was not shrewd enough to realize that it was only his ballot paper which had a number and that the counterfoil did not have any numbers.

Politics at the Power Elite Level

What groups constitute the power elite of Pakistan and how cohesive are these groups? At the very apex stands Ayub, supported by the army and the civil services, the most cohesive groups in Pakistan. But in terms of decision-making, next to Ayub are perhaps the Cabinet Ministers, the Governors, and industrialists whose ostensible political support is supposed to rest upon the Pakistan Muslim League organization. We have seen that in West Pakistan the political machinery consists of mostly the landlords and the *pirs*. In East Pakistan the organization takes a more political form and consists of the Governor and certain political oligarchs with their respective areas of support.

So far as the President's political supporters are concerned, the different layers in the political hierarchy consist of the village influentials at the lowest tier and the Governors, Cabinet Ministers, and some of the well-known *pirs* and landowners at the higher levels. The President is supported by all these groups and factions, but the groups and factions do not support each other. As an example, one may cite the case of the former Foreign Minister, Zulfiqar Ali Bhutto, who draws his main support from Sind. He is a Sindhi landlord from Larkana in Upper Sind who has tried to build his support in the rest of Sind. But in the recent National Assembly elections, his supporters in Tharparkar and Thatta were defeated by the Independent candidates who supported the President.[38] The Nawab of Kalabagh, the former Governor of West Pakistan (1960–66), held unchallenged sway in most of Punjab, but his political writ did not run unchallenged in the Frontier and Sind. In East Pakistan, the Governor and some of the Central East Pakistani Ministers divide among themselves the political support that exists there. One can say that the Governor, supported by certain Central Ministers, is the strongest political figure in East Pakistan. The East Pakistan Muslim League is faction-ridden with rival groups constantly

[38] It was well known that Foreign Minister Z. A. Bhutto had campaigned actively for his supporters in Thatta and Tharparkar districts. For his campaign in Thatta, see *Dawn*, March 12, 1965. After he was appointed as acting secretary-general of the Pakistan Muslim League, he declared that action would be taken against those who had worked against the Muslim League candidates and he mentioned the case of the Muslim League candidate from Tharparkar who was defeated and against whom some of the Muslim Leaguers had worked. *Dawn*, March 27, 1965.

contending against each other. A young Central Minister from East Pakistan may try to build his political support among student groups and trade unions in East Pakistan, but the Governor may view all this with suspicion and use his government and political machinery to thwart the political ambitions of the Central Minister.

Thus, the political party that Ayub has built is somewhat similar to de Gaulle's UNR whose source of unity is the leader. After the presidential elections, it must have become apparent to Ayub that in order to maximize his political support, he cannot depend upon local or provincial oligarchs who are feuding against each other. One of the President's supporters in Khulna in East Pakistan, guided by his short-term interests, instigated his followers to resort to strong-arm tactics against industrial workers belonging to Noakhali district. The result of this action was that the President's supporter won Khulna for the President, but the President lost Noakhali. All this means that the President is not building a viable political organization. He claims that he is primarily interested in economic development and seems to think that all forms of political activity other than those severely controlled by the government are likely to impede it. He and the other oligarchs in Pakistan have not yet become aware that economic development generates new and unanticipated demands, and that any government in order to cope with or absorb these demands needs political machinery to maintain national consensus and discipline necessary for economic development and also to stimulate further economic growth.

Ayub can claim that Pakistan for the first time has held a national election and that on the whole the election was fair and free. The opposition candidate polled 36.4 per cent of the votes. All Basic Democrats cannot be dismissed as pliable tools in the hands of the government, for as many as 28,691 of them voted for Miss Jinnah. But the purpose of this election was not so much to give the country an opportunity to bring about a peaceful change of government as it was to create a sense of commitment among the electorate to the policies and decisions of the government. In several of his speeches, the President reminded the people that if the opposition candidate were elected, the nation would have "dug their grave." The result would be, perhaps, a bloody revolution unlike that of the Martial Law. Soon after he was declared elected, he said, "Thank God, Pakistan has been saved." Thus, the purpose of holding these elections was perhaps to give the electorate a sense of identification with the national objectives of the government.

But what is the role of the opposition during the elections and after their defeat in the election? Ayub does not seem to realize that the Combined Opposition Party was able to bring together regionalists like the Awami League and the National Awami Party, religious fundamentalists like the Jamaat-i-Islami, and advocates of national unity like the Council Muslim League, all under one canopy. It is true that the greatest common measure among them was their opposition to Ayub's autocratic regime. Nevertheless, the sense of unity that emerged among them during the campaign augured well for the future of Pakistan. If Ayub were farsighted and were to encourage this sense of unity instead of trying to destroy the opposition, it would mean that each of the components by modifying their extreme stands would come closer to each other and thus create a responsible opposition. Above all, this would promote national integration because the Awami League and the National Awami Party, having once modified their stands on regionalism, and the fundamentalists like the Jamaat-i-Islami, having once agreed to the nomination of a woman as the presidential candidate and to the modification of the Family Laws Ordinance (instead of insisting on its repeal), cannot easily revert to their former rigid approaches. Unfortunately, the present regime believes in imposing conformity and not creating consensus. By continuing to use the government machinery and resorting to gerrymandering tactics, the government has crippled the opposition to such an extent that in the National Assembly elections of March, 1965, they could win only 17 seats in the Assembly.[39]

Ayub can claim that the Pakistan Muslim League is a horizontal constellation of interests in which he has tried to aggregate the regional interests, the business interests, and the religious and landowning groups. In addition, he can claim that he has tried to bring about vertical integration through his system of Basic Democracy in such a way that all levels and styles of politics ranging from the most urban and sophisticated elements to the most feudal and parochial groups in the rural society coexist. Moreover, his system of local government is integrated with the national political system so that the Basic Democrats, particularly at the time of national elections, can bargain with national leaders who have to seek their support in order to have their men in different regions elected.[40]

[39] It was alleged that the constituencies in East Pakistan which underwent changes in delimitation were those where Miss Jinnah had fared well in the presidential elections. Several constituencies in Mymensingh, in Comilla, in Chittagong, and in Chittagong Hill Tracts, all constituencies of the Sylhet and Noakhali districts, underwent fresh demarcation. *The Pakistan Observer,* February 9, 1965.

[40] For example, in the Thatta district when Foreign Minister Bhutto was addressing meetings in support of the Muslim League candidate, he was asked by a Basic Democrat whether the government would agree to the demand of the landowning interests that the collection of government dues

The present regime often asserts that the new political system suits the genius and traditions of Pakistan. It may be argued that under the newly created system there is a blending of the political system with the existing social structure. Village influentials have been brought into the Union Councils and civil servants have been made advisers to give the Councils a sense of direction and to make them program-oriented. In this way the village influentials derive their authority not merely as leaders of clans and tribes, but on the basis of their performance as Union Councillors. As one moves up to the provincial and the central levels of authority, one does not come across a highly democratic constitution resting on a social structure which is basically authoritarian. One may go so far as to use Eckstein's suggestive phrase and say that there is a congruence of authority pattern in the new political system.[41] There is a centralized, stable executive to maintain national unity and facilitate economic development and an Assembly not to obstruct the exercise of executive authority, but to ventilate grievances of the public. Thus, Ayub with supreme satisfaction would say that here is a perfect blending of essential executive action with the right amount of democracy.

Even if for the sake of argument one were to admit that the former constitutions in Pakistan suffered from an excess of democracy, one cannot help feeling that under the new system an excessively centralized executive authority rests on a substructure which is basically heterogeneous. Thus, if Ayub had made efforts to accommodate most of the urban and regional elements within the political system and tried to create consensus, he might have brought into being a more stable political system. Now there is stability in terms of one man rule. If Ayub is overthrown, the factions, both inside and outside the government, will once again take up arms against each other unless another great saviour emerges to maintain national unity.

---

be postponed because of the failure of crops. The Foreign Minister asked the Deputy Commissioner to request the provincial Board of Revenue for an early decision regarding this matter.

[41] Harry Eckstein, *A Theory of Stable Democracy* (Princeton: Center of International Studies, 1961), pp. 6–12.

❈ 10 ❈

Basic Democracies and Development in the Rural Sector

Basic Democracy sounds very much like the term "basic English." As basic English was devised to enable foreigners with a limited vocabulary to communicate in English, so Basic Democracy was designed to initiate the broad masses of Pakistan, a great majority of whom are illiterate, into the workings of the democratic process. It is suggested that this can best be done by first exposing them to a form of limited democracy before they can learn to operate the more sophisticated forms. The same philosophy lies behind the system of direct elections on the basis of adult franchise for the election of Union Councillors or Basic Democrats, and indirect elections (that is, the Union Councillors or Basic Democrats forming the electoral college) for the election of the President and members of the National Assembly and two Provincial Assemblies. "Ask the question to the primary voter which the rustic mind can comprehend." His main concern is about a road connecting his village with the outside market, perhaps a primary school for his children, or loans or remission of taxes in times of drought. He cannot understand issues of foreign policy or inflation or a balanced growth of agriculture and industry. The government contends that such questions may not be beyond the comprehension or concern of the 80,000 Basic Democrats or Union Councillors, who are the rural influentials or leaders of urban areas.

For the country as a whole, the percentage of literacy is 15.9; whereas the percentage of literacy among the Union Councillors is 84.4.[1]

It is often said that institutions of local government did not strike deep roots in India. This was not only because the District Officers dominated these institutions. Perhaps a more important cause of their decay was the reluctance or unwillingness of the British to disturb or change the traditional social structure that existed in the villages. The District Officer often sought the cooperation of the landlords or tribal or caste leaders for the maintenance of law and order and collection of revenue. The British thought that they could introduce institutions of local government as a superstructure below which existed the village or caste *panchayats*,[2] the principal functions of which were to maintain law and order, dispense justice, and perform other social functions connected with the caste or village. The local government institutions atrophied because the District Officer found it more convenient to deal directly with the rural oligarchs rather than disturb the traditional social structure by facilitating a freer and more open participation of the people in the local institutions. Political participation of the rural people could only have come about if the authority and influence of traditional institutions like caste, tribe, or even religion had been deliberately undermined. This the British were unwilling to undertake.

The primary concern of the politicians most of the time during the British period was the struggle for independence and not the trans-formation of the traditional society that existed in the villages. In fact, they wanted the rural oligarchs, instead of going with their petitions to the District Officer, to come to them for the redress of their grievances. We have seen in Chapter 6 that the Deputy Commissioner (DC) in Pakistan exercises so much control over the district that the politician has not been able to aggregate rural interests under his control. During the pre-Martial Law period, the politicians did try to wrest power from the DC in the districts, but were never fully successful. The emergence of Martial Law meant that the civil servants were re-established in the full exercise of their powers. The present government is also interested in maintaining the existing social structure in the villages. Indeed, the elections of 1964–65[3] indicate that the

---

[1] *Annual Report on Basic Democracies October 27, 1959, to October 27, 1960* (Karachi: Government of Pakistan, n.d.), p. 11.

[2] A village or caste council consisting of elders or leaders. Its origin goes back to ancient Hindu India.

[3] Primary elections were held in October, 1964, and the campaign for presidential elections took place during November and December, 1964. The polling day for the presidential election was January 2, 1965.

regime has made use of the existing social structure to mobilize political support. It is clear, however, that the government is more interested in stimulating economic development in the countryside and has designed the institution of Basic Democracies to encourage rural participation in the task of economic development with this in mind.

The functions of the Union Councils and District Councils in the Basic Democracies Order, 1959, show that the major emphasis is on economic rather than on political development. The pre-Martial Law regime also tried to bring about community development in the rural areas under the Village Agricultural and Industrial Development Program, popularly known as the Village AID. But the program achieved only limited success because of its administrative and technical deficiencies and because leadership was imposed from outside the community rather than evolved within it. Under the scheme of Basic Democracies, the government is trying not only to create local leadership but to give it an institutional form. As we have indicated before, the term "Basic Democracy" does not suggest the creation of institutions over which the elected Union Councillors will exercise democratic and full control. The government has armed itself with powers of such a sweeping nature that it can easily prevent the local councils from undertaking activities which it considers undesirable. It has been argued by the government that such powers will be used only in extreme cases. At the same time a considerable measure of democracy has been introduced at the Union Council level. This suggests that the District Officers are expected to initiate economic development through popular consent and consultation. One of the crucial questions which needs to be raised in this chapter is whether there is likely to emerge under the scheme of Basic Democracies a system of democratic centralism as practiced in totalitarian countries with a significant difference that in Pakistan the instruments will be civil servants unlike party officials in Communist countries. Or would Basic Democracies usher in democratic decentralization?

Economic development of the rural areas cannot be brought about unless the seasonably unemployed and underemployed are utilized for creating some of the infrastructure needed in the rural sector. This means that in developing countries the serious handicap of overpopulation, particularly in the agricultural areas, can be converted into an advantage if the surplus manpower is mobilized for productive purposes. We have seen, for example, that in a country like China masses of peasants have been induced into working tirelessly at various irrigation and construction projects. In Pakistan, where regimentation of this sort has not been practiced, the instrument of Basic Democracies, and particularly the Thana or Tehsil Councils and the Union Councils, are being used in the Rural Public Works Program for the construction of roads, bridges, embankments, and so on.

Structure and Functions of Basic Democracies

The term "Basic Democracies" refers to the "basic democratic institutions" that have been created under the Basic Democracies Order, 1959.[4] Under this system, there are four tiers. Starting from the lowest, they are (1) Union Councils (rural areas) and Town and Union Committees (urban areas), (2) Thana (EP) or Tehsil (WP) Councils, (3) District Councils, and (4) Divisional Councils. Their numbers, membership, and relationship with each other may be seen in the Structural Chart of Basic Democracies on page 248.

Of the four Councils created by the Basic Democracies Order, only two, the Union and the District Councils, have been assigned specific functions. The Divisional and the Thana/Tehsil Councils perform mostly coordinative functions. The Union Council has been entrusted with the responsibility of agricultural, industrial, and community development in the Union. It maintains law and order through its rural police and has been given some judicial powers to try minor civil and criminal cases through its Conciliation Courts. It has also been empowered to impose local taxes to finance its activities. In addition, the elected members of the Union Council are a part of the national electoral college, consisting of 80,000 members, for the election of the President and the members of the National Assembly and the two Provincial Assemblies. However, the key clause is to be found in Article 29 of the BD Order which states that the chairmen of the Union Council are required to assist revenue and police officials and are enjoined not to interfere "in the performance by any official of his official duties." This indicates that the government would like the cooperation of the elected Councillors, but it does not expect them to bring the grievances of the people to its attention or to pressure it into taking remedial action.

The District Council has been assigned both compulsory and optional functions. Compulsory functions have been stated in Part I of the Fourth Schedule of the BD Order and optional functions in Part II of the Fourth Schedule. Some of the compulsory functions pertain to provision and maintenance of primary schools, public roads, culverts, and bridges. In addition, the District Council has also been entrusted with broad functions like agricultural, industrial and community de-

---

[4] Government of Pakistan, Ministry of Law, *The Basic Democracies Order, 1959* (Karachi: Government of Pakistan Press, 1959), pp. 1–51.

STRUCTURAL CHART OF BASIC DEMOCRACIES
Divisional Councils (16)

Chairman — Divisional Commissioner

Membership — Maximum number, 45 members. Official members are
chairmen of all District Councils in the Division and representatives of
development Departments, and an equal number of nonofficial members.
Of the latter, at least one-half are appointed from among chairmen of
Union Councils and Union/Town Committees.

District Councils (74)

Chairman — Deputy Commissioner

Membership — Maximum number, 40 members. Official members selected
from the District level officers of development Departments and an
equal number of nonofficial members. Of the nonofficial members, at
least one-half are drawn from amongst the chairmen of Union Councils
and Union/Town Committees.

Thana (EP), Tehsil (WP) Councils (655)

Chairman — Subdivisional Officer in East Pakistan, Tehsildar in West
Pakistan.

Membership — Official members are Thana/Tehsil level officers of various
government departments and an equal number of representative members all of whom are the chairmen of the constituent Union Councils
and Union/Town Committees.

Union Councils (rural areas),
Town and Union Committees (urban areas) (7,300)

Chairman — elected

Membership — Usually about 15 members. Two-thirds of the members are
elected representatives from constituencies of roughly 1,200 people
spread over a number of villages and one-third consist of nominated,
nonofficial members appointed by the government.

In addition to these bodies, there are Municipal Committees and Canton-
ment Boards. This chart is based on the *Basic Democracies Order, 1959.*
Some of the changes to be brought about in the future are discussed on
p. 249.

velopment, promotion of national reconstruction, and development of
cooperative movement and village industries. Optional functions have
been detailed under broad headings like education, culture, social
welfare, economic welfare, public health, and public works. But, again,
the crucial question is whether the nonofficial members of the District
Council will exercise much initiative in formulating developmental

programs or independence in reviewing the work of the departments, particularly when the official representatives of these departments are present in the District Council. They enjoy such powers under Article 34, but the ethos and traditions of the district administration, presided over by the Deputy Commissioner, who is also chairman of the District Council, have been built on an autocratic and paternalistic pattern. Therefore, it is difficult to say that in the near future the District Councils will be pulsating with a new democratic vigor generated by the independence and initiative of some of the chairmen of the Union Councils present in the District Councils.

It may be seen from the Structural Chart of Basic Democracies that even in the Union Council, a third of the members are appointed. In the upper tiers, with the exception of Thana/Tehsil Councils, all the nonofficial members in the District and Divisional Councils are to be appointed by Deputy Commissioners and Commissioners, respectively. The system of Basic Democracies has been criticized because of the way democracy has been diluted through this principle of appointments. The government has decided that there would be no nominations to Union Councils in the future. In the past, the practice was for the Subdivisional Officer in East Pakistan and the Deputy Commissioner in West Pakistan to appoint a certain number of members, not exceeding one-half of the total number of elected members, to Union Councils. In the case of Municipal Committees like Karachi and Lahore, the practice of picking only a limited number of chairmen of Union Committees to serve on Municipal Committees has been discarded, and in the future the chairmen of all Union Committees will become members of the Municipal Committees. This means that the Basic Democracies Order, 1959, will be amended accordingly.[5]

In addition to the autocratic and paternalistic nature of the district administration, the new technical departments responsible for most of the developmental work are likely to feel that all their technical or professional ability in agriculture or public health is being wasted in tiresome and tedious arguments with rustics or ill-informed people. It has been reported that the Department of Education has tried to wrest the control of primary schools from the Union Councils. In the case of high schools, which were being run by the District Councils and Town Committees in parts of West Pakistan like the Punjab, Bahawalpur, and Sind, the provincial government has decided that such schools would be brought under its control through a phased program extending over a period of three years.[6] Does this suggest

[5] For decisions of the Governors' Conference regarding these matters, see *Dawn*, June 5, 1965.

[6] *The Pakistan Times*, December 15, 1964.

that the government is not serious in its announced intentions to bring about democratic decentralization of power and responsibility at the local level? Perhaps it would not be fair to criticize the government in this sweeping fashion because different areas in Pakistan are at different stages of development. Government circles may argue that the Basic Democracies Order, though uniform in its scope and application to all parts of Pakistan, will have to be tailored to the needs and special conditions prevailing in different areas. Similarly, as we shall see, the Union Councillors in East Pakistan or the Union Committee chairmen in the city of Karachi are more conscious and jealous of their rights and responsibilities than their counterparts in some of the areas of West Pakistan.

In the presidential election of 1965 as many as 18,434 (or 46.6 per cent) of the votes cast in East Pakistan, were given to the opposition candidate, Miss Jinnah; whereas in West Pakistan she obtained only 10,257 votes (or 26.1 per cent). Does this suggest that the Union Councillors in East Pakistan are more independent? It may be argued that Basic Democrats, as Union Councillors, are more amenable to official pressure or government patronage through an instrument like the Rural Public Works Program. Therefore, when 46.6 per cent of the voters in East Pakistan can withstand this pressure and vote for the opposition candidate, it redounds to their credit as independent voters. Another explanation offered is that since the opposition parties were better organized in East Pakistan than they were in West, a substantial number of the Basic Democrats who voted for Miss Jinnah were probably party workers or solid supporters of their respective parties and thus could withstand the pressure or temptation to vote for the government candidate.

We showed in Chapter 9 that most of the rural areas in West Pakistan are dominated by a traditional or semifeudal social structure. But as we also indicated in that chapter, the district bureaucracy, backed by the power of the central and provincial governments, is even more powerful than the religious *pirs* or the feudal landlords. The result is that in such an environment a symbiotic relationship exists between the district administration and the feudal-cum-religious social order. District administration, which collects land revenue and maintains law and order, enlists the cooperation and support of the feudal and religious oligarchs; but feudal and religious leaders are hopelessly divided and compete against each other for government favors. The government, on the other hand, has the monopoly of coercive power in its hands. It is in such a setting that one has to see whether the system of Basic Democracies with its initial and primary emphasis on economic development will generate certain social changes that are likely to transform the rural society.

Characteristics and Performance
of Union Councillors

It may be seen from the following table that there is a difference of 28 per cent in the percentages of literacy among Union Councillors in East and West Pakistan. It is also significant that the percentage of literacy in East Pakistan is even higher than that in Karachi.

Educational Qualifications of Union Councillors

	West Pakistan	East Pakistan	Karachi	Overall Percentage
Matriculates and above	1,993	4,298	185	8.1
Literates	24,828	34,814	1,065	76.1
Illiterates	11,636	888	139	15.8
Percentage of literacy	69.7%	97.7%	90%	84.2%

Source: *Annual Report on Basic Democracies October 27, 1959, to October 27, 1960* (Karachi: Government of Pakistan, n.d.), p. 11.

In East Pakistan, 43.5 per cent of the Union Councillors are in the 30–44 age group and 36.4 per cent are in the 45–59 age group.[7] A sample study of two districts in West Pakistan also indicates that 47 per cent of the Union Councillors are in the 30–45 age group, and 36 per cent are in the 46–60 age group.[8] Two other sample studies of the districts of Rawalpindi and Nowshera in West Pakistan indicate that 70 per cent of the members are fifty years of age or less.[9]

In East Pakistan, 87.4 per cent of the Union Councillors are agriculturists; businessmen and professionals number 7.9 and 3.3 per cent respectively. In West Pakistan, on the whole, the proportion of agriculturists is higher and that of businessmen slightly lower than in

[7] The Bureau of National Reconstruction and The Pakistan Academy for Village Development, *An Analysis of the Working of Basic Democracy Institutions in East Pakistan* (Dacca: 1961), p. 38.

[8] Inayatullah, *Basic Democracies District Administration and Development* (Peshawar: Pakistan Academy for Rural Development, 1964), p. 52. Although the author does not disclose the names of the two districts that he has studied, it is clear from details like area and population of the two districts that he has given that they are Mardan in the former N.-W.F.P. and Campbellpur in former Punjab.

[9] See Inayatullah, *A Study of Selected Union Councils in Rawalpindi Division* (Peshawar: West Pakistan Academy for Village Development, 1961), and Inayatullah, *A Study of Union Councils in Nowshera Tehsil* (Peshawar: West Pakistan Academy for Village Development, 1961).

East Pakistan.[10] However, the term *agriculturist* in West Pakistan, so far as the membership of the Union Councils is concerned, means that the Councillors are much bigger landlords than their East Pakistani counterparts. But a large number of Union Councillors in West Pakistan who list their occupation as agriculturists belong to the category of small or medium-size landowners. The sample studies in that province indicate that about 70 per cent of the Union Councillors own forty acres or less.

The same kind of disparity emerges in the incomes of East Pakistani and West Pakistani Councillors. The majority of the East Pakistani Councillors have a yearly income below Rs. 5,000. The mean is Rs. 3,570, and the median is Rs. 3,940.[11] In West Pakistan, on the other hand, 38 per cent of the Councillors have incomes of Rs. 6,000 with 8 per cent making as much as Rs. 24,000 and above. Fifty per cent of the Councillors in West Pakistan have incomes ranging between Rs. 1,200 and 6,000.[12]

Both in East and West Pakistan, the chairmen of the Union Councils are drawn from more wealthy and influential groups than the Councillors. In East Pakistan, 58.5 per cent of the chairmen have incomes above Rs. 5,000. Their mean income of Rs. 6,950 and median income of Rs. 5,550 indicate that their income is higher than the salary of any government official working at the Thana level.[13] In West Pakistan, the sample study indicates that the chairmen are also better educated and bigger landowners than the Union Councillors.[14] It may also be pointed out that the Union Councils in West Pakistan contain a large majority drawn from the influentials in the area covered by the Union Council.[15]

[10] In Mardan and Campbellpur, 88 per cent are agriculturists and 6.3 per cent are businessmen. See Inayatullah, *Basic Democracies District Administration and Development*, pp. 58–59. In Nowshera, 97 per cent of the Union Councillors are landowners and 3 per cent are tenants. See Inayatullah, *A Study of Union Councils in Nowshera Tehsil*, p. 7. In Peshawar, 66 per cent are agriculturists and 24 per cent are businessmen. See Inayatullah, *An Analysis of Functioning of Seven Union Councils in Peshawar Tehsil* (Peshawar: West Pakistan Academy for Village Development, 1961), p. 7.

[11] *An Analysis of the Working of Basic Democracy Institutions in East Pakistan*, p. 41.

[12] Election Authority of West Pakistan, *Election Report* (Lahore: 1960).

[13] *An Analysis of the Working of Basic Democracy Institutions in East Pakistan*, p. 41.

[14] Inayatullah, *Basic Democracies District Administration and Development*, p. 66.

[15] In Rawalpindi, Nowshera and Peshawar, 80 per cent of the influentials are in the Union Councils. See Inayatullah, *A Study of Selected Union Councils in Rawalpindi Division*, p. 9. In the Mardan and Campbellpur

We have referred to the paternalistic attitude of the bureaucrats, particularly at the district and rural level. Under the system of Basic Democracies, it is true that the objective is to make the Union Councillors increasingly self-reliant in the discharge of their developmental duties. But in the near future, when Union Councillors have to acquire experience in their new tasks, formulate budgets, explore new ways for mobilizing political support, and inject a sense of dynamism in the villages, they may constantly seek the assistance and guidance of government officers. According to a survey in East Pakistan, 81 per cent of the chairmen and 70 per cent of the Union Councillors said that the Circle Officer had helped them in framing the budget while an even greater number said that the Circle Officer had audited the accounts.[16] Furthermore, it is said that approximately 85 per cent of the items on the agenda in Union Council meetings in East Pakistan have originated not from the members of the Council, but from government officials through their correspondence, and, in some cases, as a result of their visits to the Councils.[17]

In West Pakistan, the paternalistic attitude of the bureaucrats is even more pronounced. Even though the field employees of the Agriculture Department and revenue officials like the *patwaris* were instructed to attend the meetings of the Union Councils, the evidence shows that they rarely attended them. Actually, most of the correspondence flowed in the direction of the departments from the Union Councils with not much response from the departments.[18] In the Conventions of Basic Democrats held at Dacca and Lahore, it has been reported that a large number of Union Councillors complained bitterly regarding the "apathy and callousness" of the police, revenue, and judicial authorities towards them.[19] But we should note two factors in the matter of these bitter complaints regarding the attitude of bureaucrats. In the first place, bureaucrats are not usually as highhanded in East Pakistan as they are in West. Even in West Pakistan, district officials are more autocratic in certain backward or feudal areas of Sind

---

study, 83 per cent of the highly influential are in the Union Councils. See Inayatullah, *Basic Democracies District Administration and Development*, pp. 68 and 72.

[16] *An Analysis of the Working of Basic Democracy Institutions in East Pakistan*, p. 52.

[17] A. T. R. Rahman, *Basic Democracies at the Grassroots* (Comilla: Pakistan Academy for Village Development, 1962), p. 31.

[18] Inayatullah, *Basic Democracies District Administration and Development*, pp. 143–144.

[19] Candidus, "Role of Basic Democracies In Our Developing Economy — II," *The Pakistan Times*, June 26, 1962.

or Punjab than in other parts. In the second place, under the system of Basic Democracies, Union Councillors are starting with considerable disadvantages in power and influence compared to government officials. But as we shall see, particularly in the case of the Rural Public Works Program in East Pakistan, government officers have found that the success of their program depends very much upon the kind of active cooperation that they receive from the Union Councillors.

What are the kinds of activities that interest the Union Councils? What priority do they attach to these activities? In East Pakistan, it seems that the order of priority runs as follows: adult education, increased food production, cooperative movement, communications, primary education, and public health.[20] In West Pakistan, 54 per cent of the resolutions passed by thirty-seven Union Councils in Mardan and Campbellpur were in areas like education, communications, agriculture, health, and sanitation.[21]

Union Councils have also set up Conciliation Courts to try minor civil and criminal cases. In Multan district in West Pakistan, 5,943 cases were filed during 1961–63 and, out of these, compromises were brought about in 3,656 cases by the chairmen of Union Councils who presided over Conciliation Courts.[22] In East Pakistan too, Conciliation Courts tried such cases. A government report states: "Many courts discretely avoided any mention of innocence or guilt but recorded the terms of the compromise."[23] It is significant that both in East and West Pakistan, Conciliation Courts have been keen in bringing about compromises. This indicates that factionalism is so rampant in the rural areas that if the Conciliation Courts were to decide such cases in favor of one party or the other, factional strife would increase and might eventually affect the working of the Union Councils adversely.

As may be seen in the Chart (p. 248), half of the members of the Thana Council are officers of various government departments. According to the Basic Democracies Order, only the District and the Union Councils were assigned specific functions; whereas the Thana/Tehsil Councils were intended to be bodies where development plans submitted by Union Councils were to be coordinated and scrutinized. The idea was that the chairmen of Union Councils would sit in the Thana or Tehsil Council in concert with the various government offi-

[20] *An Analysis of the Working of Basic Democracy Institutions in East Pakistan,* p. 86.

[21] Inayatullah, *Basic Democracies District Administration and Development,* p. 145.

[22] *Dawn,* April 11, 1963.

[23] Bureau of National Reconstruction, *Four Years of Basic Democracies* (Dacca: Government of East Pakistan, 1963–64), p. 6.

cers and in the scrutiny of the development schemes, the administrative efficiency of officers would be matched by the political wit and skill of the chairmen of the Union Councils. At first the Thana Councils were not very active in East Pakistan, but the Rural Public Works Program seems to have transformed them into lively institutions. Under the Rural Public Works Program, allocations to District Councils in East Pakistan have declined from 50 per cent in 1963 to a planned 21 per cent in 1965 while there has been a remarkable increase in allocations to Thana and Union Councils (27 per cent in 1963, 64 per cent in 1964, and a planned 65 per cent in 1965). The idea of the Rural Public Works Program, initiated during 1962–63, was to utilize the surplus manpower in the agricultural sector to create the necessary infrastructure in the rural economy in the form of roads, bridges, drainage canals, embankments, etc. During 1962–65, Rs. 800 million have been invested in the rural areas under the Rural Public Works Program out of which Rs. 550 million were invested in East Pakistan and Rs. 250 in West Pakistan. It may be noted that this injection of purchasing power into the rural sector would have created inflationary pressures were it not for the fact that the funds invested in the Rural Public Works Program had been realized by the sale of American surplus foodstuffs and other commodities under the P.L. 480 program.

Under the Rural Public Works Program in East Pakistan, the Thana Council has been strengthened as a planning and coordinating agency. It is in the Thana Council that projects involving more than one Union are discussed, and when some of these inter-Union schemes are rejected, the decision is taken only after consulting the chairmen of Union Councils involved in the schemes concerned. This has meant that the chairmen have not only come to respect decisions of the Thana Council, but are also developing political skills in wheeling and dealing whereby one Union Council chairman may agree to vote for the scheme of another chairman this year in return for the latter's promise to support his scheme next year.[24]

The success of the Rural Public Works Program should be judged not only in terms of the infrastructure that it has created in the rural sector, but also whether it has been instrumental in achieving some of the objectives of the system of Basic Democracies. Its social and political impact may be judged on the basis of the following criteria: (1) Has it improved the relationship between officers and chairmen of Union Councils without weakening the representative capacity of the chairmen? (2) Has its impact been wide enough to draw the support

[24] *An Evaluation of the Rural Public Works Programme East Pakistan 1962–63* (Comilla: Pakistan Academy for Rural Development, 1963), p. 23.

of the local leadership outside the Union Councils? (3) In what way has it helped the leaders to stimulate the motivational resources of the people in a given area? (4) Has it brought about any attitudinal change among the rural people?

The results of the Rural Public Works Program have been encouraging so far as East Pakistan is concerned. According to one survey, in nearly two-thirds of the cases, there were conflicts between Circle Officers and Union Council chairmen in considering Thana Council schemes. It seems that the Circle Officers tended to look at these schemes from the point of view of the Thana as a whole; whereas the Union Council chairmen were influenced by the interests of their Unions and sometimes even their own constituencies. It seems that in 60 per cent of the cases, Circle Officers were able to persuade the chairmen to consider the interests of the Thana as a whole. In 23 per cent of the cases, Circle Officers had to alter the plans and estimates prepared by the Union Councils so that they might conform to Thana interests. But in 17 per cent of the cases, the Union Council chairmen were able to mobilize majority support in the Council for their proposals and the Circle Officers had to yield.[25] After the approval of the schemes, Project Committees were formed to implement one or more of these projects. These Project Committees usually functioned in the area of each Union Council and consisted of a member or the chairman of the Union Council as well as other members—local leaders or workers of the area—drawn from outside the Union Council. As a result of working in these Project Committees, the members developed certain skills and experience. The Project Committees were responsible for employing laborers, for paying their wages, for maintaining proper accounts of the projects, etc. But even all these skills were not enough for the successful completion of the projects unless the members of the Project Committee displayed qualities of leadership in creating confidence and, above all, in injecting energy and enthusiasm among the rural people.

In West Pakistan, out of an allocation of Rs. 100 million during 1963–64, there was a shortfall of Rs. 17.9 million in the actual utilization of these funds.[26] As noted earlier, conditions in West Pakistan differ from area to area, and in several areas, both skilled and unskilled laborers were not available. But there has been a remarkable change in the attitudes of the people. In the words of a Divisional Commissioner in West Pakistan:

[25] A. T. Rafiqur Rahman, *An Evaluation of the Rural Public Works Programme East Pakistan 1963–64* (Comilla: Pakistan Academy for Rural Development, 1964), p. 27.

[26] Planning Commission, Government of Pakistan, *The Third Five Year Plan 1965–70* (Karachi: May, 1965), p. 530.

People do not come to you with exorbitant requests for general favours any more. Now they have specific requests, which usually relate to the sinking of tube-wells, distribution of cheap fertilizer, and the proper maintenance of irrigation channels.[27]

In order to inject a sense of new hope and dynamism into the rural sector through the system of Basic Democracies, a new kind of political leadership is needed. It is significant that so far most of this leadership has come from civil servants. As we have seen in Chapter 6, the role of the Deputy Commissioner is not restricted to that of a district administrator. In addition to being the administrative agent of the provincial and central governments, he also performs certain "political" functions. In maintaining law and order, he does not rely entirely on coercive instruments like the police that he has at his disposal. He operates through the local gentry, and for the right combination of coercion and persuasion, he is expected to develop in himself that rare quality of *hikmatamali* (judicious management) which has been the pride and joy of his illustrious predecessors in the ICS (Indian Civil Service). The response he is expected to provide to the new challenge of transforming the traditional rural society is much more difficult. He has to persuade the people in the rural areas that merely changing their techniques is not enough; an appreciable increase in agricultural productivity leading to prosperity involves a radical change in their cultural and behavior patterns as well. In addition, the process of modernization implies that the villager has ceased to be a member of an isolated village community. He not only becomes aware that by acquiring new skills and knowledge, he can improve his material lot; he must realize that there are district or provincial or even national authorities who are willing to offer him certain facilities and resources. He thus moves from a parochial political culture, where he expects nothing from the political system, to a subject political culture, where he develops new orientations toward the output aspects of the system.[28]

However well organized or structurally sound the system of Basic Democracies may be, it cannot become meaningful to the peasants unless they find that they can use this system to raise their living standards and resolve some of the problems that rural society is faced with. This means that the peasant is not the only one who has to adopt a positive orientation towards the system; much depends upon how the district officials themselves are willing to change the character of their administration. In other words, will the district officials reconstruct

---

[27] "Rural Works Programme Supplement," *The Pakistan Times*, March 7, 1966.

[28] Gabriel A. Almond and Sidney Verba, *The Civic Culture* (Princeton: Princeton University Press, 1963), pp. 17–19.

their administration on a different scale of priorities so that they attach greater importance to matters like raising the agricultural productivity in their district rather than merely maintaining law and order and collecting land revenue? Again, will the district officials realize that agricultural productivity can best be raised not so much by a paternalistic administration but by the willingness and the capacity of the peasant to participate in programs designed for such purposes? There are some indications to suggest a marked change has taken place in the attitudes of district officials.

Quite apart from the changes that have taken place in the training of CSP officials and the greater emphasis given to welfare administration in Pakistan, much of the credit for the liveliness and vigor that the experiment of Basic Democracies has displayed in East Pakistan goes to the pioneering activities of men like Akhter Hameed Khan, a former member of the ICS who resigned in order to undertake social work in East Pakistan. Akhter Hameed Khan has been the main inspiration behind the activities of the Pakistan Academy for Rural Development in Comilla. In this Academy, he has been able to assemble a band of dedicated CSP officers, officials from other technical and agricultural departments, and village workers from the district of Comilla.[29] The Rural Public Works Program started as a pilot project under the guidance of the Comilla Academy in Comilla Kotwali Thana in 1961. It was only when it proved to be successful that it was extended to the whole of East Pakistan during 1962–63, and started in West Pakistan during 1963–64. Under the Comilla experiment, a Thana Development and Training Center was established where village workers were given intensive training and sent back to their villages to function as catalytic agents to initiate development work. Other major accomplishments of the Comilla Academy have been to develop a cooperative structure with multipurpose cooperatives at the village level (with functions of banking, marketing, equipment leasing, etc.), specialized commercial cooperatives in small towns (rickshaw drivers, weavers, etc), and a Central Cooperative Association at the Thana level.

Similarly, attempts are being made to orient the farmer in East Pakistan toward productivity. This does not mean, however, that he will be given a set of directives or lectures on how to increase the rice

[29] Akhter Hameed Khan was for several years the Director of the Pakistan Academy for Rural Development, Comilla, and even though his present official title is Vice-Chairman, Board of Governors, Pakistan Academy for Rural Development, he continues to be the driving force of the Academy. Another officer who also deserves credit for organizing rural development through the system of Basic Democracies is A. M. S. Ahmed, Secretary, Basic Democracies and Local Government Department, Government of East Pakistan.

yield of his farm by agricultural experts. The plan is to make him aware of what his problems are so that he may become interested in resolving them by his own efforts as well as by seeking the assistance of the government departments. In this way, an ingenious scheme called the Program Building Concept of Agriculture Extension was evolved in late 1961 after a series of conferences of the agriculture officials of the government of East Pakistan and United States AID advisers. To implement their plans, the system of Basic Democracies at the Union level has been used. In each Union, an Agricultural Development Committee, consisting of the Union Council Chairman as ex-officio Committee chairman, the Union Agriculture Assistant as member-secretary, three Council members, and at least one farmer from each village of the Union, has been set up. The first task of each new Union Agriculture Committee is to organize a house-to-house survey to determine the social and economic conditions in terms of population, agriculture production, education, ·credit, health, etc., in the Union. After the completion of the survey, the Agriculture Development Committee, sitting in concert with interested farmers, tries to identify the precise problems that the Union is facing. After the problems have been identified and a scale of priorities established, the Committee undertakes to devise measures whereby the people may be induced and trained to solve each of these problems. For each problem area like crops, livestock, fisheries, education, health, etc., a subcommittee consisting of a Union Council member as chairman and two or more farmers is formed. This subcommittee becomes the unit through which improved techniques and methods are taught and demonstrated. It is the responsibility of the Union Agriculture Assistant to obtain the aid of provincial government departments. Under this scheme, more than 40,000 rice improvement demonstrations have been carried out showing that the average yield of paddy per acre could be as high as 40.1 *maunds* (1 *maund* = 82 lbs.) as compared to an average yield of 15 *maunds* when the traditional methods are used. Similarly, in Mymensingh district, nearly 500,000 farmers have attended harvesting demonstrations. Under the program of adult literacy organized by the Education Subcommittee, more than 100,000 farmers are attending night schools. The Health Subcommittee in Mymensingh district has organized mass immunization programs under which, during the past two years, more than 4.3 million persons have been immunized against contagious diseases. This experiment of the Program Building Concept of Agriculture Extension was first started in the district of Mymensingh as a pilot project and, after its success, was extended throughout the province.[30]

[30] For a detailed description of this project, see U.S./AID Pakistan, *Rural Development in East Pakistan* (typescript) (April 2, 1965), pp. 21–26.

As we have indicated earlier, East Pakistan has made more rapid strides than West Pakistan in community development under the system of Basic Democracies because of two principal factors. First, there has been much less social stratification and greater egalitarianism in East Pakistan because of the absence of big landlords. Secondly, ever since the British days, because of geographical and historical reasons, the administration in East Pakistan has been much less overbearing in its controls and paternalism than its counterpart in West Pakistan. The peasant, therefore, being less parochial, seems to be moving more rapidly towards a subject political culture than the West Pakistani peasant. But in West Pakistan, too, significant changes are afoot. There the medium-size landowner is asserting himself. In Sind, these medium-size landowners, being chairmen of the Union Councils, attend meetings of the Tehsil and District Councils. In this way, they are becoming aware of the business and commercial opportunities that exist in towns and cities so that instead of handing over their cash crops like rice or cotton to the big landlords, they would like to market these crops themselves in the towns. There have also been instances when some of the Union Councillors in West Pakistan have lodged complaints to the President against the big landlords, pointing out how they still impose feudal taxes and maintain a system of oppression and terror in their areas. It has become possible for medium-size landlords to take a stand against big landlords because they find that in Union or Tehsil Councils they can act together not only as landlords but also in combination with other professional classes like traders and lawyers, and in some of the military districts of West Pakistan, with retired military officers. It may be noted that the Union Councils have not yet reached a stage of development when they become exposed to pressures from various interests in a rural society. However, it is clear that they themselves are emerging as pressure groups in demanding certain amenities and facilities from the government. Some of the Union Councillors and chairmen, who, both in East and West Pakistan, represent medium income groups, are actively engaged in pressuring the government to locate certain industries in their particular areas. In doing this, they not only develop political skills, but find that in order to maximize their pressure, they have to combine their efforts with those of social and political workers and business circles of the district.[31]

[31] For an instance when Basic Democrats have demanded the setting up of new sugar mills in Sheikhupura in West Pakistan, see *Dawn*, January 1, 1966.

Foreign Relations

It is well known that every country pursues its foreign policy in accordance with its national interests. In doing so it has a scale of preferences in which the maintenance of its national security or independence occupies first place. Next in order of importance — particularly in developing countries — are economic interests. A developing country would like to establish and maintain cordial relations with those states with whom it can maximize its trade relations or from whom it can obtain maximum economic aid. Following these interests and sometimes intertwined with them is the pursuit of ideological objectives. Thus, a developing country like Pakistan would like to achieve the objective of Islamic solidarity or the promotion of Afro-Asian unity through its foreign policy. Foreign policy also has a considerable impact on the political development of a country; it may align itself with totalitarian or democratic blocs. Of even more crucial importance, perhaps, is the fact that the government of a developing country in pursuing an ambitious foreign policy may not only strain its economic resources, but in times of stress and tension may also suppress the opposition or suspend the civil rights of its citizens.

Any country as strategically placed as Pakistan is would be concerned about its security and independence. West Pakistan with its seaport and airport of Karachi and with the oil-rich areas of the Middle East situated nearby provides the only outlet to large parts of landlocked Asiatic Russia, Afghanistan, and China. It is through the northwestern areas of West Pakistan that all the invaders, except the British, entered India. In addition, Pakistan with its province of East Pakistan is also a part of Southeast Asia. The greatest Chinese threat to India in the 1962 conflict came through the North-East Frontier Agency, which is one of the easily accessible areas along the Himalayan Frontier. A deep penetration of Indian territory by the Chinese would bring them into contact with the northern borders of East Pakistan.

These geopolitical factors have obviously influenced, as we shall see later, the foreign policy of Pakistan. But Pakistan has always attached far greater importance to its relations with India. Most of its border adjoins the territory of India and, in addition, Indian territory separates the two parts of Pakistan. India is four times as large as Pakistan in area and more than four times as large in population. Its industrial base is probably ten times that of Pakistan. The martial races of West Punjab and the former North-West Frontier Province constituted some of the best fighting divisions of the former Indian Army; yet Pakistan emerged after Partition as a much weaker military power than India. India refused to transfer the military assets which were allotted to Pakistan when the subcontinent was divided. Out of the forty ordnance depots which contained reserves of all types of stores, equipment, ammunition, and vehicles, only five small retail depots were situated in Pakistan territory. All the seventeen ordnance factories which the British had established were located in Indian areas. Before India's border clash with China in 1962, Pakistan's armed forces never exceeded a third of India's, although Pakistan was receiving United States military aid.

These factors reinforce the deeply held Pakistani belief that Hindus, who constitute the great majority in India, not only opposed the very establishment of Pakistan, but have not yet reconciled themselves to its separate and independent existence. Pakistanis cite the long-cherished belief held among the Hindus regarding the sacred unity of India, the ancient land of Hindus. The fact that India has not agreed to the holding of a free and impartial plebiscite in Kashmir, where Muslims are in the majority, indicates that India questions the very basis of Pakistan, which was established on the theory that contiguous areas in which Muslims constituted a majority would be separated from India and constitute the state of Pakistan. Pakistan has also accused India of fomenting separatist tendencies in East Pakistan. Out of a total population of 50.8 million in East Pakistan, there are about 9.4 million Hindus (1961 census). Pakistanis suspect that India is likely to use this considerable Hindu population, particularly the Caste Hindus, who number about 4.4 million, to create conflict between East and West Pakistan in the hope of ultimately detaching East Pakistan from West Pakistan and encouraging it to join India. During the tense period following the September, 1965, armed conflict with Pakistan, the Indian press and the All-India Radio highlighted such separatist tendencies and even went to the extent of suggesting that East Pakistanis were in a state of revolt against West Pakistanis and that an East Pakistan Revolutionary Council had been formed to establish an independent republic of East Pakistan.[1] All these factors have intensified the historic animosity which has existed between the two communities for centuries. *Dawn* in an editorial observed: "If the main concern of the Christian West is the containment of Chinese Communism, the main concern of Muslim Pakistan is the containment of militarist and militant Hinduism."[2]

Indian hostility towards Pakistan, particularly as reflected in the speeches of its leaders or even in the press, may not be as outspoken, but the feeling of bitterness runs as deep. First of all, India complains that Pakistan, by constantly claiming that it was established as a homeland for Muslims and suggesting that India with all its secularism is no more than a Hindu state, has made the task of India in building a secular state on noncommunal lines extremely difficult. Another cause of Indian hostility is that, according to India, the sole objective of Pakistan's foreign policy is to undermine the influence of India and demonstrate to the world that Pakistan is in no way a smaller power than India. The Indian Ambassador in Washington declared that India and Pakistan could live together in peace only when Pakistan had learned "to accept that it is less than a quarter of India's size and cannot hope to alter this fact of geography either by break-up of Indian unity or by borrowed strength from abroad."[3] India has often bitterly denied Pakistan's accusation that Muslims in India have been treated as second-class citizens. Moreover, Indian leaders from time to time have been suspicious of Pakistan encouraging some of the Muslim groups in India to undertake anti-Indian activities. Muslims constitute in numerical terms the most important minority in India. They number 46.9 million, or 10.7 per cent, of the population. Indian bitterness is reflected in the view put forward by some Indians that "just as the United States has come to view the aims of the Soviet leadership as the greatest threat to its security, so India looks on Pakistan as the main threat to its security."[4]

The Kashmir conflict is easily the greatest hurdle that stands in the way of long-term peaceful relations between India and Pakistan. It was on January 1, 1948, that India complained to the Security Council that Pakistan was involved in the invasion of the state of Jammu and Kashmir launched by Pathan tribesmen in October, 1947. Since then,

[1] See *The Times of India,* October 18, 1965, and also *The Statesman,* December 30, 1965.
[2] *Dawn,* April 26, 1963.
[3] *The Times of India,* October 25, 1965.
[4] Phillips Talbot and S. L. Poplai, *India and America* (New York: Harper and Brothers, 1958), p. 68.

the Security Council has met so far 136 times to consider this dispute between India and Pakistan. India at first rested its case on legal grounds. The Hindu Maharaja of Jammu and Kashmir, when faced by the invasion of Pathan tribes, acceded to India on October 27, 1947. India's argument has been that since the paramountcy exercised by Britain over the Indian Princes lapsed when the British withdrew from India, the Indian Princes had a sovereign right to accede to whichever Dominion they desired. Pakistan's answer is that the wishes of the people should be a paramount factor in deciding the question of accession. Pakistan has argued that indeed India itself had disregarded the sovereign right of the Princes when it occupied Junagadh in September, 1947, in spite of the fact that the Nawab had acceded to Pakistan. Similarly, India ignored the wishes of the Nizam of Hyderabad, who wanted to remain independent, when it sent its troops to that state in September, 1948.

India has argued that it did agree to holding a plebiscite in Kashmir provided that Pakistan withdrew its troops and nationals from the State of Jammu and Kashmir. It has rested its case on the resolutions of the United Nations Commission on India and Pakistan of August 13, 1948, and January 5, 1949. Part B, 1, of the resolution of August 13, 1948, states:

> When the Commission shall have notified the Government of India that the tribesmen and Pakistani nationals referred to in Part II, A, 2, hereof have withdrawn, thereby terminating the situation which was represented by the Government of India to the Security Council as having occasioned the presence of Indian forces in the State of Jammu and Kashmir, and further, that the Pakistani forces are being withdrawn from the State of Jammu and Kashmir, the Government of India agrees to begin to withdraw the bulk of its forces from that State in stages to be agreed upon with the Commission.

Since Pakistan, according to India, has consistently refused to withdraw its troops, the UN resolutions calling for a plebiscite have become obsolete. "If they are not accepted, they terminate. If an offer is made, and it is not accepted or not implemented, it cannot stand forever."[5] "The passage of time" and several other factors have made the resolutions regarding plebiscite obsolete. First of all, it is obvious that India repudiates the two-nation theory advanced by Jinnah according to which Hindus and Muslims are two separate nations. India takes its stand on secular democracy and regards Kashmir as a symbol of that ideology. India has argued that if a plebiscite were held and Kashmiris were offered an alternative in terms of acceding to Muslim Pakistan or

[5] *United Nations Security Council Official Records,* 1090th Meeting. Nineteenth Year. 10 February 1964, S/PV. 1090, p. 17.

Hindu India, this would fan the flame of communal passions which would engulf the entire subcontinent. A further argument is: "India today is perhaps the only country which can stand up to Chinese expansion and aggression. If India failed, there would be nothing to control the Chinese forward policy."[6] This plea is also reinforced by military arguments which suggest that India needs the territory of Kashmir in order to defend Ladakh against Chinese threats. Thus, Mr. Chagla, the Indian representative, declared in the Security Council on February 5, 1964: "I wish to make it clear on behalf of my Government that under no circumstances can we agree to the holding of a plebiscite in Kashmir."[7]

Pakistan, on the other hand, rests its case on the principle of the Kashmiri people's right to self-determination and argues that this right can only be exercised through a free and impartial plebiscite held under UN auspices. Pakistan has expressed its willingness to withdraw its troops from Azad Kashmir (Pakistan-held Kashmir) provided India also undertakes to effect a similar withdrawal of its troops from India-held Kashmir.

In February, 1950, General A. G. L. McNaughton, a Canadian, was entrusted by the President of the Security Council to work out details for a plebiscite. After his talks with Indian and Pakistani representatives, he presented a plan to the Security Council according to which both India and Pakistan were to bring about a simultaneous and progressive demilitarization of the territories under their control. Pakistan accepted these proposals with certain minor reservations, but India insisted upon the complete withdrawal of Pakistan forces and the occupation of the northern areas of Baltistan and Gilgit by the Indian army.[8] Later, Sir Owen Dixon, a prominent Australian jurist, also failed to bring about an understanding between India and Pakistan on the question of a plebiscite. He reported to the Security Council in September, 1950:

> In the end, I became convinced that India's agreement would never be obtained to demilitarization in any such form, or to provisions governing the period of the plebiscite of any such character, as would in my opinion permit the plebiscite being conducted in conditions sufficiently guarding against intimidation, and other forms of influence and abuse by which the freedom and fairness of the plebiscite might be imperiled.[9]

[6] *Ibid.*, 1088th Meeting. Nineteenth Year. 5 February 1964, S/PV. 1088, p. 25.

[7] *Ibid.*, p. 14.

[8] Josef Korbel, *Danger in Kashmir* (Princeton: Princeton University Press, 1954), p. 167.

[9] *United Nations Security Council Official Records.* Fifth Year. Supplement for September through December, 1950. Document S/1791, p. 36.

These attempts at mediation were followed by those of the American, Dr. Frank Graham, but he also reported failure in March, 1953. During 1953–54, the Prime Ministers of India and Pakistan, Jawaharlal Nehru and Muhammad Ali Bogra, carried on direct negotiations, but these were terminated when the Indian Prime Minister declared that the whole situation had changed because of Pakistan's defense alignment with the United States in the form of military alliances.

India has never really favored holding a plebiscite in Kashmir simply because the Muslim majority there would vote to join Pakistan. In the Indian-occupied state of Jammu and Kashmir, Muslims number 2.4 million and the rest of the population, including Hindus, Sikhs, Buddhists, and others, number 1.1 million, according to the 1961 census figures. The population of Pakistan-held Kashmir, which is overwhelmingly Muslim, is fewer than a million strong. In a plebiscite of the whole area of Jammu and Kashmir, therefore, Muslims would constitute over 70 per cent of the population. A correspondent asked Krishna Menon when he was Defense Minister why India had consistently refused to agree to carry out the UN plebiscite. Krishna Menon's reply was: "Because we would lose it. Kashmir would vote to join Pakistan, and no Indian government responsible for agreeing to the plebiscite would survive."[10]

Pandit Nehru was completely captivated by the beauty of Kashmir, which was the original home of the Kashmiri Brahmin Nehrus. But above all, Nehru had sincerely tried to prove to the Muslims of India that India as a secular democracy was capable of being just and generous toward the Muslims. He hoped that if this plan were to succeed, particularly in Kashmir, peoples throughout India and Pakistan would become disenchanted with the two-nation theory and a foundation would be laid for a better understanding or even confederation between the two countries. Nehru's plans went awry because his personal good will and sincerity were not enough to eliminate a conflict which had continued for centuries. Sheikh Abdullah, the Prime Minister of Kashmir from 1947 to 1953, and a trusted friend of Nehru, was suspected of being pro-Muslim and was accused of attempting to establish an independent Kashmir. He was removed from office in 1953 and imprisoned by the Indian government. During 1953 to 1965, India has tried to integrate Kashmir administratively and constitutionally, but the attempt has failed politically because the Muslims in the Kashmir Valley are still antagonistic to regimes supported by India. Elections held during 1957 and 1962 were not accepted as free and fair and were not regarded as a substitute for a plebiscite either by

[10] Arthur Bernon Tourtellot, "Kashmir: Dilemma of a People Adrift," *Saturday Review* (March 6, 1965).

Pakistan or by others not only because the great majority of the seats were uncontested,[11] but also because such elections were held when the Indian army was in occupation of Kashmir.

India has often accused Pakistan of fomenting the religious passions of Muslims in Kashmir against the Indian government. There was widespread agitation in the Kashmir Valley over the question of the theft of the Prophet's relic from a mosque in December, 1963. There were demonstrations in favor of the release of Sheikh Abdullah who was released in April, 1964, and imprisoned again in May, 1965. India's admission that pro-Pakistani elements had gained a foothold in Kashmir and the fact that Muslims, particularly the urban and educated ones in Srinagar, can paralyze the life of the city by strikes and demonstrations indicate that the Indian policy of political integration of Kashmir has not succeeded.[12] Early in August, 1965, Pakistan was again accused of having sent armed infiltrators across the truce line in Kashmir, and this alleged action led to war between India and Pakistan during September, 1965. It is often said that the people of Kashmir, as a result of continued oppression through the centuries, have become so docile that only the issue of religion can stir them into defiant action against the government. This explains why Pakistan and Muslim leaders in Kashmir itself have continued to stress the religious issue.

Pakistan has also pointed out that economically and strategically Kashmir should form an integral part of West Pakistan, for most of the natural and other means of communication of Kashmir have been with that province. Even after eighteen years of occupation, India has not been able to establish all-year communications by air or land with the capital of Kashmir, Srinagar. In addition, Pakistan has pointed out that the three western rivers which are vital for its agriculture originate in Kashmir. India has, according to the Indus Waters Treaty signed in September, 1960, undertaken forever not to interfere with the flow of the western rivers into Pakistan. According to this treaty, India after a period of ten years will be entitled to the use of the three eastern rivers; whereas the three western rivers have been allotted for the use of Pakistan. This treaty was brought about largely through the good offices of the World Bank. Commonwealth countries, the United States, and West Germany have agreed to offer financial aid to Pakistan for the construction of works to replace the water of the three eastern rivers allotted to India.

---

[11] See B. Shiva Rao's letter to the editor, *The Statesman,* December 24, 1965.

[12] *The Times of India,* February 26, 1964, and *The Statesman,* December 3, 1965. Sometimes Indian newspapers take the view that pro-Pakistani feeling is strong only in a few cities without realizing that often political agitation starts in cities and then spreads to the surrounding rural areas.

Relations With Big Powers — U.S., China and U.S.S.R.

All Pakistani leaders — political, bureaucratic, and military — have agreed in believing that the most imminent threat to Pakistan's security came from India. When India threatened Pakistan by massing its troops on the West Pakistan border in March, 1950, "Pakistan was practically defenceless. It was necessary for our Prime Minister to go to India and to arrive at a settlement and stave off this impending invasion."[13] Political leaders were not clear in their minds as to how the country should meet the Indian threat. Pakistan's first Prime Minister, Liaquat Ali Khan (1947–51) was, like Nehru, an advocate of a policy of neutrality and nonalignment in foreign affairs. In July, 1951, Pakistan was again faced with Indian concentration of troops on Pakistan's borders and in August, 1951, General Ayub Khan, the Commander-in-Chief of the Pakistan Army, started thinking in terms of a military alliance with the United States.[14] Military leaders in Pakistan must have felt that West Pakistan, besides being a strategic area with India as its next-door neighbor and big powers like the U.S.S.R. and China quite close to it, did not have much depth in terms of area for its forces to fall back in and fight if overpowered and thrown back initially by a lightning offensive of the enemy. The only way to deter such an attack was for Pakistan to obtain armaments and air power by aligning itself with a power like the United States. In addition, West Pakistan had to defend physically separate East Pakistan, which had hardly any troops of its own. Pakistan's military leaders were also aware that the former Commander-in-Chief of the British Indian army, Field-Marshal Auchinleck, in a note to the Viceroy on the strategic implications of the setting up of an independent Pakistan had observed ominously:

> . . . from the purely military and strategical aspect . . . it must be concluded that the provision of adequate insurance in the shape of reasonably good defensive arrangements for Pakistan would be a most difficult and expensive business, and that no guarantee of success could be given.[15]

Military leaders like the Defense Secretary, Iskander Mirza (later President), and General Ayub Khan, the Commander-in-Chief, soon

[13] H. S. Suhrawardy, *Statement on Foreign Relations and Defence,* February 22, 1957. (Karachi: Government of Pakistan, n.d.), p. 10.

[14] Major-General Fazal Muqeem Khan, *The Story of the Pakistan Army* (Karachi: Oxford University Press, 1963), p. 154.

[15] John Connell, *Auchinleck* (London: Cassell, 1959), p. 877.

found that after the death of Prime Minister Liaquat Ali Khan in October, 1951, political leadership in the country had become so ineffective that they could seize the initiative in negotiating with the United States for military assistance.[16]

Pakistan signed the Mutual Defense Assistance Agreement in May, 1954, and joined the Southeast Asia Treaty Organization (SEATO) in September, 1954, and the Baghdad Pact (now the Central Treaty Organization — CENTO) in February, 1955. It was obvious that Pakistani leaders in signing these pacts were motivated primarily by their desire to improve the defensive capacity of Pakistan against India. At the Manila Conference in September, 1954, when SEATO came into being, Pakistan succeeded in getting aggression defined in general terms.[17] The United States, however, insisted on interpreting the term only as Communist aggression and it inserted an "understanding" to that effect into the text of the treaty.

How could the United States agree to give military assistance and invite Pakistan to join military pacts when it was clear that Pakistan's main concern was the alleged Indian threat? At the time the Baghdad Pact and SEATO came into being, the United States believed that there was a real threat of Communist attack and subversion both in the Middle East and Southeast Asia. In the Middle East there was the possibility of Soviet penetration, and in Southeast Asia the French had suffered a diasastrous defeat at Dien Bien Phu. Thus, the United States must have felt that Pakistan, because of its unique geographical position, could become one end of the northern tier opposing the Soviet Union in the Middle East and could provide protection to Southeast Asia on its western flank. Pakistan also became a part of the Western strategy of ringing the U.S.S.R. with military and air bases. It may be recalled that the famous U-2 plane took off from Peshawar in 1960 on its flight over the Soviet Union. It has also been

---

[16] In a biography of General Ayub, an army officer has written that the military aid program with the United States was negotiated during 1953–54 almost entirely through the initiative and efforts of General Ayub Khan. According to the same source, the Americans did not have a high opinion regarding the competence of Pakistan's political leaders and, therefore, welcomed having the Pakistan army on their side. Colonel Mohammad Ahmed, *My Chief* (Lahore: Longmans, Green & Co., 1960), pp. 73–76.

[17] Article 4 of the Southeast Asia Collective Defense Treaty of September 8, 1954, states: "Each Party recognises that aggression by means of armed attack in the treaty area against any of the Parties or against any State or territory which the Parties by unanimous agreement may hereafter designate, would endanger its own peace and safety, and agrees that it will in that event act to meet the common danger in accordance with its constitutional processes. Measures taken under this paragraph shall be immediately reported to the Security Council of the United Nations."

pointed out that these military bases in West Pakistan have listening and radar devices which enable the United States to watch Soviet military movements along a part of its southern border in Central Asia. In addition to these broad strategic considerations, there was also the danger of the Soviet Union starting a subversive military and political war against Pakistan by giving military support to the Afghan irredentist claims against Pakistan's Pathan areas.

What advantages accrued to Pakistan as a result of its alliance with the United States? In terms of the badly needed military hardware, the total assistance extended to Pakistan from 1954 to 1965 amounted to between $1.2 to $1.5 billion.[18] But economic assistance in the form of Public Law 480 or other agricultural commodity programs, grants for economic development, technical assistance development grants, and loans of various kinds was much larger. Over the period from 1947 through June 30, 1965, economic assistance of this nature amounted to $3 billion. It may also be noted that out of a total developmental outlay of $5.5 billion during the Second Five Year Plan, the United States contributed $1.7 billion in the form of loans, grants and other assistance or about 30 per cent of the total outlay.[19]

However, Pakistan also had to assume certain burdens and disadvantages arising from its membership in the United States-sponsored military alliances. In August, 1953, after a series of bilateral negotiations, a joint communiqué was issued by the Prime Ministers of India and Pakistan that the Kashmir dispute should be settled through a fair and impartial plebiscite and that the plebiscite administrator for this purpose should be appointed by the end of April, 1954. But when Mr. Nehru came to know that Pakistan was engaged in preliminary negotiations with the United States regarding an alliance, he warned Pakistan in December, 1953, that the agreement set out in the joint communiqué of August, 1953, would not be carried out because the "whole context" of the Kashmir agreement "will change if military aid comes to Pakistan."[20] In May, 1954, Pakistan signed the Mutual Defense Assistance Agreement with the United States. After that, it was clear to Pakistan that the Indian Prime Minister would repudiate the joint communiqué on Kashmir. Pakistan did try to save the agreement when the Prime Ministers met in May, 1955, but failed. Similarly, the Soviet Union, which had maintained a neutral stand on the Kashmir

[18] The figures mentioned are usually $1.2 or $1.5 billion. According to Selig S. Harrison, *The Washington Post,* August 12, 1965, it is $1.2 billion. According to *The New York Times,* August 29, 1965, it is $1.5 billion. Similarly, in *The Times of India,* November 29, 1965, it is $1.5 billion.

[19] Figures regarding American economic assistance to Pakistan have been furnished to the author by the Agency for International Development, Department of State.

[20] *The New York Times,* December 24, 1953.

dispute, in 1955 accused Pakistan of becoming a member of "an aggressive Western alliance" and Mr. Khrushchev declared that Kashmir was an integral part of India. After that, the Soviet Union vetoed every resolution of the Security Council on Kashmir that was opposed by India. As we shall see later, the Soviet Union has started veering round to a more neutral position.

It was pointed out in the House of Representatives that one of the advantages the United States derived from its military alliance with Pakistan was this: "In its relations with other Moslem states and with other members of the Afro-Asian bloc, Pakistan can be an efficacious advocate of Western policies and can exert a moderating influence on the extreme nationalism and anti-Western attitudes of some of the members of these groups."[21] But so far as Pakistan was concerned, its alliance with the United States turned out to be a serious liability in its relations with Afro-Asian countries. India often contemptuously referred to Pakistan as a country which had degraded itself by becoming a camp follower of a Western power.[22] The hostility that Pakistan incurred in the Arab world, particularly because it was one of the founder members of the Baghdad Pact, which was bitterly opposed by President Nasser, was even stronger than that of India. As a result, the Arab world was not prepared to support Pakistan in its stand on Kashmir even though Pakistan was a Muslim country claiming to struggle for the self-determination of Kashmiri Muslims.

In 1962 it looked as if American policy in South Asia had turned full circle. When the United States signed the Mutual Defense Assistance Agreement in May, 1954, it was followed by deterioration in Indian-American relations and an improvement in India's relations with China. When the United States decided to extend military aid to India in the wake of the Sino-Indian border war in October, 1962, relations between the United States and Pakistan took a sharp turn for the worse, and relations between Pakistan and China were lifted to a higher level of cordiality. But a reappraisal of American policy towards India and Pakistan had been going on ever since President Kennedy came to power in 1961. Even before, some of the liberal intellectuals in the Democratic Party had put forward the view that India, being the most influential and powerful democracy in Asia, should be supported by the West in the ideological and power struggle that was taking place in Asia between the Free World and a Communist

[21] *Mutual Security Act of 1958.* Hearings before House Committee on Foreign Relations, 85th Congress, 2d sess., April 15–16, 1958 (Washington: 1958), p. 1753.

[22] See Nehru's speech in the Bandung Conference in April, 1955. Cited in K. Sarwar Hasan, *Pakistan and the United Nations* (New York: Manhattan Publishing Co., 1960), p. 73.

power like China.[23] Selig Harrison of the *New Republic* had expressed this view in blunt terms: "India is the great power of South Asia: it is not the business of the U.S. to subsidize Pakistan as a permanent garrison state with a military capability swollen out of all proportion to her size."[24] Similarly, some of these leaders did not view with sympathy the historical depth and intensity that lay behind Pakistan's Muslim nationalism.[25] This lack of sympathy towards Pakistan was also reinforced by Pakistan's suspension of democratic processes in 1958. Pakistani fears, which had been aroused by the writings and statements of the New Frontiersmen, were heightened when Vice-President Lyndon Johnson declared in 1961 during his visit to Asia that "at President Kennedy's request" he had "urged Mr. Nehru to extend his leadership to other areas in South-East Asia."[26] Later, in September, 1964, Senator Humphrey, who had already received the Democratic nomination for the Vice-Presidency, declared the United States must realize that in the long run, the only possible defense against Communism in Southeast Asia was an Asian coalition of powers "with India as its main force."[27]

Another factor which brought about a change in American thinking was the decreasing dependence of the United States on military bases in foreign countries as a result of the development of intercontinental ballistic missiles. Henry Kissinger, often described as an adviser of President Kennedy on international affairs, declared in a press conference at New Delhi in January, 1962, that he had been against the formation of the NATO alliance, but "at that time [we] were suffering from a disease called 'pactitis.'" Pakistani leaders were also aware of this change in American thinking. Foreign Minister Muhammad Ali Bogra, who as Prime Minister (1953–55) had been one of the architects of Pakistan's alliances with the United States, declared in the National Assembly in 1962 that the great powers were not attaching much importance to pacts and regional security arrangements. "The whole military thinking has become different."[28]

[23] For Chester Bowles' and Kennedy's statements, see Selig S. Harrison, *India and the United States* (New York: Macmillan, 1961), pp. 28 and 64.

[24] Selig S. Harrison, "India, Pakistan and the United States." Reprint from August 10, August 24, and September 7, 1959, issues of *The New Republic*.

[25] See Chester Bowles, *Ambassador's Report* (New York: Harper, 1954), pp. 70–71 and 251–253; Adlai Stevenson, *Call to Greatness* (New York: Harper, 1954), p. 23; and also *The Round Table*, LIII (1962–63), 397.

[26] *The Round Table*, LI (1960–61), 408. Mr. Johnson tried to calm Pakistani suspicions by explaining what he really meant.

[27] *The New York Times*, September 13, 1964.

[28] *National Assembly of Pakistan Debates*, I, No. 12 (June 27, 1962), pp. 621–622.

President Ayub Khan was not only aware of these shifts in American policy; he was even prepared to cooperate with India in forging a common front against the inroads of Communism in Asia. Ayub Khan, who had spent a considerable part of his active life serving in the British Indian army, genuinely believed, like other senior military officers in the Pakistan and Indian armies, that the subcontinent of India and Pakistan could only be defended against outside powers like China and the Soviet Union by the creation of a joint defense arrangement between the two countries. In other words, President Ayub was in basic agreement with the overall objectives of the American policy of containing Communism in Asia. In pursuing this policy, he wanted to work in partnership with India and not under its leadership. But the most essential condition for this cooperation so far as Pakistan was concerned was the settlement of the Kashmir problem.

During 1959–60, serious differences arose between Delhi and Peking over Chinese oppression in Tibet, Chinese incursions beyond the McMahon Line, and Chinese occupation of territory around Aksai Chin in Ladakh. Chinese probings beyond the McMahon Line in the northeast also provided a threat to East Pakistan. In an interview with a British correspondent, Ayub had gone on record to say that: "A Russian-Chinese drive to the Indian Ocean is a major aim in the Communist drive for world domination."[29] Believing therefore that Nehru would be more receptive to arguments of strategy and defense than to the demand for a plebiscite in Kashmir, which was linked to the two-nation theory, Ayub approached Nehru on September 1, 1959, for a settlement of their disputes and the creation of joint defense arrangements. Nehru is reported to have dismissed the offer and snapped back: "Joint defence against whom?"[30]

Even at a time when India was faced with a military conflict with China in 1962, President Ayub Khan wrote to Mr. Nehru that "the intensive military activity" on India's frontier was "endangering the peace and stability of a region in which Pakistan was vitally interested." He also assured Mr. Nehru that Pakistan was wedded to peace and friendly relations, "especially with India."[31] It is said that this attitude enabled India to transfer some of the troops from the Pakistan frontier to the Chinese border.[32]

Pakistan's relations with Communist China may roughly be divided into two phases. During the first phase (1950–60), starting with Pakistan's recognition of the People's Republic of China (P.R.C.) on

[29] *The Pakistan Observer*, November 19, 1959.
[30] *The Round Table*, LIII (1962–63), 182.
[31] *The Times of India*, November 14, 1962.
[32] *The Economist*, September 4, 1965, p. 853.

January 4, 1950, it tried to combine friendship with the West with a "correct" attitude towards the growing power of Communist China. During the second or current phase (1961–   ), Pakistan's relations have become increasingly cordial, but it has found that it could not carry this cordiality too far in view of American pressure and the threat to cut off economic and other assistance, and also because of Russian attempts to insulate the subcontinent of India and Pakistan from excessive Chinese influence or pressure.

During the first phase, even though Pakistan became a member of the SEATO alliance, which was designed largely to counteract the growing Chinese influence and power in Southeast Asia, the Pakistani Prime Minister, Muhammad Ali Bogra, assured Chou En-lai that Pakistan's membership in SEATO did not imply that Pakistan was against China or that Pakistan feared aggression from Communist China.[33] Significantly, the Chinese did not react in a hostile fashion towards Pakistan. They probably knew that Pakistan's membership in SEATO and other pacts was largely motivated by its fear of India. Actually, Pakistan's role in the SEATO pact was extremely modest and, with the exception of the Pakistan Navy, Pakistani troops had not participated in SEATO military exercises. United States military aid to Pakistan seemed to be directed against Moscow and not Peking.[34] It may also be noted that even though Pakistan until 1960 continued to support the Western-sponsored resolutions postponing consideration of the question regarding UN membership for Communist China, the Chinese did not come out in favor of India on the Kashmir question. In contrast, the Soviet Union turned against Pakistan over the matter of Kashmir after Pakistan joined the Baghdad Pact. The U.S.S.R. vetoed several Security Council resolutions designed to settle the Kashmir dispute either through plebiscite or bilateral negotiations. In the Bandung Conference of April, 1955, the Chinese Prime Minister, Chou En-lai, took advantage of India-Pakistan differences and rivalry and tried to play the role of a mediator.[35]

[33] See Chou En-lai's statement, *The Statesman,* April 30, 1955. This statement was confirmed by Muhammad Ali Bogra, *National Assembly of Pakistan Debates,* I, No. 12 (June 27, 1962), pp. 622–623.

[34] "There is no evidence in the shape of military planning, ground, air or naval exercises, or public statements that preparations have been laid for any SEATO military assistance to Pakistan. United States military aid for Pakistan seems oriented against the U.S.S.R. rather than China (except in so far as it is used to strengthen forces deployed against India), and on either count has little relevance to SEATO purposes." George Modelski, ed., *SEATO: Six Studies* (Vancouver: The University of British Columbia, 1962), p. 133.

[35] Mohamed Abdel Khalek Hassouna, *The First Asian-African Conference Held at Bandung, Indonesia (April 18–24, 1955)* (Cairo: League of Arab States, 1955), pp. 99–101 and 129, and Hasan, p. 73.

The second phase of Pakistan's relations with the P.R.C. started with a concrete gesture of friendship: Pakistan voted in December, 1961, in favor of seating the P.R.C. in the United Nations. It took some time for Pakistan to veer round to this point of view. As we have noticed earlier, in September, 1959, India had turned down Pakistan's offer for joint defense. At a news conference on October 23, 1959, President Ayub Khan announced his intention to approach the Chinese authorities for a peaceful settlement of the Chinese-Pakistan border. Pakistan had some cause to be concerned about its border with the P.R.C. because the government of Pakistan had seen Chinese maps showing large parts of Pakistan's northern regions as Chinese territory. The government was also aware that the Chinese were maintaining infantry forces along the Sino-Pakistan frontier; whereas the Pakistani side of the border was so inaccessible that they could maintain only border police posts.[36] This border had considerable geopolitical importance as the P.R.C. was involved there in conflict both with the U.S.S.R. and India.

Pakistan's border with the P.R.C. extended along a line starting from the tri-junction of Pakistan, Afghanistan, and the P.R.C. to the Karakoram Pass in the East — a distance of 200 miles. In this area Pakistan's frontier with the P.R.C. consisted of Hunza and Gilgit, which were parts of Kashmir under Pakistani control and which India claimed as its own because of the Maharaja of Jammu and Kashmir's decision to accede to India in 1947. On the Chinese side, it may be noted that the province of Sinkiang (the Sinkiang-Uighur Autonomous Region) reached as far as the tri-junction of Pakistan, Afghanistan and the P.R.C. The majority of the people of this province were the Uighurs and Kazakhs, who belonged to the same group as the Turkic-Muslim peoples living in neighboring Soviet Kazakhstan. During 1962 and 1963, there were serious differences between the Chinese and the Russians, and the Chinese accused the Soviet Union of having lured thousands of Chinese citizens from Sinkiang into Russian territory. The Russians, on the other hand, accused the Chinese of oppressing the non-Chinese nationalities in Sinkiang.[37] This area, therefore, was of vital importance to the P.R.C. A revolt in Sinkiang organized by the Muslim tribes with Soviet help would isolate the Chinese position in Tibet. A major purpose of the P.R.C.'s claim to the Aksai Chin area of Ladakh and its subsequent attack on Indian outposts in Ladakh was to safeguard the road the Chinese had built through Sinkiang and Ladakh into Tibet.

[36] President Ayub's interview with *The Daily Mail* correspondent, *The Pakistan Observer*, November 19, 1959.

[37] Geoffrey Wheeler, "Sinkiang and the Soviet Union," *The China Quarterly*, No. 16 (October/December, 1963), p. 59.

Although the Pakistan government announced their intention to approach the Chinese regarding a border settlement in October, 1959, it was in January, 1961, that the Pakistani Foreign Minister announced that the P.R.C. had agreed in principle to demarcate its border with Pakistan. After that, again more than a year elapsed before the two governments announced on May 3, 1962, that they had decided to negotiate an agreement regarding their borders. It was on October 12, 1962, at the time that the P.R.C. and India were engaged in a border war, that actual talks began in Peking. Similarly, when Pakistan and India were engaged in bilateral talks regarding Kashmir, the Pakistani Foreign Minister left in March, 1963, for Peking in response to an invitation from the P.R.C., and the border agreement was signed in Peking in 1963. According to Indian claims, Pakistan surrendered 2,050 square miles of Pakistani-held Kashmir. But a careful analysis of the terms of the border agreement shows that both sides made concessions. The area in dispute was about 3,400 square miles. The compromise arrived at left about 2,050 square miles of the disputed area on the P.R.C.'s side. Pakistan, however, gave up only claims on maps, whereas the P.R.C. agreed to withdraw its frontier forces and administration from about 750 square miles. Pakistan insists that the territory it conceded to the P.R.C. had neither been under its control nor under the control of its predecessors, the British authorities.[38]

The border pact was followed by a Civil Aviation Agreement in August, 1963, between Communist China and Pakistan. This air agreement linked the Chinese cities of Canton and Shanghai with Dacca and Karachi. The United States State Department reaction was that the agreement was "an unfortunate breach of the free world solidarity" and that the air link between Pakistan and Communist China would "have an adverse effect on efforts to strengthen the security and solidarity of the subcontinent which the Chinese Communists want to prevent."[39]

Why were Pakistan's policy-makers building such close links with the P.R.C.? Mian Mumtaz Daultana, a former Chief Minister of West Punjab and for a brief period the Central Defense Minister, assessed the situation in November, 1962, in this way:

The rivalry for Asian domination which both China and India consider to be their "manifest destiny," the ethnic and historical ties of

[38] Alastair Lamb's book, based on British records, seems to support Pakistan's case. Alastair Lamb, *The China-India Border* (London: Oxford University Press, 1964), pp. 105–114. See also *The Times,* March 4 and 6, 1963. For an official statement of Pakistan's position, which is in agreement with Lamb's account, see *United Nations Security Council Official Records.* 1114th Meeting. Nineteenth Year. 11 May 1964, S/PV. 1114, pp. 11–12.
[39] *The Round Table,* LIII (1962–63), 396.

the disputed areas with China, the stringent Chinese ideological emphasis on "conflict" rather than "co-existence" as the operative springs of Communist dialectics, the austerities of the Chinese internal situation, the reckless wooing of India by the West, point to a deeper alienation. My own tentative interpretation is this. The cold war between India and China is likely to be prolonged, the hot war is a very temporary phase, which many circumstances impugn to bring to an early close.[40]

Pakistan's policy-makers knew that the West, and particularly the United States, had been engaged in a bitter confrontation with Communist China and now that the conflict between India and the P.R.C. had erupted, the United States would regard India as a bastion of democracy and Western interests against Chinese Communism. Therefore, the United States was bound to extend massive military and economic assistance to India. Because of this, Pakistan would be placed at a serious disadvantage, for India might not only use American military assistance against Pakistan, but would be in a position to tighten its hold over Kashmir, pointing out to the Americans that it could not defend Ladakh against Chinese incursions without maintaining its firm foothold in the Kashmir Valley. The United States and Britain rushed military assistance to India in the order of $120 million in December, 1962, after the Chinese troops had penetrated Indian territory. Later, in June, 1964, the United States announced that military aid between $500 million to $525 million would be extended to India for the next five years.[41] Pakistan thought that if India, strengthened by American military assistance, were to embark on aggression against Pakistan, the P.R.C., which had also become a nuclear power, might come to the assistance of Pakistan. Both Foreign Minister Bhutto and President Ayub Khan suggested that Pakistan expected Chinese support in the event of an Indian attack.[42] A bitter press campaign started against the United States in the Pakistani press, and the United States was openly accused of interfering in Pakistan's domestic politics and fomenting conflict between East and West Pakistan.

The Chinese extended their support to Pakistan in careful and calculated stages. Before the border agreement was reached, they took the position that Kashmir was a disputed area. After the border agree-

[40] Cited in *ibid.,* p. 289.

[41] According to *The Washington Post,* June 7, 1964, military aid of about $100 million a year on a long-term basis was announced. According to an article by Sharokh Sabavala in *The Christian Science Monitor,* July 22, 1964, military assistance was in the order of $525 million for the next five years.

[42] For Bhutto's statement, see *The Round Table,* LIII (1962–63), 398. For Ayub's statement, see *The Washington Post,* September 12, 1963.

ment and other understandings, they came out fully in support of Pakistan's stand on Kashmir. The Ayub-Chou joint communiqué of February 23, 1964, indicated a much greater area of understanding than previous professions of Chinese friendship for Pakistan had.

> They expressed the hope that the Kashmir dispute would be resolved in accordance with the wishes of the people of Kashmir, as pledged to them by India and Pakistan. It would be of no avail to deny the existence of these disputes and to adopt a big-nation chauvinistic attitude of imposing one's will on others.[43]

It seemed that the Chinese attempts to forge close links with Pakistan were ultimately directed towards driving a wedge between Pakistan and the United States. Following Ayub's visit to the P.R.C. in March, 1965, a China-Pakistan joint communiqué was issued which extolled Asian-African solidarity and referred to colonialism and racial discrimination as obstacles to national independence and world peace. The communiqué, without mentioning the United States by name, alleged that by introducing nuclear weapons into the Indian Ocean, it had posed a threat to the independence of the countries concerned and had undermined Asian-African solidarity. In the communiqué Pakistan expressed its opposition to the schemes for creating two Chinas and the Chinese supported the Pakistani demand for plebiscite in Kashmir.[44]

Pakistan also supported Chinese attempts to summon the Second African-Asian Conference in 1965 in Algeria, which could not be held owing to political upheaval in that country when the host government of Ben Bella was overthrown. By associating closely with Communist China and Indonesia, Pakistan was trying to become one of the influential countries in Asia. Foreign Minister Bhutto pointed out that the role of nonaligned nations like India had greatly diminished since the Cold War had been practically eliminated; whereas "the need for the development of African-Asian solidarity as a world force had on the other hand become even greater."[45]

As we have noted earlier, during 1954–55, when Pakistan entered into the Mutual Defense Assistance Agreement with the United States and joined the SEATO and the Baghdad Pact (now CENTO) alliances, there was broad agreement between Pakistan and the United States, but by no means perfect parallelism of interests. The American decision to give military aid to India in 1962 and Pakistan's increasing friendship with Communist China altered their relationship into one

---

[43] *Dawn*, February 24, 1964.

[44] *Peking Review*, No. 11 (March 12, 1965), pp. 9–10.

[45] Press Information Department, Government of Pakistan. Handout, "Foreign Minister's Statement at Press Conference," (April 21, 1964), p. 2.

in which they exerted pressure tactics against each other. Pakistan wanted the United States not to give military assistance to India because, in Pakistan's view, the Chinese threat to India was not serious enough to warrant massive military aid, and above all, because such military assistance would ultimately endanger Pakistan's security. Pakistan also felt that if the United States insisted on giving military aid because of the threat of Chinese Communism in Asia, then it should at least pressure India into settling the Kashmir dispute with Pakistan. Indeed, the Pakistanis finally concluded that since the United States was not willing to exert the necessary pressure on India for the settlement of the Kashmir dispute and since Pakistan's security was in danger, it had a right to seek Chinese protective friendship. The Americans, for their part, warned Pakistan that its increasing friendship with Communist China could lead to a reappraisal of United States aid.[46]

Pakistan seemed to be aware of American sensitivity regarding Communist China and its own dependence on American economic and military aid. Foreign Minister Bhutto, a consistent advocate of increasing Pakistan's friendship with Communist China, signed the communiqué issued by the SEATO Council in London in May, 1965. The communiqué charged that the aggression against the Republic of Vietnam was organized and directed by the Communist regime in North Vietnam.[47] During early July, 1965, however, at the request of the United States, the Aid-Pakistan Consortium meeting scheduled for July 27, 1965, was postponed for two months. (The Aid-Pakistan Consortium consisted of nine countries — the United States, West Germany, United Kingdom, Canada, France, Japan, Belgium, Netherlands, Italy.) Pakistan was seeking $500 million from the Consortium for the first year of its Third Five Year Plan which began on July 1, 1965. The official American position was that without congressional authorization the United States could not pledge 40 per cent of the $500 million that Pakistan had asked for. Pakistani reaction was bitter because the United States had pledged $940 million to India well in advance of authorization by Congress. Pakistan's Foreign Minister also pointed out that the United States, besides postponing the Consortium meeting, had suggested to the Pakistan government that "other problems should also be discussed."[48] In September, 1965, when the meeting was to be held, Pakistan and India were engaged in an armed

[46] For Hearings before the House Appropriations Sub-Committee on Foreign Operations, see *Dawn*, June 25, 1965.

[47] *Pakistan Documents Series*, II, No. 1 (Embassy of Pakistan, Washington, D.C.: June, 1965), pp. 2–4.

[48] Press Information Department, Government of Pakistan. Handout, "Consortium" (July 15, 1965), p. 3.

conflict over the question of Kashmir, and the United States suspended military and economic aid to both countries.

Why did Pakistan allow guerrillas from Pakistan-held Azad Kashmir to infiltrate the cease-fire line in August, 1965? It looked as if Pakistan hoped that India, faced by internal unrest in Kashmir and guerrilla activity from across the cease-fire line, with the Chinese waiting to pounce upon them from the Ladakh side, would be forced into reopening the Kashmir question with a view to reaching a settlement. These calculations went awry when India retaliated with a massive military attack on Lahore and Sialkot in West Pakistan. The fighting, however, reached a stalemate and both sides knew that if the war continued each would face economic disaster. Ayub, the architect of Pakistan's military alliances and under whose regime Pakistan had made impressive economic progress, perhaps felt that he could not take any more risks. During the course of the fighting itself, he appealed to President Johnson for his intervention and said that the President should tell both India and Pakistan, which depended on large United States aid programs, that the United States "will not stand for this conflict" and that the two countries should arrange a purposeful and permanent cease-fire.[49] Later, after the cease-fire had been brought about under the Security Council resolution of September 20, 1965, Ayub visited Washington on December 14 and 15, 1965. According to Ayub, his meeting with President Johnson cleared the misunderstanding that existed between the two countries regarding Pakistan's relationships with China, which, according to the Pakistani view, had been dictated by "compulsions of geo-political factors."[50] Since the December meeting, relations between the two countries have improved. The United States, which was interested in political stability and economic development in South Asia, particularly in view of the Chinese threat, wanted Pakistan and India to reach an accord. Presumably it was made clear to both countries that economic assistance would be resumed only if they were at peace with each other. But Pakistan of course expected the United States to do its best in persuading India to settle the Kashmir conflict; the Pakistanis felt that without such a settlement a long-term peace between the two countries would be most difficult.

In no other area of the world did there ever emerge such a coincidence of interests between the United States and the U.S.S.R. as when fighting broke out between India and Pakistan in September, 1965. Both countries were concerned that if the fighting continued, the Chinese would profit from it immensely. Both supported the UN effort in bringing about a cease-fire and creating a machinery for the settle-

[49] *The Washington Daily News,* September 15, 1965.
[50] *The Times,* December 20, 1965.

ment of outstanding disputes between the two countries, including the Kashmir problem. It was also clear that this cooperation was triggered by the Chinese threat to start military activity against India on the Sikkim border. Significantly, the Chinese denounced both the American and Soviet efforts, calling the former as those of "imperialists" and the latter as those of "revisionists." But Pakistan appreciated Chinese support during the war. Foreign Minister Bhutto said that the first two September resolutions of the Security Council could be characterized as "India's resolutions" because they served India's interests by simply trying to restore the status quo. The resolution of September 20, 1965, on the other hand, not only ordered a cease-fire, but pointed out that such a cease-fire would be an essential first step towards "a peaceful settlement of the outstanding differences between the two countries on Kashmir and other related matters." According to Mr. Bhutto, this was "China's resolution" because "the Chinese ultimatum to India had shaken the United Nations and the great powers into realizing the danger of war on the subcontinent and that only a political settlement could allow permanent peace."[51]

Students of South Asian history are aware of the desire of both the Czarist and Communist regimes in Russia to gain access to the warm water ports of the Indian Ocean, particularly Karachi, which also provides an outlet to the oil-rich areas of the Middle East. Behind every major policy decision of the British pertaining to the northwestern parts of India, there lurked the fear of Russian penetration of these areas. The American policy of extending the Baghdad Pact to Pakistan was a continuation of the British policy to prevent Russian expansion. As we have noted earlier, the Russians were extremely annoyed by Pakistan's alliances with the United States and tried to penalize Pakistan in the matter of the Kashmir problem. But it seems that as Pakistan became increasingly alienated from the United States during 1962–65 and cordial towards the Chinese, the Russians started adopting a neutral attitude towards the Indo-Pakistan conflict. When an armed conflict flared up between India and Pakistan in April, 1965, over the Rann of Kutch, the Russians advised both India and Pakistan not to weaken each other and threaten the peace in Asia, and pointed out that only "the imperialist circles of the Western powers" would profit from such conflicts.[52] The change in Russian policy was succinctly stated by *Pravda* when it wrote that "we should like good Soviet-Pakistan relations, just as our traditional friendship with India, to be a stabilizing factor in Asia."[53] The Tashkent agreement of January 10,

[51] *Ibid.*, October 6, 1965.
[52] *Pravda*, May, 9, 1965.
[53] Cited in *The Times,* January 3, 1966.

1966, between India and Pakistan represented a highwater mark of Russian diplomacy. The cease-fire brought about by the Security Council resolution of September 20 had often been observed in the breach and there was no immediate prospect of the two countries agreeing to withdraw their troops to the positions they held prior to August 5, 1965. At Tashkent the two countries agreed to withdraw all armed personnel to their former positions and, in addition, they agreed to restore diplomatic relations and consider measures for the restoration of economic and trade relations. Furthermore, they agreed to discontinue propaganda against each other and to try to settle their disputes through peaceful means.

Why are the Russians interested in promoting peaceful relations between India and Pakistan and the maintenance of political stability in those two countries? One cannot do better than to quote from a violent attack on the Tashkent talks in the Peking *People's Daily* for the motives behind the Russian policy.

> The course taken by the Soviet leaders in the Vietnam, India-Pakistan, and Japan questions completely conforms with the requirements of imperialism, and especially with the latter's policy of encircling China.[54]

There are several reasons why Pakistan would seek the good will and assistance of the Soviet Union both in settling its disputes with India and in its efforts to maintain a steady pace of economic development. In the first place, Pakistan cannot afford to ignore the Russian presence in adjacent Afghanistan, which has sometimes tried to stir the Pathans living in the Frontier area of Pakistan to demand a separate state. In the second place, Pakistanis know that the Russians have acquired considerable influence in India by providing military and economic assistance to that country and, above all, by offering India protection against China's growing nuclear power. Thus, Pakistan hopes that the Russians, through their influence in India, may be able to help Pakistan in the settlement of the Kashmir dispute. Finally, the Soviet Union is a richer country than Communist China. Its economic aid to India has amounted to more than a billion dollars and credit for military aid has approached $300 million.[55] In 1961, the Soviet Union offered Pakistan a credit of $30 million to purchase Soviet equipment for the exploration of oil. It also trained Pakistani engineers and sent Soviet experts to Pakistan. In 1964, the Soviet Union extended a credit of $10 million for the purchase of heavy earth-moving machinery and

---

[54] See *Peking Review*, IX, No. 6 (February 4, 1966), p. 12.
[55] Selig S. Harrison, "Troubled India and Her Neighbors," *Foreign Affairs* (January, 1964), p. 326.

other accessories. The two countries are also linked through a commercial airline flying between Moscow and Karachi. Early in 1966, Pakistan entered into barter agreements with the Soviet Union under which, for the export of rice, cotton, jute, etc., Pakistan can obtain Soviet vehicles and agricultural machinery. Pakistan's planners would like to have alternative sources for credit and capital goods because they sometimes run into difficulties in obtaining such facilities from Western countries.

Relations with Britain, the Commonwealth and Muslim Countries

It is true that in terms of economic and military assistance the United States has been the most influential country in Pakistan. Since 1962, Chinese support, as that of a great power and particularly against India, has been warmly appreciated. For British influence, however, one has to look deeper to see how it has had a decisive impact on the army, the bureaucracy, and the judiciary. An observer would find many similarities in the Secretariats of New Delhi and Islamabad were he to walk through them, even after nearly two decades of separate existence often marked by deep hostility.

But the formal ties that bind Britain and Pakistan are few. The Queen is the Head of the Commonwealth, a symbolic office with neither authority nor influence. There is, of course, the Commonwealth Prime Ministers Conference, which is like a seminar where differences are openly aired and the participants assemble more to gather information and insight into each other's problems and difficulties than to reach common agreement or policy decisions. In matters of behind-the-door diplomacy, however, Britain continues to wield considerable influence. If there is a sharp disagreement between Pakistan and the United States and if the British sense any danger that American impatience is likely to drive Pakistan into an anti-Western posture or commitment, one is told that British officials intervene to caution against any hasty moves or decisions. Pakistani leaders tend to draw on British experience and advice at London before they go to Washington for talks or consultation. Similarly, Washington respects British advice because it is based on centuries of experience. British influence in India sometimes carries even greater weight than it does in Washington. It may be recalled that it was largely British mediation which brought about a settlement between India and Pakistan over the Rann of Kutch dispute in April, 1965.

We have already seen that nearly 30 per cent of the developmental outlay of the Second Five Year Plan has come in the form of loans and economic assistance from the United States. Table 14 shows that the Commonwealth's share of economic assistance, compared to countries other than the United States, continues to be considerable. In terms of individual countries, the share of Germany and Japan is higher than that of any Commonwealth country. However, it may be pointed out that in most of the cases, with the exception of Canada, the bulk, and sometimes the whole of economic assistance, has been extended in the form of loans. In the case of Canada, $76.49 million out of $88.49 million have been contributed in the form of grants and the rest in the form of loans.

Table 14

Foreign Grants and Loan Commitments
(July 1, 1960–March 31, 1965)

	In Million Dollars
Australia	6.38
Canada	88.49
France	24.00
Germany	207.00
Japan	138.68
U.K.	127.56
U.S.S.R.	41.00
World Bank	120.00

Source: Economic Adviser to the Government of Pakistan, *Pakistan Economic Survey 1964–65* (Karachi: Manager of Publications, Government of Pakistan), pp. 196–197.

For several years after its establishment Pakistan was an enthusiastic supporter of close cooperation among Muslim countries. But it soon discovered that Arab nationalists in the Middle East or in Indonesia did not attach as great an importance to Islam as the Pakistanis did. They took Islam for granted and did not have to invoke their religious faith to maintain their national identity as Pakistan had to do in its relations with India. Above all, Pakistan found that the Islamic bond was not enough to resolve its differences with Afghanistan over the question of Pakhtunistan — the demand supported by Afghanistan for a separate state of the Pakhtuns carved out of certain areas of Pakistan. Afghanistan actually voted against Pakistan's admission into the United Nations. Furthermore, when Pakistan became a member of the Western-sponsored defense alliances, especially of the Baghdad Pact, during 1954–55, it provoked intense Arab indignation in large parts of the Middle East. Pakistan has not always been able to win support over the question of Kashmir, particularly in an influential country like the U.A.R. In 1962, for example, when the U.S.S.R. vetoed the Security Council resolution which merely urged India and Pakistan to enter into negotiations on the question of Kashmir, the U.A.R. abstained. Pakistan's deep disappointment was expressed by its Foreign Minister when he said:

> Our hearts cry out in anguish at the agonizing thought that a country
> — a great Muslim country . . . should have deemed it appropriate
> to withhold her support in an issue of such vital importance not
> only to us but to millions of Muslims of Jammu and Kashmir held
> in colonial subjugation by India.[56]

Pakistan has often found it difficult to evoke support from the U.A.R. in the name of Islamic brotherhood because of the U.A.R.'s close ties with India. But Pakistan's relations with a predominantly Muslim country like Indonesia have become so close that Pakistan not only received support over the question of Kashmir but also military equipment after its reserves had become depleted as a result of the war with India in 1965. Similarly, Pakistan's relations with Afghanistan have also improved.

Pakistan has been much more successful in cementing ties with the Muslim countries of Turkey and Iran. They, like Pakistan, have been members of the CENTO pact ever since its inception. Its cultural relations with these countries have also been closer than with the Arab world. Persian has exercised probably a greater influence over West Pakistan's languages than Arabic. The Mughal emperors who ruled India during the seventeenth and eighteenth centuries were of Turkish origin. In addition to these cultural ties, the three countries have also been able to cooperate with each other because the ruling elites of each have on the whole been conservative and moderate.

The ruling circles in Pakistan have often wondered whether their country as a whole can survive as a viable entity in the long run, not only because of the threat of India, but because of the physical and cultural separation that exists between East and West Pakistan. In addition, they have also worried about their country's ability to resist a long-term economic pull towards confederation with India. Therefore, the idea of a confederation or federation between Pakistan and Afghanistan or Pakistan and Iran has been mentioned, but not pursued in view of the existing difficulties and obstacles.

In the CENTO pact, there was provision for an economic committee and some steps were taken to initiate better communications through roads and railways among the three Muslim countries. Since the CENTO treaty had been sponsored and financed largely by Western initiative, however, the heads of state of Turkey, Iran, and Pakistan perhaps felt that economic and cultural cooperation should be initiated

[56] *National Assembly of Pakistan Debates*, I, No. 10 (June 25, 1962), p. 390.

and pursued by their countries outside the CENTO framework; therefore they announced a new scheme of cooperation entitled Regional Cooperation for Development (RCD) in July, 1964. The aims of this scheme were freer movement of goods through trade agreements, improvement of air, road, and rail links between the three countries, close collaboration in the field of shipping with a view to establishing a joint maritime line or conference, provision of technical assistance to each other, and abolition of visa formalities among the three countries.[57] Since the announcement in July, 1964, many meetings have been held, a Secretariat established in Iran, and the groundwork laid for the establishment of the RCD Chamber of Commerce and Industry. In addition, it was announced in December, 1965, that the RCD shipping line, with headquarters in Istanbul, would start operating in April, 1966. But the problem which has constantly cropped up in East Pakistan is that the RCD is purely an alliance between Iran, Turkey, and West Pakistan, and the long-term outcome of such an alliance, if successful, would mean that West Pakistan would become closer to the two Middle East countries than to East Pakistan. In order to counter such criticism and also as a result of closer understanding with Indonesia, Pakistani leaders have talked of extending RCD arrangements to Indonesia as well. In December, 1965, an agreement in principle to set up a joint Pakistan-Indonesia Chamber of Commerce and Industry was announced. Trade between Pakistan and Indonesia, however, has not yet assumed an appreciable proportion, and the distance between the two countries is so considerable that large-scale regional cooperation between them is not likely to take place.

Pakistanis are impressed by the fact that they have drawn handsome dividends from their new "independent foreign policy," of which the former Foreign Minister Z. A. Bhutto can claim to be the supreme architect. During the war with India in September, 1965, Indonesia, Iran, and Turkey offered both moral and military support. Chinese support was even more impressive because of their threatening posture towards India. Prime Minister Harold Wilson of the United Kingdom condemned the Indian attack. Pakistan also claimed to have enjoyed French support with regard to the Kashmir dispute in the Security Council. Furthermore, Pakistan was supported for the first time by all the Arab countries during the war; indeed, they passed a resolution to this effect at Casablanca[58] — much to Pakistan's elation. In contrast, Indians complained that during the September, 1965, war "there was

---

[57] *Pakistan Document Series,* I, No. 1 (Washington, D.C.: Embassy of Pakistan, August, 1964), p. 1.

[58] Foreign Minister Bhutto in his speech in the National Assembly gave a complete list of all countries that had supported Pakistan. *Dawn,* November 22, 1965.

not in the whole gamut a single nation, great or small, rich or poor, that was openly and wholeheartedly on our side."[59]

We have seen all along that Pakistan's foreign policy revolves around its relations with India and that Kashmir is the crux of its tense relations with India. We have seen how the two countries are in the habit of putting up their respective "semantic smoke screen" every time they debate about the problem of Jammu and Kashmir. Pakistanis maintain that, according to the Security Council resolutions, the people of Jammu and Kashmir should be allowed to exercise their right of self-determination through an impartial plebiscite. Indians, on the other hand, point out that Pakistanis have been violating Security Council resolutions in not withdrawing their troops from certain parts of the state of Jammu and Kashmir. Since Pakistan has persisted in such a violation for a long time, India's undertaking to the holding of a plebiscite could not be carried out and such an undertaking has lapsed. Various proposals regarding the partition of Jammu and Kashmir have been made, but both countries have rejected them. The heart of the dispute is actually the Valley of Kashmir. It is likely that Pakistan will agree to India retaining its hold over Jammu, but will insist that the Valley of Kashmir, which is predominantly Muslim and from which the River Jhelum flows, should come to Pakistan. Sir Owen Dixon, UN representative for India and Pakistan, also suggested a solution along these lines in December, 1950.[60] President Ayub in an interview in 1960 said that he was prepared to discuss any proposal provided it gave Pakistan control of the Chenab waters in Kashmir and did not leave the Muslim inhabitants of the Valley under Indian rule. He did not refer to a plebiscite, talked of joint defense with India, and was willing to discuss partition of the state of Jammu and Kashmir.[61] India has so far resisted all such proposals on the plea that Pakistan is merely giving up claims; whereas India is being called upon to surrender territory.

As Pakistan's relationship with India is of paramount importance, Pakistan views all other relationships in terms of attempts to keep India off balance. By pursuing a friendly relationship with Communist China, Pakistan feels that its international stature will improve and that it will not be taken for granted by powers like the United States and the U.S.S.R. Indeed, Pakistan feels that as its cordiality towards the Chinese increases, perhaps both the United States and the U.S.S.R. will

[59] J. B. Kriplani, "Axe in the Jungle of Administration," *The Times of India,* December 12, 1965.

[60] *United Nations Security Council Official Records.* Fifth Year. Supplement for September through December, 1950. Document S/1791, pp. 44–45.

[61] Interview with Kingsley Martin. See Kingsley Martin's letter to the editor, *The Sunday Statesman,* February 13, 1966, p. 6.

pay more heed to its complaints and make efforts to persuade and pressure India into settling the Kashmir dispute. But Pakistan hopes to draw even more direct dividends from its policy toward China. The Western powers have argued that if China attacks and weakens India, Pakistan's turn will come next. The Pakistanis believe, however, that China has no major territorial designs against India and that the Sino-Indian conflict of 1962 was with regard to certain border adjustments. Pakistan contends that China knows it will provoke a major confrontation with India and the West if it overextends itself into Indian territory. But Pakistan feels confident that both its friendship with China and the latter's menacing attitude toward India are factors which are likely to weaken India's position internally and externally, since India will increasingly have to depend on foreign economic and military aid. Pakistan insists that it made positive friendly gestures toward India by even suggesting a joint military alliance in 1959, but that the offer was spurned by India because Pakistan had attached a rider to this proposal — namely, the settlement of the Kashmir problem. Thus, the Pakistanis have concluded they had no alternative except to turn to China, particularly in view of the fact that the West was reluctant to exert too much pressure on India for a settlement of the Kashmir problem. Pakistanis think that this policy suits them admirably, even if they fail to wrest Kashmir from India's hold, because the major objective of their policy is a weak India. Pakistan with its divided territory would be a difficult proposition if such an existence were not predicated upon the presence of a weak neighbor. This thinking was abundantly confirmed by the Indo-Pakistan war of September, 1965, when India, contrary to all expectations, confined its military activities to West Pakistan, leaving East Pakistan alone. Pakistan's inference from this was that if India had attacked East Pakistan, this move would have provoked Chinese attacks along Sikkim, Bhutan, and the North-East Frontier Agency. Foreign Minister Bhutto even suggested in the National Assembly that East Pakistan was "quarantined" from war as a result of some kind of understanding between the United States, China, and India.

Why did India not raise its little finger against East Pakistan? he asked. He said he could not answer the question directly but anybody was welcome to deduce the answer from the fact that the representatives of the United States and of the People's Republic of China brought the question of defence of East Pakistan under discussion in Warsaw during the 17-day war. It was also during that period that the American Ambassador brought a proposal to Pakistan Government that East Pakistan should be quarantined from war.[62]

[62] *The Pakistan Times,* March 17, 1966.

The foreign policy of a developing country has a decisive impact on political development. Pursuing an ambitious or independent foreign policy may help a country like Pakistan to promote national consensus or integration. It was reported that a leftish leader like Maulana Bhashani in East Pakistan did not campaign actively against President Ayub because opposition to Ayub might upset the government's pro-Chinese foreign policy. The government of Pakistan has also tried to rally support internally by pointing out that as a result of its independent foreign policy, Pakistan has become an influential country in international politics. President Ayub once claimed, "When Mr. Chou En-lai, China's Prime Minister, recently visited Pakistan, half of my talks with Mr. Chou were on relations with the United States."[63] Alignment with Communist China and the promotion of Afro-Asian solidarity, also reflect the predispositions of young men in their thirties and forties who are becoming increasingly influential in Pakistan's power structure. These men are to be found in the Civil Service of Pakistan and the Pakistan army. They have been to the universities and participated in or watched the flowering of nationalist movements into independence in large parts of Asia and Africa. It is to this group of young men that the former Foreign Minister, Zulfiqar Ali Bhutto, belongs. He thinks in terms of historic forces or world currents, and conceals beneath a suave exterior scars of racial bitterness against the West. He dreams of the unity of the Afro-Asian world, which to him "is a world of the proletariat." In a speech in the National Assembly, Bhutto declared:

Asians wanted to fashion their societies in their own way. These ways were not known to Americans who had never been in the region. As classical imperialists even the British and the French, who ruled these regions, knew the Asians only as servants and not as human beings with aspirations.[64]

However, foreign policy in developing countries which results in war or conflict with neighboring countries can also impose strains on national unity. Particularly in a country like Pakistan with its territory divided into two parts and separated by a thousand miles of Indian territory, a conflict with India is likely to leave East Pakistan, with its weaker defenses, isolated and vulnerable. Thus, an East Pakistani member of the National Assembly, referring to the September, 1965, conflict with India, asked why the security of fifty million people of East Pakistan was placed in dire danger for the liberation of five million Kashmiris.[65] In developing countries like India and Pakistan,

[63] *Morning News,* July 14, 1964.
[64] *The Pakistan Times,* March 17, 1966.
[65] See *ibid.*

where democratic institutions are still in their fragile and formative state, another consequence of an ambitious and aggressive foreign policy leading to military conflicts could be the suspension of civil liberties. This was the experience in both India and Pakistan during the September, 1965, conflict.[66]

We have seen how Pakistan, by cultivating cordial relations with Communist China, has increased its importance in the eyes of both the United States and the U.S.S.R. in the sense that neither of them would like Pakistan to get too close to Communist China. But Pakistan also has to pursue its relations with Communist China with considerable adroitness and skill so that the United States may not be provoked into suspending its military and economic aid to Pakistan. In a revealing statement, Foreign Minister Bhutto has declared: "Some countries are very good experts on being aligned and non-aligned. We have yet to learn the art of being both aligned and non-aligned."[67] What does a power like the United States seek to achieve through its economic aid to Pakistan? It is clear that the United States will be anxious that Pakistan should not align itself so closely to Communist China that the Chinese begin to interfere in Pakistan's domestic politics and, above all, through their influence may pressure Pakistan into pursuing the foreign policy objectives of Communist China. But the long-term objectives of American aid policy are probably to use economic aid so skillfully as to shape the direction of economic and political development in Pakistan along what Americans consider right or desirable lines. To some extent, the United States has already achieved success in their policy objectives. Thus, it may be argued that the American announcements of general commodity assistance loans have enabled Pakistan to liberalize its import program and thus offer a wider scope to private enterprise "in which it can operate freely unhindered by the shackles of price and distribution controls."[68] Perhaps the United States believes that there is a positive correlation between political competitiveness and economic development in which private enterprise plays an important role. Perhaps, too, American support to the Rural

---

[66] In India, the government was accused of using Defence of India Rules against opposition leaders. This legislation was first introduced during the conflict with China in 1962. In Pakistan, where the National Assembly enjoys fewer powers than its counterpart in India, the Fundamental Rights were suspended during the conflict with India in 1965.

[67] Press Information Department, Government of Pakistan, "Question-Answer Part of Mr. Bhutto's Press Conference At The Old National Assembly Hall, Karachi On 19.2.1964," p. 14.

[68] Economic Adviser to the Government of Pakistan, Ministry of Finance, *Pakistan Economic Survey 1964–65* (Karachi: Manager of Publications, 1965), p. 29.

Public Works Program through the sale of American surplus foodstuffs and other commodities under the P.L. 480 program and the assistance that AID advisers have given to the Program-Building Concept of Agriculture Extension (referred to in the previous chapter) are all designed to ensure that there be not only greater political participation on the part of the people, but also that leaders of Pakistan may be able to broaden the base of their political support.

These objectives of United States policy with regard to Pakistan, when viewed by Pakistanis in the context of American support to India against China and American unhappiness regarding Pakistan's cordiality towards China, have aroused Pakistani suspicions and created the impression that the United States is trying to undermine the influence of Pakistan's Central Government in certain areas of Pakistan. Particularly American interest in the economic development of East Pakistan has heightened these suspicions. The government of Pakistan often finds it to its advantage to take a stand against the United States for in this way it can mobilize political support in the country. These reactions also indicate the inherent weakness of Pakistan's political system in the sense that it is dominated far too much by the bureaucracy and has not been able to create adequate political support either among the urban elements or regional forces like those of East Pakistan. In addition to all this, as we have suggested earlier, Pakistan occupies such a strategic importance in the global policies of powers like the United States, the U.S.S.R., and Communist China that all three countries are engaged in increasing their influence in Pakistan. Particularly East Pakistan with its proximity to Communist China is likely to become a political battleground. Communist China, if it succeeds in establishing a firm foothold in East Pakistan, and the United States, with its influence in India, are likely to compete against each other for political support in this part of the world.

SELECTED BIBLIOGRAPHY

Genesis of Pakistan

The bibliography of the genesis of Pakistan may be divided into three headings: (1) books which are historical and descriptive (2) government reports and other publications, All-India Muslim League publications, and others (3) books, Gazetteers and reports on the social and economic conditions of Muslims living in the Muslim-majority provinces of British India.

I. Historical and Descriptive

Ahmad, Jamil-ud-Din, ed. *Speeches and Writings of Mr. Jinnah.* 2 vols. Lahore: Ashraf, Vol. I, 6th ed., 1960; Vol. II, 1964.

Albiruni, A. H. *Makers of Pakistan and Modern Muslim India.* Lahore: Ashraf, 1950.

Ambedkar, B. R. *Pakistan, or the Partition of India.* 3rd ed. Bombay: Thacker, 1946.

Azad, Maulana Abul Kalam. *India Wins Freedom.* Calcutta: Orient Longmans, 1959.

Besant, Annie. *How India Wrought for Freedom.* Madras: Theosophical Publishing House, 1915.

Bevan, Edwyn. *Indian Nationalism.* London: Macmillan, 1913.

Blunt, Sir Edward. *The I. C. S. The Indian Civil Service.* London: Faber, 1937.

Bolitho, Hector. *Jinnah, Creator of Pakistan.* London: John Murray, 1954.

Brecher, Michael. *Jawaharlal Nehru: A Political Biography.* London: Oxford, 1959.

Campbell-Johnson, Alan. *Mission With Mountbatten.* London: Robert Hale, 1953.

Casey, R. G. *An Australian in India.* London: Hollis and Carter, 1947.

Chaudhuri, Nirad C. *The Autobiography of An Unknown Indian.* New York: Macmillan, 1951.

Chirol, Valentine. *Indian Unrest.* London: Macmillan, 1910.

Coatman, I. *Years of Destiny: India, 1926–1932.* London: Jonathan Cape, 1932.

Coupland, R. *The Indian Problem.* New York: Oxford, 1944.

Cumming, John. *Political India, 1832–1932.* London: Oxford, 1932.

Dar, Bashir Ahmad. *Religious Thought of Sayyid Ahmad Khan.* Lahore: Institute of Islamic Culture, 1957.

Dutt, R. Palme. *Modern India.* London: Communist Party of Great Britain, 1927.

Gandhi, M. K. *Communal Unity.* Ahmedabad: Navajivan Publishing House, 1949.

Garratt, G. T. *An Indian Commentary.* London: Jonathan Cape, 1928.

Gopal, Ram. *Indian Muslims: A Political History (1858–1947).* Bombay: Asia Publishing House, 1959.

Gopal, S. *The Viceroyalty of Lord Irwin, 1926–1931.* Oxford: Clarendon, 1957.

Griffiths, Sir Percival. *The British Impact on India.* London: Macdonald, 1952.

Gwyer, Sir Maurice, and Appadorai, A., eds. *Speeches and Documents on the Indian Constitution 1921-47*. 2 vols. London: Oxford, 1957.

Gwynn, J. T. *Indian Politics: A Survey*. London: Nisbet, 1924.

Horne, E. A. *The Political System of British India*. Oxford: Clarendon, 1922.

Hunter, W. W. *The Indian Mussalmans*. Lahore: Premier Book House, 1964. Reprinted from 1st ed. of 1871.

Husain, Azim. *Fazl-i-Husain*. Bombay: Longmans, 1946.

Iqbal, Afzal, ed. *My Life A Fragment. An Autobiographical Sketch of Maulana Mohamed Ali*. Lahore: Ashraf, 1946.

————. *Select Writings and Speeches of Maulana Mohamed Ali*. 2nd ed. 2 vols. Lahore: Ashraf, 1963.

Jack, J. C. *The Economic Life of a Bengal District*. Oxford: Clarendon, 1916.

Jung, Nawab Dr. Nazir Yar. *The Pakistan Issue*. Lahore: Ashraf, 1943.

Khaliquzzaman, Choudhry. *Pathway to Pakistan*. Lahore: Longmans, 1961.

Kiernan, V. G., trans. *Poems From Iqbal*. London: John Murray, 1955.

MacMunn, Lieut.-General Sir George. *The Martial Races of India*. London: Sampson Law, n.d.

Malik, Hafeez. *Moslem Nationalism in India and Pakistan*. Washington, D.C.: Public Affairs Press, 1963.

Mallick, Azizur Rahman. *British Policy and the Muslims in Bengal 1757–1856*. Dacca: Asiatic Society of Pakistan, 1961.

Manshardt, Clifford. *The Hindu-Muslim Problem in India*. London: Allen & Unwin, 1936.

Mehtar, M. A. *Whys of the Great Indian Conflict*. Lahore: Ashraf, 1947.

Menon, V. P. *The Transfer of Power in India*. Princeton: Princeton University, 1957.

Moon, Penderel. *Divide and Quit*. Berkeley and Los Angeles: University of California, 1962.

————. *Strangers in India*. New York: Reynal & Hitchcock, 1945.

Mukherjee, Haridas, and Uma. *India's Fight for Freedom or The Swadeshi Movement (1905-1906)*. Calcutta: Firma K. L. Mukhopadhyay, 1958.

————. *'Bande Mataram' and Indian Nationalism (1906-1908)*. Calcutta: Firma K. L. Mukhopadhyay, 1957.

Murphy, Gardner. *In the Minds of Men*. New York: Basic Books, 1953.

Nehru, Jawaharlal. *An Autobiography*. London: The Bodley Head, 1958.

————. *A Bunch of Old Letters*. Bombay: Asia Publishing House, 1958.

————. *The Discovery of India*. London: Meridian Books, 1956.

Nichols, Beverley. *Verdict on India*. New York: Harcourt, Brace, 1944.

Noman, Mohammed, ed. *Our Struggle, 1857-1947*. Karachi: Pakistan Publications, n.d.

O'Dwyer, Sir Michael. *India As I Knew It, 1885-1925*. London: Constable, 1925.

Pirzada, Syed Sharifuddin. *Evolution of Pakistan*. Lahore: All-Pakistan Legal Decisions, 1963.

Prasad, Rajendra. *India Divided*. Bombay: Hind Kitabs, 1947.

Rajput, A. B. *Muslim League Yesterday and To-Day*. Lahore: Ashraf, 1948.

Rawlinson, H. G. *The British Achievement in India*. London: William Hodge, 1948.

Roy, Sir Bijoy Prasad Singh. *Parliamentary Government in India*. Calcutta: Thacker, 1943.

Saiyid, Matlubul Hasan. *Mohammad Ali Jinnah (A Political Study)*. Lahore: Ashraf, 1953.

Sayed, G. M. *Struggle for New Sind*. Karachi: 1949.

Sayeed, Khalid Bin. *Pakistan, The Formative Phase*. Karachi: Pakistan Publishing House, 1960.

Schuster, Sir George, and Wint, Guy. *India and Democracy*. London: Macmillan, 1941.

"Shamloo," ed. *Speeches and Statements of Iqbal*. 2nd ed. Lahore: Al-Manar Academy, 1948.

Sitaramayya, B. Pattabhi. *History of the Indian National Congress*. 2 vols. Bombay: Padma Publications, Vol. I, 1946; Vol. II, 1947.

Smith, Vincent A. *The Oxford History of India*. Oxford: Clarendon, 1958.

Smith, Wilfred Cantwell. *Modern Islam in India*. Lahore: Minerva Book Shop, 1947.

Spear, Percival. *India, Pakistan and the West*. 3rd ed. London: Oxford, 1958.

Suleri, Zia-ud-Din Ahmad. *My Leader*. 3rd ed. Lahore: Lion Press, 1946.

Tahmankar, D. V. *Lokamanya Tilak*. London: John Murray, 1956.

Thompson, Edward. *The Reconstruction of India*. London: Faber & Faber, 1930.

————, and Garratt, G. T. *Rise and Fulfilment of British Rule in India*. Allahabad: Central Book Depot, 1958.

Thorburn, S. S. *Asiatic Neighbours*. Edinburgh and London: William Blackwood, 1894.

————. *Musalmans and Moneylenders*. Edinburgh and London: William Blackwood, 1886.

Tuker, Lieut-General Sir Francis. *While Memory Serves*. London: Cassell, 1950.

Tyabji, Husain B. *Badruddin Tyabji: A Biography*. Bombay: Thacker, 1952.

Wasti, Syed Razi. *Lord Minto and the Indian Nationalist Movement, 1905 to 1910*. Oxford: Clarendon, 1964.

Woodruff, Philip. *The Men Who Ruled India. The Guardians*. London: Jonathan Cape, 1954.

Yeats-Brown, F. *Martial India*. London: Eyre & Spottiswoode, 1945.

Yunus, Mohammad. *Frontier Speaks*. Bombay: Hind Kitabs, 1947.

II. *Government Reports and Other Publications, All-India Muslim League Publications, and Others*

A. Government Publications

Government of India Act, 1935. 26 Geo. 5. Ch. 2. London: H. M. Stationery Office.

Indian Independence Act, 1947. 10 & 11 Geo. 6. Ch. 30. London: H. M. Stationery Office.

Report on Indian Constitutional Reforms (the Montagu-Chelmsford Report). Cmd. 9109. Calcutta: Superintendent, Government Printing, 1918.

Report of the Indian Statutory Commission (the Simon Commission). Cmd. 3568–9. 2 vols. London: H. M. Stationery Office, 1930.

B. All-India Muslim League Publications

The Constitution and Rules of the All India Muslim League. (Constitutions for the years 1928, 1940, 1941, 1942, 1944 and 1946). Delhi: All India Muslim League.

It Shall Never Happen Again. Delhi: All India Muslim League, 1946.

List of the Members of the Council of the All India Muslim League. (Lists for the years 1940, 1941 and 1942). Delhi: All India Muslim League.

The Report of the Inquiry Committee Appointed by the Council of the All-India Muslim League to Inquire into Muslim Grievances in Congress Provinces (Pirpur Report). Delhi: All India Muslim League, 1938.

Rules and Regulations of the All India Muslim League. Aligarh: The Institute Press, 1909.

C. Others

All Parties Conference, 1928. Report of the Committee Appointed by the Conference to Determine the Principles of the Constitution for India (Nehru Report). Allahabad: All India Congress Committee.

Constitutional Proposals of the Sapru Committee. Moradabad: Sapru Committee, 1945.

The Indian Annual Register. (For the years 1919–1947.) Calcutta: The Annual Register Office.

III. *Books, Gazetteers and Reports on Social and Economic Conditions*

Annual *Administration Reports* of the Provinces of Bengal, Punjab, the North-West Frontier Province, and Sind.

Darling, Malcolm Lyall. *At Freedom's Door.* London: Oxford, 1949.

————. *The Punjab Peasant in Prosperity and Debt.* London: Oxford, 1932.

————. *Rusticus Loquitur or the Old Light and the New in the Punjab Village.* London: Oxford, 1930.

Griffen, Sir Lepel H. *Chiefs and Families of Note in the Punjab.* 2 vols. and Appendix vol. Lahore: Superintendent, Government Printing, Punjab, 1940.

Hunter, Sir William Wilson. *The Imperial Gazetteer of India.* 2nd ed. 14 vols. London: Trübner, 1885–87. See also *Imperial Gazetteer of India* Provincial Series. Calcutta: 1908. For more detailed information regarding castes, tribes, social and religious customs of Muslims, see *Punjab District Gazetteers, Baluchistan District Gazetteers, N.-W. F. Province Gazetteers, Gazetteer of the Province of Sind,* and *Bengal District Gazetteers,* and *Final Report on the Survey and Settlement Operations* (of the various districts of Bengal). For Muslim merchant classes, see particularly *Gazetteer of the Bombay Presidency,* Vol. IX, Part II, Gujarat Population Musalmans and Parsis. Bombay: 1899.

Ibbetson, Sir Denzil. *Punjab Castes.* Lahore: Superintendent, Government Printing, Punjab, 1916.

Trevaskis, Hugh Kennedy. *The Punjab of To-Day.* 2 vols. Lahore: Civil & Military Press, 1931.

STRUCTURE OF GOVERNMENT SINCE INDEPENDENCE

I. *Books*

Ahmad, Muhammad Aziz, ed. *Proceedings of the Third All Pakistan Political Science Conference, 1962.* Karachi: University of Karachi, n.d.

Ahmad, Mushtaq. *Government and Politics in Pakistan.* 2nd ed. Karachi: Pakistan Publishing House, 1963.

Ahmed, Colonel Mohammad. *My Chief*. Lahore: Longmans, 1960.
Ali, Syed Amjad. *Aaj Aur Kul* (Today and Tomorrow). Karachi: Ferozsons, 1959.
Beg, Aziz. *The Quiet Revolution*. Karachi: Pakistan Patriotic Publications, n.d.
Birdwood, Lord. *India and Pakistan: A Continent Decides*. New York: Praeger, 1954.
Brohi, A. K. *Fundamental Law of Pakistan*. Karachi: Din Muhammadi Press Publications, 1958.
Callard, Keith B. *Political Forces in Pakistan, 1947–1959*. New York: Institute of Pacific Relations, 1959.
———. *Pakistan: A Political Study*. London: Allen & Unwin, 1957.
———, and Wheeler, Richard A. "Pakistan," in George McT. Kahin, ed., *Major Governments of Asia*. 2nd ed. Ithaca: Cornell, 1963.
Campbell, Robert D. *Pakistan: Emerging Democracy*. Princeton: Van Nostrand, 1963.
Choudhury, G. W. *Constitutional Development in Pakistan*. Lahore: Longmans, 1959.
———. *Democracy in Pakistan*. Dacca: Green Book House, 1963.
Dil, Anwar S. *Perspectives on Pakistan*. Abbottabad: Bookservice, 1965.
Feldman, Herbert. *A Constitution for Pakistan*. Karachi: Oxford, 1955.
Gledhill, Alan. *Pakistan: The Development of Its Laws and Constitution*. London: Stevens, 1957.
Jennings, Sir Ivor. *Constitutional Problems in Pakistan*. Cambridge: Cambridge University, 1956.
Jinnah, Mohamed Ali. *Speeches by Quaid-i-Azam Mohamed Ali Jinnah Governor-General of Pakistan*. 3rd June 1947 to 14th August 1948. Karachi: Government of Pakistan, n.d.
Kayani, M. R. *Not the Whole Truth*. Lahore: Pakistan Writers' Co-Operative Society, 1963.
Khan, Major-General Fazal Muqeem. *The Story of the Pakistan Army*. Dacca: Oxford, 1963.
Khan, Liaquat Ali. *Pakistan: The Heart of Asia*. Cambridge, Mass.: Harvard, 1950.
Khan, Field Marshal Mohammad Ayub. *Speeches and Statements*. 6 vols. Karachi: Pakistan Publications, published during 1961–64.
———. *Pakistan Perspective*. Washington, D.C.: Embassy of Pakistan, n.d.
Mahmood, Sh. Shaukat. *The Constitution of Pakistan, 1962*. Lahore: Pakistan Law Times Publications, n.d.
Mahmud, Syed Hassan. *A Nation Is Born*. 1958.
Maniruzzaman, Talukder. *Political Development in Pakistan, 1955–58*. Unpublished Ph.D. thesis, Queen's University, Kingston, Canada, 1966.
Maron, Stanley. *Pakistan: Society and Culture*. New Haven: Human Relations Area File, 1957.
Metz, W. S. *Pakistan: Government and Politics*. New Haven: Human Relations Area File, 1956.
Sayeed, Khalid Bin. *Pakistan, The Formative Phase*. Karachi: Pakistan Publishing House, 1960.
Smith, Harvey H., *et al*. *Area Handbook for Pakistan*. Washington, D.C.: Govt. Printing Office, 1965.
Spear, Percival. "The Political Evolution of Pakistan: A Study In Analysis," in Saul Rose, ed., *Politics in Southern Asia*. London: Macmillan, 1963.

Stephens, Ian. *Pakistan.* London: Ernest Benn, 1963.
Suleri, Z. A. *Pakistan's Lost Years.* Lahore: The Progressive Papers Ltd., 1962.
————. *Whither Pakistan?* London: Eastern Publishers, n.d.
Symonds, Richard. *The Making of Pakistan.* London: Faber, 1950.
Tinker, Hugh. *India and Pakistan: A Political Analysis.* New York: Praeger, 1962.
Von Vorys, Karl. *Political Development in Pakistan.* Princeton: Princeton University, 1965.
Weekes, Richard V. *Pakistan. Birth and Growth of a Muslim Nation.* Princeton: Van Nostrand, 1964.
Wilbur, Donald N. *Pakistan. Its People, Its Society, Its Culture.* New Haven: Human Relations Area Files, 1964.
Wilcox, Wayne Ayres. *Pakistan: The Consolidation of a Nation.* New York: Columbia University, 1963.
Williams, L. F. Rushbrook. *The State of Pakistan.* London: Faber, 1962.

II. *Documents*

A. Constitutions, Debates, Reports, Acts and Ordinances

The All-Pakistan Legal Decisions (PLD) (1955–   ).
A Collection of the Central Acts and Ordinances (1947–1959). 13 vols.
Constituent Assembly of Pakistan Debates (1947–1954).
Constituent Assembly of Pakistan Debates (1955–1956).
Constituent Assembly (Legislature) of Pakistan Debates (1948–1954).
The Constitution of the Islamic Republic of Pakistan. 1957.
The Constitution of the Islamic Republic of Pakistan. (As modified up to the 12th October, 1964.)
Draft Constitution of the Islamic Republic of Pakistan. 1954.
The Gazette of Pakistan Extraordinary (1947–   ).
The Government of India Act, 1935 (26 Geo. 5 Ch. 42) *With Indian Independence Act, 1947, as Adapted in Pakistan by (Provisional Constitution) Order, 1947, and Amended Up to April, 1955.*
Martial Law Regulations & Orders. Central & Zone "B" with President's Orders. (As amended up to 13–10–59.)
National Assembly of Pakistan Debates (1956–1958).
National Assembly of Pakistan Debates (1962–   ).
Orders of the Governor-General 1947–1950.
Orders of the Governor-General 1951–1956.
The Political Parties Act, 1962. Act No. III of 1962.
The Press and Publications Ordinance (XV of 1960) (As modified up to the 1st September, 1964).
Report of the Constitution Commission, Pakistan. 1961.
Report of the Council for Administration of West Pakistan. 1955.
The Report of the Sind Special Court of Enquiry.
The Transitional Constitutions of India and Pakistan. Calcutta: Indian Law Publications, 1947.
The University of Karachi Ordinance, 1961. Ordinance No. V of 1962.
West Pakistan Criminal Law Amendment Act, 1963, & Criminal Law Amendment Rules, 1963, with Frontier Crimes Regulation. (III of 1909) (As amended up to the 10th August, 1963).

B. Budgets and Other Public Finance Documents. (For other documents, see also Bureaucracy and Development.)

Budget. Each year the Finance Ministry publishes documents like the following: *Basic Facts About the Budget; The Budget in Brief; The Budget Speech of the Finance Minister; Demands for Grants and Appropriations; Explanatory Memorandum; Financial Statement; Pakistan Budgets* (Central, Provincial, Railway); *Pakistan Economic Survey.*

Raisman, Sir Jeremy. *Financial Enquiry Regarding Allocation of Revenues between the Central and Provincial Governments.* Karachi: 1952.

Report of the National Finance Commission 1964.

Report of the National Finance Commission 1964–65.

BUREAUCRACY AND DEVELOPMENT

I. *Books*

Ahmad, Muneer. *The Civil Servant in Pakistan.* Karachi: Oxford, 1964.

Andrus, J. Russell, and Mohammed, Azizali F. *The Economy of Pakistan.* 2nd ed. London: Oxford, 1958.

Ansari, Salam, ed. *Social Research in National Development.* Peshawar: Pakistan Academy for Rural Development, 1963.

Aslam, A. H. *The Deputy Commissioner. A Study in Public Administration.* Lahore: University of the Panjab, 1957.

Braibanti, Ralph. "Public Bureaucracy and Judiciary in Pakistan," in Joseph LaPalombara, ed., *Bureaucracy and Political Development.* Princeton: Princeton University, 1963.

————. *Research on the Bureaucracy of Pakistan.* Durham: Duke University, 1966.

————, et al. *Asian Bureaucratic Systems Emergent from the British Imperial Tradition.* Durham: Duke University, 1966.

Chaudhuri, Muzaffar Ahmed. *The Civil Service in Pakistan.* Dacca: National Institute of Public Administration, 1963.

Douie, James M. *Land Administration Manual.* Lahore: 1908.

————. *Punjab Settlement Manual.* Lahore: Superintendent, Government Printing, West Pakistan, 1962.

Gable, Richard W. *Introduction to District Administration* (mimeographed). Lahore: 1963.

Goodnow, Henry Frank. *The Civil Service of Pakistan.* New Haven: Yale, 1964.

Habib, Hassan, and Birkhead, Guthrie, S., eds. *Selected Papers on Development Economics and Administration.* Lahore: Pakistan Administrative Staff College, 1963.

Haq, Mahbub ul. *The Strategy of Economic Planning. A Case Study of Pakistan.* Lahore: Oxford, 1963.

Inayat, M. R., ed. *Perspectives in Public Administration.* Lahore: Civil Service Academy, n.d.

Inayatullah, ed. *Bureaucracy & Development in Pakistan.* Peshawar: Academy for Rural Development, 1963.

————, ed. *District Administration in West Pakistan.* Peshawar: Pakistan Academy for Rural Development, 1964.

Masihuzzaman. *District Administration and Other Essays* (mimeographed).

300 SELECTED BIBLIOGRAPHY

Platt, George M. *Administration and Agricultural Development in Pakistan* (mimeographed). Syracuse: Maxwell Graduate School of Citizenship and Public Affairs, 1962.

Swerdlow, Irving, ed. *Development Administration Concepts and Problems.* Syracuse: Syracuse University, 1963.

Waterston, Albert. *Developing Planning: Lessons of Experience.* Baltimore: Johns Hopkins, 1966.

———. *Planning in Pakistan.* Baltimore: Johns Hopkins, 1963.

II. *Reports of Committees and Commissions, and Planning Commission Publications*

Central Public Service Commission Annual Report for the Year 1962. Karachi: 1963.

Central Public Service Commission Annual Report for the Year 1963. Karachi: 1964.

Civil List of Class I Officers Serving Under Government of Pakistan (separate *Lists* for the years 1960–64). Rawalpindi: Establishment Division, President's Secretariat.

Decisions of the Cabinet on the Report of the Provincial Administration Commission. Rawalpindi: Cabinet Division, President's Secretariat, 1962.

The East Pakistan Civil List. (separate *Lists* for the years 1960–64). Dacca: Deputy Secretary, Home (O & M) Department.

Egger, Rowland. *The Improvement of Public Administration in Pakistan.* Karachi: 1953.

Gladieux, Bernard L. *Reorientation of Pakistan Government for National Development* (mimeographed). Karachi: 1955.

Government of Pakistan, Central Statistical Office. *Pakistan Statistical Yearbook, 1962.* Karachi: 1962.

———. *Report on Socio-Economic Survey of Korangi.* December 1960-January 1961. Karachi: 1961.

Government of Pakistan, Efficiency and O & M Wing, Establishment Division, President's Secretariat. *Report of the Administrative Reorganisation Committee.* Karachi: 1963.

Government of Pakistan, Ministry of Finance. *Finance Services Academy Brochure, 1963–64.* Lahore.

———. *Government Sponsored Corporations.* Rawalpindi: 1965.

———. *Report of the Economy Committee Appointed to Review the Expenditure of Central Government and Suggest Economies.* Parts I–III. Karachi: 1957.

Government of Pakistan, National Planning Board. *The First Five Year Plan, 1955–60.* Karachi: 1958.

Government of Pakistan, Planning Commission. *Central Development Programme 1965–66 as Approved by the National Economic Council.* Karachi: 1965.

———. *Development Programme 1964–65 as Approved by the National Economic Council.* Karachi: 1964.

———. *Mid-Plan Review. Evaluation of Progress During the First Three Years of the Second Five-Year Plan.* Karachi: 1964.

———. *Mid-Plan Review of Progress in 1960/61–1961/62 Under the Second Five-Year Plan.* Karachi: 1963.

———. *Preliminary Evaluation of Progress During The Second Five Year Plan.* Karachi: 1965.

Government of Pakistan, Planning Commission. *The Review of Progress in 1961/62 Under The Second Five Year Plan.* Karachi: 1963.

——. *Schemes Approved by the Economic Committee of Cabinet/Executive Committee of the National Economic Council.* Karachi: 1963.

——. *The Second Five Year Plan (1960–65).* Including Revised Estimates November 1961. Karachi: 1960.

——. *The Third Five Year Plan (1965–70).* 1965.

Government of Pakistan, Taxation Enquiry Committee. *Report on Provincial Taxation.* Karachi: 1959.

Gradation List of the Civil Service of Pakistan (separate *Lists* for the years 1958–65). Karachi: Establishment Division, President's Secretariat.

History of Services of Officers Holding Gazetted Appointments in the Civil Service of Pakistan, Ministry of States and Frontier Regions, Ministry of Foreign Affairs and Commonwealth Relations and Baluchistan Administration. Corrected up to 1st July 1952. Karachi: Manager of Publications, 1955.

History of Services of Officers Holding Gazetted Appointments in the Civil Service of Pakistan, Ministry of States and Frontier Regions and Ministry of Foreign Affairs and Commonwealth Relations. Corrected up to 1st July, 1959. Karachi: Manager of Publications, 1963.

Mahbub ul Haq. *Planning Machinery in Pakistan.* 1965.

Manual of Powers and Functions of Commissioners and Deputy Commissioners Under Various Central and Provincial Laws. 2 vols. Lahore: Superintendent, Government Printing, West Pakistan, 1961

Niaz, M. Shafi and Khoja, M. H. *Land Reforms in Pakistan.* Karachi: Planning Commission, 1959.

Parnwell, L. *Organisation and Methods in the East Pakistan Government* (mimeographed). Dacca: 1958.

Report of the Administrative Enquiry Committee. Karachi: Manager of Publications, 1953.

Report of the Commission on National Education. Karachi: Ministry of Education, 1961.

Report of the Food and Agriculture Commission. Karachi: Ministry of Food and Agriculture, 1960.

Report of the Government Hari Enquiry Committee, 1947–48. Government of Sind.

Report of the Jute Enquiry Commission. Karachi: Ministry of Commerce, 1960.

Report of the Land Reforms Commission for West Pakistan. Lahore: Superintendent, Government Printing, West Pakistan, 1959.

Report of the Scientific Commission of Pakistan. Karachi: Ministry of Industries, 1960.

Report of the West Pakistan Administrative Organisation Committee. Lahore: 1955.

Ruddock, Grenfell. *Towns & Villages of Pakistan.* Karachi: Planning Commission, 1964.

Shoaib, Mohammed. *Pakistan's Economic Growth Since 1958.* Karachi: 1963.

Taxation Enquiry Committee Report. Vol. I. Karachi: Manager of Publications, 1963.

The West Pakistan Civil List (separate *Lists* for the years 1958–64).

III. *Census of Pakistan, 1961 Reports*

Government of Pakistan, Ministry of Home Affairs. *Provisional Tables of Population.* Bulletin No. 1.

————. *Final Tables of Population. Sex, Urban-Rural, Religion.* Bulletin No. 2.

Government of Pakistan, Ministry of Home & Kashmir Affairs. *Age, Sex and Marital Status.* Bulletin No. 3.

————. *Literacy and Education.* Bulletin No. 4.

————. *Economic Characteristics.* Bulletin No. 5.

————. *Cottage Industry 1960.* Bulletin No. 6.

————. *District Census Report.* There are Census Reports for each of the Districts in East and West Pakistan. In addition, there is also a Census Report of Tribal Agencies (in West Pakistan).

Government of Pakistan, Ministry of Food & Agriculture. *1960 Pakistan Census of Agriculture. Final Report — East Pakistan.* Vol. I.

ISLAM AND NATIONAL UNITY

Ahmad, Khurshid, trans. and ed. *An Analysis of the Munir Report.* Karachi: Jamaat-e-Islami Publications, 1956.

————, trans. and ed. *Islamic Law and Constitution* by Syed Abul 'Ala Maudoodi. Karachi: Jamaat-e-Islami Publications, 1955.

————, ed. *Marriage Commission Report X-Rayed.* Karachi: Chiragh-e-Rah Publications, 1959.

Ali, Mohamad. *The Task Before Us.* Karachi: Pakistan Publications, 1952.

Ali, Syed Ameer. *The Spirit of Islam.* London: Christophers, 1922.

Anderson, J. N. D. *Islamic Law in the Modern World.* New York: New York University, 1959.

Annual Report of the Proceedings of the Advisory Council of Islamic Ideology for the Year 1964.

Arberry, A. J. *The Koran Interpreted.* 2 vols. London: Allen & Unwin, 1955.

Aslam, Q. M. and Ansari, M. A., eds. *Observations and Recommendations Made by a Conference of Psychologists Held on September 21-26, 1959 Under the Auspices of the Bureau of National Reconstruction.* Karachi: Bureau of National Reconstruction, n.d.

Binder, Leonard. *Religion and Politics in Pakistan.* Berkeley and Los Angeles: University of California, 1961.

Gibb, H. A. R. *Modern Trends in Islam.* Chicago: University of Chicago, 1945.

————, and Kramers, J. H., eds. *Shorter Encyclopaedia of Islam.* Leiden: Royal Netherlands Academy, 1953.

Husain, A. F. A. *Human & Social Impact of Technological Change in Pakistan,* 2 vols. Dacca: Oxford, 1956.

Iqbal, Javid. *The Ideology of Pakistan and Its Implementation.* Lahore: Sh. Ghulam Ali, 1959.

Iqbal, Dr. Sir Muhammad. *The Reconstruction of Religious Thought in Islam.* Lahore: Javid Iqbal, 1960.

Levy, Reuben. *The Social Structure of Islam.* Cambridge: Cambridge University, 1957.

Maudoodi, Sayyed Abul Ala. *Political Theory of Islam*. Pathankot: Published by the author, n.d.

Qureshi, Ishtiaq Husain. *The Muslim Community of the Indo-Pakistan Subcontinent, 610–1947: A Brief Historical Analysis*. 's-Gravenhage: Mouton, 1962.

———. *Pakistan: An Islamic Democracy*. Lahore: n.d.

Report of the Activities of the Bureau of National Reconstruction. Dacca: East Pakistan Government, 1962.

Report of the Court of Inquiry Constituted Under Punjab Act II of 1954 to Enquire into the Punjab Disturbances of 1953. (Munir Report). Lahore: Superintendent, Government Printing, Punjab, 1954.

Report of the East Bengal Educational System Reconstruction Committee. Dacca: Government of East Bengal, 1952.

Report of Enquiry into Sectarian Trouble in Lahore During Moharram, 1963. Lahore: Superintendent, Government Printing, West Pakistan, 1964.

Rosenthal, Erwin I. J. *Political Thought in Medieval Islam*. Cambridge: Cambridge University, 1958.

Schacht, Joseph. *An Introduction to Islamic Law*. Oxford: Clarendon, 1964.

Smith, Donald E., ed. *South Asian Politics and Religion*. Princeton: Princeton University, 1966. (See the Third Section on Pakistan.)

Smith, Wilfred Cantwell. *Islam in Modern History*. Princeton: Princeton University, 1957.

POLITICS OF REGIONALISM

Abbas, Zainab Ghulam, comp. *Folk Tales of Pakistan*. Karachi: Pakistan Publications, 1960.

Ahsan, Syed Qamarul. *The New Proletariat*. Habiganj: Syed Iqbal Jawid Ahsan, 1960.

Al-Razee, Dr. Aleem. *Process of Economic Disparity*. Dacca: Ferdoush Publications, n.d.

Ansari, Sheikh Sadik Ali Sher Ali. *A Short Sketch Historical and Traditional of the Musalman Races Found in Sind, Baluchistan and Afghanistan. Their Geneological Sub-Divisions and SEPTS Together with a Niethnological and Ethnographical Account*. Sind Government Press, 1954.

Azam, M. A. *A Soul Grows in the East: An Autobiography*. Karachi: Ma'aref, 1961.

Baluch, Muhammad Sardar Khan. *History of Baluch Race and Baluchistan*. Quetta: 1958.

Barth, Fredrik. *Political Leadership Among Swat Pathans*. London: The Athlone Press, 1959.

Caroe, Olaf. *The Pathans*. London: Macmillan, 1958.

Choudhry, Mohammad Iqbal. *Pakistani Society: A Sociological Analysis*. Lahore: Noorsons, 1964.

East Pakistan. Karachi: Pakistan Publications, n.d.

Government of East Pakistan, Finance Department. *Economic Survey of East Pakistan, 1963–64*. Dacca: 1964.

Government of East Pakistan, Information Department. *East Pakistan on the March, 1963*. Dacca: 1963.

———. *Years of Progress, 1958–1962*. Dacca: 1962.

Government of East Pakistan, Planning Department. *Economic Disparities Between East and West Pakistan.* Dacca: 1963.

Government of East Pakistan, Public Relations Department. *East Pakistan.* Dacca: 1958.

——. *One Year of Popular Government in East Pakistan.* Dacca: 1957.

Haq, Dr. Md. Enamul. *Muslim Bengali Literature.* Karachi: Pakistan Publications, 1957.

Howell, Evelyn. *Mizh: A Monograph on Government's Relations With the Mahsud Tribe.* Simla: Government of India Press, 1931.

——, and Caroe, Olaf, trans. *The Poems of Khushhal Khan Khatak.* Peshawar: University of Peshawar, 1963.

Husain, Muhammad. *East Pakistan: A Cultural Survey.* Karachi: Pakistan P. E. N., 1955.

Husain, Mrs. Muhammad, trans. *Poems from East Bengal.* Karachi: Pakistan P. E. N., 1954.

Husain, S. Sajjad, ed. *Dacca University Seminars on Contemporary Writing in East Pakistan.*

——, ed. *East Pakistan: A Profile.* Dacca: Orient Longmans, 1962.

Ikram, S. M., and Spear, Percival, eds. *The Cultural Heritage of Pakistan.* Karachi: Oxford, 1955.

Islam, Nurul, ed. *East Pakistan Annual, 1962.* Chittagong: The Tempest Publications, 1962.

Johnson, B. L. C. *How People Live in East Pakistan.* London: Educational Supply Association, 1961.

Kabir, Humayun, ed. *Green and Gold. Stories and Poems from Bengal.* Bombay: Asia Publishing House, 1957.

Karim, Nazmul. *Changing Society in India and Pakistan.* Dacca: Oxford, 1956.

Khan, Ghani. *The Pathans: A Sketch.* Peshawar: University Book Agency, 1958.

National Association for Social and Economic Progress. *The Challenge of Disparity.* Dacca.

——. *The Challenge of Education.* Dacca.

——. *Pre-requisites of Democracy in Pakistan.* Dacca.

Owen, John E., ed. *Sociology in East Pakistan.* Dacca: Asiatic Society of Pakistan, 1962.

Rahman, Choudhury Shamsur. *Life in East Pakistan.* Dacca: Pakistan Co-operative Book Society, 1956.

Report of Five Members of the Finance Commission. Dacca: January 18, 1962.

Sadeque, A. *The Economic Emergence of Pakistan.* 2 parts. Dacca: Part I, East Bengal Government Press, 1954; Part II, Planning Department, Government of East Pakistan, 1956.

——. *Pakistan's First Five-Year Plan in Theory and Operation.* Dacca: Government of East Pakistan, 1957.

Sayeed, Khalid B. "Pathan Regionalism," Reprint No. 13, Program in Comparative Studies on Southern Asia, Commonwealth Studies Center, Duke University.

Sen, Rai Saheb Dineshchandra. *The Folk-Literature of Bengal.* Calcutta: University of Calcutta, 1920.

Spain, James W. *People of the Khyber. The Pathans of Pakistan.* New York: Praeger, 1963.

——. *The Pathan Borderland.* The Hague: Mouton, 1963.

ELECTIONS, PARTIES AND INTEREST GROUPS

Ali, Syed Anwer. *Election Laws in Pakistan*. Karachi: Syed Publications, 1965.

Chamber of Commerce and Industry, Chittagong. *Memorandum & Articles of Association*. Chittagong: 1959.

Chamber of Commerce and Industry, Karachi. *Memorandum & Articles of Association*. Karachi: 1959.

Chief Election Commissioner. *Pakistan General Elections 1962*. Karachi: 1963.

Election Commission Studies (mimeographed). *Criticisms on General Elections 1962; Extension of Franchise; Report on the Elector-Candidate meeting held on 12.11.1963, in connection with the Bye-election to the National Assembly Constituency No. NE-73 Chittagong-III that is vacancy caused by the unseating of Jamalus Sattar; Report on visits to polling stations during the bye-election to Constituency NE-37 Faridpur-cum-Dacca held on 17.11.63; A Review of the Publicity Programme of the General Elections Held in 1962 for Pakistan National and Provincial Assemblies*.

Faruki, Kemal A. *Franchise Commission Report, 1963*. Karachi: Pakistan Publications, 1964.

The Federation of Pakistan Chambers of Commerce and Industry. *Brief Report of Activities 1961–62*. Karachi: n.d.

Government of Pakistan, Department of Investment Promotion and Supplies, *Tax Concessions for Industries*. Karachi: 1964.

Government of Pakistan, Ministry of Law. *Report of the Franchise Commission 1963. An Analysis*. Karachi: 1964.

Leghari, A. M. *Report on the Sargodha District Board Elections, 1952–53*. Lahore: Superintendent, Government Printing, Punjab, 1955.

Leishman, R. J. W. *The Interest Group Approach to the Study of Political Systems of Transitional Societies*. B. A. thesis, Queen's University, Kingston, Canada, 1964.

Millen, Bruce H. *The Political Role of Labor in Developing Countries*. Washington, D.C.: The Brookings Institution, 1963.

Political Parties Publications Prior to 1958.

Jamaat-e-Islami. *Jamaat-e-Islami Pakistan* (organizational structure, literature, program, etc.). Lahore: 1957; *Manifesto of Jamaat-e-Islami Pakistan* (mimeographed). 1958.

National Awami Party. *Constitution of the National Awami Party*. Karachi: n.d.

Pakistan Awami League. *Rules and Regulations of East Pakistan Awami League* (Bengali). Dacca. 1954; *Two-Nation Point of View and The Issue of Electorate* (Urdu). Karachi:n.d.

Pakistan Muslim League. *Constitution of the East Pakistan Provincial Muslim League*. Dacca: n.d.; *Constitution & Rules of the Pakistan Muslim League*. Karachi: 1952; *Manifesto of the East Pakistan Provincial Muslim League*. Dacca: 1956. *Text of Resolutions of the Working Committee of Pakistan Muslim League 1949–1950 and Budget of the Central Office* (mimeographed).

Pakistan Nizam-i-Islam. *The Constitution of The Pakistan Nizam-i-Islam Party*. Lahore: 1958; *The Manifesto of Nizam-i-Islam Party*. Lahore: n.d.

Political Parties Publications after 1962.
Combined Opposition Parties. *Mohtrima Madar-i-Millat and Her Critics.* Lahore: n.d.; *The Presidential Contest and Pakistan's Stability.*
Jamaat-e-Islami. *White Paper on Malpractices and Irregularities in the Elections in Karachi* (mimeographed).
National Democratic Front. *Declaration of Objectives.* Dacca: 1964.
Pakistan Muslim League. *Constitution of the Pakistan Muslim League.* Rawalpindi: 1964; *Draft Constitution of the East Pakistan Provincial Muslim League.* Dacca: 1962; *Ayub's Manifesto.* Rawalpindi: n.d.; *Socio-Economic Programme of the Pakistan Muslim League.* Rawalpindi: n.d.
Pakistan National Awami Party. *Constitution Aims and Objectives* (Urdu). Karachi: n.d.; *Pakistan's Foreign Policy and the Stand of Pakistan National Awami Party* (Urdu). Lahore: n.d.
Presidential Election Result 1965. Rawalpindi: Election Commission Pakistan, 1965.
Report of the Franchise Commission, Pakistan, 1963.
Report on the General Elections to the Punjab Legislative Assembly, 1950–51. Lahore: Superintendent, Government Printing, Punjab, 1952.
Rose, Saul. *Socialism in Southern Asia.* London: Oxford, 1959.
Shafi, M. *Annual Review of Labour Problems, 1960.* Karachi: Bureau of Labour Publications, 1961.
Sufrin, Sidney D. *Unions in Emerging Societies. Frustration and Politics.* Syracuse: Syracuse University, 1964.
———, and Sarwar, Syed A. *The Status of Trade Unions in Pakistan* (mimeographed). Syracuse: Maxwell Graduate School of Citizenship and Public Affairs, 1962.

BASIC DEMOCRACIES

Akhtar, Dr.S.M. *Village Life in Lahore District.* Lahore: University of the Panjab, 1960.
Bureau of National Reconstruction. *Annual Report on Basic Democracies October 27, 1959, to October 27, 1960.* Karachi: n.d.
Cambridge University Asian Expedition. *The Budhopur Report: A Study of the Forces of Tradition and Change in a Punjabi Village in the Gujranwala District, West Pakistan.* Lahore: University of the Panjab, 1962.
Falcon, Walter P., and Gotsch, Carol H. *Agricultural Development in Pakistan: Past Progress and Future Prospects* (mimeographed). Cambridge, Mass.: Center for International Affairs, Harvard University, 1966.
Government of East Pakistan, Basic Democracies and Local Government Department. *Report on the Working of District Boards, Local Boards and Union Boards in East Pakistan During the Year 1953–54.* Dacca: 1963.
———. *Works Programme Through Basic Democracies 1963–64.* Dacca: 1963.
———. *Works Programme Through Basic Democracies 1964–65.* Dacca: 1964.
Government of East Pakistan, Law Department. *The Conciliation Courts Manual.* Dacca: 1962.

Government of Pakistan, Ministry of Law. *The Basic Democracies Order, 1959*. Karachi: 1959.

Haider, Agha Sajjad. *Village in an Urban Orbit*. Lahore: University of the Panjab, 1960.

Hasan, Masud ul. *Law and Principles of Basic Democracies*. Lahore: Pakistan Social Service Foundation, 1960.

Inayatullah. *Basic Democracies District Administration and Development*. Peshawar: Pakistan Academy for Rural Development, 1964.

―――. *An Experiment in Village Development*. Peshawar: Pakistan Academy for Village Development, 1961.

Khan, A. Majeed. *Rural Pilot Family Planning Action Programme. First Annual Report March 1961-May 1962*. Comilla: Pakistan Academy for Rural Development, n.d.

Khan, A.Z.M. Obaidullah. *The Comilla District Development Project*. Comilla: Pakistan Academy for Rural Development, 1964.

Khan, M.K.H. *Attitudes of the Union Councillors Towards Adoption of Family Planning Programme as a National Policy*. Lahore: Family Planning Association of Pakistan, n.d.

―――. *Knowledge of and Attitudes Towards Family Planning*. Lahore: Family Planning Association of Pakistan, n.d.

Luykx, Nicolaas. *The Role of Rural Government in Agriculture Development* (mimeographed).

Mohsen, A.K.M. *The Comilla Rural Administration Experiment. History and Annual Report, 1962–63*. Comilla: Pakistan Academy for Rural Development, 1963.

Pakistan Academy for Village Development. *Third Annual Report*, June 1961–May 1962. Comilla: 1962; *Fourth Annual Report*, June 1962–May 1963. Comilla: 1963; *Fifth Annual Report*, June 1963–May 1964. Comilla: 1964.

Rahman, A.T.R. *Basic Democracies at the Grass Roots*. Comilla: Pakistan Academy for Village Development, 1962.

―――, and Bausch, James J. *An Evaluation of the Rural Public Works Programme East Pakistan, 1962–63*. Comilla: 1963.

Rahman, A.T.R. *An Evaluation of the Rural Works Programme East Pakistan, 1963–64*. Comilla: Pakistan Academy for Rural Development, n.d.

Roy, Naresh Chandra. *Rural Self-Government in Bengal*. Calcutta: University of Calcutta, 1936.

Rizvi, S.M.Z., ed. *A Reader in Basic Democracies*. Peshawar: West Pakistan Academy for Village Development, 1961.

Siddiqi, M.T. *An Analysis of the Working of Basic Democracy Institutions in East Pakistan*. Dacca: Bureau of National Reconstruction, 1961.

Slocum, W. L., Akhtar, Jamila, and Sahi, Abrar Fatima. *Village Life in Lahore District*. Lahore: University of the Panjab, 1959.

Social Sciences Research Centre, University of the Panjab. *A Study on Knowledge and Attitudes Towards Basic Democracies*. Lahore: Bureau of National Reconstruction, West Pakistan, 1960.

Stevens, Robert D. *A Test of Theory of Agricultural Development in Early Transition — Some Evidence from Comilla* (mimeographed).

Tinker, Hugh R. *The Foundations of Local Self-Government in India, Pakistan and Burma*. London: London University, 1954.

US/AID Pakistan. *Rural Development in East Pakistan* (typescript). 1965.

FOREIGN RELATIONS

Ahmad, Mushtaq. *The United Nations and Pakistan.* Karachi: 1955.

Bhutto, Zulfikar Ali. *Foreign Policy of Pakistan.* Karachi: Pakistan Institute of International Affairs, 1964.

————. *A South Asian View.* Washington, D.C.: Embassy of Pakistan, n.d.

Brecher, Michael. *The Struggle for Kashmir.* Toronto: Ryerson Press, 1953.

Brown, W. Norman. *The United States and India and Pakistan.* 2nd. ed. Cambridge, Mass: Harvard, 1963.

Callard, Keith. *Pakistan's Foreign Policy: An Interpretation.* New York: Institute of Pacific Relations, 1957.

Chaudhri, M. A. *Growth of International Law and Pakistan.* Karachi: 1965.

Chaudhuri, Nirad C. *The Continent of Circe.* New York: Oxford, 1966.

Daultana, Mian Mumtaz Muhammad Khan. *Kashmir Dispute in Present-day Perspective.* Lahore: Punjab Literary League, n.d.

Embassy of Pakistan, Political Division. *Pakistan Documents Series.* Vols. I-III. Washington, D.C.: 1964–66.

Gupta, S. *Kashmir, Study of India-Pakistan Relations.* Bombay: Asia, 1964.

Hasan, K. Sarwar. *Pakistan and the United Nations.* New York: Manhattan Publishing Co., 1960.

Korbel, Josef. *Danger in Kashmir.* Princeton: Princeton University, 1954.

Lamb, Alastair. *The China-India Border. The Origin of the Disputed Boundaries.* London: Oxford, 1964.

Pakistan-China Boundary Agreement. Karachi: Government of Pakistan, Department of Films and Publications, 1963.

Palmer, Norman D. *South Asia and United States Policy.* Boston: Houghton Mifflin, 1966.

Qureshi, Ishtiaq Husain. "The Foreign Policy of Pakistan," in Joseph E. Black and Kenneth W. Thompson, eds., *Foreign Policies in a World of Change.* New York: Harper, 1963.

Reports on Kashmir by United Nations Representatives. Karachi: Government of Pakistan, 1958.

Sayeed, Khalid B. "Pakistan and China: The Scope and Limits of Convergent Policies," in A. M. Halpern, ed., *Policies Toward China: Views from Six Continents.* New York: McGraw-Hill, 1965.

Sherwani, Latif Ahmed, *et al. Foreign Policy of Pakistan: An Analysis.* Karachi: Allies Book Corporation, 1964.

Siddiqi, Aslam. *Pakistan Seeks Security.* Lahore: Longmans, 1960.

————. *A Path for Pakistan.* Karachi: Pakistan Publishing House, 1964.

Talbot, Phillips, and Poplai, S. L. *India and America.* New York: Harper, 1958.

United Nations Security Council. *Official Records. Supplement for September through December 2, 1950.* Fifth Year. S/1791 (incorporating S/1791/Add.1). (Report of Sir Owen Dixon, U.N. Representative for India and Pakistan.)

————. *Official Records.* Nineteenth Year. 1964. S/PV.1088–1090, 1105, 1112, 1117, and 1140.

Wilcox, Wayne. *India, Pakistan and the Rise of China.* New York: Walker, 1964.

INDEX

Abdali, Ahmad Shah, 2
Abdullah, Sheikh, 266, 267
Advisory Council of Islamic Ideology, 165–166
Afghanistan, 179, 284, 285
African-Asian Conference (Second), 278
Aga Khan, 13
Agency for International Development (AID—U.S.), 148, 259, 291
Agricultural Development Bank, 98
Agricultural Development Corporation, 158
Agriculture, 98, 206, 259; see also Rural areas
Agriculturists, 251–252
Ahmad, Abul Mansur, 258 n.
  quoted, 187
Ahmad, Aziz, 64
Ahmad, Farid, 219
Ahmad, Mirza Ghulam, 179
Ahmadis, 169, 177
  agitation against, 68–70, 179–180, 194
Ahrars, 70 n.
Aid-Pakistan Consortium, 279
Ali, Ameer, 33, 161
Ali, Chaudhri Muhammad, 75, 80, 81, 87 n., 99, 105, 154, 169, 219, 234
  quoted, 170
Ali, Choudhry Rahmat, 39
Ali, Muhammad, 4, 7, 14, 20, 21, 23, 24, 25
  quoted, 28
Ali, Shaukat, 21, 23, 24
Ali Bogra, Muhammad, 71, 72, 73, 75, 80, 83, 266, 272, 274
Alienation, 178
Aligarh, Muslim college at, 12, 14, 16
All-India Muslim League, objectives of, 14; see also Muslim League
All-Parties Conference (1928), 27
Allahabadi, Akbar, 7
Amin, Nurul, 65, 108
Anandamath (The Abbey of Bliss) (Chatterjee), 3, 37
Anglo-Oriental College, 12

Apter, David E., quoted, 182
Arab world, Pakistan and, 271, 284–286
Arabic, inability to read and write, 174, 176
Arains, 87 n., 219, 235
Army, 102, 103, 204, 262, 289
  anti-smuggling drive of, 86
  in British days, 130
  East and West Pakistanis in, 66–67, 194, 195–196
  improved, 119
  officers of, 88
  power of, 66, 67, 71, 74, 75, 76, 78, 211
  support of Ayub by, 115, 221
Articulation of economic and regional demands, 196–203
Assam, 18, 29, 45
Attlee, Clement, 49
Auchinleck, Field Marshal, quoted, 268
Aurangzeb, 1–2
Authoritarianism, 104, 170, 242
Autocracy, constitutional, 101–126
Awami League, 65, 81, 85, 86, 87, 88, 90, 91, 92, 108, 176, 192, 193, 210, 211 n., 217, 219, 242
Awans, 235
Ayub Khan Muhammad, 75, 76, 80, 92, 268
  authoritarianism of, 170, 242
  and China, 275, 277, 278
  and election of 1965, 113, 114, 214, 220, 221, 222, 223, 227–228, 233, 235
  and Johnson, 280
  and Nehru, 273
  and new Constitution, 105–111
  political ideas of, 102–105, 117
  power of, 118, 119, 122–123, 125, 181, 213, 215–216, 220, 229, 242
  as President, 93–100, 101, 112, 120, 161, 165, 166, 172, 181, 204, 211, 213, 243
  quoted, 93, 102, 104, 105, 117, 118, 120, 210, 289
  steps of, to reform Islamic institutions, 166–167